Tackling Alcohol Together

Tackling Alcohol Together

The Evidence Base for a UK Alcohol Policy

Edited by
Duncan Raistrick
Ray Hodgson
and
Bruce Ritson

FREE ASSOCIATION BOOKS / LONDON / NEW YORK

First published in 1999 by
FREE ASSOCIATION BOOKS
57 Warren Street
London W1P 5PA

Copyright © Society for the Study of Addiction 1999

The right of the Society for the Study of Addiction
to be identified as the author of this work has
been asserted in accordance with the
Copyright, Designs and Patents Act 1988.

A CIP catalogue record for this book is available
from the British Library.

ISBN 1 85343 457 4 hbk; 1 85343 458 2 pbk

Designed and produced for
Free Association Books Ltd by
Chase Production Services, Chadlington OX7 3LN
Printed in the EC by T.J. International, Padstow

Contents

Preface
The Tackling Alcohol Together Project

Tackling Alcohol Together is a Society for the Study of Addiction project. The Society is an independent organisation whose membership is elected on the basis of an interest in and commitment to the addiction field. The membership is international comprising, in the main, scientists who are practitioners and academics.

The Society publishes two international journals: *Addiction* is edited by Professor Griffith Edwards and *Addiction Biology* is edited by Professor Tim Peters. The Society also supports an Annual Conference and ad hoc projects of which Tackling Alcohol Together is one. Information about the Society can be found on its Website: http://www.addiction-ssa.org/

Tackling Alcohol Together was launched with a two-day conference in Leeds, 25–26 April 1996, which was intended to raise the profile of alcohol policy issues in the UK. The government Green Paper *Our Healthier Nation* (Department of Health, 1998) signalled an intention to have a national alcohol policy. This book seeks to place the evidence base for a national policy within a contemporary and historical perspective. The resulting policy mix (see Chapter 12) is not intended to be prescriptive, rather it is about a way of thinking and an attempt to encourage new partnerships for the future. The policy mix includes proposals for both national and local measures – no one set of measures will suit every situation nor will the measures required remain constant over time.

The project has been driven by a Steering Group which set, as its first task, the commissioning of position papers from experts in subject areas. The Steering Group debated the position papers and edited them into the chapters that make up this book. Additional topic contributions were commissioned to fill out gaps. The Steering Group wishes to acknowledge the collaborative spirit of the scientists who have written this book and their generosity in giving free rein to the use of their material.

Duncan Raistrick, Project Manager for
the Society for the Study of Addiction.

Contributors

Eric Appleby BA (Hons), Director, Alcohol Concern, Waterbridge House, 32 Loman Street, London SE1 0EE.
Author of policy in practice sections.

Robert Baggott PhD, Reader in Public Policy, Department of Public Policy, De Montfort University at Leicester, Scraptoft Campus, Leicester LE7 9SU.
Author of position paper on alcohol controls policy.

Christopher Cook MD, Professor of the Psychiatry of Alcohol Misuse, Kent Institute of Medicine and Health Sciences, University of Kent at Canterbury, Kent CT2 7PD.
Author of position paper on risk.

Tony Clamp MA, Graduate Teaching Assistant, School of Community and Health Studies, University of Hull, Hull HU6 7RX.
Author of section on culture.

Colin Drummond MD, Reader in Addictions, Department of Psychiatry of Addictive Behaviour, St George's Hospital Medical School, University of London, Level 6 Hunter Wing, Cranmer Terrace, London SW17 0RE.
Author of position paper on alcohol related problems.

Griffith Edwards DM, Editor-in-Chief, *Addiction*, National Addiction Centre, 4 Windsor Walk, London SE5 8AF.
Author of position paper on the history of alcohol policy.

David Foxcroft PhD, Senior Research Fellow, National Co-ordinating Centre for Health Technology Assessment, University of Southampton, Southampton SO16 7PX.
Co-author of position paper on schools-based education.

Ian Fry Workplace Policy Officer (1995–97), Alcohol Concern, Waterbridge House, 32 Loman Street, London, SE1 0EE.
Author of workplace section.

Eilish Gilvarry FRCPsych, Joint Head of Clinical Services and Consultant Addiction Psychiatrist, Northern Regional Drug and Alcohol Services, Newcastle NHS Mental Health Trust, Plummer Court, Carliol Place, Newcastle upon Tyne NE1 6UR.
Author of position paper on young people.

Christine Godfrey BA (Hons), Professor of Health Economics and President of the Society for the Study of Addiction, University of York, Centre for Health Economics, Heslington, York YO1 5DD.
Author of position paper on the health economics of alcohol.

Richard Hammersley PhD, Director, Social Science Research Training Unit, Sociological Studies, University of Sheffield, Elmfield House, Northumberland Avenue, Sheffield S10 2FL.
Author of position paper on crime.

Larry Harrison MA, Reader in Addiction Studies, Head of School of Community and Health Studies, University of Hull, Hull HU6 7RX.
Author of position paper on mass media.

Gordon Hay BSc, Research Fellow, Centre for Drug Misuse Research, University of Glasgow, 11 The Square, Glasgow G12 8QC.
Co-author of position paper on epidemiology.

Nick Heather PhD, Consultant Clinical Psychologist, Professor and Director, Centre for Alcohol and Drug Studies, Newcastle City Health NHS Trust and University of Northumbria at Newcastle, Plummer Court, Carliol Place, Newcastle upon Tyne NE1 6UR.
Co-author of position papers on generalist and specialist treatments.

Ray Hodgson PhD, Director, Cardiff Addiction Research Unit, Centre for Applied Public Health Medicine, Lansdowne Hospital, Cardiff CF1 8UL
Co-editor; author of policy in practice sections and school education section.

Deborah Lister-Sharp PhD, Research Fellow, NHS Centre for Reviews and Dissemination, University of York, York YO1 5DD.
Co-author of position paper on schools-based education.

Geoff Lowe PhD, Senior Lecturer, Department of Psychology, University of Hull, Hull HU6 7RX.
Co-author of position paper on schools-based education.

Jane Marshall MRCPsych, Senior Lecturer in the Addictions, National Addiction Centre, Institute of Psychiatry and Maudsley Hospital, 4 Windsor Walk, London SE5 8AF.
Author of position paper on individual and population level risks.

Pip Mason MSocSc, Assistant Director (1989–98), Aquarius, 116 Watford Road, Kings Norton, Birmingham B30 1PB.
Co-author of position paper on generalist treatments.

Steve McCarthy MAppSc, Joint Head of Clinical Services and Consultant Clinical Psychologist, Northern Regional Drug and Alcohol Service, Newcastle

City Health NHS Trust, Plummer Court, Carliol Place, Newcastle upon Tyne NE1 6UR.
Co-author of position paper on specialist treatment.

Neil McKeganey PhD, Professor of Drug Misuse Research and Director, Centre for Drug Misuse Research, University of Glasgow, 11 The Square, Glasgow G12 8QC.
Co-author of position paper on epidemiology.

Annie Ogletree MSc, Social Policy Tutor (1995–99) Leeds Addiction Unit, 19 Springfield Mount, Leeds LS2 9NG.
Compiler of policy landmarks (Appendix 1); author of policy in practice sections; editorial assistant.

Duncan Raistrick FRCPsych, Clinical Director and Consultant Addiction Psychiatrist, Leeds Addiction Unit, 19 Springfield Mount, Leeds LS2 9NG.
Editor and author; author of policy in practice sections.

Gerda Reith BA (Hons), Lecturer, Department of Sociology, University of Glasgow, 11 The Square, Glasgow G12 8QC.
Co-author of position paper on epidemiology.

Bruce Ritson MD, Senior Lecturer and Consultant, Department of Psychiatry, Edinburgh University, Royal Edinburgh Hospital, Morningside Terrace, Edinburgh EH10 5HF.
Editor and author; author of policy in practice sections.

Betsy Thom PhD, Senior Research Fellow, School of Social Science, Middlesex University, Queensway, Middlesex EN3 4SF.
Author of position paper on the history of treatment.

Gillian Tober BA (Hons), Head of Training and Psychologist, Leeds Addiction Unit, 19 Springfield Mount, Leeds LS2 9NG.
Author of position paper on training.

The editors also acknowledge the contributions of Jonathan Chick, Peter Rorstad and Russell Webster.

Part I
Setting the Scene

1
Alcohol Policy History

Alcohol policy is too important a public issue to leave to chance or to market forces. If there is no coherent alcohol policy there will undoubtedly be sectional policies in abundance, often competing and costly in their consequences. Those who produce, sell and distribute alcohol have policies and aims, for instance, to maximise profitability. There are policies concerning licensing and restrictions on availability in the interests of public order. There are policies about the staffing of Accident and Emergency departments where alcohol problems make a huge impact on workload; policies for allocating costly liver transplants to individuals whose drinking has caused irreparable damage; policies concerning child protection and the family lives affected by alcohol; policies concerning drinking and driving; policies concerning sports sponsorship and advertising, and so on. Given these circumstances, the delineation of a coherent alcohol policy is an exciting challenge to both national government and the local community. It presents unique dilemmas, ambivalences, conflicts and unanswered questions but at the same time it offers an opportunity to effect a significant change in the quality of our environment and lives of the many who suffer from the consequences of alcohol misuse.

Alcohol problems have too often been left to ebb and flow. It is the job of policy, so far as possible, to capture and control that tide in the public interest (Edwards, 1995). Because it is a 'favourite drug', almost all of us have mixed feelings about restricting the availability of alcohol, while, at the same time, most recognise the damaging effects that alcohol has on the quality of life. It is not the aim of this book to decry its benefits and attractions in facilitating social discourse or as an important economic commodity. However, alcohol is not a simple commodity like any other. It is one which potentially damages health, contributes to crime, impairs productivity and disrupts family life. The effect on young people is particularly evident and has been the source of widespread concern. The damage to and by young people as a result of excessive drinking far exceeds the harm attributable to illicit drugs and yet there is a clear policy in relation to drug misuse.

It is clear from a reading of history that this is not the first time that the government has been concerned about a policy for alcohol. It is also clear that without some coherent strategy it is quite possible to descend into the kind of excesses and harm which were evident in Britain in the nineteenth century and are currently causing so much concern in Eastern Europe where unfettered availability and commercial pressure is having such a baneful effect on public health. This is not an academic or marginal concern but something which is central to all our lives and to the quality of our environment. These concerns are not new and it is instructive first to learn about the experiences of previous generations who have confronted these issues. Sometimes they have been forthright in their resolution to achieve a balanced response and at other times governments have turned a blind eye until damaging consequences made it an inescapable public concern. We can try to avoid these extremes possibly by instituting an informed debate and coherent understanding of the elements which need to be included in a national policy, and of the many different facets of public life and community concern that need to be drawn into this debate.

It is helpful to identify a few of the main themes which have arisen in the long and complex history of Britain's relationship with drinking rather than wishing to suggest that there are easy lessons to be taken from history. We would argue only that a knowledge of what has gone before may, in some way, serve to sensitise us to the nature of the current problems and encourage a rethinking of current remedies. Within the space available, the intention can be no more than a modest one of pointing out issues and pertinent questions. For a more detailed historical analysis there are several recommended texts (see, for example, French, 1884; Shadwell, 1902; Wilson, 1940; Glatt, 1958; Harrison, 1971). Here, in the first of two scene-setting chapters we focus on:

- drunkenness as the time-honoured cause for concern about alcohol
- past responses to a situation out of control
- drinking and drinking problems in the twentieth century
- what has counted in the twentieth century as the problem with drink
- contemporary history.

Drunkenness as the Time-honoured Cause for Concern about Alcohol

Over many centuries and until approximately the end of the seventh century or a little earlier, Britain was predominantly a beer-drinking country with some taste for wine. During the Saxon, Dane, Norman, Tudor, Stuart, revolution and restoration periods there were repeated references to the effects of drunkenness. It was a theme with many variations but centred upon the threat to godliness, good order and decency which was likely to result from drunken disinhibition. A quotation from a statute of 1604 (cited in French, 1884) provides a fair representation of those apprehensions:

> Whereas the loathsome and odious sin of drunkenness is of late grown into common use, being the root and foundation of many other enormous sins, as bloodshed, stabbing, murder, swearing, fornication, adultery with suchlike, to the great dishonour of God and our nation, the overthrow of many good arts and manual trades, the disabling of divers workmen and the general impoverishment of many good subjects, abusively wasting the good creature of God.

And 'the good creature of God' was, of course, drink. For centuries the outcry was very generally against drunkenness but not against drink for the reason that beer was a staple household commodity and vastly preferable to contaminated water as a drink. If, during this lengthy period, the primary focus of concern was the *fact* of drunkenness, a related concern came to be attached to the tavern or ale house as the place where the drinking was done. Thus Robert Burton, in his *Anatomy of Melancholy* (1621), wrote:

> What immoderate drinking in every place! How they flock to the tavern! as if they were born to no other end but to eat and drink, as so many casks to hold wine ... No disparagement now to stagger in the streets, reel, rave, etc, but much to his renown ... 'Tis the *summum bonum* of our tradesmen, their felicity, life, and soul, to be merry together in an ale house or tavern ... They will labour hard all day long to be drunk at night and will spend totius anni labores on a tippling feast.

Such pronouncements usually tended to suggest that every generation was becoming more prone to drunkenness than the previous one. We are left with a rich store of anecdotes with which to chart the history of drunkenness and concern over drunkenness during these many centuries, but data are not such as to allow a quantification or a detailed, objective chronology of the course of British drinking and drunkenness during that time. A reasonable guess, however, would be that although drunkenness had always been seen as some kind of problem and there had been no age of absolute temperate innocence, until a time toward the end of the seventeenth century the national co-existence with drink was a matter of reasonable balance. Preachers might pronounce their anathemas and lay authority express its concern and engage in a little bit of legislation, but there were sufficient societal and economic factors to militate against mass drunkenness to any great extent. Society had strong traditional informal controls in good repair and there was no significant drinks industry or organised commercialisation to promote consumption.

By the end of the seventeenth century, however, the problem set by drunkenness seems radically and suddenly to have changed, and the eighteenth and nineteenth centuries were to experience drunkenness of a kind and degree never before seen in Britain. It is again wise to note that the analysis which is being offered here is a best-guess interpretation of what occurred rather than anything approaching a definitive analysis supported by detailed scholarship.

What, in essence, seems to have occurred was the emergence of a number of influences which in sum caused the overthrow of an old equilibrium, with the population's relationship with alcohol skidding out of control. Here, to give an image of that shift, is an account of London life as given by Lord Lonsdale in a speech to the House of Lords in 1743 (cited in Shadwell, 1902):

> In every part of this great metropolis whoever shall pass along the streets will find wretchedness stretched upon the pavement, insensible and motionless, and only removed by the charity of passengers from the danger of being crushed by carriages or trampled by horses or strangled by filth in the common sewer … No man can pass a single hour in public places without meeting such or hearing such expressions as disgrace human nature – such as cannot be looked upon without horror or heard without indignation.

Tobias Smollett in his *History of England* (1757) described the scene which pertained around the time in the following vivid terms:

> Such a shameful degree of profligacy prevailed … that the retailers of this poisonous compound (gin) set up painted boards in public inviting people to be drunk for the small expense of one penny, assuring them that they might be dead drunk for 2d and have straw for nothing: they accordingly provided cellars and places strewed with straw, to which they conveyed those wretches who were overwhelmed with toxication: in these dismal cellars they lay until they had recovered some of their facilities, and then they had recourse to the same mischievous potion. (cited in Shadwell, 1902)

The forces which conspired to bring about this situation included the availability of cheap imported gin and later of the cheap home-manufactured product. The nineteenth century also saw the growth of an industrialised brewing industry as an early triumph and exemplar of entrepreneurial capitalism. But if increase in supply was part cause for the old ecological balance being destroyed, a vitally important concurrent element was an increase in demand. The demand-side was fed by the establishment of the new mass of the working-class urban poor whose labour was the engine of the Industrial Revolution. Old informal social controls were weakened as the people left their villages to move into the urban slums. One may turn to works such as William Booth's *In Darkest England and the Way Out* (1890) or Jack London's *The People of the Abyss* (1903) for contemporary pictures of an awful, impoverished, broken, drink-sodden urban landscape.

Past Responses to a Situation Out of Control

The responses which various sectors of society made to the emergence of a drink problem of a kind and degree which might fairly be called a national disaster, were several, and to an extent we live with the legacy of those responses today. For the first time in history there was a drink problem to which society did indeed have to respond.

First, there were a variety of reactions to drink at government level. These included a sequence of Acts which aimed to control the sale of spirits or cut off foreign imports, and the concurrent imposition of taxation. The Duke of Wellington's Beer Act of 1830 sought to engineer the situation by allowing a massive increase in the number of ale houses with the hope of reducing the sale of spirits. James Silk Buckingham, a sea captain turned radical MP, chaired a parliamentary committee which reported in 1834 (Select Committee, 1834) and which analysed the problem in terms of its social origins and proposed a number of social remedies. Among these were a limitation on the number of liquor outlets, annual licensing, and a range of environmental measures in addition to those aimed directly at drinking establishments and drinking behaviour. It is salutary to compare this strategy with the component tasks set out by Holder (1998), and discussed in Chapter 2, for the new century. Key elements of strategy in 1834 were:

1. the keepers of such houses to be subject to progressively increasing fines for disorderly conduct, and forfeiture of licence and closing up of the houses for repeated offences ... the closing of all such houses at an earlier hour in the evening than at present ... and making of all Retail Spirit Shops as open to public view as other shops where wholesome provisions are sold.

2. The discontinuance of all issues of ardent spirits (except as medicine under the direction of the medical officers) to the Navy and Army.

3. The prohibition of the practice of paying the wages of workers at public houses ... [and] payment of such wages to every individual his exact amount ... so as to render it unnecessary for men to frequent the public houses, and spend a portion of their earnings to obtain change.

4. The payment of wages at or before the breakfast hour in the mornings of the principal market day in each town to enable the wives to lay out their earnings in necessary provisions at an early period of the market, instead of risking its dissipation at night in the public house.

5. The establishment of public walks, and gardens, or open spaces for athletic and healthy exercise in the open air, in the immediate vicinity of every town, of an extent and character adapted to its population: and of district and parish libraries, museums and reading rooms, accessible at the lowest rate of charge; so as to admit of one or the other being visited in any weather, and at any time; with rigid exclusion of all Intoxicating Drinks.

6. The reduction of the duty on tea, coffee and sugar, and all the healthy and unintoxicating articles of drink in ordinary use; so as to place within the reach of all classes the least injurious beverages on much cheaper terms than the most destructive.

7. The removal of all taxes on knowledge and the extending of every facility to the widest spread of useful information to the humblest classes of the community.

That the then contemporary perspective on the problem was social rather than medical is emphasised by the fact that there were no medical doctors on Buckingham's committee.

Besides these responses to alcohol at the national level, individual cities at times launched campaigns against their local drinking problem. One such city was Liverpool. Over the years 1889–99 that city had such great success in reducing the incidence of public drunkenness as to attract deputations from other jurisdictions (Rowntree and Sherwell, 1903). Contemporary reports insist that the decline in arrest rates reflected a real downturn in public drunkenness rather than an administrative artefact. Table 1.1 shows that over these eleven years there was a steady decline in arrest rates from 30.6 per 1000 population to 6.0 and arrests had thus been cut to one-fifth of their original level. Meanwhile, the overall levels for drunkenness arrest recorded for England and Wales over these years were almost stationary.

As for measures which were employed in Liverpool to effect these changes, the mix included strict supervision of licensed premises by the police, the enforcement of licensing laws, and the removal of licences from badly conducted premises. There was also a 'refusal to give drink to those verging on intoxication', thus foreshadowing modern ideas on server training and liability. But despite the beneficial reduction in the public manifestations of the drink

Table 1.1   Drunkenness arrests in Liverpool, 1889–99

Year	Drunkenness offences per 1000 population
1889	30.6
1890	28.2
1891	21.9
1892	17.3
1893	15.2
1894	10.8
1895	8.1
1896	7.6
1897	7.7
1898	6.5
1899	6.0

Source: Rowntree and Sherwell (1903).

problem, the per capita consumption of alcohol in Liverpool probably remained unaltered. As Rowntree and Sherwell (1903) put it:

> The poverty inseparable from a high drink expenditure, and the resultant physical deterioration, continue. There has apparently been little or no progress in this vital direction.

Second, a further sustained and significant type of social response to the drink problem came with the emergence of the Temperance movement which might be seen as the people themselves turning against the destructive influence of drink. In Britain, Temperance was a grass-roots working-class movement which had close connections with the Nonconformist churches. The Temperance movement was already well established in the US when the first Total Abstinence Association on this side of the Atlantic was set up in Preston in 1832. These founding fathers took the unequivocal view that alcohol was 'the enemy of the race'. Temperance was in part a self-help movement which rescued the drunkard and supported individual abstinence, but it exerted pressure at the political level also. It was, additionally, an educational movement which aimed to reach people at a young age with the abstinence message, using music and magic lantern shows at weekly meetings of the Bands of Hope. Although the movement spoke out against the slum conditions which it saw as contributing to the drink problem, it held consistently and unambiguously to the view that the problem with drinking was quite simply the drink, and within that perspective the only rational response to that problem for individuals and society alike was to get rid of the drink. That position was a long way from alcohol as 'the good creature of God' with its drunken abuse the only problem.

A third type of response to the drinking problem which can be seen as having gradually emerged over this same period was the theory that some people who drank excessively might be doing so because they were driven to drink by a disease state which impaired their personal control over drinking. The first full exposition of that view was given in 1804 by an Edinburgh doctor, Thomas Trotter, in his remarkable *Essay on Drunkenness* (1804). He declared that 'the habit of drunkenness is a disease of the mind' and described a sensitive and empathetic approach to the treatment of the diseased patient which centred on the breaking of habit. There had been doctors in the eighteenth century who had earlier employed this kind of disease concept but their writings did not approach Trotter in scope or detail (Porter, 1985).

Trotter's views probably had little direct impact on society, but by the latter part of the nineteenth century they had become accepted within the medical profession which was by then persistently and publicly declaring that inebriety was a disease. The corollary to that conclusion was that inebriety was a medical problem requiring medical intervention. Further, and within the perspective of the time, the appropriate treatment was to incarcerate these diseased drinkers in special institutions similar to the lunatic asylums which were to be a memorial to the Victorian age. Thus the drinking problem was in some measure redefined as being rooted in the diseased disposition of the individual rather than being due to alcohol as the intrinsically evil agent or to any predisposing social conditions. However, it should be emphasised that at this point the redefinition of inebriety as a disease was of limited rather than widespread acceptance. Many of the doctors who championed the disease concept as the rational basis for government and supported institutional treatment for these supposedly diseased persons, doubled as Temperance advocates and believed that a prime cause for the disease of inebriety was the individual's exposure to alcohol and society's excessive drinking. It was thus eminently possible to have things both ways. The prime champion of this disease formulation and of institutional treatment was Dr Norman Kerr. He had tried to set up a total abstinence society while still a medical student in Glasgow and in 1884 became the first president of the Society for the Study and Cure of Inebriety (Kerr, 1889).

The Habitual Drunkards Act of 1879 had allowed for non-criminal inebriates to submit themselves for voluntary detention in state-funded retreats for drunkards, and in 1898 Parliament passed the Inebriates Act which allowed for compulsory detention of inebriates in institutions which were to be termed 'reformatories' in contrast to the rather more upper-class 'retreats'. The institutional treatment of the diseased inebriate was not a great success. It was an expensive scheme and difficult to administer. In addition, it was not funded on a scale to match the size of the problem and was thus more tokenism than solution. None the less, by the latter part of the nineteenth century a movement had developed which individualised the problem and which believed it could be removed from society and treated, and this was a portent of things to come.

Before moving on from the nineteenth century to more recent times one further element in the development of responses deserves to be noted. That century saw the rise of a drinks industry as a force in its own right. It responded to the social appetite for drink by manufacturing and selling more alcohol, but it also became organised and forcefully defended its activities against the Temperance campaigners. The drinks industry provided an early example of organised parliamentary lobbying and the brewerage entered the House of Lords. As Wilson (1940) put it in *Alcohol and the Nation*:

> In the earliest days, when … thousands of public houses and many private householders brewed their own beer, when the publican was, in an arguable sense, 'mine host' and the public house the principal social centre of the neighbourhood, the influence of the Trade as a corporate entity was comparatively small. The public house, regardless of party, at election times was at the disposal of any candidate who wished to bribe the electors. When, however, the nation began to realise the necessity for legislative control and restriction of the sale of liquor in the public interest, the Trade, in its turn, realised that necessity for combined efforts in defence of its own interests, which has resulted in the creation of a political combination, which, down at any rate to the war, was probably the most powerful in the country.

Thus the nineteenth century witnessed a polarity of responses to the drink problem in terms of those who saw drink as the root of a social problem and those who viewed drink as an opportunity for great profit, while somewhere between those opposed forces was a little band of medical practitioners who wanted to persuade society that the diseased individual needed to be treated. Those themes, unresolved and conflicting, went forward into the next century.

Drinking and Drinking Problems in the Twentieth Century

The trajectory of alcohol intake which Britain has experienced can be charted over the last hundred years. The data matter in their own right but their size and direction are also important in terms of the salience likely to be given to drink and the drink problem as a public issue, and the types of response which were then elicited.

Figure 1.1 represents the estimated per capita alcohol intake for England, Wales and Scotland in terms of litres of absolute alcohol per head. For data up to 1986 we are grateful to the Royal College of Physicians for allowing us to reproduce material from its report on alcohol (Royal College of Physicians,

1987), while we have ourselves updated that run of data to 1997. Several sources of error are likely to affect the accuracy of these data so they are offered here as providing an approximate rather than absolutely accurate picture of a drinking century.

Source: Royal College of Physicians 1987, p. 21, and Brewers and Licensed Retailers Association 1998

Figure 1.1   Per capita consumption 1900 to 1997

From Figure 1.1 two broad conclusions can be drawn:

1. *Over the period of a century per capita consumption has shown considerable variations.* The trough of consumption between the two world wars was at about one-third the level experienced at either the beginning or the end of the century. Since the 1960s the trend has been toward an increase in per capita consumption that has effectively reversed the decline in consumption which marked the first part of the century. The strong conclusion which stands out, whatever the noise and inaccuracies in the data, is that far from the level of alcohol consumption being fixed for all time it is capable of very large downward or upward movement over the course of decades. The First World War and the control regulations introduced at that time (Smart, 1974) produced an acute short-term fall of a kind not

otherwise seen, but consumption was on a downward trend anyhow which continued during the economically depressed years between the wars. The Second World War saw a slight increase in overall consumption, with a decline once more in the post-war years. Drinking then followed a rising curve which, with a few dips and plateaux, has been the story of the last 40 years.

2. *Within the totality of change there have often been different trends evident between beer, wines and spirits.* Beer consumption has not fluctuated as greatly as that of other beverages; spirits consumption slumped steeply and has never climbed back to quite the old level, while wine consumption has risen dramatically since the 1960s. Similar changes towards a more mixed pattern of consumption can be seen in many other European countries over the same period (Edwards *et al.*, 1994).

Factors which may help to explain the picture of change depicted in Figure 1.1 are considered in Chapter 5. Here we would simply note that the influences are undoubtedly multiple. At each of the time-points shown (1900, 1950 and 2000) Britain was a profoundly different society in which to live – and in which to drink. Control systems over the period became stricter and then more lax, while marketing and promotion became much more sophisticated and determined and the demography of the population changed. Behind all these other influences were the impacts of price and income, and distribution of income. For the most part, and with the exception of the 1914–18 period when heavy alcohol controls were introduced because of anxiety about industrial efficiency, most of the changes that came about appear to have been unplanned and accidental; a result of the ebb and flow of drinking history rather than the product of intentional policy.

What has Counted in the Twentieth Century as the Problem with Drink?

By the beginning of the twentieth century, the visibility of drinking problems and public drunkenness which had provided much of the impetus behind medical and temperance campaigns, was on the wane. Legislation passed at the turn of the century to control the worst excesses, reforms to tackle problems of environmental and social deprivation associated with inebriety, moves to nationalise the drink trade, the social upheaval of the First World War, and the economic depression of the 1930s, all contributed to a continuing decline in alcohol consumption (Turner, 1980; Williams and Brake, 1980). In the interwar years, interest in alcohol treatment both at policy and professional levels was at a low ebb. At national level, led by the activities of the Temperance movement with its strong parliamentary links, attention had shifted towards the public health approach with an interest in alcohol and in prevention, but there was little policy action (Williams and Brake, 1980; Rutherford, 1991).

It is probably fair to conclude that by the 1950s the overall British view was that drink was not very problematic and the great drinking issues of the last century had become non-issues. Drink was not a problem and neither was drunkenness – no one remembered Trotter or Kerr. The British could pride themelves on their national sobriety: per capita consumption was not only at an all-time low but much lower than in most other European countries. Anyone who wanted at that time to persuade the government, the public or the medical profession to take Britain's drinking problems seriously, was likely to discover that they were pushing a lost cause uphill. The glory days of the Temperance movement were well and truly over.

However, in the 1950s something rather curious happened. The nascent National Health Service (NHS) began to realise that it was without established ways of dealing with 'alcoholics' who were presenting – albeit in small numbers – for treatment. The particular influence at this juncture of Dr Max Glatt (Glatt, 1983) deserves to be recognised. Glatt established a pioneering in-patient unit at Warlingham Park in 1952, and in 1962 the Warlingham Unit was taken up by the NHS as the model for the establishment of regional Alcoholism Treatment Units throughout the country.

These units marked the beginning of a new willingness on the part of government to take the drinking problem seriously, but only in the restricted terms of the individual victim of alcoholism as a subject of concern. Nineteenth-century understanding of inebriety as a disease was rediscovered, and once again the establishment of institutional treatment moved to the fore as a reforming cause. This time around there was, however, one large difference: whereas their nineteenth-century predecessors had been closely allied with the Temperance cause, the doctors who led this new movement were eager to assert that there was nothing wrong with drink. They were rather more likely to insist that alcoholism was the problem, and their alliance was with Alcoholics Anonymous (AA) which championed exactly that view. From the 1950s onwards AA was becoming an important presence in Britain and its approach further reinforced the message – carried to and espoused by government – that the problem was with the disease of alcoholism rather than with alcohol itself. The following quotations may serve to illustrate the nature of post-war consensus which emerged to support that notion.

Alcoholism is disease.(Opening line in Dr Lincoln Williams's *Tomorrow Will Be Sober* (Williams, 1960), an important book written by a leading specialist of that era.)

We believe that any measures, fiscal or other, which would limit the sales of spirits while favouring beer or wine would probably reduce the number of alcoholics. (Kessell and Walton 1965). The authors of this very successful paperback were two distinguished psychiatrists. Neil Kessell became Consultant Adviser on Alcoholism to the Department of Health and Chairman of the Department's Advisory Committee on Alcoholism. The view on spirits was heterodox, but alcohol *per se* was clearly not the problem.)

Intoxicating liquors are part of our way of life – I do not complain of that ... Informed opinion is today prepared to accept that intoxication and alcoholism are not to be regarded as crimes to be punished, so much as diseases to be cured if possible. (Stonham (1969). Viscount Stonham was at the time Minister of State at the Home Office.)

We are fortunately emerging from the era in which the chronic alcoholic was rejected by public and doctors alike. The medical profession, the Department of Health and Social Security and many members of the public are coming to appreciate that alcoholism is a disease, a disease that can be prevented and cured. (Rosenheim (1970). Max Rosenheim, later Lord Rosenheim, was to become President of the Royal College of Physicians.)

We live in a society where it is customary to drink. It is the abstainer who strikes us as the more abnormal ... Repeated minimal intoxication is expected of our leading figures, soldiers, statesmen, businessmen, dons. We know that this sort of drinking, open and well moderated, is for the most part harmless and seems conducive to good relationships. (Kessell and Walton, 1965)

The cluster of quotations is arbitrary in its selection, but each person we quote here spoke at the time with significant authority. Further quotations from other authors might usefully fill out the picture, but the main features of that post-war consensus are clear. The disease of alcoholism was the core issue which defined and delineated the vision of the drink problem in the years following the end of the Second World War.

In addition to the main focus on the disease of alcoholism it is possible to identify two other, more minor, themes which emerged at this time. One was the drink driving question, concern over which resulted in the introduction in 1967 of the statutory 80 mg% blood alcohol concentration (BAC) level, supported by the new technology of the breathalyser. Drink driving stands out as an example of a concern about the impact of alcohol on society quite beyond anything that could be put under the disease heading and thus as an issue ahead of its time. The second theme was an intense but rather short-lived concern with a type of drinker who was then usually referred to as 'the chronic drunkenness offender', echoing nineteenth-century anxieties about 'habitual drunkards'. In the mid-twentieth century, however, it was argued that drunkenness offenders deserved compassionate help because they were 'real alcoholics'. This reforming movement, with its concern about habitual drunkenness, achieved a number of legislative and policy successes over a few years and catalysed voluntary agency endeavours (Cook, 1975), but it rather soon faded, for reasons which are not entirely clear. Only for a remarkably brief period did the government revisit concern with the public inebriate and ministers address meetings on the topic, but with due historical roundedness there was at the time some talk of reviving the Inebriates Act.

Contemporary History

What looked like firm consensus on the nature of the problem proved to be remarkably short-lived. A number of people may still find it useful to see alcoholism as a disease and that certainly remains the tenet of AA, but the scientific validity of such a formulation has been strongly questioned (Heather and Robertson, 1997). Medical and social concerns have widened beyond any single inebriety or alcoholism-as-disease formula, and have embraced the host of greater or lesser, acute or chronic, social and physical and psychological problems which can be caused by drink. Alcoholism has, as it were, been deconstructed and disaggregated and where a few decades ago there was a sharp focus on one core disease entity, the modern vision embraces a wide-angled awareness of alcohol problems as a disseminated public health issue. At the same time, the proposition that alcohol has nothing to do with the drink problem has been rejected by most experts. Nineteenth-century questions are again being asked about the degree to which the level of alcohol consumption by the population is an issue for public health concern. Further, these questions are being raised at a time when the political climate is favourable to deregulation.

The 1970s saw the start of a transformation from a largely medical response to alcoholism to a social, community-based response to problem drinking. Policy began to focus on a range of interventions which encompassed a control strategy – the control of availability of alcohol through, for instance, price or licensing regulations – demand reduction approaches using, for example, public awareness and health education campaigns, early intervention in problem drinking which drew in primary health and social care services, and the provision of specialist care for individuals with severe drinking problems – the more traditional treatment and rehabilitation services. Although the Department of Health (DoH) did not claim responsibility for all these aspects of alcohol policy, policy discourse on treatment was now located within a more comprehensive framework which included consideration of prevention and control responses. Thus, by the 1990s, policy was concerned with an effective response to, rather than the treatment of, alcohol problems.

At practice level, adopting a broader perspective meant that service approaches became more diversified as treatment agencies began to broaden their role to include, for example, early intervention approaches, outreach work, the provision of training for health professionals, the development of courses for drink drivers, and so on. Even within more traditional treatment services, therefore, this broadening of their role meant that by the 1990s management had become a more accurate descriptor of agency activities than treatment.

The shifts and developments in policy approaches and service delivery in the alcohol field have to be seen within the political, social and economic contexts of the times. The history of post-war alcohol policy is intimately linked with the history of change in the organisation and funding of health and welfare services, change in the relationship between the voluntary sector and the state, increasing professionalisation in the 'caring' occupations, and shifts in the laws, sanctions and fashions which help to shape public views on alcohol use and misuse. More particularly, the emergence of the new public health model of alcohol problems was located within general trends in public health towards employing an epidemiological and economic perspective on health and social problems, visible, for instance, in approaches to tobacco smoking or the intake of salt as well as in alcohol consumption (Rose, 1992).

Another important influence on these developments was the underlying rise in alcohol consumption portrayed in Figure 1.1. The upward swing of the last 40 years was not an event on the scale of the gin epidemic but it was enough to cause strain and questioning. And, rather fortuitously, research began to inform policy at this time: it was shown that alcohol problems go beyond 'alcoholism' (Edwards *et al.*, 1987), alcohol has a lot to do with the genesis of alcohol problems, control of supply is a necessary component to prevention (Bruun *et al.*, 1975), and intensive individual treatment of the dependent drinker might not be very effective as a core strategy (Orford and Edwards, 1977). Thus to a considerable extent it was the evidence of research rather than whim or fashion which overthrew the existing consensus.

We believe therefore that this book is written at a time when ideas are in flux, when new research evidence of great potential policy relevance is coming to hand at a steep and accelerating pace, and at a time marked by much con-structive and energetic debate about what the problem is and what constitutes the most appropriate responses. In the chapters which follow we offer some evidence to inform that debate and seek to define a new and evidence-based consensus on how to view the drinking problem and what should be done about it. We are still faced with old themes but there is significant new knowledge to illuminate data and inform the decision making.

2
Whose Alcohol Policy?

The success of a national alcohol policy will depend upon setting out broad aims that most people will wish to support. These aims might include preventing violence and crime, promoting good health, and encouraging sensible drinking patterns. While the diversity of culture, the vested interests and the personal ambivalences of policy stakeholders will make it difficult to secure a consensus which is sustained into the details of policy, there is much that can be readily agreed.

Although there are many unanswered questions, research evidence is building up an impressive foundation of understanding of the biological effects and benefits as well as harms that arise from drinking and also of effective treatments and prevention policies which would reduce harm without seriously impairing the social benefits. The fact that such evidence now exists makes it particularly timely that there should be an open debate about the development of a purposeful and effective alcohol policy. Green Papers in both Scotland and England have pointed to a new commitment to public health policy. We also have the model of *Tackling Drugs to Build a Better Britain* (Home Office, 1998) which has shown one way in which different sectors can be encouraged to work together to a common purpose in dealing with alcohol and other drug misuse. In this second scene-setting chapter we discuss:

- the rationale for a national policy
- stakeholders and vested interests
- alcohol as part of British culture
- the Community Systems Model
- an overview of current issues.

The Rationale for a National Policy

Most people would agree that it is the job of government to have in place an effective foreign policy, an economic policy, and so on. Why government should have anything to do with people's drinking behaviour and whether there is public support for a national alcohol policy is a more difficult question. Prior to the Green Paper *Our Healthier Nation* (DoH, 1998) no UK government had deemed it necessary to propose a national alcohol policy, whereas, and in sharp contrast, the need for a national drugs policy has been long accepted. Equally the principal statute controlling the supply and use of drugs other than alcohol, the Misuse of Drugs Act (1971), is of a different order to alcohol control measures (see Appendix 1). *Tackling Drugs Together* (DoH, 1995a) and the policy update *Tackling Drugs to Build a Better Britain* (Home Office, 1998) have been broadly welcomed, not necessarily because everybody supports every statement made or even all of the major policy directions, but because the policy goes at least some way towards clarifying the roles of different agencies and setting out a framework for collaborative action with clear objectives. Perhaps the single most important effect of the national drug policy has been to inspire and to cajole agencies including Drug Action Teams, health authorities, social services, probation, police, service providers and education authorities into working together with a common purpose.

If a national drugs policy is such a good thing, why is there a reluctance to have a national alcohol policy? Is alcohol policy really that different? In order to justify a national alcohol policy there needs to be an acceptance that alcohol has a profound effect upon society as a whole and that in the interest of the public good there is a need to combine the regulation of alcohol use with actions to attenuate actual or potential adverse consequences. It is, of course, the debate on the balance between benefits and harms that separates alcohol and illicit drug policy – this is probably not a distinction shared by users of illicit drugs. Comparing alcohol to illicit drugs should not be taken too far. Drugs differ in their addictive potential and potential to cause harm. It follows that different policies might be applied to different drugs. Equally it is logical that there should be a general set of principles applied to all psychoactive substances.

Heath (1996, p. 279) describes how politicians have used the rhetoric of a war on drugs as a 'device virtually guaranteed to galvanise public opinion, demonstrate the speakers' decisiveness, rally support, and draw a sharp line between *us* and *them'* – in this case a division between people who drink and people who use other drugs. UK drugs policy has flirted with war rhetoric (Strang *et al.*, 1997) but has also failed to appreciate the frequency of recreational drug use (see Parker *et al.*, 1998). Rather than perpetuate this divide between licit and illicit substances the longer-term project should now be the bringing together of alcohol and other drug policies. The shorter-term project is an alcohol policy which boldly acknowledges and balances the conflicting interests for the community. The *European Charter on Alcohol* (WHO, 1995) sets out some guiding principles:

- All people have the right to a family, community and working life protected from accidents, violence and other negative consequences of alcohol consumption.
- All people have the right to valid impartial information and education, starting early in life, on the consequences of alcohol consumption on health, the family and society.
- All children and adolescents have the right to grow up in an environment protected from the negative consequences of alcohol consumption and, to the extent possible, from the promotion of alcoholic beverages.
- All people with hazardous or harmful alcohol consumption and members of their families have the right to accessible treatment and care.
- All people who do not wish to consume alcohol, or who cannot do so for health or other reasons, have the right to be safeguarded from pressures to drink and be supported in their non-drinking behaviour.

Stakeholders and Vested Interests

Citizens

All citizens are stakeholders in a national alcohol policy. Alcohol has always been the accepted and available psychoactive drug in the four countries that constitute the United Kingdom. Alcohol is ingrained deep into UK culture. This is not to say that the meaning of alcohol use, patterns of drinking, and use among population subgroups is by any means static. In fact the social acceptability and availability of drugs other than alcohol has once more become fashionable over the latter part of the twentieth century and alcohol should now be seen as among the repertoire of drugs that people use rather than the only substance which is deemed culturally acceptable. We should remember that tobacco, opium and cocaine have all been accepted and legal drugs in the twentieth century.

Some citizens will choose to be non-drinkers and many of these people can be expected to favour policies which support abstinence from alcohol. Religious conviction is the pre-eminent reason for lifelong abstention; however, non-drinkers also include former heavy drinkers, people with illnesses that prevent drinking, older people, and so on. Most people in the UK drink and, while people wanting alcohol-free environments will undoubtedly be a small minority, their views should none the less be recognised. The extreme policy of alcohol prohibition has been attempted by a number of nation states but, with the possible exception of some Islamic countries, the measure has been dropped in the face of widespread disruption of society from lack of public support, bootlegging, police corruption, deaths from sales of contaminated alcohol and loss of tax revenues. Heath (1995, p. 290) has argued that, since ancient times, selective and inconsistent prohibition has been used as a form of social control and applied particularly to minority or low-status groups.

Swings in social value systems that favour a more relaxed approach to drinking have been tempered by a sense that there are times and places when drinking is inappropriate. A contemporary example is drinking at work which is increasingly seen as unacceptable and there are now few businesses or organisations that provide structures supportive of drinking in the workplace. For most people drinking is a leisure-time activity. The most popular leisure activities away from the home, for both men and women, are visiting a public house and having a meal in a restaurant (ONS, 1998a, p. 221). However, eating and drinking out accounts for only one-fifth of the time spent watching television or listening to the radio, averaged at 2.5 hours per day. Of course both watching television and visiting friends might be accompanied by drinking; indeed, it can be difficult to find recreational activities where alcohol is not available.

In summary, the citizen stakeholder is likely to have a vested interest in there being constraints on drinking, typically where drinking leads to violence or accidents, but thereafter is likely to want a relaxed approach to the availability and use of alcohol. To what extent does this ambivalence to alcohol emerge from an informed position?

Public Debate

At present there is very little real debate about the impact of alcohol on society, certainly when compared to the high level of interest in other drugs. In everyday conversation people tend to distance themselves from problem drinking by making 'drunks' or 'alcoholics' a repository for evidence relating to the harmful consequences of alcohol. Most people will disapprove of drink driving but will applaud an upwards re-evaluation of safe drinking limits. Beyond these well publicised topics there is little knowledge or discussion about alcohol. The alcohol field itself is uncomfortable with the mass media fearing that coverage acceptable to television or newspapers will portray either positive alcohol use – for example, in soap operas – or 'horror' documentaries, rather than offering a more balanced position. However, Casswell (1995) has identified a number of mass media influences on public debate: (i) entertainment material (television, video, film, computer games), (ii) advertising, (iii) media education campaigns, (iv) news coverage and (v) academic discourse.

From a social and psychological point of view smoking and drinking are very similar behaviours. Arguably any smoking is harmful and so health promotion messages are more clear cut than messages about safer drinking levels. None the less, public opinion has successfully been turned against smoking, particularly smoking in public places. This experience may have relevance for alcohol policy. It is noticeable that any 'good news' stories about alcohol are reported with great enthusiasm, whereas stories about problems resulting from drinking often receive a subdued media response unless they are directed at safe targets such as drink driving or the behaviour of young people. Casswell *et al.* (1989) suggest that the promotion of safer drinking needs to comprise a combination of both mass media campaigning, which is seen as a means of sensitising the public to alcohol policy issues, and local action to deliver actual changes in drinking attitudes and behaviours.

Pendleton *et al.* (1990) sampled public opinion across the UK on various aspects of alcohol policy. They found very strong support for control measures which included enforcing the law on under-age drinking (92%), enforcing drink driving laws (91%), banning alcohol at sporting events (80%) and also support for educational policies such as labelling alcoholic drinks (88%), schools education (89%) and taxing drinks advertising to pay for health education (73%). There was little enthusiasm for restricting the availability of alcohol: only 47% of respondents supported restricting the hours of off-licence sales and 46% supported reducing the total number of outlets for alcohol. A more recent study in Australia by McAllister (1995) found a remarkably similar profile of opinion regarding the regulation of alcohol. It may be that people are inclined to endorse measures to limit the use of alcohol provided that those measures do not affect them personally, or it may be that attempts to curtail the availability of alcohol are somehow seen as an attack on personal freedom and therefore not endorsed. Whatever the reasons, the dilemma for the policy makers is that restricting the availability of alcohol, widely believed to be an effective measure, does not seem to have public support. There is considerable variation in support for alcohol policies among different groups in the population; not surprisingly, non-drinkers, women and older people tend to be more in favour of more controls. The point to underline here is that support or otherwise for policy measures is not obviously informed by a knowledge of the facts (see HEA, 1997, pp. 15–17).

Personal Freedom and Responsibility

The freedom to use psychoactive drugs raises difficult moral and legislative questions. Mill's (1859) view is the classical liberal stance on the individual's pre-eminent right to self-determination:

> The only purpose for which power can be rightfully exercised over any member of a civilised community, against his will, is to prevent harm to others. His own good, either physical or moral, is not a sufficient warrant. He cannot rightfully be compelled to do or forbear because it will be better for him to do so, because it will make him happier, because in the opinion of others, to do so would be wise, or even right ... The only part of the conduct of anyone, for which he is amenable to society, is that which

concerns others. In the part which merely concerns himself, his independence is, of right, absolute. Over himself, over his own body and mind, the
individual is sovereign.

This position is often contrasted with the interventionist control of 'the nanny
state' or, in more extreme form, the totalitarian state. This dichotomy is a
caricature of both viewpoints and Mill himself introduced a number of caveats
to his thesis and stressed that the sovereignty of the individual over his own
body and mind applied only to adults making rational and informed choices.
This, of course, raises the question of the extent to which an individual who
has become addicted or besotted by alcohol, is able to make truly independent
choices. This argument may justify a degree of intervention. We should be
willing to debate the limits of intervention which are acceptable without
eroding the rights of the individual. History shows that these limits of acceptable
behaviour are frequently being redrawn and also that they are applied in ways
which are far from logical. Consider again the attitudes towards drunkenness
with those that exist towards behaviour induced by any form of illicit drug use
which we discussed at the beginning of this chapter.

There is a very significant difference between controls that are a reflection
of social influences and those that are imposed by government edict. The
customs and informal controls which have arisen around drinking in every
society are potent influences on behaviour. The view that 'no man is an island'
contrasts with Mill's position without undermining it. There are many circumstances in which intervention can be justified; for example, to protect
others who also have rights, and to ensure public safety and the quality of the
environment. The community has a right to be concerned about the quality
of its environment. 'The spirit of the community' identified by Etzioni (1995)
points to the need to balance individual rights with responsibilities including
a concern for the quality of life of others and their surroundings. A logical and
effective alcohol policy needs to take into account this delicate balance of
individual freedoms and the responsibilities incumbent on living within an
interdependent community. There is also a justifiable expectation that
government will, if necessary, back up these rights by appropriate legislation.

Drinks and Leisure Industries

The production and sale of alcoholic drinks is the main business of brewers
and distillers who, between them, make a significant contribution to the UK
economy. In 1996 the industry delivered a positive UK trade balance of £893.6
million on an exports:imports ratio of 1.43:1. In 1996/97 the government
revenue from alcoholic drinks was £10,037 million, representing 4.8% of total
government tax revenue (Alcohol Concern, 1998a). There are costs and benefits
to any industry and it is not within the remit of this review to comment on

individual companies or the cost benefits of the industry as a whole, but rather to draw attention to the influence that can be wielded, for both good and bad, by such a large sector of productive UK industry. It is the scale of these industries that needs to be underlined. Room (1998) sees the globalisation of the drinks industry as cause for concern. The major players in the industry have a combined wealth that exceeds the gross national product of most non-industrialised countries and their capacity to influence governments is immense. In the sphere of illicit drug use the global market is controlled by organised crime. In contrast, the production and distribution of alcohol is controlled by a highly regarded and influential sector of legitimate industry. This does not mean that similar equations of supply and demand may not operate, but the legitimacy and government support for the one as opposed to the other is plain.

Different entertainment businesses will see the profits from the sale of alcohol quite differently. The sale of drinks at a cinema will, for example, represent a small proportion of profit as compared to, say, the sale of drinks in a nightclub. Football clubs may welcome drink sponsorship and corporate hospitality while regretting declining gates due to reports of drunken hooliganism. Similarly, the accumulation of litter and vandalism associated with drunkenness may diminish some of the profits arising from sales in city-centre pubs. The advertising industry poses a different dilemma: the profits for them in the advertising of alcohol are much greater than the profits in health promotion, though both are presumably to their advantage. Newspapers have the added problem of relying on advertising for their profits. If drinks advertising is a major component of this, then they may not wish to disturb the goose that lays the golden eggs. While profit may be the motivation for large corporations, employees have a vested interest in security of employment. The brewers and distillers and the entertainment industries that are mainly concerned with the sale of alcohol are major employers, accounting for over 1 million jobs between them (see Table 2.1). This is not to say that a significant number of these jobs would be lost if alcohol consumption was markedly reduced – there is much overlap with the provision of food and non-alcoholic beverages.

Table 2.1   Employment in brewing and related industries

Description	1990	1994	1997
Production	83,000	65,000	53,000
Hotels and accommodation	314,000	317,000	327,000
Restaurants	303,000	311,000	344,000
Public houses and bars	446,000	362,000	376,000
Totals	1,146,000	1,055,000	1,100,000

Source: Brewers and Licensed Retailers Association (1998).

Responsibility of Drinks and Leisure Industries

The principles that should underpin a national alcohol strategy have been defined within the *European Charter on Alcohol* (WHO, 1995). Today the drinks and leisure industries are often seen to pursue profit and influence with scant regard for these principles. Two issues, marketing strategy and funding of research, have provoked debate on the responsibility of the industry. The arguments on both sides have been well rehearsed and will be reviewed only briefly here.

The ethical marketing of a product such as alcohol which has both beneficial and harmful effects is bound to be difficult. Brewers and distillers bring benefits to the economy, and individuals derive pleasure from drinking; however, alcohol is also a factor behind accidents, ill health and family breakdown and so on. Edwards (1998) articulates the view that the industry will not behave responsibly without recourse to legislation. He makes the case that the industry wilfully disregards and misrepresents scientific evidence; most crucially he points to the industry's rejection of the relationship between per capita consumption and harm in favour of locating alcohol misuse within the individual. He also characterises the industry funded Portman Group as a public relations front for the drinks industry rather than the watchdog that it is portrayed to be and he calls for independent regulation on the industry. How best to include the contributions of industry in a national policy will no doubt continue to be debated.

The drinks industry has funded significant medico-social research but doubts have been raised about the independence and ethical basis of this activity. The arguments against receiving funding from the drinks industry are twofold: first, direct funding almost always has strings attached; second, the drinks industry has sufficient funds available to distort the volume of research in areas that are favourable to the industry view. Hannum (1998) has argued that neither of these propositions are necessarily true and that opportunities to conduct important research should not be rejected simply because funding comes from the drinks industry. These same arguments have been raised against receiving support for research, or even scientific meetings, from the pharmaceutical industry. Openness and transparency of any possible vested interests should be the underpinning principle guiding clinicians and researchers. One solution to these dilemmas would be to challenge the good will of the industry by inviting it to put funds into a truly independent research body.

The Alcohol Services Providers

The separation in the 1980s and 1990s of the roles of purchasers and providers of services has created a more commercial atmosphere in the public sector – in effect, turning service providers into small businesses. Alcohol Concern's

Services Directory for 1998/99 lists a total of 544 specialist providers in England and Wales: 342 are non-statutory, 144 are statutory, 49 are private and 9 are partnerships. There are no data available on the numbers of staff employed by or total expenditure on these agencies.

The provision of alcohol services is not limited to agencies providing direct client interventions. Included under this heading are health promotion services and people engaged in prevention work of all kinds: research workers spanning the basic sciences, psychology, sociology, and medicine; people involved in training professionals and others to deal with problem drinking. The resources allocated for all alcohol related work – research, treatment and prevention – are modest and alcohol services have to compete with more popular health or social services, such as children's services and cancer units, for limited public money. It follows that providers of alcohol services need to be able to demonstrate that they deliver value for money.

Responsibilities of the Alcohol Services Agencies

The image of alcohol prevention, treatment and research agencies has generally benefited from the public perception that these agencies are poorly funded and struggling to help an unpopular group of people. The reality is probably somewhat different but, either way, agencies have a responsibility to behave ethically and to serve the public good. It cannot be assumed, however, that a kind of profit motive does not exist in the alcohol treatment and research communities. Personal advancement, the status of 'gurus', the curricula vitae of agency advisors will depend upon the size of an organisation and possibly upon promoting outmoded paradigms in the face of evidence to the contrary. Therefore, the first responsibility of agencies is to demonstrate that they do indeed deliver value for money based on scientific evidence of effectiveness.

Two major themes which can be seen running through the Department of Health's review of the effectiveness of alcohol treatments (Raistrick and Heather, forthcoming) have a bearing on value for money. First, we have a great deal of knowledge about which treatments are effective and it is therefore incumbent upon agencies to use these therapies (see also Chapters 9 and 10). Second, we know that many therapists in the addiction field have no formal qualification of competence – it follows that there must be more accredited training of therapists backed by a greater openness of what goes on in therapy sessions (see also Chapter 11). Attention to these two responsibilities could improve the quality of alcohol services without increasing costs. Recognising the need for agencies to be effective, Alcohol Concern and the Standing Conference on Drug Abuse (1998) have collaborated on a project to improve standards: QUADS – Quality in Alcohol and Drug Services – is an audit tool that covers both organisational and clinical aspects of agencies' responsibilities.

The State

The state is a very special kind of stakeholder in that it is responsible for the well-being and prosperity of all its citizens. The interests of the member countries of the British Isles are entrusted to a single elected government with a variety of arrangements for devolving power away from the centre. Checks and balances are provided by institutions which may or may not be independent of government. Local government has a responsibility for the environment, and social services, education and health authorities and the criminal justice system are among the more obvious state institutions to be concerned with alcohol policy. In the case of alcohol policy we believe that the machinery of government needs to be coordinated as if it were a single stakeholder acting for the public good. The *European Alcohol Action Plan* (WHO, 1993) calls on all member states of the European Community to act in a coordinated way and to follow the ethical principles and goals of the *European Charter on Alcohol* (WHO, 1995).

We have argued that the state is a special kind of stakeholder in that it is empowered to balance the different vested interests that might pull and push a national alcohol policy in different directions. While the ethical principles and goals woven into the *European Charter on Alcohol* set standards that few would argue against, it is the translation of these principles into meaningful action that causes difficulty.

The state is governed through departments that can be expected to have conflicting views on the balance of elements within a national alcohol policy. The Treasury will be keen to keep up tax revenues from alcohol. The Department of Trade and Industry and the Ministry of Agriculture, Fisheries and Food will want to encourage world class businesses and keep up UK employment – we have already referred to data supporting the economic and employment benefits of the drinks and leisure industries. However, a benefit to one department may well be a cost to another. What is certain is that alcohol has an impact on all government departments:

- of unmarried people, 35% of males and 21% of females drink in excess of safe limits (21 and 14 units of alcohol weekly for men and women respectively) – corresponding figures for married men and women are 24% and 13%. Consumption is rising in women across all age groups and also in young men. The figures for drinking at harmful levels are 6% for men and 2% for women (ONS, 1998a).
- In 1996 the UK spent over £28,000 million on alcohol which generated in excess of £10,000 million revenue for the government. Pre-tax profits to the six leading alcohol companies exceeded £3200 million in 1995 and

in 1996 £190 million was spent on promoting alcohol (Alcohol Concern, 1997a).

- It is calculated from the national census of treatment (Luce *et al.*, 1998 – see Appendix 2) that, on a typical day, some 10,000 individuals seek help for their own or someone else's drinking problem.
- It has been estimated that 60% of para-suicides, 30% of divorces, 40% of domestic violence and 20% of child abuse cases are associated with alcohol misuse. About a third of all domestic accidents are alcohol related and a quarter of all alcohol related deaths are due to accidents (HEA, 1997).
- Estimates of alcohol related mortality, which reflect the more general use of health resources, range from 4000 to 40,000. In 1996 there were 4484 deaths reported as directly alcohol related – this figure does not take account of the alcohol attributable fraction in deaths due to, for example, cancer, heart disease, accidents, and so forth (Alcohol Concern, 1998b).

Politicians and policy makers know all about conflicting interests – that is their business. The potential for conflict is highlighted here in order to strengthen the argument for a strong, ministerial-level steer on a national alcohol policy. We return to the organisational issues of policy in Chapter 12.

Alcohol as Part of British Culture

We have said that alcohol is deeply embedded within British culture. The veracity of this statement rather depends upon our understanding of the meaning of 'culture'. Consider, for example, terms such as 'Western culture', 'Eastern culture' and 'multiculture'; 'high culture' and 'mass culture'; 'cult', 'subculture', 'mainstream culture' and 'counterculture'. Which, if any, of these is implied when the influence of culture is referred to? The word is conceptually complex (Williams, 1976) which has implications for its capacity to transmit meaning accurately.

A distinction can be made between an *aesthetic* notion of culture, which refers to the creative arts, and a much broader *sociological* notion which incorporates all activities and practices of a society. This understanding, which has its roots in anthropology, was encapsulated in an early definition as, 'that complex whole which includes knowledge, belief, art, morals, laws, customs, and any other capabilities and habits acquired by man as a member of society' (Tylor, 1870, p. 1). While this clarifies the focus of anthropological concern, it is somewhat lacking in explanatory power. Rather, it emphasises the catch-all nature of the term and the problems inherent in trying to combine these different aspects into a unifying concept of what culture is. Perhaps the simplest analysis of culture is that is represents the 'personality of society'.

For our purposes we might suggest that both the sociological and the aesthetic notions of culture have relevance to an understanding of British society's drinking behaviour. Social norms, law and practices all impact upon beliefs and regulate behaviour in relation to drinking. At the same time, belief and behaviour are represented within the creative arts which, in turn, feed back into social norms and practice. The relationship of alcohol to culture has been studied largely from two broad perspectives. First, anthropologists have catalogued the normative role of alcohol within cultures. Second, alcohol specialists have been concerned with the links between the development of alcohol problems, successful treatment and cultural influences. Early anthropological work tended to focus on ethnographic studies of 'primitive societies' (Pittman and Snyder, 1962a, p. 3), such as Heath's (1962) study of the Bolivian Camba. This developed into the investigation of minority cultures, such as Bales's (1962) study of Irish Americans, and Snyder's (1978) work on Jewish Americans and alcohol. Here the focus was on cultural differences in the use of alcohol and consumption patterns, and particularly the role of religion, in affecting the different rates of alcohol dependence within these communities. The tradition was continued by, for example, Heath *et al.* (1981), who investigated, amongst other groups, Native Americans.

Focusing mainly on minority populations within large cultures, these approaches rarely investigated majority populations. Where they did (for example, Pittman and Snyder, 1962b), attention was given to the individual person's 'alcoholism', but the social problems associated with alcohol consumption, such as interpersonal violence, were largely ignored. Room (1984) has alleged that the anthropologists have *deflated* the extent of alcohol related problems within societies. This has been denied by Heath (1995), who has pointed to the benefits of alcohol consumption in most societies and suggested that those who highlight alcohol's negative consequences have an interest in doing so. Sociologists have replied by emphasising the influence which mainstream culture has on alcohol consumption patterns, and therefore on problem development (for example, Cahalan and Room, 1974). This has been taken further by MacAndrew and Edgerton (1969), who have claimed that the occurrence of violence and other antisocial behaviours as consequences of heavy drinking are also a result of cultural expectations.

Scientific analysis of the types of problems experienced, the relationship of these to culturally influenced consumption patterns, levels of drinking, and expectations, has been undertaken (for example, Knibbe *et al.*, 1987; Norström, 1995). This has created firmer ground from which to consider the influence of culture not only on problematic, alcohol related behaviour, but also on associated health problems. In an account of alcohol and work in pre-industrial England, Warner (1995) surmises that there were no boundaries between work and leisure and no boundaries between drinking and non-drinking times. To drink a gallon of beer a day was seen as desirable, a means to fend off hunger and tiredness. The Industrial Revolution brought with it the need for people to work regular hours and to be fit to operate machinery. At about the same time the Temperance movement became a major player in changing public attitudes (see Chapter 1 for a more detailed discussion). Dean (1995) has mapped drinking patterns in the Hebridian culture from the sixteenth through to the twentieth century. Over the study period drinking patterns and preferred beverage adapted markedly in response to social, economic and religious changes within the islands.

These two studies are unusually clear illustrations of how, viewed through a sufficiently long time-frame, drinking cultures can be seen to change. Not surprisingly major shifts in social value systems are mirrored in major shifts in alcohol policy. Some of the time, drinking patterns just become more visible; some of the time, real changes occur. Study of this area will be of increasing importance as the impact of globalisation (Simpura, 1997, pp. 34–6) affects established drinking patterns. For example, the European Union has seen significant changes in consumption in the past 40 years. Countries which used to have higher levels of consumption have reduced them significantly, while those which had lower levels have increased their consumption. Preferred types of beverage and patterns of drinking have also altered (Simpura, 1996). There will be resulting changes in future alcohol related problems which will present challenges to those responsible for provision of services. In Chapter 5 we discuss how, on a much larger scale, European patterns of drinking tend to be moving closer both for per capita consumption rates and for beverage choice.

The Community Systems Model

Policy making is more inclusive than prevention alone – it is a balancing act with the public good as its guiding principle. The ideal of any policy might be to prevent all alcohol related harms but the reality will be to achieve a balance of risks that results in an acceptable level of 'casualties'. It follows that policy must be rooted in an understanding of alcohol consumption in the community and a model of prevention. Holder (1998, pp. 8–9) makes a strong case for a new paradigm of alcohol prevention and, in support, lists six propositions:

- Alcohol and other drug problems are the natural result, or output, of dynamic, complex, and adaptive systems called *communities*.
- Working only with high-risk individuals or small groups produces, at best, short-term reductions in alcohol problems, because the system will produce replacements for individuals who leave high-risk status, and the system will adapt to changes in the composition and behaviour of subgroups and populations.

- Interventions in complex adaptive systems do not always yield the desired results, and they often produce undesired and unexpected outcomes that are counter-intuitive – 'not what we thought would happen'.
- The most effective prevention strategies are those that seek to alter the system that produces alcohol problems.
- Prevention strategies historically have been single solutions; that is, they have attempted to accomplish a goal by one, usually massive, programme or strategy, rather than by concurrent, mutually reinforcing approaches.
- Without an understanding of the community as a dynamic system – that is, without a model that increases our ability to understand and effectively change the system – it is unlikely that effective long-term prevention of alcohol problems will occur in practice.

So, the 'Community Systems Model' described by Holder (1998) is fundamentally different from conventional approaches to policy and prevention. Real communities are *complex*, meaning that many variables are needed to describe the character of the community accurately – key factors might include the size of population, unemployment rates, local economy, and more esoteric variables such as weather patterns or incidence of football matches. Real communities are also *dynamic*, meaning that they are constantly changing in order to adapt to new events occurring within the system. What is important is that whenever a new event occurs the consequences are difficult to predict because each consequence is the product of a number of probabilities. Holder and colleagues have developed a dynamic computer model of community systems which can be used at national, regional and local levels. Computer modelling is relatively new to health and social care in the UK; however, we believe that computer modelling is a research and policy evaluation tool that merits more widespread utilisation. Holder's Community Systems Model is made up of six subsystems (see Figure 2.1). It is the interactions between the subsystems that is all-important in devising a computer model of a real community.

The *Consumption* subsystem is the anchor point of the model and refers to patterns of consumption among different groups of the population, notably age and gender. The *Sales and Production* subsystem refers to the number of outlets, such as public houses, off licences, supermarkets and corner shops, and includes home production and illegal supply of alcohol. The *Formal Controls* subsystem reflects national legislation, by-laws and the degree to which these are enforced within a community – this subsystem is about the availability of alcohol. The *Social Norms* subsystem is a way of capturing what we have described as the 'culture' which may be supportive of or antagonistic towards drinking. The *Legal Sanctions* subsystem refers to laws that proscribe the use of alcohol in specific situations; for example, in public places, when driving, while responsible for children, and so on. The *Social, Economic and Health*

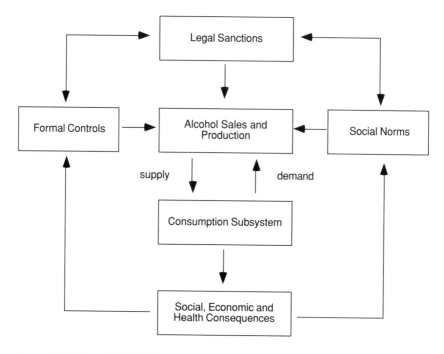

Source: Adapted from Holder (1998, p. 22).

Figure 2.1   Conceptual Community Systems Model for alcohol use

Consequences subsystem measures the impact of alcohol on health, the economy and the well-being of society more generally.

It is not difficult to see how a description of each subsystem might be constructed – for some subsystems there will be good-quality data and for others data will be lacking. Having described the subsystems, the important next step is to think about the possible interactions. From a cursory inspection it is obvious that change in any one subsystem is likely to upset the community system in its entirety. If policy makers and practitioners understand the dynamic nature of their community, whether at national or more local level, then they will also understand the need for coordination across a number of government departments and cultivate a commitment to collaborative working.

An Overview of Current Issues

We said at the beginning of this chapter that one of the appeals of the alcohol field is that we are constantly facing new challenges. It is also true that there are recurring themes. As far as current issues are concerned we have used this chapter to marshal some of the ambivalences about alcohol that are manifest in many different, often gross ways. For example, we have suggested that the state, on the one hand, likes to receive tax revenue from alcohol but, on the other hand, recognises the adverse effects of alcohol on health and social well-being; the drinks industry is criticised for putting profit first but praised for its employment record; at the individual level there is some wish to see all problems related to drinking as belonging to '*them*, not *us*'.

The title rather than the content of this chapter implies a second, important current issue, namely a more inclusive and community orientated alcohol field. In recent years our understanding of treatment mechanisms and the range of specific alcohol interventions has been expanded and evidence on effectiveness has accumulated. In the US the influential Institute of Medicine report *Broadening the Base of Treatment* (1990) is an authoritative update on where and how treatment should now be delivered; the trend to shorter community-based therapy is clear. In the UK the Advisory Council on the Misuse of Drugs goes a step further and looks at drug misuse and the environment (1998). The need to broaden the subject base is welcomed by many in the alcohol field and needs to be supported by broadening the professional base and training of people working in the alcohol field.

Part II

Patterns of Drinking and Associated Risks

3
Drinking in Different Population Subgroups

The consumption of alcohol is, for the majority of the adult population, a normal and unremarkable part of their lives. Self-reported data (HEA, 1997) show that 93% of men and 86% of women aged 16 or over claim to drink alcohol, many of whom will experience no serious problems as a result. However, neither levels of consumption nor the existence of alcohol related problems are evenly spread throughout the population. To understand the relationship between drinking and resultant harms, it is necessary to examine more closely *patterns* of consumption. The intention of this chapter is to present such an examination, first by setting out the evidence for consumption in the general population and subsequently by exploring in greater detail drinking patterns and drinking problems within some population subgroups. In this chapter we discuss:

- alcohol consumption in the general population
- young people
- students
- homeless people
- older people
- people at work
- criminality
- people in prison
- people with alcohol problems and psychiatric disorders.

Alcohol Consumption in the General Population

Customs and Excise

Because the trade in alcohol has raised money for governments through taxation for the last 300 years, fairly good historical estimates on alcohol consumption

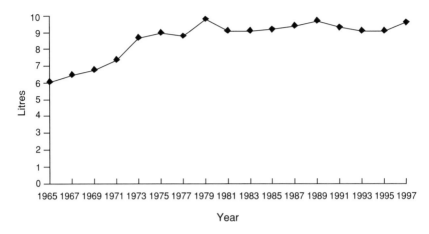

Source: Brewers and Licensed Retailers Association (1998, p. 37).

Figure 3.1   Litres of 100% alcohol per head of population aged 15 and over

are available (Brewers and Licensed Retailers Association, 1998). When records began, drinking per head of population was far in excess of today's levels. Alcohol consumption during the twentieth century has risen from the low levels recorded during the Depression and the war years. Figure 3.1 charts the litres per head of 100% alcohol consumed by the population aged 15 and over in the UK from 1960 onwards and shows that, after the previously steady increase, consumption has reached a plateau. The types of drinks being consumed have changed, however, with a particular recent increase in the consumption of wine (Brewers and Licensed Retailers Association, 1998).

Data of this kind from Customs and Excise give a reasonably objective indication of the UK's drinking, albeit that only alcohol on which duty is paid is included – so consumption will be underestimated because: (i) imports from outside the UK are excluded, (ii) home brewing is excluded, and (iii) returns may be incomplete.

The General Household Survey

Information on alcohol consumption and alcohol related problems can be gathered from the series of General Household Surveys that are undertaken in Great Britain. Every other year since 1978 there has been a section on alcohol consumption. Self-reported data from population surveys such as the 1996 General Household Survey (ONS, 1998a) show lower levels of alcohol use than do excise data, and also underestimate population consumption, because: (i) a unit of alcohol issued at home may be larger than one served on licensed premises but is still recorded as a unit, (ii) the heaviest drinkers may be under-represented in a household survey, (iii) sales include those to non-residents, (iv) there may be under-reporting, and (v) some age groups may be excluded.

Information for the General Household Survey is gathered in the autumn, which means that the increased drinking in the festive season will not be accounted for in the survey. Furthermore, the influence of tourist consumption noted above is difficult to disentangle – tourists who drink in this country inflate national consumption but, equally, British residents will drink unrecorded quantities when abroad. As there are many difficulties in accurately assessing the quantity of alcohol that respondents drink, especially in surveys that are not solely concerned with alcohol consumption, the responses are coded into alcohol consumption levels (see Table 3.1). In the summary charts (see Figures 3.2 and 3.3) the two lowest and the three highest consumption levels are collapsed into one 'low' and one 'high' category.

Table 3.1 Alcohol consumption levels as units of alcohol by sex and age

	16–24 years %	25–44 years %	45–64 years %	>65 years %	Total %
Men					
Non-drinker	8	5	6	12	7
Very low (under 1)	6	5	9	14	8
Low (1–10)	32	33	35	39	35
Moderate (11–21)	18	26	24	18	23
Fairly high (22–35)	16	16	15	10	145
High (36–50)	9	7	6	4	7
Very high (51+)	10	6	5	3	6
Mean weekly units	20.3	17.6	15.6	11.0	16.0
Base = 100%	880	2612	2214	1445	7151
Women					
Non-drinker	9	8	13	24	13
Very low (under 1)	13	14	21	30	20
Low (1–7)	36	42	38	29	37
Moderate (8–14)	20	19	15	10	16
Fairly high (15–25)	12	11	9	5	9
High (26–35)	4	3	2	1	2
Very high (36+)	5	2	2	1	2
Mean weekly units	9.5	7.2	5.9	3.5	6.3
Base = 100%	968	3179	2508	1836	8491

Source: ONS (1998a, p. 188).

Comparing the data for men and women, it can be seen that males drink more than females and that the older age groups on average drink less. The

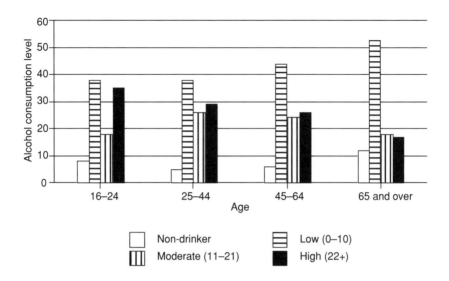

Source: ONS (1998a, p. 188).

Figure 3.2   Alcohol consumption level and mean weekly number of units for males

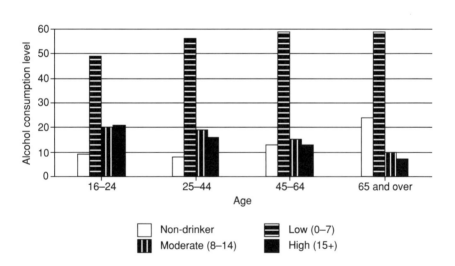

Source: ONS (1998a, p. 188).

Figure 3.3   Alcohol consumption level and mean weekly number of units for females

number of non-drinkers is lowest in the 25–44 age group. Although the percentage of men drinking over the recommended limits has remained fairly stable, the percentage of women drinking in the higher brackets has been increasing (ONS, 1998a, p. 180). Alcohol consumption levels can also be examined in relation to weekly income. Table 3.2 shows that, in general and except for men amongst the lowest income group, the higher an individual's disposable income, the more he or she is likely to drink.

Table 3.2   Alcohol consumption (mean weekly units) by sex and household income

	<£100	>£100 to £150	>£150 to £200	>£200 to £250	>£250 to £300	>£300 to £400	>£400 to £500	>£500
Men	17.1	9.6	13.3	15.8	13.7	15.8	15.7	19.1
Women	4.4	4.5	5.3	6.1	5.8	6.1	7.2	8.2

Source: ONS (1998a, p. 192).

Regional differences in reported alcohol consumption can also be examined. In Table 3.3 data from the 1996 General Household Survey are presented by sex and region. This shows that the highest reported mean alcohol levels are in men from the North and North West of England. Northern Ireland is not shown but has a much higher percentage of abstainers than other areas of the country (ONS, 1998b).

Table 3.3   Alcohol consumption by sex and region

Region	Male: mean weekly units	Female: mean weekly units
North	19.1	5.9
Yorkshire and Humberside	16.8	6.6
North West	18.4	7.9
East Midlands	15.3	5.8
West Midlands	16.2	5.9
East Anglia	13.7	5.5
South East:	15.2	6.2
Greater London	14.5	5.6
Outer Metropolitan	15.4	6.4
Outer South East	15.8	6.7
South West	15.0	6.1
England	16.1	6.3
Wales	15.0	6.8
Scotland	16.2	5.5
Great Britain	16.0	6.3

Source: ONS (1998a, p. 189).

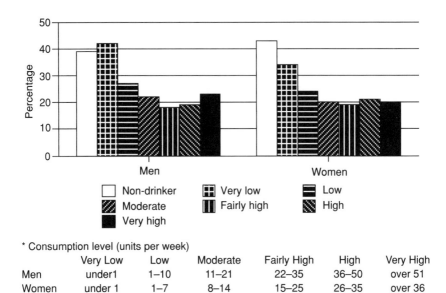

* Consumption level (units per week)

	Very Low	Low	Moderate	Fairly High	High	Very High
Men	under1	1–10	11–21	22–35	36–50	over 51
Women	under 1	1–7	8–14	15–25	26–35	over 36

Source: ONS (1998a, p. 195).

Figure 3.4   Percentage of persons with limiting longstanding illness by sex and alcohol consumption level

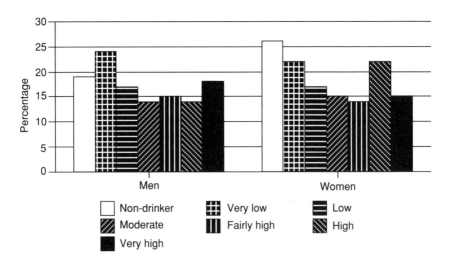

See Figure 3.4, note.

Source: ONS (1998a, p. 195).

Figure 3.5   Percentage of persons with restricted activity by sex and alcohol consumption level

The statistical relationship between health and alcohol consumption can be examined by comparing the prevalence of longstanding illness and restricted activity of those that report different alcohol consumption levels. Figures 3.4 and 3.5 give data from the 1996 General Household survey. Both these figures show the highest levels of illness are in the category that do not drink or drink very low levels. This is, in part, due to non-drinkers often abstaining from drink for medical reasons. Age is also a confounding factor in that older people, while being less likely to drink, as demonstrated by Figures 3.2 and 3.3, are also more likely to be ill. There are probably other social influences in addition, and correlations that should make us cautious about interpreting these data (Fillmore *et al.*, 1998a).

Other General Population Surveys

For recent years when the General Household Surveys have not been undertaken, similar data on alcohol consumption are available from the Health Survey for England (OPCS, 1995a). Both surveys examine alcohol and excessive alcohol consumption. However, neither specifically examines alcohol problems or alcohol dependence. The psychiatric morbidity survey by the Office of Population Censuses and Surveys (OPCS) in 1993 (OPCS, 1995b) examined alcohol dependence as a psychiatric problem, not a clinical diagnosis which may not have been completely realistic for a general population survey. Respondents were classified as being dependent on alcohol if they agreed with at least three of the twelve statements taken from the National Alcohol Survey carried out in the US in 1984 (Clark and Hilton, 1991).

The results, which are charted in Figure 3.6, show the prevalence of alcohol dependence by age and sex. These high levels, which show almost one in five men aged 20–24 as being dependent on alcohol during the preceding twelve months, are more likely to be a reflection of the screening instrument used to ascertain alcohol dependence than a true measure of the extent of clinical dependence. This survey also examined alcohol dependence by socio-demographic groupings, and found it to be less common among West Indian or African respondents and rare in Asian or Oriental respondents. Single people were more likely to be dependent on alcohol, as were those who were unemployed, who were unskilled manual workers or who were renting property. Regional differences are also apparent in this survey with the North East Thames and the Mersey Regional Health Authority areas as well as Scotland and Wales having higher levels of alcohol dependence.

Harrison *et al.* (1997) summarised a series of studies among different ethnic groups on the prevalence of problems associated with substance use. The authors noted that UK studies have consistently found consumption levels substantially lower than those of the native British reported by men and women

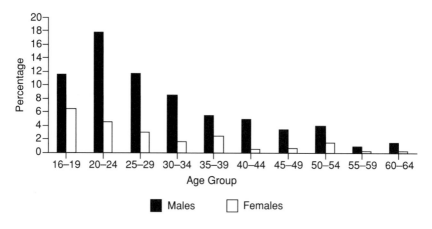

Source: OPCS (1995b).

Figure 3.6　Prevalence of alcohol dependence by age and sex

of African-Caribbean origin or born on the Indian Subcontinent. Men born in Ireland, however, report considerably higher levels of drinking.

Other ad hoc surveys of alcohol consumption in general populations have been carried out. Goddard (1991), for example, looked at alcohol consumption in the late 1980s, examining the changes in alcohol consumption around the time of a relaxation in licensing laws in England and Wales. This survey showed that despite the increase in the hours which licensed premises were allowed to open, there was no significant increase in alcohol consumption at the population level, although the possible influence of background economic changes was not controlled. There have also been health surveys undertaken in England in 1993 and 1995 (OPCS, 1995a), the information from which can be analysed with respect to other data, such as that relating to income and health.

Young People

The term 'young people' is a relative rather than an absolute term, applied in different circumstances to groups of individuals who may be years apart in terms of age. Reports on alcohol consumption in 'young people' should be read with this in mind. Findings from studies of school-age children, for example, may have little relevance to our understanding of potential problems in a wider total population of 'all young people'.

Equally, the term 'young person' can have different meanings in terms of local authority responsibility, under the Criminal Justice Act, within child and adolescent mental health services and in different funding streams. A 'young person' can be someone less than 16, less than 18, less than 19 or less than 25 years old. Under the Children Act (1989) young people are usually defined, in terms of local authority responsibilities, as those under 18 years or younger, although in exceptional cases this is sometimes extended to 21 years.

Prevalence

The consumption of alcohol by young people can be examined using population surveys; for example, the OPCS survey *Teenage Drinking in 1994* (OPCS, 1996c), which analysed the questions on alcohol consumption from surveys on smoking in secondary school children. In total, 24% of those aged 11–15 in England and 25% in Wales, and 20% of those aged 12–15 in Scotland, had drunk in the preceding week.

Balding (1996) has published the results from a national survey of children's health which included information on alcohol consumption. In the 1994 survey, the number of units of alcohol consumed in the last seven days by those in year 8 (aged 12–13) and year 10 (14–15) were presented. Although almost 60% of boys aged 12–13 did not consume an alcoholic drink in the preceding week, 15% consumed 1 or 2 units of alcohol and 2% consumed more that the recommended safe level of consumption for adult men. Similarly, 6.6% of boys and 9.4% of girls aged 14–15 drank over the recommended level for adults.

The findings from the literature demonstrate that by the age of 13, most young people have tasted alcohol, and that boys drink more than girls and older adolescents more than younger. Recent research (Newcombe *et al.*, 1995) has noted a changing pattern, with young people drinking considerably more alcohol on any one occasion: this may be related to regional differences or to the availability of high-strength drinks now being promoted.

Drinks Attractive to Young People

In recent years the alcohol industry has introduced and promoted new fortified wines, spirit mixers and strong ciders. Increasingly, concern has been raised that such drinks might appeal particularly to adolescent drinkers, due to their sweet taste and stylish packaging (McKeganey *et al.*, 1996; Hughes *et al.*, 1997). The reports by McKeganey *et al.* and Hughes *et al.* appear to confirm concerns about the extent to which young people might be attracted to such drinks, and their association with heavier alcohol consumption, greater intoxication and drinking in less controlled environments. Both studies found that pupils who reported drinking white ciders or fruit wines were significantly more likely to have been drunk. The peak age for consumption of the white ciders was 14 but Hughes *et al.* reported an age differential in terms of choice of alcoholic drinks. The 12- and 13-year-olds were mainly experimenters with any available drinks; those aged between 14 and 15 preferred drink to be strong, inexpensive and sweet; while those aged 16 and 17 had developed a taste for drinks such as spirits and bottled beer. It is noteworthy that alcohol use is a common precursor to smoking or the use of illicit drugs. The risk of smoking and drug use is particularly high in adolescents who report high levels of drunkenness.

Alcohol Related Problems in Young People

A significant minority of young people are at risk of chaotic intoxication: 6% of 11–16-year-old boys and 5% of similarly aged girls drank more than recommended adult limits weekly. With an older group (16–19 years), 15% of males and 8% of females drank in excess of the safe limits as defined at the time of the study (HEA, 1992). Those who were more regular drinkers were more likely to be regular smokers and to have used illicit drugs. Miller and Plant (1996), in examining a representative sample of young people born in 1979, noted that almost all had used alcohol, 77% reported intoxication at some time, 50% reported consumption of more than 5 units in a row in the previous 30 days and 48% had been intoxicated in the same period. Of this group, 36% had smoked cigarettes in the past 30 days, while 42% had tried an illicit drug, usually cannabis.

Lack of clarity in defining categories leads to confusion and uncertainty about the presence or severity of problems, the nature of these problems, and the need for and availability of services. Definitions of use, misuse or abuse often depend on a society's acceptance or tolerance of the recreational use of alcohol and other drugs among young people. Alcohol use is seen as more acceptable by both young people and adults.

The terminology of substance use disorders has been developed for adults with little or no empirical evidence for its appropriateness in adolescents. The terms used with alcohol and drugs include 'experimenter' and 'recreational user', and these have typically referred to 'non-pathological' use. However, the boundaries with regard to frequency, quantity or consequences are unclear. Equally unclear is the meaning of terms such as 'chaotic', 'heavy', or 'extensive' (Kaminer, 1991). Furthermore, the literature on defining problematic alcohol use among adolescents shows noteworthy disagreement (Dunn *et al.*, 1993). Ellickson and Hays (1991) used frequency of binge drinking; Jessor (1987) adopted the number of times intoxicated as a sole measure of problem use; while others, such as Dielman *et al.* (1989), defined misuse using negative consequences (problems with family, argument with peers, trouble with teachers, and so on) as an indicator. Hays and Ellickson (1996) surveyed alcohol experts in the US and noted that exact agreement over frequency/quantity and negative consequences was rare. Adolescent alcohol use differs from that of adults in that frequency/quantity measures have different significance, dependence is unusual and levels that may be reasonable for the older adolescent may not be appropriate for the younger person.

The Inter-relationship of Substance Use and Delinquency

It is now clear that a range of adult problems can be predicted from behaviour and psychological factors in childhood. The adult problems which can be predicted include alcohol dependence, dependence on other drugs, depression and neurotic disorders, as well as antisocial behaviours including violence and other crime (Robins and McEvoy, 1991; Moffitt *et al.*, 1996). It is not possible to predict precisely which problems a child is going to develop in the future; the problems tend to develop together and exacerbate each other. A youth with two or more problems has a poorer adult prognosis than a youth with only one problem. As drug use has become prevalent among adolescents, it has ceased to be a simple matter clearly to separate out the role of alcohol from the role of other substances. Drug misusers tend to have misused alcohol under age, younger than their peers and prior to use of most or all illegal drugs (Jessor and Jessor, 1977; Golub and Johnson, 1994). It therefore makes little sense to single out alcohol at this stage as being more or less benign than the other substances of misuse. It is not known why some substance misusers become dependent on one substance, such as alcohol, and others on another, such as heroin, while most avoid dependence and grow out of substance misuse, or grow into a relatively stable and controlled pattern of alcohol or other drug use as adults.

Adolescent delinquency and substance misuse share common developmental predictors (Jessor and Jessor, 1977; Elliott *et al.*, 1985; Brook *et al.*, 1996). Delinquents and substance misusers tend to: (i) have disrupted family backgrounds, (ii) do poorly in school/truant, (iii) have poor social skills, (iv) associate with delinquents, (v) have been in care (and later on remand or in prison), (vi) have a history of age-inappropriate behaviour (doing things younger than approved of by society), (vii) have been sexually or physically abused, and (viii) have low psychological well-being (depressed, anxious, low self-esteem, and so on).

The alcohol–crime connection may be increased by the recent increase in the quantities of alcohol consumed per drinking session in the young population (Measham, 1996). In addition there is some evidence that alcohol is particularly associated with violent crime (see, for example, Wiley and Weisner, 1995; Windle and Windle, 1995; Fergusson *et al.*, 1996). However, longitudinal research has concluded that the question of whether alcohol misuse causes crime is ill-conceived because both develop together. In particular, alcohol, alcohol misuse and alcohol dependence do not *cause crime* in any straightforward way. Alcohol use is one thing which adolescents with problem behaviours do, and alcohol can be one – often one of many – factor which worsens delinquent and problem behaviours.

For alcohol and crime, it is also important to emphasise the difficulties of separating out alcohol problems from other drug problems. In the generations born after about 1965, criminality will often co-occur with a pattern of poly-drug use, commonly including alcohol, cannabis, amphetamines, ecstasy, LSD and perhaps opiates and cocaine (Parker, 1996). In that context alcohol may affect people's behaviour even if they present with another drug problem, and people who present with alcohol problems may also misuse other drugs. This applies both to substance misuser samples (Hammersley, *et al.*, 1990a) and offender samples (Keene, 1997). Both alcohol and benzodiazepine misuse are acutely related to crime (Wiley and Weisner, 1995; Hammersley and Pearl, 1997a), as is dependence on opiates, cocaine or amphetamines. The relationship between alcohol and crime will be examined further later in this chapter.

Students

It has been found that many students, across faculties and throughout the UK, are drinking alcohol above sensible limits. Students are vulnerable to excessive drinking because (i) university and college bars sell low-price drinks, (ii) there are peer groups supportive of drinking behaviour, and (iii) there are unfamiliar academic and social pressures to deal with. The full extent of alcohol related problems – sexual, violence, poor work performance, vandalism – is not known.

Table 3.4   Alcohol use among second year university students

Weekly use (units)	Men (n=1610)		Women (n=1447)	
Mean	31.8		17.3	
Median	26	(1–195)	14	(1–96)
0	10.9%	(176)	10.6%	(153)
1–14	22.5%	(363)	46.5%	(673)
15–21	12.3%	(198)	16.9%	(245)
22–28	12.4%	(200)	10.9%	(158)
29–35	10.3%	(166)	5.7%	(82)
36–50	15.9%	(256)	7.3%	(105)
>50	15.6%	(251)	2.1%	(31)

Source: Webb *et al.* (1996).

A survey of 260 medical students by Collier and Beales (1989) found mean alcohol consumption to be 20.5 units per week for male students and 14.6 units per week for females. Of the respondents, 23% of males drank over 35 units per week and 22% of females drank over 21 units a week. Of the 59 students exceeding these limits, 51 responded positively for a standard screening test for alcohol abuse, 40 reported that they may have a drinking problem, and 138 reported that alcohol had affected their academic performance at some time. Howse and Ghodse (1997) described the reported drinking behaviour of students at 13 United Kingdom Medical Schools. Of these students, 23% of males and 10% of females reported drinking above sensible limits in a typical week. These levels are somewhat lower than those reported by studies of students overall. Regular use of tobacco was reported by those who drank in a hazardous way compared to 18% of moderate drinkers. A similar association was observed with cannabis use (see Table 3.4).

Webb *et al.* (1996) gathered information about alcohol, tobacco and drug use from 3075 second year university students from ten UK universities. They found that 11% of the students were non-drinkers. Among drinkers, recommended levels (1–14 units per week for women; 1–21 for men) were exceeded by 61% of men and 48% of women. 'Binge drinking', defined as drinking over half the recommended number of units per week in one session, was reported by 31% of men and 24% of women.

Homeless People

A pronounced rise in homelessness in both the UK and the US occurred throughout the 1970s and 1980s (Harrison and Luck, 1996), although an exact estimate of the number is difficult to obtain, since official figures record only those who come forward for help (George *et al.*, 1991; Shanks *et al.*, 1994). In 1987, local authorities in England and Wales estimated that some 120,000 households (350,000 people) were homeless, although this number excluded most of the population of young, single homeless, estimated by Shelter to be around 150,000 (George *et al.*, 1991). There is general agreement that the demographic characteristics of the homeless have changed over the past 30 years, and that the new homeless population tends to be younger and more heterogeneous than the old 'skid row' population, with a higher proportion of unmarried and single-parent women, adolescents and ethnic minorities (Harrison and Luck, 1996).

The term 'persistent street drinker' has been used to describe 'people who drink in public places and whose behaviour is seen to require intervention for reasons of public order or to prevent a continuing nuisance to the public or for their own safety'. There are no estimates of the number of persistent street drinkers. A proportion will meet the definition of habitual drunken offenders – people who have been arrested at least three times in a year for a drunkenness offence – and of these there are estimated to be between 5000 and 8000 (Mental Health Foundation, 1996).

Prevalence

The 1994 national survey of psychiatric morbidity among homeless people in Britain found that 44% of people using night shelters were alcohol dependent, of whom 31% were severely dependent. Of rough sleepers using day shelters, 51% were found to be dependent, of whom 36% were severely dependent (OPCS, 1996b). A study of 96 inhabitants of a shelter in London found a strikingly high prevalence of 'alcoholism', 53%, and alcohol dependence, 27% (Reed *et al.*, 1992). A survey of 371 individuals sleeping rough in Central London found just under half to have an alcohol problem, a third to have poor mental health and one in five to have a problem with drugs (Homeless Network, 1996). Of the 340 single homeless respondents in George *et al.*'s (1991) Sheffield survey, 28% reported a history of alcoholism, compared with 9% who reported drug misuse and 34% who gave a history of psychiatric illness.

Alcohol Related Problems of the Homeless

A relationship between alcohol problems and homelessness exists, although its precise nature is less obvious. For some, being homeless exacerbates problems that already exist, while for others, alcohol problems may develop as a result of being homeless (Weaver, 1997). Surveys of attenders at General Practitioner (GP) clinics for homeless people have shown in Oxford that 60% of consultations were for alcohol related problems. In Manchester, self-described alcoholism accounted for 48% of such consultations, while 36% in London were for problems associated with alcohol abuse (Royal College of Physicians, 1994). One study (Gelberg and Leake, 1993) found no evidence that homelessness *per se* was independently associated with either alcohol or illegal drug misuse, although the authors were careful to point out that their findings contradicted other studies where a significant relation was found. Whatever the direction of causality, research has shown that alcohol problems among the homeless are intertwined with crime, violence and physical and mental illness (Dunne, 1990; George *et al.*, 1991; Reed *et al.*, 1992; Gelberg and Leake, 1993; Shanks *et al.*, 1994; Harrison and Luck, 1996; OPCS, 1996b).

It is recognised that single homeless people with alcohol problems have higher rates of ill-health than do the general population (Dunne, 1990; Harrison and Luck, 1996), suffering all the illnesses associated with excessive drinking as well as those associated with an unsettled lifestyle and rough sleeping. Studies have shown that almost half of all street drinkers receive less than one meal a day, while the remainder eat irregularly, and generally the food is of low nutritional content (Moore, 1987; Wake, 1992).

A survey of 521 homeless individuals in seven local authority districts by Drake *et al.* (1981) found that alcohol and health problems vary with age. Intermediate age groups (30–44 years) reported higher rates of 'alcoholism' and mental illness (5–9% and 15–16% respectively) than the elderly, of whom only 2% suffered from 'alcoholism' and 3–12% from mental illness. This pattern also applied to the researchers' separate sample of 6531 clients of a referral agency. Of 100 young homeless people interviewed in a Glasgow study, 16% scored more than 9 on the standardised Severity of Dependence Scale, classing them as severely dependent (Hammersley and Pearl, 1997b).

Exclusion from Services

Because of a lack of specific services for homeless problem drinkers, because many services for the homeless exclude those with alcohol problems, and because many services for those with alcohol problems exclude the homeless, members of this group frequently move between tertiary sources of health care, temporary shelter and alcohol treatment services without ever receiving a comprehensive package of care. Homeless individuals with alcohol problems are excluded from health care services which are available to those *with* secure accommodation (Lamb, 1995; Weaver, 1997). Homeless people not registered with a GP often find difficulty in obtaining medical help. Similarly, those seeking access to rehabilitation centres normally approach their local authority for assessment and funding under community care. However, for the transient, without proof of an address and periods of residence, an already difficult process becomes fraught with problems (Weaver, 1997). Problems with keeping appointments, responding to or receiving letters and budgeting can all contribute to a situation in which the individual becomes practically excluded from a range of essential services. Homeless people who drink can find themselves excluded from generic services set up for the homeless. For example, some housing agencies will not accept homeless people who continue to drink, nor provide shelter for those who relapse. It is in this climate that groups such as Alcohol Concern have argued for a range of accommodation services to provide both for those who aim for abstinence and for those who do not.

Older People

Alcohol consumption commonly declines with age. At least in part, decline with age can be attributed to increased mortality amongst excessive drinkers or increasing physical illnesses causing individuals to cut back their drinking. Socio-economic factors may restrict opportunities for drinking or make drinking less rewarding. There is also the possibility of a cohort effect so that the apparent decline with age reflects the drinking habits of that generation rather than a true age-related decline. If this is the case, then the recent increase in reported consumption may prove to be a reflection of the prevailing pattern in the generation that now constitutes the elderly. General Household Surveys show an increasing proportion of older (age 65+) people in Britain drinking at hazardous levels. In 1984, 12% of men and 3 % of women aged 65 or over were drinking above 21 and 14 units respectively. By 1996 this figure had risen to 18% of men and 7% of women. Heavy drinking was not uncommon, 3% of older men drinking 51 units or more and 1% of women 36 units or more per week (ONS, 1998a). Clinical studies suggest that of those older people who have more serious drinking problems, in at least two-thirds of cases this has been a longstanding problem. A smaller proportion developed alcohol problems later in life often in response to retirement, bereavement or other forms of loss (see Wattis, 1983).

Older people are more vulnerable to the effects of alcohol and this makes it all the more important that those who are drinking excessively are recognised and advised appropriately. Unfortunately, problem drinking is often overlooked in older people because it does not accord with prevailing stereotypes. Although a minority, we may see a greater number of older people with alcohol problems in the future. Their needs must not be overlooked in the development of services and training is required to ensure prompt identification and adequate support.

People at Work

Historically, alcohol has always played a role in relieving the stress and monotony of work. At various times it has been used as 'payment in kind', and to desensitise manual workers to long hours, strenuous physical labour and poor conditions (Warner, 1995), in much the same way as cannabis has been smoked on West Indian plantations and coca leaves chewed in Peruvian mines (Tyler, 1986).

Today, alcohol continues to play its part in and around work, both as an antidote to the pressures of the modern workplace and as a lubricant of business and personal relations. Social pressures to drink, stress, lack of supervision, boredom, anxiety about status, remuneration and job security are all factors which may contribute to alcohol use and misuse at work. While the positive effects of work-related drinking, such as group celebrations and team-building social activities cannot be disregarded, the perceived benefits are difficult to measure and little research has been done in this area. A number of studies have shown that light, social drinkers seem to be better at handling work stress than either abstainers or heavier drinkers and have lower sickness absence rates than the other two groups (see Vasse *et al.*, 1998). Of more immediate concern to industry and society are the negative effects of alcohol misuse at work, which can be defined as consumption which reduces workers' capacity to perform to acceptable standards of quality, safety and presentation, and includes the costs of accidents, absenteeism, lost revenue, disciplinary problems arising from occasional inappropriate drinking, and the longer-term management and reha-bilitation of alcohol-dependent workers.

The socio-economic status of a job influences reported consumption even within occupational categories. A study amongst civil servants in Whitehall showed that the pattern and quantity of drinking differed by employment grade. For men there was a striking increase in the prevalence of non-drinkers in the lower grades: 32% per cent of the men employed in the top grade fell into the moderate drinking category (11–21 units per week); this fell progressively to 16% in the lowest grade. Women similarly showed a gradient in the prevalence of abstinence more frequent in the lower grades and a higher proportion of moderate drinkers in the higher grades. There was little difference in the proportion of people in the heaviest drinking categories by grade for men, while for women, the higher the grade, the greater the prevalence of heavy drinking (Marmot *et al.*, 1991).

Occupational Mortality

Those who work in certain occupations have higher levels of alcohol related mortality than others. According to the OPCS report (1995c), *Occupational Health: Decennial Supplement*, publicans, doctors, lawyers and seafarers are the four occupations most at risk from deaths caused by liver cirrhosis, a major indicator of the prevalence of drinking problems. At least 70% of such mortality in Britain is alcohol related. The occupational health survey analyses all deaths recorded between 1979 and 1990 in England and Wales for individuals aged between 20 and 74, and notes eight causes of death known to be related to alcohol: cirrhosis of the liver; cancers of the oral cavity, pharynx, oesophagus, liver and larynx; falls on stairs; 'other alcohol related diseases', which includes alcohol dependence syndrome; non-dependent use of alcohol; alcoholic cardiomyopathy; alcoholic liver damage and accidental poisoning by alcohol.

The survey also identified the prevalence of alcohol related *problems* in specific occupations. Among men, the following patterns were found.

- *Farmers* from Somerset, Hereford and Worcester showed high rates of mortality from oesophageal cancer. These are areas where cider apples are grown, and, as alcohol is an established cause of this type of cancer, it is possible that the consumption of the rough cider made in these farms is a factor in its incidence. Slightly increased rates were also noted in Devon and Dorset, where cider is also made.
- *Aircraft flight deck officers and air traffic controllers* have increased mortality rates from 'other alcohol related diseases'. The latter group also have a higher than average level of liver cancer deaths, and the report speculates that occupational stress may contribute to the high alcohol consumption of this group.

- *Publicans and bar staff/brewery workers* figure highly in all alcohol related categories. This probably reflects not only easy availability of alcohol, but also a predilection for such work among people who drink heavily.

Amongst women, slightly different patterns were found.

- *Publicans and bar staff* displayed an almost threefold excess of deaths from 'other alcohol related diseases', and the rates for cirrhosis were even higher.
- *Literary and artistic occupations* showed increased mortality rates from cirrhosis, cancer of the oesophagus and oral cavity and 'other alcohol related diseases'.
- *Hairdressers* had significantly raised mortality rates from cirrhosis, cancer of the oral cavity and 'other alcohol related diseases'.
- *Health related professions* showed lower than expected death rates from alcohol related causes.

Interventions

The UK does not have a strong culture of workplace policies and help for employees. Rightly or wrongly, occupational health departments are often seen as an arm of management rather than an independent service and have not been used as a conduit for alcohol interventions.

The workplace is a special setting which offers opportunities for both preventive work and early intervention. Trice and Beyer (1984) describe a strategy of constructive confrontation, which is designed to take advantage of the coercive opportunities in the workplace setting. Using this approach they found that 70% of employees improved their work performance to a satisfactory level and a further 10% improved but with relapse; more severe forms of discipline were negatively associated with work performance. This approach has given way to Employee Assistance Programmes which have demonstrated high levels of acceptability across the workforce (see Delaney *et al.*, 1998).

Criminality

There is a worrying catalogue of associations between alcohol consumption and crime. Many perpetrators and victims of crimes of disorder or violence, including murder, as well as perpetrators of acquisitive crimes, such as burglary and theft, have alcohol in their blood at the time of the offence (see, for example, Bennett and Wright, 1984; Choquet *et al.*, 1991; Lindqvist, 1991; Avis, 1996; Rossow, 1996). Furthermore, as with other drugs, heavier users of alcohol are more likely to have criminal records and to admit to criminal acts than are lighter users or abstainers (Elliott *et al.*, 1985; Yu and Williford, 1994).

Such links are striking, but do not mean that alcohol causes the crime. Control studies examining the equivalent blood alcohol levels of people who have not offended are rarely conducted. Drugs, including alcohol, are often regarded as being the sole explanation of bad behaviours when they are only one contributing factor. There is a danger, however, of underestimating the impact of alcohol on crime, for society tends to minimise some of the common bad behaviours which accompany alcohol and stigmatise more criminal acts as behaviours restricted to a deviant alcoholic, violent or criminal minority. The tendency is to simplify and polarise the issue insisting either that alcohol causes crime, or that it does not, whereas the evidence is more balanced.

Common-sense Explanations of the Alcohol–crime Relationship

One common-sense explanation, widely favoured by drinkers and the drinks industry, is that since most drinkers do not commit crimes, alcohol use itself obviously does not cause crime. Rather, crimes associated with alcohol should be blamed on the deviant or 'alcoholic' nature of the drinker, on the social setting where drinking and crime occurred, or on some other factors. Human behaviours, however, are rarely caused by single direct effects. Alcohol may be neither a necessary nor a sufficient *cause* of crime, but may nonetheless *affect* crime.

The opposing explanation is that, as alcohol is at the root of much human misery, it is obvious that alcohol must influence crime, both directly and indirectly. *Directly*, alcohol triggers some crimes which would not have happened without it. It is argued, for example, that intoxication may shift some people over the threshold from contemplating crime to committing it. From this perspective, alcohol can become a scapegoat for human misbehaviour, whereas the picture is usually more complex (Davies, 1992; Coggans and McKellar, 1995). Public disorder, for instance, is commonly linked to open-air drinking by young people. Bans on drinking outside are easier to implement than more considered responses to disorder by youth, but may fail to address the causes of disorder, as well as ignoring the fact that open-air drinking only rarely involves intoxication (McGowan, 1995). *Indirectly*, alcohol is believed to affect crime in the following ways: (i) alcohol use can serve as a financial motive for crime, (ii) alcohol problems can produce a home environment conducive to antisocial behaviours, (iii) adolescent alcohol use can interfere with development leading to a more antisocial adult, (iv) alcohol can trigger or facilitate aggression, (v) drunk people may be amnesic regarding the negative consequences of their criminal actions, thus failing to learn from them, and vi) alcohol intoxication can reduce inhibitions and judgement.

Such explanations are hampered by the difficulties in distinguishing cause and effect in a mass of related social and personal problems. Given the psychological effects of alcohol, which one could say at minimum impairs judgement and thought processes, it would be surprising if it had no effect on crime. It is more surprising that the established effects are relatively variable, subtle and often indirect despite high levels of alcohol consumption. None the less, at the population level alcohol and crime appear to be related (Ensor and Godfrey, 1993).

The commonly accepted view is that *crime* is one coherent set of activities which is engaged in by a small minority of the population called *criminals*. If this were true then it might be plausible that some criminals are partly fuelled by alcohol and others consume large quantities of alcohol as part of their general antisocial character. In reality, crime constitutes a diverse set of law-breaking activities. The study of alcohol and crime largely neglects crime other than violence, including sexual assault; disorder; and acquisitive crimes such as theft, burglary and shoplifting. There is an unknown potential association between alcohol and fraud, tax evasion, smuggling, fiddles in the workplace and other 'white collar' crimes. There is also a probable, but largely unresearched, connection between intoxication and minor offences other than road traffic offences, including urinating in the street, parking offences, skipping fares or restaurant bills, vandalism and others.

Unfortunately, information is lacking on the very types of crime that are probably most likely to be committed by non-dependent drinkers. In terms of numerical evidence, it is not really possible to assess the truth of the proposition that *people in general are more likely to do things which are wrong when they are drunk*. Yet this seems very likely on the basis of everyday drinking experiences and fits with the known experimental psychological effects of alcohol, which impairs cognitive functioning, including decision making, forward planning and perceptual judgements (Finnigan and Hammersley, 1992), as well as increasing the occurrence of aggressive behaviour in situations which facilitate aggressive responding (Gustafson, 1993).

The Criminality of Drinkers

This issue remains surprisingly under-researched, compared to interest shown in the criminality of heroin or cocaine users. Many studies have found that a higher proportion of prisoners or arrestees have alcohol problems than one would find in the general population (see, for example, Heather, 1982; Hollin, 1983) and this includes those who have committed serious offences such as homicide or arson (Rasanen *et al.*, 1995). However, offenders have higher rates of virtually any psychological or social problem and it would be unwise to infer causality.

Only a proportion of alcohol dependent people commit criminal acts (deLucia, 1981). As with drugs and delinquency, the same factors tend to predict alcoholism and criminality (see, for example, Vaillant, 1995). Again, no simple causal model is appropriate. It would be reasonable to assume that alcohol dependence and criminality tend to exacerbate each other over the years. An offender is probably more likely to reoffend unless he or she ceases or moderates drinking – equally, the difficulties of being a prisoner, then an ex-prisoner, may well worsen or prevent improvement of an alcohol problem.

Outside of the offender population, it is more difficult to assess the relationship between problem drinking and crime. Many alcohol problems are hidden for years until a serious health, legal or social problem brings them to light. Some alcohol-dependent people appear to drink heavily and regularly without ever breaking the law, though it is not clear whether crime is hidden along with the drinking. For example, are all dependent drinkers at risk of violent offending against their families or friends, or are many dependent drinkers not violent? The various factors already reviewed suggest that alcohol problems and criminal behaviour will be strongly associated but causality cannot be inferred.

People in Prison

Relatively little research focusing exclusively on alcohol and prisons exists. Rather, it tends to be conflated with substance use in general, or studied as a factor involved in suicide and psychiatric disorder in prison (see, for example, Backett (1987) on the relation of alcohol and drug misuse to suicide or Brooke *et al.* (1996) on the relation of alcohol and drug use to psychiatric disorder). The literature on alcohol and prisoners is also deficient with respect to female prisoners. Thus, studies by Cookson (1992), McMurran and Hollin (1989), McMurran and Baldwin (1989) Brooke *et al.* (1996), McKeown *et al.* (1996) and Hodgins and Lightfoot (1988) are all conducted exclusively with males.

Research on alcohol use amongst prisoners shows a high proportion to be heavy or problem drinkers (Royal College of General Practitioners, 1986; National Association for the Care and Resettlement of Offenders, 1992), and tends to find that drinking is frequently related to offending (McMurran and Hollin, 1989; Cookson, 1992). Many prisoners themselves report a relationship between drinking and offending (Myers, 1983). Of Heather's (1982) sample, 63% claimed to have offended under the influence of alcohol, while Hollin (1983) reported that 38% of his sample of young male English offenders said they had been intoxicated when committing their crimes.

In a sample of young male offenders, McMurran and Hollin (1989) found the average self-reported alcohol consumption to be 58 units, compared with an average intake of 28 units per week in a normative sample (Wilson, 1980). Other research has measured the incidence of problem drinking among prison populations, with definitions and criteria varying across studies. Heather (1982), for example, identified 27% of prisoners in a sample of Scottish male offenders as having a drink problem. A consecutive case study of remand prisoners screened at reception for substance misuse revealed that 11% misused alcohol and 21% were alcohol-dependent. These figures were similar for those reporting drug dependency (Mason *et al.*,1997).

Prisoners, Alcohol and Mental Health

In 1991 the Gunn Report to the Home Office published a study of the mental health of the sentenced prison population based on interviews with 2042 prisoners serving sentences of six months or more: around 5% of the prison population (Home Office, 1991). Over 400 inmates were diagnosed as having substance misuse problems – by far the largest single diagnostic category in the study. Another study of mental disorder, this time amongst unconvicted male prisoners, was conducted in three young offenders' institutions and thirteen adult men's prisons by Brooke *et al.* (1996). A total of 750 prisoners, representing 9.4% of the unconvicted male population, were interviewed to determine the prevalence of mental disorder. Psychiatric disorder was diagnosed in 63% of inmates, of which substance misuse at 38% was the highest category. However, the authors did not distinguish between dependence on, or harmful use of, drugs or alcohol (Brooke *et al.*, 1996).

McKeown *et al.*'s (1996) study of the Forensic Addictive Behaviours unit at Broadmoor Special Hospital reported that 7% of patients had severe alcohol problems and that 33% had been drinking at the time of their offence. Norris (1984) surveyed males discharged from Broadmoor during the second half of the 1970s and found that around one in five had an alcohol problem and that this group was much more likely to reoffend. A study of male patients in Rampton Special Hospital noted that those with a history of alcohol related problems prior to admission had more previous convictions and were responsible for a disproportionately higher number of homicides (Thomas and MacMillan, 1993). A pilot mental health assessment scheme conducted by Greenhalgh *et al.* (1996) found 77% of prisoners to be suffering from a psychiatric disorder and almost half to be suffering from alcohol or drug dependence. Quayle and Clarke (1992) found that 7% of Broadmoor patients had severe alcohol dependence, 15–17% were in the high dependence category, and as many as 33% of patients had been drinking at the time of the offence which led to their admission. It has been concluded that 'alcohol use alone poses a formidable problem for Special Hospital patients' (McKeown *et al.*, 1996, p. 27).

People with Alcohol Problems and Psychiatric Disorders

Psychiatric comorbidity can be defined as the co-existence of an alcohol misuse or alcohol dependence problem and one or more additional mental illness or behavioural disorders. For present purposes, comorbidity and 'dual diagnosis' are taken to be synonymous. A great deal has been published on comorbidity but the research to date has been dominated by an epidemiological perspective, with relatively little attention given to the effectiveness of treatment or the best management of different dual diagnoses.

Prevalence of Comorbidity in the UK

There are formidable difficulties to estimating the size and the nature of comorbidity, including difficulties with diagnosis, differences in the time-frames used to assess comorbidity, evaluation of the part played by drugs other than alcohol in comorbid problems and differences in methods of recruitment and the settings in which studies are carried out.

There are good data from large-scale epidemiological surveys upon which to base estimates of the possible demand on services from problem drinkers with comorbidity. The Epidemiological Catchment Area Study database, generated from 10,291 interviews, was analysed by Regier *et al.* (1990) to give the prevalence of comorbid alcohol, other drug, and mental disorders in the US total community and institutional population. The lifetime prevalence in the survey population was 13.5% for any alcohol disorder, 6.1% for any other drug disorder and 22.5% for any mental illness; among those with alcohol disorders, 36.6% had at least one mental illness and 21.5% had another drug disorder. The lifetime odds ratio for experiencing problem drinking associated with schizophrenia was 3.3, affective disorder 1.9, anxiety 1.5, and antisocial personality 21.0, as compared to the general population. In specialist alcohol treatment services more than half the clients had comorbid mental disorder. In a similar analysis of the US National Comorbidity Survey of 8098 persons aged 15–54 years, Wittchen *et al.* (1996) calculated prevalence rates and odds ratios for a more comprehensive range of mental disorders which are compared to the total survey population in Table 3.5. For over 80% of respondents the mental illness disorder antedated substance misuse and this sequencing was strongest for conduct disorders and anxiety states.

With regard to the prevalence of psychiatric disorders among clients of alcohol treatment services, Glass and Jackson (1988) reported that, over a twelve-year period in two psychiatric hospitals in London, a consistent 30–40% received an additional psychiatric diagnosis. Associations were shown between alcohol problems and neurosis (10–16% of alcoholism diagnoses), personality disorders (10–24%), affective psychoses (2–3%), schizophrenia (1%) and dependence on other drugs (5%). A study of 171 inner-city London patients in contact with psychiatric services found a one year prevalence for alcohol problems of 32% amongst subjects with psychotic illness (Menezes *et al.*, 1996). Using various sources of data, Rorstad and Checinski (1996) calculated that in a population of 500,000 there will be nearly 6000 problem drinkers with comorbid mental health problems. Ward and Applin (1998) reported on the role of alcohol and drug misuse in the reports of inquiries into homicides by mentally ill people. Although the role of substance misuse was clear in the majority of cases, little attention had been given to improving this aspect of the services proposed.

Table 3.5   One year prevalence of mental disorder for the total (n=8098) NCS sample and comorbidity prevalence and odds ratios (OR) for problem drinkers

	Total Sample %	Alcohol Misuse %	OR	Alcohol Dependence %	OR
Generalised Anxiety	2.0	1.1	(0.4)	16.2	(4.6)
Panic	1.3	1.4	(0.5)	7.4	(1.7)
Social Phobia	6.6	5.2	(2.3)	10.5	(2.8)
Agoraphobia	1.7	2.7	(1.1)	10.4	(2.6)
Major Depression	7.7	2.8	(1.1)	12.1	(3.7)
Dysthymia	2.1	2.6	(1.0)	15.1	(3.9)

Sources: Kessler *et al.* (1994); Wittchen *et al.* (1996).

Psychiatric Comorbidity in Young People

Research suggests a major contribution from alcohol or other drug use in the etiology and progress of mental illness such as affective disorder, conduct disorder, anxiety syndromes, attention deficit and hyperactivity disorder. Rohde *et al.* (1996) looked at psychiatric comorbidity with problematic alcohol use in high school students aged 14–18 classified in five groups, from abstainers to misuse and dependence. More than 80% of adolescents with an alcohol disorder had a psychiatric disorder. The likelihood of a comorbid diagnosis with alcohol use appeared to be dose related, systematically increasing at each level of problematic alcohol use.

The rates of suicide among males have been increasing in most countries in the last two decades, with the biggest increase occurring in the 15–24-year-old group. Alcohol may be an important precipitant to both deliberate self-harm and suicide (Kerfoot and Huxley, 1995). Approximately one-third of young suicides are intoxicated with alcohol at the time of death (Williams and Morgan, 1994). An association between eating disorders and alcohol use has been frequently reported among females, with high levels reported in both general populations and clinic samples. Suzuki *et al.* (1995) reported significantly more alcohol use among both males and females with bulimic symptoms. Lavik and Onstad (1986) also noted the association with bulimia and alcohol intoxication. Eating disorders were present in 30% of those with alcohol problems, while 27% of those with eating disorders had alcohol problems.

Summary of Main Arguments

- The evidence shows that there is nothing fixed or unchanging about drinking habits and that they are responsive to social pressures and fashion. Subgroups of the population have distinctive and diverse patterns of consumption.
- The evidence base for planning prevention and service delivery depends upon having regular, consistent surveys of drinking habits available and reported alcohol related problems. Surveys should include all age groups and population subgroups who are often hard to reach, such as ethnic minorities or the homeless.
- The drinking habits of children and young people are important both in their own right and as predictors of subsequent problems. There is a close relationship between alcohol, other drug use (including tobacco) and future mental health problems.
- The workplace is well suited to identifying people at risk of drinking problems. The workplace is also a good environment in which to deliver prevention and treatment interventions.
- The homeless have a high level of alcohol related problems and suffer from various forms of social exclusion which exacerbate their special needs. Homeless drinkers are one of the few subgroups for whom special services are appropriate.
- Alcohol and drug misuse are common amongst offenders and convicted prisoners. The relationship between criminality and alcohol misuse is complex and varied; however, evidence suggests that alcohol initiatives instigated by the criminal justice system have been effective in a number of settings.

4
Intoxication in Social and Environmental Contexts

Through legislation and state institutions society sets minimum standards for the use of alcohol within certain contexts with the broad aims of protecting vulnerable individuals, improving public health, preventing crime and promoting social well-being. In some social and environmental contexts simply drinking alcohol may be a problem in itself. For example, any drinking in some workplace situations may be a dismissable transgression, and drinking in a public place may be against the law, so that in these contexts the consumption of alcohol constitutes a social or legal problem regardless of the extent to which an individual is intoxicated. Intoxication may impair performance, and increase the likelihood of accidents and aggressive behaviour. In certain contexts, any or all of these consequences of intoxication may pose an unacceptable risk.

In this chapter we move on from looking at people and their drinking to looking at drinking and the specific risks associated with intoxication. We stress again that the three chapters in Part II of the book need to be taken as a whole. The interactions between people, their environments and drinking are complex – the structure we have chosen is intended to focus minds on policy opportunities and is of necessity reductionist. In the real world it is seeing each policy opportunity within the community system that matters. In this chapter we discuss:

- blood alcohol concentrations and risk
- drunkenness, aggression and violence
- accidents
- behaviours facilitated by alcohol.

Blood Alcohol Concentrations and Risk

Pharmacokinetics

The rate at which alcohol is absorbed into the bloodstream is dependent upon several factors, including whether food is present in the stomach, and the type of alcohol consumed: beverages in the region of 15% alcohol by volume (abv) are most rapidly absorbed. The sex of the drinker is also relevant. Alcohol is water soluble and is not, therefore, distributed in fatty tissues; given that women's bodies have a greater ratio of fat to water – thus less water to dilute the alcohol – women have a higher blood alcohol concentration (BAC) than men for an equivalent amount of alcohol consumed, but also metabolise the alcohol more quickly than men (Cole-Harding and Wilson, 1987).

Most people will be familiar with the positive social and psychological effects of alcohol when taken at moderate doses. At relatively low levels alcohol leads to a pleasant sense of well-being; as the level increases, psychological and physical impairment is seen. Impaired judgement and coordination present particular threats to appropriate social behaviour, as well as the safety of the drinker and others. Ultimately the BAC may reach levels that lead to overdose and potentially to death. Gross intoxication is particularly dangerous in young people who are relatively naive to the effects of alcohol. While death through alcohol overdose on its own is relatively uncommon, in suicide attempts alcohol is more commonly taken in conjunction with other drugs that depress the central nervous system, so adding to the risk of death. Furthermore, alcohol can begin to impair coordination and driving ability at a relatively low level. A BAC of 40 mg% can be achieved by a male consuming only 2 units of alcohol (1 unit = 8 g alcohol = 1 glass of wine). Thus it must be emphasised that the context in which intoxication occurs is an important variable in determining adverse consequences.

The relationship between BAC and impairment is not a simple linear relationship. Zador (1991), for example, found that the risk of a fatal road traffic accident increased by a factor of eleven for drivers with BACs between 50 and 90 mg% compared with non-drinking drivers. At a BAC of between 100 and 140 mg% the risk increased by 48, and by 385 at levels of greater than or equal to 150 mg%. Thus the risk associated with each successive drink increases exponentially. In the same study, younger drivers were found to be at greater risk of fatality at a given BAC and the relative risk for females increased more steeply than for males. These findings emphasise the importance of individual risk factors in the relationship between alcohol consumption and adverse consequence (see Figure 4.1).

In practice it is extremely difficult to predict the exact effect of a given dose of alcohol. Numerous factors – including personality, mood, sex, level of

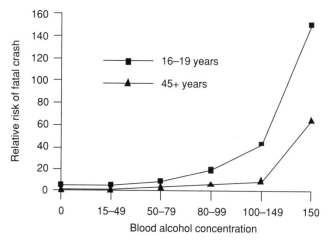

Source: Romelsjö (1995).

Figure 4.1   Blood alcohol content and risk of accident

tolerance to alcohol, and the physical, social, and cultural context in which alcohol is consumed – can magnify or diminish the effects of alcohol. For any particular function there will be a range of impairment around an average; it is this range that makes alcohol such a potentially dangerous drug. An individual's level of experience in drinking alcohol is not a reliable guide to its effects. What may be an acceptable or 'safe' level on one occasion, or for one person, may lead to serious adverse consequences on another occasion or for another person. It is not possible, therefore, to provide a definitive public health message as to what constitutes a 'safe' amount of alcohol to consume on a single occasion.

While there is individual variation in the rate of alcohol metabolism, typically alcohol is broken down at a rate of 1 unit per hour. It follows that individuals who are significantly intoxicated during the evening may still have a high blood alcohol concentration the following morning, so increasing the risk of a road accident or arrest for driving whilst intoxicated with alcohol.

Prevalence

A distinction must be made between intoxication and drunkenness. Intoxication is a physiological state which does not always result in clear behavioural consequences. Drunkenness, on the other hand, is a form of behaviour having less than perfect correlation with blood alcohol concentration. Nevertheless, figures on the prevalence of drunkenness provide some indication of relative levels of intoxication.

Drunkenness offence figures were routinely published until 1995. Changes in these figures may often only reflect changes in police practice or local by-laws. Although the penalty of imprisonment for the offence of being drunk was removed in the Criminal Justice Act of 1967, many habitual drunkenness offenders continue to find their way into prison because of the non-payment of fines (Robertson *et al.*,1995). Thus, while 94% of the 122,000 convictions for drunkenness in England and Wales in 1980 resulted in a fine, many of those fined may subsequently have been imprisoned for non-payment. These so-called habitual drunken offenders pass in and out of prison, usually serving frequent, short sentences.

Health surveys for England have included questions about 'drunkenness' since 1991. In 1994, amongst 'current drinkers' (consuming alcohol at least once every couple of months), 23% of men and 11% of women reported that they had been drunk three or more times during the previous three months (Colhoun and Prescott-Clarke, 1994). This included 12% of male current drinkers (10% of all men) and 5% of female current drinkers (4% of all women) who reported having been drunk on average once per week in the previous three months. Furthermore, 32% of young male drinkers (aged 16–24) reported being drunk at least once a week on average, and 79% at least once in the past three months. Intoxication is therefore extremely common in the general population, particularly amongst young males.

Drunkenness, Aggression and Violence

Although it is often imagined that there is a direct link between intoxication, drunkenness and aggression, the reality is rather different. There is certainly a robust correlation between alcohol consumption and aggressive behaviours (see, for example, Pihl and Peterson, 1995; Valdez *et al.*, 1995; Wiley and Weisner, 1995), but the causes of aggression are complex (Coggans and McKellar, 1995). The popular explanation of the correlation between crime and drinking alcohol is that alcohol has disinhibitory effects on people, causing behaviours to emerge that are normally controlled or suppressed (see Wight, 1993). It is often assumed that (i) aggression is a primitive instinct controlled by our social inhibitions or ego, (ii) *aggression* is virtually synonymous with *violence*, and (iii) alcohol disinhibits people, so aggressive behaviours emerge.

However, aggressive acts are skilled, learned behaviours which often occur because they are rewarded (Bandura, 1977; Baron and Richardson, 1994). Alcohol is not simply disinhibiting; indeed, the decreased arousal resulting from alcohol consumption should reduce the likelihood of aggression. Instead, alcohol tends to impair cognitive and intellectual functioning, including decision making: after alcohol consumption people will tend to make poor decisions (Steele and Josephs, 1990; Finnigan and Hammersley, 1992). In some circumstances alcohol can make aggression less likely (Steele and Josephs, 1990).

Aggression and violence do not comprise a single type of behaviour (see, for example, Baron and Richardson, 1994). In considering aggression and violent crime it is useful to distinguish (a) aggressive displays, (b) violent interpersonal conflict, and (c) premeditated violent offending. However, as premeditated violence is probably not related to alcohol intoxication, only aggressive displays and violent interpersonal conflict will be discussed.

Aggressive displays include verbal threats of violence, aggressive appearance and postures, perhaps a show of weapons, possible property damage and maybe even minor violence such as hitting without causing significant injury. Aggressive displays resolve without violence when the aggressor achieves his or her goal; for example, the victim complies, or shows fear, or the situation is broken up by other people. Aggressive displays occur either because the aggressors have learned that they can get their own way with aggression, or out of fear or strong arousal.

Violent interpersonal conflicts usually occur when an aggressive display has not achieved the aggressor's goal, when two or more parties are equally aggressive, when no one intervenes or when violence seems to be the only appropriate response. Violence can become serious if the aggressors have weapons, outnumber the victim or continue the assault when the victim is unable to escape and no one intervenes.

Offenders often view the violence that they have inflicted on others as being situationally caused; the unintended result of a routine interpersonal conflict, for instance (Hammersley *et al.*, 1990b); or as a justifiable protection of honour, possessions or territory (Carpenter *et al.*, 1988, p. 99). An act of violence may be regarded as an accident, or even as the victim's fault for not having backed down. Given such perceptions, alcohol may be regarded as irrelevant by some offenders and as a further mitigation of violence by others (Wight, 1993, pp. 160–1).

Most experimental and quasi-experimental research has examined aggression rather than violent and illegal behaviours. While the two are perhaps linked (Pihl and Peterson, 1995), aggression channelled in non-violent ways may often be appropriate and socially positive. A number of studies have examined the role of the drinking situation in determining drunken behaviour, including aggressive behaviours. Four key points have emerged. First, some people choose drinking settings where aggression is more likely. Some men choose settings which confirm a particular masculine self-image, which may include a willingness to fight (Alasuutan, 1992; Wight, 1993). Others even seek out fights, using alcohol as a facilitator (Moore, 1990). Naturally, these choices are culture-specific but this kind of masculinity appears to influence binge-style drinking; such cultures can be found in Finland (Alasuutan, 1992), Scotland (Wight,

1993), the US (Cavan, 1966; MacAndrew and Edgerton, 1969) and Australia (Moore, 1990; Homel *et al.*, 1992). People who drink more heavily or behave badly after drinking are likely to seek out environments where this is tolerated. They will tend to drink with friends who also drink heavily, in places where no one stops them (Alasuutan, 1992).

Second, the social setting of the bar or pub may be conducive to aggression. Pubs can facilitate social interactions between lots of people and thus the potential exists for increased levels of all sorts of interaction, including aggression, in addition to the difficulties that arise from random contacts or conflicts with strangers (Homel *et al.*, 1992).

Third, aspects of the drinking environment affect behaviour after drinking (Homel *et al.*, 1992). Environments which increase arousal and anxiety may promote aggression. Some of the factors which are known to have this effect are heat, noise, overcrowding, problems in obtaining service, unpleasant or aggressive staff and cut-price alcohol (Stockwell *et al.*, 1993). Thus a cheap drinks night in an overcrowded pub with inadequate ventilation, a loud sound system and poorly trained staff, including perhaps aggressive doormen, constitutes an environment in which aggression may thrive.

Fourth, drinking environments which tolerate or encourage heavy alcohol consumption tend to lead to more behaviour problems after alcohol is consumed. A key feature is the behaviour of staff. In premises where staff actively encourage heavy drinking – for example, via drinking games – the rates of aggression tend to be higher (Homel *et al.*, 1992). As already noted, some drinkers seek such environments. Staff in other premises will follow a range of procedures to limit and manage violence.

It appears that aggression after alcohol occurs for a number of reasons:

1. The social settings, such as some pubs and clubs, where alcohol is consumed make aggression more likely. One reason for this is that many licensed premises remain male preserves where less 'civilised' behaviour is tolerated (Mass Observation, 1943; Wight, 1993).
2. After consuming alcohol communication skills can be impaired. It is then difficult to diffuse awkward situations without aggression, and signals from others may be misinterpreted as threats (Steele and Josephs, 1990). Aggressive displays may be more likely to escalate into violence.
3. People will be less able accurately to calculate the likely effects of aggression or violence. Interpersonal violence may become more serious than it would without alcohol. A drunk may hit someone without realising what damage he or she will do, or the legal problems that he or she will face.
4. There are varying cultural expectations about drunken behaviour (see, for example, Miller, 1966; Alasuutan, 1992; Wight, 1993). For males, it may be deemed 'unmanly' not to respond aggressively after alcohol to certain

types of challenge that would be passed over when sober (see, for example, Wight, 1993).

5. Alcohol can disinhibit the unassertive. Those who are unwilling to express their feelings when sober may find it easier to do so after alcohol (Wight, 1993). When the inhibited feelings include anger and resentment, then aggression is more likely after drinking, although people who are assertive and able to express negative feelings appropriately while sober are less likely to become aggressive when drunk. Even after alcohol, however, aggressive displays are more common than actual violence.

6. All these factors apply also to bystanders; intoxicated onlookers may be less likely to intervene and prevent aggressive display escalating to violence. If they do intervene, then they may do so less effectively, perhaps even getting drawn into the violence themselves.

In short, the drinker, the drinking setting, the bystanders and alcohol combine to create aggression, but alcohol alone is not sufficient to cause violence. This is well illustrated by the continued rarity of female violence, even though women's drinking has increased markedly over the past 30 years. It may be useful to regard alcohol as a drug which can facilitate aggressive or violent behaviour if there is potential for such to occur. If the potential for aggression is absent, then no amount of alcohol will induce it.

The Determinants of Serious Violent Crimes, Such as Murder

Serious violent crimes remain quite unusual events. Alcohol may play a contributory role in some of these crimes (Eronen, 1995; Avis, 1996), but it appears rarely to be the main cause of such offending. In some cases it is possible that the crime would not have occurred, or the injuries would not have been so serious, if the offender – or, indeed, the victim – had not been intoxicated (Shepherd, 1994a), but controlling alcohol is unlikely to be an effective method of controlling violent crime. Other factors, such as a personal or family history of violence and psychopathology, are better predictors of reoffending (Lattimore *et al.*, 1995).

However, some violent and sexual offenders may use intoxication as a means of summoning the courage to commit their offences. These are either offences which they find frightening when sober, such as armed robbery, or offences which they may struggle to avoid committing when sober, such as sexual assaults. In the right conditions, activities which are only fantasies when sober may be acted out when the person is drunk. Case histories of violent offenders point to individual differences in the extent to which people become drunk in order to facilitate the acting out of their fantasies, or act out behaviours because they are disinhibited by alcohol. However, neither alcohol use nor severity of psychiatric symptoms predict reoffending (Teplin *et al.*, 1994).

The Interaction of Substance Use, Mental Illness and Crime

The relationship between mental illness and crime is not as strong as is sometimes supposed (Teplin *et al.*, 1994). There is probably no particular relationship between mental illness and acquisitive crime, except that people with antisocial personality traits are more likely to break the law and drink heavily. Some people with psychotic disorders commit violent crimes; most do not. For example, schizophrenics are responsible for about 6% of murders (Eronen *et al.*, 1996). However, people with psychotic disorders may be adversely affected by heavy consumption of alcohol or other drugs, which may incline them to cease taking their medication and may also worsen their mental status, possibly making them more paranoid and delusional. Thus, alcohol intoxication may trigger or contribute to violence among those people whose psychotic disorders do predispose them to violence.

People who suffer from more than one mental disorder tend to have more difficulties and be harder to treat (see, for example, Vaillant, 1995). This includes people with psychotic disorders who also suffer from alcohol abuse or alcohol dependence. Violent crime may feature among the problems of this group (Rasmussen and Levander, 1996) and schizophrenics are more than twice as likely to commit murder if they are also alcohol dependent (Eronen *et al.*, 1996).

Domestic Disharmony

Alcohol can adversely affect families in a variety of direct and indirect ways. Orford *et al.* (1998) describe a 'rare experience' which is independent of culture, the substance used or the relationship with the problem person: (i) finding the problem person unpleasant to be with, (ii) experiencing financial difficulties, (iii) concerns over the problem person's health or performance, (iv) concern about the effect on the whole family and the home, (v) personal anxiety and worry, and (vi) feeling helpless, despairing, low or depressed. These researchers found that the coping strategies used by family members to deal with their experiences are complex – there are important implications for family interventions.

Domestic violence and other dysfunctional behaviour within the family context is a significant problem within most societies. National surveys of drinking problems in the US routinely ask respondents about a variety of social problems. Marital strain due to drinking is the most commonly reported problem. For example, in the 1984 National Alcohol Survey (Hilton, 1991) 9% of respondents (including 13% of men and 5% of women) reported a moderate problem with their spouse related to their drinking, and 4% of respondents (5% of men and 2% of women) reported at least a moderate problem with belligerence, such as getting into fights or arguments while drinking. Further, alcohol misusers experience a higher level of separation and divorce than non-alcohol misusers. Domestic violence is related to the frequency and amount of drinking by partners (Kantor and Straus, 1987). Physical conflict with wives was acknowledged by 44% of men interviewed in one survey who met a diagnosis of alcohol dependence, compared to 14% of those who did not. Domestic violence related to alcohol is not, however, a consequence of excessive drinking by the perpetrators alone. Alcoholic women are more likely to be victims of moderate and severe violence than non-alcoholic women (Miller *et al.*, 1989).

Murder occurs most commonly where victim and perpetrator are related. Welte and Abel (1989) concluded that alcohol use was most likely to be detected in murders that emerged spontaneously from personal disputes. Alcohol abuse by either or both partners can also contribute indirectly to domestic violence by exacerbating economic problems, child care difficulties or other family stressors (Leonard and Jacob, 1988).

Child Abuse and Neglect

Child abuse includes physical, emotional and sexual abuse. All of these forms of child abuse are associated with heavy drinking in parents. An association between child abuse and parental alcohol misuse has been identified in families involved in child care proceedings (Famularo *et al.*, 1986), although not all studies show these trends (for example, Steele and Pollock, 1974; Dawson, 1992). Children taken into care commonly have a history of parental 'alcoholism'. Famularo *et al.* (1986) found that in a group of severely abused children taken into care, 50% of the fathers and 30% of the mothers had a history of alcoholism, compared with 6% and 9% of controls.

Parental alcohol misuse is implicated in child sexual abuse, particularly in father–daughter incest (Julian and Mohr, 1979). Further, adults who were sexually abused as children commonly report that the perpetrators misused alcohol (Herman and Hirshman, 1981). It is important to note, however, that parental alcohol misuse is associated with child sexual abuse even when the abuser is someone other than the parent (Downs and Miller, 1996; Moncrieff *et al.*, 1996). This may be an indirect effect of alcohol due to parental unavailability and the failure of alcohol misusing parents to protect children from visitors to the home.

Accidents

Many activities are associated with the risk of accidents. Whenever alcohol is consumed prior to the activity then the risk of an accident increases. This applies to leisure activities, driving and other forms of transportation, and activities within the workplace and the home. Many accident victims present at hospital Accident and Emergency (A & E) departments and studies of these attendances provide evidence of the size of the problem.

Transport

Drinking accidents are associated with some particularly risky but ubiquitous activities, such as driving. They frequently involve people whose drinking is otherwise 'normal' and who therefore do not see themselves as having a drinking problem. Drinking and driving is perhaps the most prevalent contextual drinking problem world-wide. In fact, drinking poses a hazard in most forms of travel, including rail (Havard, 1991), water (Wright, 1985; Howland *et al.*, 1995) and air (Cook, 1997a, 1997b). In all of these cases, the activity is one in which there is a need for precision, safety and unimpaired performance.

There are three sources of information on drinking and driving: coroners' reports, breath test data from road accidents and police breath test data. None of these data sources are complete, although estimates can be produced from the available information. It is widely accepted that the consumption of alcohol prior to driving increases the risk of accident for both drivers and pedestrians (Mayou and Bryant, 1995; Cherpitel 1996; Deery and Love, 1996; Kennedy *et al.*, 1996), with estimates of intoxication as a cause of road injury varying from between 20% (Mayou and Bryant 1995) and 33% (Hansen *et al.*, 1996). A recent study of the role of alcohol in A & E admissions resulting from road traffic accidents concluded that 10% of all road accidents causing injury result from drivers with excess blood alcohol concentration and that 25% of all road accident fatalities have blood alcohol levels greater than 80 mg% (Green *et al.*, 1993). As Roizen (1989, p. 52) summarises: 'There is by now considerable evidence that there is a positive relationship between severity of injury and drinking. Patients who have been drinking ... are more likely to be seriously injured than others.'

A Scottish study (Bradbury, 1991) found that young males (aged 20–29) were the highest risk group of intoxicated pedestrians, sustaining traffic injuries as a result of the impairment of judgement and reaction time needed to cross roads. Another study (Irwin *et al.*, 1983), which used controls to compare levels of intoxication in victims of road accidents, found that of 50 consecutive pedestrian accidents, 18 had blood alcohol concentrations of 80 mg/100 ml contrasted with only 7 of the controls. The researchers calculated that the relative risk of a pedestrian with a blood alcohol concentration of this level being involved in an accident was 3.6. They concluded that 'there is a strong positive correlation between blood alcohol levels and road accidents to pedestrians' (Irwin *et al.*, 1983, p. 522).

Figure 4.2 charts the estimates of the number of 'fatal', 'serious' and 'slight' casualties involving illegal alcohol levels for the years 1987–97; clearly, as a single accident can result in more than one casualty, the estimates for accidents are somewhat lower. From these figures we can see that although the number

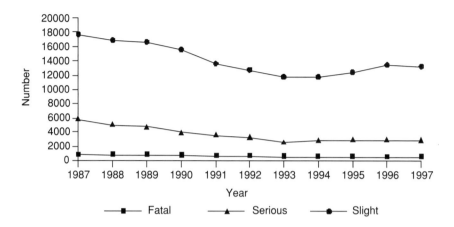

Figures for 1997 are provisional.

Source: DETR (1998, p. 23).

Figure 4.2   Estimates of casualties resulting from accidents, adjusted for under-reporting, 1987–97

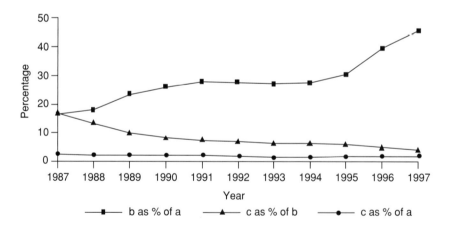

a = total involved in road injury accidents
b = total tested
c = total failed

Source: DETR (1998, p. 24).

Figure 4.3   Drivers and riders in road injury accidents: breath tests and failures, 1987–97

of casualties did decrease from 1987–93, they subsequently began to increase again. When traffic volume is taken into account, however, this increase is less obvious.

The data relating to breath tests are charted in Figure 4.3. The number of drivers tested has increased and the proportion of positive tests has decreased through the period 1987–97; however, as a proportion of number of accidents, positive tests have remained fairly constant at approximately 2%. These data suggest that, in earlier days, drivers were tested only where there was a high index of suspicion for drink driving, and hence the high proportion of positive tests. Testing has now become more routine following an accident, and hence the lower proportion of positive tests. Table 4.1 offers more detailed analysis of the blood alcohol level of road accident fatalities and shows that of the drivers who were over the legal limit, some two-thirds had blood alcohol levels in excess of 150 mg%. Of pedestrian fatalities, 37% were over the limit for driving, as were 16% of cyclists.

Table 4.1 Blood alcohol levels of fatalities aged 16 and over, 1996

| | Percentage over blood alcohol levels (mg/100 ml) | | | | | |
	9	50	80	100	150	200
Motorcycle riders	25	15	13	11	8	4
Other vehicle drivers	37	26	23	21	15	10
Passengers	39	30	24	19	13	8
Pedestrians	49	39	37	34	30	23
Cyclists	24	17	16	16	10	3

Source: DETR (1998, p. 27).

Alcohol Related Injuries Admitted to A & E Departments

Yates *et al.* (1987) attempted to identify the characteristics of 1693 patients with alcohol related problems attending two A & E departments over a two-week period. They identified four subgroups: those patients who drove to hospital to seek medical advice, unemployed men, men who had been injured at work and men who had been assaulted. No patient who had driven to hospital had exceeded the UK legal limit (80 mg% blood alcohol concentration), whereas those who arrived by taxi were the most frequently inebriated. Frequent heavy drinking was found to be commonplace amongst the unemployed men in the sample, whereas those who claimed to have been assaulted were more frequently represented in the 'occasional heavy' or binge drinking group. Of the latter, 9.3% had a blood alcohol concentration of more than 200 mg%, compared to the population mean of 2.8%. Only 40% of these patients were completely sober, in contrast to 86.3% of all attenders (Yates *et al.*, 1987). A study of facial injuries showed that alcohol was a significant factor either for the victim or the assailant in 61% of cases (see Magennis *et al.,* 1998). In their study of Emergency Room patients, Walsh and Macleod (1983) found injury deriving from assault to be the type of accident most frequently associated with alcohol (see Table 4.2).

Table 4.2   Types of accident most frequently associated with alcohol

Incident	Number of patients	Positive Alcometer		Alcometer >80 mg/100 ml	
		No.	%	No.	%
Assault	56	39	69.6	28	50.0
Home	192	25	13.0	12	6.3
Road Traffic Accident	74	8	10.8	6	8.1
Work	242	19	7.9	9	3.7
Sport	79	4	5.1	1	1.3
Other	101	41	40.6	27	26.7
Not known	10	2	20.0	2	200
Total	754	138	18.3	85	11.3

Source: Walsh and Macleod (1983).

Home and Public Places

The accidents that may occur as a result of inappropriate drinking within a particular context are many and varied. The risk of falls in public places increases by a factor of three at a blood alcohol concentration of 60–100 mg%, by a factor of 10 at 105–150 mg% and by a factor of 60 at higher concentrations (Honkanen *et al.*, 1983). Furthermore, 21–77% of those involved in fatal falls, 17–35% of those in non-fatal falls (Hingson and Howland, 1987), and 25–50% of adult drowning victims (Howland and Hingson, 1988) have been exposed to alcohol. Nearly half of those who die in fires have a blood alcohol level above 100 mg% (Howland and Hingson, 1987), and alcohol consumption is also implicated in home accident injuries (Wechsler *et al.*, 1969). Alcohol involvement in sports injuries, apart from aquatic sports, is apparently rather less common (Honkanen, 1993).

The Workplace

Alcohol has been shown to contribute to a significant proportion of workplace accidents. The Health and Safety Executive measured blood alcohol concentrations in 35 of 92 fatal accidents reported to them between 1979 and 1980, of which seven (20%) exceeded the legal drink driving limit. Despite the limited size of the sample, this compares well with estimates from research elsewhere (Hutcheson *et al.*, 1995).

There are, however, reasonable grounds to assume that the involvement of alcohol in workplace accidents is greater still as the real figure may be obscured by insufficient post-incident investigation, inadequate monitoring procedures, and the possibility of 'cover-ups' by employees wishing to avoid disciplinary action and by employers concerned about invalidating insurance cover, forfeiting compensation or subsequently paying higher premiums. Similarly, it can also be reasonably assumed that many minor alcohol related accidents, knocks and falls go unreported altogether.

Absenteeism attributable to alcohol misuse, from accidents at work to the Monday morning consequences of a heavy weekend, presents further costs to employers. Current estimates indicate a loss of between 8 and 14 million working days each year, or 3–5% of all absences (Holtermann and Burchell, 1981) which the Centre for Health Economics costed at £964 million in 1990. As with accident reporting, these figures may also understate the true scale of the problem. Recording mechanisms are not uniform across industry, and employees completing self-certification forms are more than likely to report vaguely defined colds, headaches and gastric problems than hangovers and other specifically alcohol related disorders. In April 1994, changes in social security arrangements and the responsibility of employers to meet the full cost of sick pay further focused the minds of cost-conscious organisations, and of 200 employers sampled by Alcohol Concern (1995), 62% perceived absenteeism to be their biggest alcohol related problem.

Harder to assess is the cost to organisations of what may be termed 'sickness presence' where employees are at work but underperforming, with a consequent loss of productivity, competitiveness and customer satisfaction. As nine out of ten adults are regular drinkers, and an estimated 75% of 'problem' drinkers are in work, no organisation can consider itself immune from the direct or indirect consequences of inappropriate drinking. Concern about the potential damage of alcohol misuse to business has been identified by 65% of company directors and 70% of managers as a problem *'to some extent'* within their organisations. There is also growing support across industry for banning alcohol consumption throughout the working day, with 80% backing the idea in principle (Alcohol Concern, 1995).

Behaviours Facilitated by Alcohol

There are some behaviours which are more likely to be manifest if a person is intoxicated: we have called this 'alcohol *facilitation*'. It may be that the behaviour in question is something that the drinker could be ashamed of if sober, such as stealing or engaging in unsafe sex, or something to be frightened of, such as self-harm.

Suicide

Alcohol intoxication is implicated in suicide and self-harm (Kerfoot and Huxley, 1995). High blood alcohol levels in A & E patients are a determinant not only of completed suicide, but also of suicide attempts (Platt and Robinson, 1991). Kessel (1961) found that 56% of male and 23% of female self-poisoners had been drinking just before the overdose was taken, while Watson (1969) found alcohol to be implicated in 10% of the suicide attempts in his study of a London A & E department.

Shaffer *et al.* (1996) examined the risk factors for suicide and their relationship with demographic factors: previous attempts and mood disorder were major risk factors for both genders, though substance misuse was a risk in males only. They concluded that more commonly a mood disorder alone or in combination with conduct disorder or alcohol and substance misuse characterises most suicides among adolescents. Marttunen *et al.* (1995) compared suicides of males and females aged 13–22. Two-thirds of the female victims had suffered from mood disorder, half had been in psychiatric care at some time and 42% had been hospitalised. Alcohol abuse (21%) was almost as common among female as male victims and was thought to be a major factor. Indeed, it has been suggested that alcohol misuse among the young may be the determining factor in the recent rise in male suicide. Williams and Morgan (1994) suggest that focusing on drug and alcohol abuse would have a greater impact on adolescent suicide rates than any other primary prevention programme.

Sexual Risk Behaviour

Since the advent of Human Immunodeficiency Virus (HIV) and Acquired Immune Deficiency Syndrome (AIDS), there has been increasing concern about the potential for alcohol to increase the likelihood of individuals engaging in high-risk sexual behaviour. However, it is important to note that even before HIV and AIDS, promiscuous and unprotected sexual activity posed potential threats from a range of causes including other forms of sexually transmitted disease, unplanned pregnancy, sexual abuse and marital breakdown. Nevertheless, HIV has provided the impetus for the growth of research in this area. Such research has tended to focus on three main risk groups: gay men, young people, and sex workers and their clients. Some research has also been conducted with heterosexual adults.

Alcohol is commonly associated with sexual behaviour, and it is popularly believed that alcohol increases the likelihood of sexual activity, particularly in women. For example, Bagnall and Plant (1991) found that amongst young Scottish adults, 82% said that they combined alcohol and sex. Alcohol intoxication impairs rational judgement and decreases behavioural inhibitions (Leigh, 1990). Thus it is entirely plausible that alcohol should increase the risk of engaging in behaviour which violates social norms (Critchlow, 1983). Alcohol, of course, can also diminish sexual arousal, and male potency, as well as reduce fertility. Donovan and McEwan (1995) have pointed out that the relationship between alcohol and sexual behaviour is highly complex, as is the relationship between alcohol and sexual risk taking. One problem in this area is the often high prevalence of sexual risk behaviour, with or without alcohol, in many of the populations studied.

There is evidence that alcohol use is related to high risk sexual behaviour amongst homosexual males (Stall *et al.*, 1986; Valdiserri *et al.*, 1988; Siegel *et al.*, 1989). McCusker *et al.* (1990) found that during the course of a longitudinal study of homosexual men, those who increased their alcohol consumption as the study progressed were twice as likely to maintain high-risk sexual practices than those who reduced drinking. However, there are other examples of studies where no association has been found (for example, Gold and Skinner, 1992; Weatherburn *et al.*, 1993).

In a group of teenagers, Hingson *et al.* (1990) found that heavy drinkers (taking more than five drinks in a day) were nearly three times less likely than non-drinkers to report condom use; 16% said that they were less likely to use condoms immediately after drinking. Similarly, 15% of young women and 22% of young men said that they were less likely to use condoms after drinking.

Drinking also poses a risk in relation to the number of sexual encounters involving new sexual partners. Ericksen and Trocki (1992) and Leigh (1990) found that heavy drinking was related to having a greater number of sexual partners. In the former study, measures of problem drinking were strongly predictive of self-reported sexually transmitted disease. McEwan *et al.*'s (1992) study of students in England showed that drinking was independently associated with having unprotected casual sex, and with having sex with someone known to have many sexual partners. Drinking was also associated with having more sexual partners, having unwanted sexual involvement, and avoiding contraceptive precautions.

Research amongst sex workers and their clients is sparse and inconclusive. Plant, Plant and Morgan-Thomas (1990) found no significant association between alcohol use and level of condom use amongst male and female sex workers. Morgan-Thomas *et al.* (1990) reported similar findings for the clients of sex workers. However, for male clients of male sex workers, condom use was inversely proportional to alcohol consumption in the week before interview.

Alcohol and Acquisitive Crime

Alcohol as a cause of acquisitive crime appears to be a complex issue. Alcohol is sometimes used to summon the 'nerve' to commit crimes (Bennett and Wright, 1984; Hammersley *et al.*, 1990b), although intoxication can also interfere with the effective planning and committing of criminal acts (Bennett and Wright, 1984). Furthermore, criminals quite often meet in licensed premises (Bennett and Wright, 1984). However, such apparent correlations are not restricted to alcohol and crime. For example, alcohol is sometimes used to summon the courage to perform music on stage, but intoxication can interfere with performance and many performers meet beforehand and afterwards in the pub (Davies, 1978). Clearly, alcohol does not *cause* musical performances, but it may affect the nature of musical performances, as well as people's skill and willingness to perform.

In practice, then, intoxication may cause some criminals to commit crimes that they would avoid when sober because they were too frightened of the consequences, or too sensible to take such risks. Some imprisoned criminals claim that they were captured because they were drunk and took risks, which may further inflate the apparent relationship between alcohol and acquisitive crime. Drunkenness may facilitate the committing of more serious crimes, but it does not appear to be a root cause of acquisitive crime. Some means of preventing criminals from drinking would probably have no impact on the acquisitive crime rate, although it might affect the violence and severity of crime.

Accidental or Injudicious Combinations of Alcohol and Other Drugs

The clinical significance of interactions between alcohol and other drugs or medical conditions is difficult to predict. Doctors often find themselves with insufficient knowledge to give accurate advice to their patients. In fact, there are exceedingly few circumstances where light social drinking would be contra-indicated; however, as a guiding principle, doctors should be circumspect about prescribing for conditions which are likely to be alcohol related and which will resolve with a period of abstinence from alcohol; for example, anxiety (Brown and Irwin, 1991) or hypertension (Marmot *et al.*, 1994). Binge drinking is likely to exacerbate epilepsy and diabetes, though most diabetics are able to drink socially if they take food with alcohol.

Alcohol sensitising agents, notably disulfiram, may be hazardous when taken with alcohol to people with a compromised cardiovascular system. Metronidazole and chlorpropamide have similar but less severe reactions. Pharmacotherapies, such as sensitising drugs, for addictive behaviour are most effective when combined with psychosocial therapy: the indications for prescribing and the procedures to follow need to be fully understood by practitioners and explained to patients prior to the offer of treatment (Fuller, 1989).

It is generally agreed that there is a serious problem of mis-prescribing to people who misuse alcohol. The most hazardous manifestation is the prescribing of central nervous system depressant drugs to people who concurrently misuse alcohol. The summation of effect, especially respiratory depression, may be fatal: the lethal dose of barbiturate and chlormethiazole, for example is markedly reduced when taken with alcohol. Chlordiazepoxide is probably the safest depressant drug where there is a risk of drinking (Duncan and Taylor, 1996). The financial and morbidity costs of mis-prescribing are unknown. For a detailed account of alcohol and drug interactions see Lieber (1982).

Summary of Main Arguments

- There is a strong relationship between intoxication, violence and aggression. The end point is a strong complex interaction between drinking, the environment and personal characteristics. Audit of incidents is an important tool for identifying high-risk public areas and informing interventions.
- Family disharmony and long-term adverse consequences for children are strongly related to problem drinking. There is good evidence that teaching particular coping styles can help family members to manage their experience of family disharmony.
- Some sporting, social and work activities are incompatible with drinking. There is public support for separating drinking and certain high-risk activities such as driving or flying, and this culture needs to spread to lower-risk activities.
- Intoxication creates 'victims'. There are difficult legal and moral issues to settle if people were intoxicated when, for example, they were involved in events leading to an accident or when claiming not to have consented to sexual acts.
- The availability of prescribed drugs to excessive drinkers is problematic. A high proportion of prescribing to drinkers is inappropriate. This prescribing is an unnecessary financial burden to the health service; it is therapeutically unhelpful and may be hazardous.

5
Individual and Population Level Risks

In this third of our three chapters looking at patterns of drinking and related problems we move the focus to regular drinking which, in very general terms, is seen to be most directly associated with physical and psychological health though, of course, a catalogue of social problems can also be cited. We have stressed in the introduction to all three chapters that divisions are artificial and so the reader must keep in mind the interactive nature of drinking, drinkers and drink related problems. Individual genetic differences must also be considered; some drinkers will be at risk of problems at lower levels of consumption than others, because of their individual constitutional vulnerability. The common theme is the level of consumption and its impact on individual risk. In this chapter we discuss:

- measurement of alcohol consumption
- the epidemiology of risk
- all-cause mortality and morbidity
- individual levels of risk
- distribution of drinking at the population level
- international trends in per capita consumption
- drinking and drinking problems in the UK: the overall picture.

Measurement of Alcohol Consumption

There are considerable difficulties in assessing levels and patterns of alcohol consumption in surveys. Drinking patterns are varied and the outcomes multiple (Midanik, 1995). General population surveys have employed a variety of ways to measure alcohol consumption. Volume, pattern and frequency of consumption are typical measures. However, there has always been a strong emphasis on volume measurement, thus allowing calculation of a threshold beyond which drinkers have a higher risk of problems. The methods used to measure volume of alcohol consumption include quantity/frequency questionnaires and the diary method. The difficulties inherent in these approaches (Duffy, 1992) must be taken into account when comparing studies.

Most medical epidemiological studies summarise drinking patterns in terms of the single dimension of average intake of alcohol usually converted into consumption per day or per year. While measures of cumulative consumption may be important for the development of cirrhosis and other long-term physical problems, heavy drinking on a particular occasion – 'getting drunk' – is a more important determinant of social problems and injuries presenting to the A & E department.

Epidemiological studies are quite effective at measuring patterns over a relatively limited time-period. They are less effective at estimating consumption over longer time-periods when measures of consumption are then summarised further, because alcohol consumption is often just one of a series of risk factors being measured. Thus, for methodological reasons, alcohol consumption tends to be under-reported in population studies. This means that the reported relationship between consumption and risk of harm is too steep; that is, the level of risk actually corresponds to a higher level of consumption than is reported (Anderson, 1995). Many prospective studies measure drinking status once at the start of the study and use this as an indicator of subsequent exposure to alcohol. There is considerable variation in the instruments used to measure volume of alcohol consumed. Drinks per day, grams per day and units per day need to be converted to standard measures of alcohol to allow for comparison, thus influencing interpretation of results. 'Standard drinks' vary in amount from country to country.

The Epidemiology of Risk

There are two approaches to aetiology, the individual centred and the population based. The individual approach uses case control studies to determine how sick and healthy individuals differ, and cohort studies to determine which patients are more susceptible to a particular disease. Identified risk factors are tested for causality and the 'relative risk' is the basic measure of aetiological or causal importance (Rose, 1985). Relative risk can be defined as the risk in exposed individuals relative to risk in non-exposed individuals. In the case of alcohol consumption, case control and prospective studies yield dose–response relationships which give information on the individual risk of some types of harm at different levels of consumption (Lemmens, 1995).

There may be a publication bias in studies of alcohol consumption and individual risk, because studies demonstrating an association between alcohol and harm are more likely to be published (Simes, 1986). Comparison between studies is hampered by a variety of factors (Ferrence, 1995): sample sizes are small or vary; standardised definitions of diseases are not used; alcohol consumption is not measured appropriately; confounding effects may not be controlled for, and are especially important for cigarette smoking which is closely linked with alcohol consumption. For instance, the level of consumption at the time of the event under study and the accumulation and pattern of drinking over time must be considered, otherwise there is the risk that the contribution of alcohol is underestimated.

Most case control studies use older subjects who may already have developed alcohol related conditions. The use of hospital controls in case control studies may introduce bias because alcohol problems are common in this population. Prospective studies using subjects selected for insurance systems will select out healthier than average subjects because those in poor health are excluded. This limits generalisation of results to the general population.

Most studies try to control for smoking status, but the strong relationship between drinking and smoking makes this difficult. Heavy drinkers who have never smoked are rare. Many studies do not control for diet, an important factor in many diseases, including coronary heart disease, cancers, hypertension, stroke, diabetes and obesity. Different lifestyles may be associated with different patterns of drinking and are also potentially important sources of confounding. For instance, lifelong abstainers in North America are older, of lower socio-economic status, live in rural areas, are religious, have relatives with alcohol problems (Hughes *et al.*, 1985; Wannamethee and Shaper, 1988) and have higher depression scores (Neff and Husaini, 1982).

Any risk curve will reflect the characteristics of the population on which it is based. This is particularly obvious for social complications of drinking, but also holds for other complications such as physical morbidity and mortality. For instance, the risk curves for alcohol and morbidity in developing countries are different from those based on populations in Northern Europe. If we are interested in the reasons for high rates of alcohol related problems in one population, and low rates in another population, we must first know what distinguishes the two populations. In order to identify differences between the populations, we must study the characteristics of these populations, not the characteristics of the individuals. The incidence of a particular alcohol related outcome in a population is considered to be the product of two variables, the risk function for that outcome and the population distribution of alcohol consumption (Lemmens, 1995).

Risk Functions

Heavy drinkers experience high rates of alcohol related problems, but only make a small contribution to the overall level of such problems. Most alcohol problems occur in light and moderate drinkers, although such drinkers have low rates of problems (Kreitman, 1986). This underlies the so-called 'prevention paradox', which can be summarised as saying that reducing consumption among moderate drinkers will have a greater impact on improving health and social conditions in the whole population than reducing consumption among heavy drinkers.

Several risk functions have been described in association with alcohol consumption (illustrated in Figure 5.1). Empirical examples include the linear, the convex or exponential, and a U-shaped function. In the case of the linear function, the risk of harm has a direct relationship to intake and so the risk is determined by total consumption, and population problem rates depend on the per capita consumption level (Skog, 1991). This means that an increase in alcohol consumption of, say, 4 units a week carries the same increase in risk irrespective of whether a person is a light, moderate or heavy drinker. This risk function describes the dose–response relationship between alcohol and most cancers including breast cancer.

For the other two models the incidence of an illness in the population depends in varying degrees on the way consumption is distributed within that population. In the case of a convex function, small changes in distribution, especially in the tail, will have a large effect on the incidence (Lemmens, 1995); the prevention paradox does not apply to the convex function where most of the 'cases' are found among very heavy drinkers. This risk function describes the dose–response relationship between alcohol and liver cirrhosis.

The U-shaped risk function described in many epidemiological studies of total mortality means that the minimal risk for an individual is not abstention but is at a light level of consumption. This relationship between individual risk and consumption means that there is an optimum mean population level of consumption at which incidence is lowest. Skog (1991) argues that the optimum population mean level is lower than the optimum individual level, because of the large dispersion and skewness of alcohol consumption distributions. How much lower will depend on the shape of the risk function and on changes in the distribution of alcohol consumption, as the consumption level of the population changes (Edwards *et al.*, 1994). This risk function describes the dose–response relationship between alcohol and all-cause mortality or coronary heart disease.

All-cause Mortality and Morbidity

Heavy alcohol consumption is associated with increased levels of cancer (mouth, pharynx, larynx, oesophagus, liver and heart), hypertension, haemorrhagic stroke, cardiovascular disease and liver cirrhosis. In most industrialised countries the overall relationship between alcohol consumption and all-cause mortality is J-shaped for both sexes.

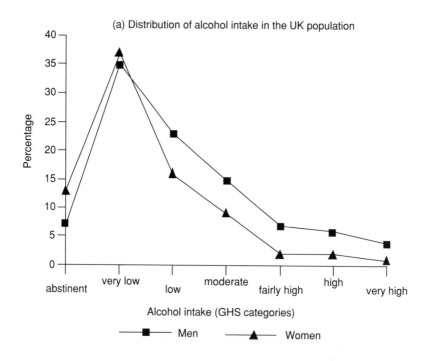

(a) Distribution of alcohol intake in the UK population

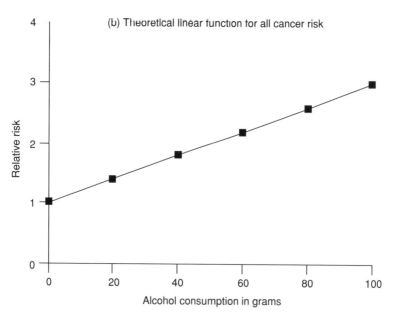

(b) Theoretical linear function for all cancer risk

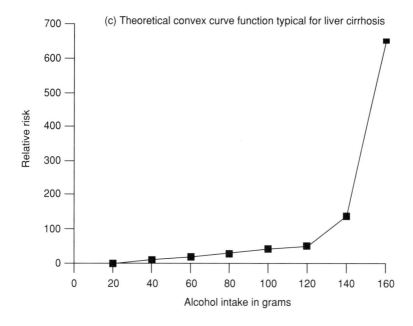

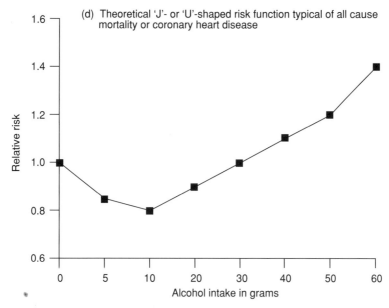

Source: Adapted from Lemmens (1995).

Figure 5.1 Distribution of alcohol consumption in the population and theoretical risk functions

This finding is based on a series of heterogeneous individual-level prospective studies which consistently report that (1) lighter drinkers have lower
mortality rates than abstainers; and (2) heavier drinkers show premature
mortality when compared with light drinkers (Marmot, 1984; Beaglehole and
Jackson, 1992; Poikolainen, 1995). These data suggest that light drinking protects
against mortality, especially coronary heart disease (CHD). The bottom of the
J-shaped risk curve is flat, indicating little difference in risk between those
drinking less than 12 g per day and those drinking 24 g per day. The risk curve
for mortality begins to rise at around 24 g per day (Royal Colleges of Physicians,
Psychiatrists and General Practitioners, 1995). In most studies the relative risk
for low-to-moderate drinkers is about 0.75, meaning that abstainers have a 33%
excess mortality. Heavy drinkers have a relative risk of 1.2–1.5, and a 60–100%
excess mortality over light-to-moderate drinkers. Although most studies have
been carried out on middle-aged men, the findings are similar for women, for
whom the relative risk of mortality starts to rise at consumption levels of 16 g
per day. Few studies have been carried out on young people; however, one such
study of Swedish conscripts (Andreasson *et al.* 1991) showed no benefit for light
drinkers compared with abstainers. This finding was also evident in another
study using subjects under the age of 40 (Klatsky *et al.*, 1992).

Certain factors need to be taken into account when interpreting these studies
(Royal Colleges of Physicians, Psychiatrists and General Practitioners, 1995).
First, the category of 'non-drinkers' is heterogeneous: it may include ex-drinkers
and people with serious illnesses. Second, methods of estimating alcohol consumption in these studies are not uniform and are often rudimentary. Third,
the conversion to the common unit is approximate. Fourth, the follow-up
period ranges from 4.5 to 22 years.

In a recent series of three papers, Fillmore *et al.* used raw data from several
general population studies containing mortality data to evaluate drinking status
and mortality risk. These studies form part of the collaborative Alcohol-Related
Longitudinal Project Archive (Fillmore, 1988). This was a portfolio of studies
originally selected for a World Health Organization review on the world's
alcohol related longitudinal literature. In the first paper, based on the raw data
of ten general population studies, Fillmore *et al.* (1998a), reported differences
between former drinkers and long-term abstainers, which may confound the
associations found between alcohol consumption and mortality risk. Compared
with long-term abstainers, adult male former drinkers were consistently more
likely to be heavier smokers, to be depressed, unemployed, of lower socio-
economic status and to have used marijuana, than long-term abstainers. Adult
female former drinkers were consistently more likely to be heavier smokers, in
poorer health, not religious and unmarried, compared to long-term abstainers.
Former drinkers and long-term abstainers were of lower socio-economic status
than light drinkers and reported poorer health. These findings support the

view that 'abstainers' are not a homogeneous group, and that certain characteristics of abstainers, such as social position, health and social integration, might account for their higher mortality compared with light drinkers.

The second paper in this series (Leino *et al.*, 1998) used the raw data of eight general population follow-up studies of men (over 68,000 subjects in total), (a) to evaluate alternative definitions of drinking pattern; (b) to conduct separate analyses for male youths and adults; (c) to separate long-term abstainers from former drinkers; (d) to control for characteristics believed to confound associations of drinking patterns and mortality risk; and (e) to conduct separate analyses by study and to synthesise the results. This meta-analysis found no evidence to support the hypothesis that abstinence was associated with greater mortality risk than light drinking. Youthful abstainers had a lower risk of dying than light drinkers. Adult men who were long-term abstainers had a lower risk of dying than their light drinking counterparts, whereas former drinkers had a higher risk of dying than light drinkers. Although these differences amongst adult men were not significant, findings were homogeneous across studies. One study of adult men had shown a significant 'age by former drinking' interaction, but this did not alter the lack of association of former drinking with mortality or the homogeneity of results across studies for this finding.

The most consistent finding was the association of heavy drinking with mortality amongst youth. In adults, frequent drinking, defined as drinking 43 or more drinks per month and drinking 21 or more times per month, was associated with increased mortality risk. On the other hand, quantity per occasion was not significantly associated with mortality risk amongst adults. These findings question the received wisdom that daily consumption of a few glasses of wine has beneficial effects.

Despite its limitations, this study showed that spurious associations may arise when studies that use limited definitions of drinking pattern do not specify age groups; treat all abstainers as a homogeneous group and do not evaluate variables that might confound the association of alcohol consumption with mortality risk – important among these are physical and mental health, social position and social isolation. The studies included in this meta-analysis all used clearly defined measures of alcohol use and quantity/frequency measures.

The third paper in this series, a meta-analysis of raw data from three general population studies of women, a total of 2489 subjects, evaluated all-cause mortality rates by drinking pattern (Fillmore *et al.*, 1998b). Lifelong abstainers and former drinkers had higher mortality rates than light drinkers, and mortality rates tended to increase as levels of alcohol consumption increased. When age was controlled, the odds of death for long-term abstainers and former drinkers were greater than those for light drinkers; odds of death for moderate and heavy drinkers were greater than those for light drinkers. When other demographic and psychosocial characteristics were controlled, neither long-term abstainers nor former drinkers were at a higher risk of dying than light drinkers. Heavier drinkers, however, had approximately twice the odds of death of light drinkers. These findings suggest that it is the demographic and psychosocial characteristics of long-term abstainers and former drinkers that accounts for their increased risk of death.

Alcohol Related Mortality

In this next section we shall discuss national data concerning alcohol related mortality. Deaths are coded into International Classification of Diseases (ICD) categories and as such some of these categories can be linked to alcohol consumption. The current classification system is the 10th Revision of the ICD codes (ICD 10), although earlier revisions were in force at the time which some data sets take as an initial point.

Figure 5.2 gives the number of alcohol related deaths per 100,000 population from England and Wales from 1968 onwards. This time-series is collated from mortality data which are published yearly. The coding of deaths has changed throughout the latter part of this century and the data from years immediately preceding a change in coding are recoded to take account of the new codes; the time-series should therefore be interpreted with care. These figures do not include deaths from other causes where alcohol was a contributory factor. Table 5.1 gives a breakdown of the causes of death for the year 1996.

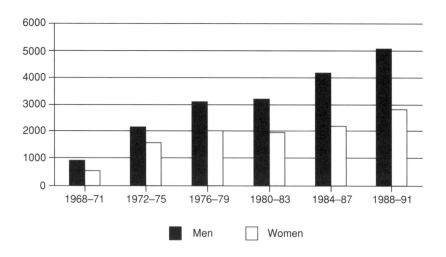

Source: Scottish Council on Alcohol (1994).

Figure 5.2   Alcohol related deaths in England and Wales

Table 5.1 Deaths from alcohol related causes, England and Wales, 1996

Cause of death	Male	Female	Total
Alcoholic psychosis	10	4	4
Alcohol dependence syndrome	172	78	250
Non-dependent use of alcohol	100	44	144
Alcoholic cardiomyopathy	116	24	140
Alcoholic gastritis	3	2	5
Alcoholic fatty liver	41	28	69
Acute alcoholic hepatitis	64	38	102
Acute cirrhosis of the liver	569	250	819
Alcoholic liver damage (unspecified)	696	373	1069
Toxic effects of alcohol	102	50	152
Total	1873	891	2764
Chronic liver disease and cirrhosis	2261	1528	3789
Total including all liver disease and cirrhosis	2754	1730	4484

Source: ONS (1998c).

Alcohol Related Morbidity

The ICD 10 codings that are applied to deaths are also applied to hospital admissions data and it is possible to chart the admissions to mental hospitals and psychiatric units. Table 5.2 presents figures extracted from the Hospital Episodes Statistics for England (DoH, 1995c) which describes the number of admissions to all NHS hospitals in England by health region. The rates per 100,000 population in England in 1994–95 are comparable to the rates in Scotland. Overall, in England the rates seem to be moving slowly upward both for men and women.

Although in Scotland there has been a decrease in mental illness admissions with a primary diagnosis of alcohol related disorder over the last few decades, trends in general hospital discharges for alcohol dependence, psychosis and misuse have increased over the 1980s. It is likely that there has been a shift from psychiatric to general hospital admissions. In the UK as a whole, the number of beds in specialist alcohol units is decreasing and the responsibility for treatment shifting to general hospitals.

Approximately 20% of general hospital beds in Britain are occupied by patients with alcohol related problems (Tolley and Rowland, 1991). In 1979, alcohol misuse was found in 27% of general medical admissions (Jariwalla *et al.*, 1979) and it contributed to 19% of acute male admissions in Glasgow in 1976 (Quinn and Johnston, 1976). However, the alcohol related nature of most of these problems frequently goes undetected (Jarman and Kellett 1979; Tolley and Rowland, 1991; Sharkey *et al.*, 1996). As Scheffler *et al.* (1987) have pointed out, it is often difficult to ascertain whether alcohol related diagnoses recorded in subsidiary diagnostic categories are related to the principal diagnosis in a causal or an associational way.

Table 5.2   Hospital episodes of main alcohol related diagnoses, by region

Health Region	Alcohol dependence syndrome	Toxic effects of alcohol	Alcoholic psychoses	Chronic liver disease	Total
Northern	1433	262	428	979	3102
Yorkshire	1696	212	340	656	2904
Trent	1461	133	308	1077	2979
East Anglia	1081	59	136	369	1645
NW Thames	1386	98	651	665	2800
NE Thames	1238	77	428	1099	2842
SE Thames	1300	195	413	1144	3052
SW Thames	1387	66	422	727	2602
Wessex	1110	144	240	566	2060
Oxford	711	91	226	471	1499
South Western	1045	165	171	697	2078
West Midlands	2345	285	378	1864	4872
Mersey	2120	109	208	940	3377
North Western	2479	364	499	1150	4492
Special HAs	158	8	44	51	261
TOTAL	20,950	2268	4892	12,455	40,565

Source: DoH (1995c).

The distribution of alcohol related problems tends to vary across surveys. While Sharkey *et al.* (1996) found the highest rates of alcohol misuse occurring in the male medical and surgical wards, at 32% and 27% respectively, Chick (1994) found the lowest rate of alcohol related problems in a London hospital, 7.2%, to be in general surgery, while Scheffler *et al.* (1987) identified the most common alcohol related diagnosis as alcohol dependence syndrome, accounting for 38.3% of patients with alcohol problems in the North East Thames area. In Chick's (1994) survey, alcohol was found to contribute to 27.7% of overdoses, 19.8% of head injuries, 17.6% of road traffic accidents and 10.5% of gastrointestinal haemorrhages. Sharkey *et al.* (1996) reported that 23% of psychiatric patients scored as misusers of alcohol on the AUDIT questionnaire. Glass and Jackson's (1988) study of psychiatric patients which identified between 9% and11% as having an alcohol problem also suggests significant levels of alcohol problems among this group.

Despite various criteria and types of studies, research into the rates of problem drinking in general hospitals tends to give estimates between 15% and 30% for males and between 8% and 15% for females in urban areas, with higher rates in hospitals serving deprived areas (Chick, 1994). These are higher rates than found in the general population.

Individual Levels of Risk

Alcoholic Liver Disease

Alcohol misuse is the commonest cause of liver damage in the UK, Europe, the US and Australia. The liver is the primary site of alcohol metabolism and is therefore particularly susceptible to alcohol related injury. Three types of alcoholic liver disease have been described: fatty liver, alcoholic hepatitis and alcoholic cirrhosis. All three may co-exist. Fatty liver, present in 90% of persistent heavy drinkers, is usually asymptomatic. Alcoholic hepatitis, an acute inflammation of the liver, occurs in approximately 40% of heavy drinkers, and is often the precursor to cirrhosis. Between 8% and 30% of heavy drinkers develop cirrhosis, typically after a 10–20-year history of heavy drinking (Sherman and Williams, 1994). For some individuals the risk of liver damage is dose-dependent and requires a threshold level of consumption to be reached. For men this is thought to be in the region of 5–6 standard drinks daily for 20 years but less for women. Thus, regular daily drinking, rather than binge drinking, is the pattern of consumption associated with cirrhosis.

The risk of developing alcoholic cirrhosis also comes under the influence of genetic and environmental factors. Women are more vulnerable to developing liver disease than men, typically presenting with shorter drinking histories and following less cumulative exposure to alcohol. This increased susceptibility occurs as a result of a lower body water and weight compared to men, which gives rise to increased bio-availability of ethanol. Further, a reduced first-pass metabolism by gastric alcohol dehydrogenase increases the percentage of ingested alcohol reaching the liver (Frezza *et al.*, 1990). For some women a daily alcohol intake of as little as 20 g may result in alcoholic hepatitis and cirrhosis.

Some people, particularly Asians of Indian origin, appear to have an increased vulnerability to liver disease. Ethnicity is also related to drinking outcomes (Mendenhall *et al.*, 1989): 40% of Orientals possess an inactive variant of the enzyme alcohol dehydrogenase, which has a reduced capacity to metabolise acetaldehyde. This results in an accumulation of acetaldehyde, even after small amounts of alcohol, which may then cause facial flushing, raised blood pressure and heart rate, nausea and vomiting. Japanese studies show that individuals possessing two copies of this mutant allele are protected from developing an alcohol problem and liver disease; on the other hand, heterozygotes develop a less toxic reaction to alcohol and appear to be more susceptible to liver disease (Shibuya and Yoshida, 1988; Enomoto *et al.*, 1991). The presence of the genetic marker known as HLA B8 appears to be associated with a more rapid development of cirrhosis (Saunders *et al.*, 1982).

Infection with hepatitis C (HCV) increases the risk of liver damage in chronic heavy drinkers. These individuals are at risk of developing liver disease at a younger age and at a lower cumulative dose than individuals without HCV (Maher, 1997). Problem drinkers who smoke more than 20 cigarettes per day have a threefold risk of cirrhosis compared with non-smokers. Curiously, drinkers who consume four or more cups of coffee per day have a reduced risk of cirrhosis (Klatsky *et al.*, 1992).

Dietary deficiencies of the amino acid glutathione or of vitamins A or E can decrease the liver's protection against toxic free radicals. Nutritional factors can induce enzymes which increase protective free radical activity. Chronic alcohol consumption promotes absorption and storage of iron, which also promotes free radical production.

Cancers

Heavy alcohol consumption is associated with an increased risk of cancers of the oropharynx, larynx, oesophagus and liver in men and women, and possibly with breast cancer in women (International Agency for Research on Cancer, 1988; Duffy and Sharples, 1992; Anderson *et al.*, 1993: Doll *et al.*, 1993). Most studies show a linear dose–response relationship (see Figure 5.1).

Cardiovascular Disorders

Alcohol related cardiovascular disease includes raised blood pressure, stroke, arrythmias, cardiomyopathies and coronary heart disease (Anderson *et al.*, 1993; Edwards *et al.*, 1997). There is evidence of a dose–response relationship between levels of alcohol consumption and risk of raised blood pressure and stroke. Approximately 7–11% of raised blood pressure in men can be attributed to alcohol consumption of over 40 g per day. Binge drinking may be particularly implicated. The figure is nearer 1% in women because of their lower levels of consumption. There is also a relationship between heavy drinking and risk of arrythmias and of cardiomyopathy, but not enough is known about this association to comment on whether or not it conforms to a dose–response pattern. Finally, there is evidence for a protective effect of alcohol consumption on risk of coronary heart disease. The risk of alcohol consumption for stroke and coronary heart disease will be discussed in more detail.

There are two broad categories of stroke, ischaemic and haemorrhagic. In ischaemic stroke, thromboembolism causes cerebral infarction. Haemorrhagic stroke is due to either intracerebral haemorrhage or sub-arachnoid haemorrhage. There appears to be no association between alcohol consumption and ischaemic stroke. Indeed, there is even some suggestion that low levels of consumption reduce the relative risk for this variety of stroke. In contrast, there appears to be a dose-dependent relationship between the level of alcohol consumption and the risk of intracerebral and sub-arachnoid haemorrhage (Stampfer *et al.*, 1988; Anderson, 1995). This risk is present even at levels of consumption of 20 g per day. A two- to threefold increase in risk is seen at consumption levels of over 30 g daily.

Population-based epidemiological studies indicate a J-shaped or U-shaped relationship between, on the one hand, alcohol consumption, and, on the other hand, coronary heart disease and all-cause mortality. (Edwards *et al.*, 1994). This association suggests that non-drinkers have higher rates of morbidity and mortality than light-to moderate drinkers, and that heavy drinkers have an elevated risk. Studies reporting this association have controlled for other factors such as cigarette smoking, obesity and hypertension.

This so-called 'cardio-protective effect' is evident in men and women, but is stronger in men over 40 years and in post-menopausal women. The reduced risk for CHD occurs at alcohol consumption levels of as little as 10 g per day and remains similar up to about 30–40 g per day. Beyond 20–30 g per day for men and 15–20 g per day for women, advantages for the heart will be outweighed by other risks. Individuals drinking in excess of these levels have an increased incidence of coronary heart disease which is dose-related (Edwards *et al.*, 1994). The 'protective' effect of alcohol is independent of the association between fat intake and CHD mortality (Hegsted and Ausman, 1988; Renaud and de Lorgeril, 1992).

Evidence confirming a protective effect has been obtained from case control and prospective cohort studies in Western populations (Marmot, 1984; Marmot and Brunner, 1991), and the finding has been supported by the male British doctors study (Doll *et al.*, 1994) and a more recent study of middle-aged men in China (Yuan *et al.*, 1997). The Alameda County study of Lazarus *et al.* (1991) is the only major study not to show such a relationship. Consumption of wine has been posited as the reason for the low risk of CHD in France (Renaud and de Lorgeril, 1992), and confirmed by results of a prospective study in Copenhagen (Gronbaek *et al.*, 1995). Other studies, however, have not found any differential effects of beverage type, and it is likely that much of the benefit is derived from alcohol, rather than from other components of each beverage type (Rimm *et al.*, 1996). These studies do not uniformly indicate that heavy drinkers have a higher risk of cardiovascular disease than moderate drinkers; rather, it is the case that heavy drinkers have higher mortality rates from a variety of other causes (Marmot and Brunner, 1991).

Studies describing a J-shaped or U-shaped curve are not without their flaws. However, the finding is consistent across different populations, ranging from British civil servants to Puerto Ricans and Japanese physicians (Royal Colleges of Physicians, Psychiatrists and General Practitioners, 1995). The fact that a large number of studies using different methodologies reports similar findings reduces the risk of artefact (DoH, 1995a). The principal criticisms of these epidemiological data are discussed below.

The 'sick quitter' hypothesis states that non-drinkers are likely to include individuals who have given up alcohol because they were unwell. Such ex-drinkers would be expected to have higher rates of illness, and their inclusion in the non-drinker category would inflate the mortality rates seen in that group (Shaper *et al.*, 1988; Shaper *et al.*, 1994). Studies separating out the mortality rates of lifelong teetotallers have confirmed that they have higher rates of CHD than the moderate drinkers (Yano *et al.*, 1977; Kono *et al.*, 1986; Klatsky *et al.*, 1990). The Klatsky *et al.* (1990) study also showed that ex-drinkers who had stopped drinking for medical reasons had higher mortality rates from non-cardiovascular causes. Thus it seems that the inclusion of 'sick quitters' does not account for the higher mortality rates in non-drinkers.

The 'burden of health' hypothesis states that abstainers may have a greater burden of ill-health than moderate drinkers, and that this factor contributes to their higher rates of CHD (Shaper, 1990). One would infer from this that ill people are less likely to take up drinking. A number of studies have controlled for this factor and the hypothesis does not hold up to scrutiny (Marmot and Brunner, 1991).

Lifelong teetotallers could be an unusual group who differ from drinkers in ways that might explain their high risk of CHD (Shaper, 1990; Shaper *et al.*, 1988). However, the higher risk of CHD among non-drinkers has been reported among Japanese-Americans, of whom 47% were non-drinkers, and in British studies where 6% of men were non-drinkers (Marmot and Brunner, 1991).

Social class is an important compounding variable, because the apparent protective effect of wine as distinct from other beverages could be attributed to the fact that low-to-moderate wine drinkers tend to be of higher social class than non-drinkers. Higher social class is, of itself, associated with fewer risk factors of CHD, including lower prevalence of smoking, lower mean blood pressure and higher levels of physical activity in leisure time. The Whitehall study (Marmot *et al.*, 1981) and British Regional Heart Study (Shaper *et al.*, 1994) controlled for social class and the protective effect is still evident in various cultures where factors associated with social class are likely to vary.

Foetal and Post-natal Development

Drinking alcohol during pregnancy is associated with a range of harmful consequences to the foetus. Foetal alcohol syndrome (FAS) abnormalities include brain damage, pre-natal and post-natal growth retardation, and facial malformations, but it is relatively uncommon even amongst heavy drinking pregnant women. One estimate suggests a FAS prevalence of 1 per 3000 live births (Abel and Sokol, 1991). When FAS occurs, however, it can have profound effects on child development, including mental impairment, as well as developmental and behavioural problems. It has been suggested that FAS is the leading preventable cause of learning disabilities in the Western world, and carries considerable costs to society. However, isolated abnormalities related to drinking in pregnancy, such as low birth weight and prematurity, are relatively common. Pratt (1981) has calculated that for every 15 g of alcohol consumed daily by a pregnant woman, there is approximately a 2.5% increased risk of the newborn having a developmental anomaly and approximately a 1.5% risk of growth retardation.

It has proved extremely difficult to establish a precise level of drinking in pregnancy below which foetal development and pregnancy outcome are unaffected. The most vulnerable period of foetal development is also unclear. Animal studies suggest that heavy drinking in early pregnancy is associated with physical abnormalities, whereas heavy drinking later in pregnancy is associated with neurological damage. This has led some health departments to recommend avoiding any alcohol during pregnancy, although it has been argued that this is overly restrictive (Knupfer, 1991).

Distribution of Drinking at the Population Level

Two principal sources of data provide estimates of the level of alcohol consumption in the population: sales and surveys. Data from the Brewers' Society Statistical Handbook show that per capita alcohol consumption in the UK has been above 9 litres for people aged 15 years and over for about 20 years. Assuming 8 g of alcohol per unit, this is equivalent to an average of 17.3 units per week for each person aged 15 and over in the population (Royal Colleges of Physicians, Psychiatrists and General Practitioners, 1995).

In the General Household Survey (OPCS, 1994) the mean consumption (units per week) for men and women aged 15 years and over in Great Britain was 10.2 units per week. The mean consumption for men overall was 15.9 units per week, and for young men aged 16–24 it was 19.1 units per week. In the 1996 General Household Survey, 27% of men and 14% of women exceeded the recommended weekly limits of 21 units for men and 14 units for women (ONS, 1998a).

There are regional variations in levels of alcohol consumption and alcohol related problems in Britain. The North and North West of England have the highest proportion of heavy drinkers (ONS, 1998b). Scottish teenagers are more likely to be heavy and infrequent drinkers than their counterparts in England OPCS, 1986b; Plant and Foster, 1991; Anderson *et al.*, 1995). Women are more likely to be abstainers and to drink smaller quantities than men. However, women of all ages are drinking more (see also chapter 3).

The Single Population Theory

The single population theory states that the distribution of alcohol consumption moves up or down as a whole and that drinking behaviour is under 'collective influence' (Ledermann, 1956; Skog, 1985; Rose and Day, 1990). This theory suggests that any increase in mean consumption for the whole population is likely to lead to an increase in the prevalence of heavy drinking. The background to this theory will be discussed, and supported by examples from the literature.

Studies investigating alcohol consumption and mortality in France, before, during and after the Second World War, led demographer Sully Ledermann to hypothesise a very strong mathematical relationship between overall alcohol consumption in a population and excessive consumption (Ledermann, 1956). Ledermann's theory has excited controversy and debate over the years. Proponents have argued that it contains important insights (Bruun *et al.*, 1975; Royal College of Psychiatrists, 1979), whereas opponents have criticised its assumptions and dismissed its relevance for prevention (Skog, 1971; Miller and Agnew, 1974; Duffey and Cohen, 1978). It has been tested against survey data from many countries. While these data confirm that the distribution of alcohol is highly skewed, the distributions did not appear to have well defined mathematical properties and the variance of the distribution was often quite different from the value predicted by the Ledermann model (Skog, 1985). Although the Bruun *et al.* (1975) report discarded the Ledermann formula, it also recognised that, where populations have similar levels of consumption, the formula gives a reasonable approximation to actual distributions. None the less, Skog has called for a more accurate alternative approach to describe the relationships that do exist and has argued that a theory of the distribution of alcohol consumption ought to be based on hypotheses about the factors influencing human drinking behaviour.

Factors Influencing Human Drinking Behaviour

Hypothesis I: Factors Combine Multiplicatively

Individual drinking behaviour is influenced by a variety of factors: biological, psychological and environmental. How do these independent factors combine and interact to determine drinking behaviour?

Skog (1985) hypothesises that these factors combine multiplicatively. In statistical terms this implies an interaction between effects. According to this hypothesis the increase in consumption should be approximately proportional to the initial level of consumption. If we assume subjectively that the two changes are equal; that is, the objective changes are equal in relative terms, then we can presume that the behavioural response to a stimulus will be relative as well. This implies that the same stimulus will more or less produce the same response, measured subjectively, among drinkers at different levels of consumption (Skog, 1985). Skog (1971) has tested the hypothesis of multiplicativity against survey data and found that it gave a good approximation.

Hypothesis II: Social Interaction

This hypothesis states that an individual's drinking habits are strongly influenced by the drinking habits of his or her friends and those in their social network. These influences can be direct and indirect. Drinking in groups is a direct influence. Most drinking occurs in groups and this pattern of drinking exerts a powerful influence on drinking behaviour. Indirect influences include expectations of significant others; for example, the absent wife has an effect on her husband's drinking. A third form of influence is related to the fact that alcohol is discussed, even when people are not drinking, and this influences knowledge, behaviour and attitudes. The social interaction hypothesis is also supported by research (see Skog, 1985). The implication of these factors with respect to the distribution of alcohol consumption will be discussed below.

The Skewness of the Distribution

Empirical distributions of alcohol consumption are strongly skewed, with a long tail towards high consumption levels (Skog, 1971; 1980). Examination of skewed empirical distributions from national surveys of self-reported alcohol consumption reveals no cut-off points distinguishing 'normal' from 'heavy drinking'. The transition from light to heavy drinking is gradual. In skewed distributions the arithmetic mean is much larger than the median and the ratio of mean consumption to median consumption can be used as a single measure of skewness. Skog (1985) estimated this ratio from distribution data for 21 general population surveys in 9 countries and found that the mean level was typically twice as large as the median.

The skewness ratio was smaller in populations with a high mean consumption level at about 1.5 in populations where the average annual consumption exceeded 10 litres. About two-thirds of the populations drink less than the mean, but this decreases somewhat as the mean consumption level increases. He also calculated that roughly every seventh drinker in a population exceeds twice the mean of the population. Skog (1985) postulates that this skewness is largely due to 'approximate multiplicativity', resulting from the law of proportionate effects. By this he means the multiplicative nature of the process underlying change in consumption. For instance, if we start off with a group of drinkers, all consuming the same amount, and follow them up over a period of years, we would find that their consumption levels spread out in a highly skewed distribution.

It has been argued that the skewness of empirical distributions is due to the proportion of 'alcoholics'. However the population does not consist of two distinct types of drinkers, normal drinkers and 'alcoholics', with the latter occupying the tail of the distribution. The proportion of 'alcoholics' is estimated at between 1% and 5%. This implies that the majority of drinkers in the tail of the distribution cannot be labelled as 'alcoholic', and that they cannot be responsible for the skewness of the distribution. It is likely that the 'normal' drinkers are skewed and overlap with the distribution of the 'alcoholic'.

Empirical studies confirm one aspect of the Ledermann theory, namely that there is a relationship between prevalence of heavy drinking and the overall consumption level in the population. The prevalence of heavy drinking varies as one moves from cultures with a low per capita consumption level to cultures with a high per capita consumption level. All drinkers, not just heavy drinkers, tend to increase their consumption on moving from a culture with a low level of consumption to a culture with a higher level of consumption. This implies a collective change across all consumption levels from light to heavy. It has been argued that this trend can be explained by cross-cultural patterns of consumption; however, it has also been shown in longitudinal data (Bruun *et al.*, 1975; Skog, 1985; Lemmens *et al.*, 1990). Abstainers are not included in these data sets and mean consumption is calculated per drinker not per capita. Caution is needed where abstainers are included.

It would appear, from the above, that an individual's risk of becoming a heavy drinker depends on the 'wetness' of the drinking culture to which that individual belongs. An individual's drinking habits are therefore strongly influenced by the drinking habits in his or her personal and social network (Skog, 1980). This social interaction theory explains why the drinking habits of someone living in a 'wet' environment where alcohol is cheap, are different from those living in a 'dry' environment. By the same token the drinking habits of a seasoned rugby or football player will be different from those of someone training to be a Baptist minister. The collective patterns observed in population consumption distribution are likely to occur as a result of social and cultural mechanisms.

The above data describe societies where there is little formal social control on individual drinkers. Distribution data can be modified by other factors, as was seen in Sweden between 1914 and the mid-1950s when there was an individual rationing system, the Bratt system, resulting in the reduction of the variance of the distribution and the prevalence of heavy drinking, compared with other countries having a similar mean consumption level. The value of a longitudinal sample survey in investigating the strength of the relationship between per capita consumption, drinking patterns and alcohol related problems was highlighted by a study carried out by Cartwright *et al.* (1978a). This study described changes in the pattern of alcohol consumption in the population of a London suburb interviewed in 1965 (n = 928) and 1974 (n = 286). There was no difference between the two samples in the proportions of drinkers or abstainers, and very little change in overall drinking habits. The mean total consumption was 47% higher in 1974, compared with 1965, and due mainly to a 56% increase in average drinking day consumption. There was a shift towards drinking on weekdays and drinking at home, which was explained by changes in the retail distribution of alcohol over the period. There was a trend for consumption in lower status occupational groups to increase and approximate that of the higher status group. Changes in drinking habits within this suburb which did not replicate national statistics were related to factors specific to the suburb; for example, women in the suburb reported only a 12% increase in consumption. This was confirmed by the decrease in the number of women in the suburb being admitted to psychiatric services with a diagnosis of 'alcoholism' or alcoholic psychosis when, over the same period, such admissions for women had more than doubled in England and Wales.

The increase in mean consumption between 1965 and 1974 did comprise a redistribution of increased proportions of drinkers into higher consumption categories, in agreement with the Ledermann theory. There was also a general trend towards increased scores on an alcohol problems index and a relationship between increased consumption and increased prevalence of problems, correlation coefficient 0.79. Furthermore there was a consistent correlation between individual consumption and individual scores on the index of alcohol related problems, 0.45 in the 1965 sample, 0.43 in 1974 and 0.44 for the combined samples. When the samples were broken down into subgroups, it was clear that the relationship between consumption and problems was not straightforward. Although the consumption of younger males of occupational group III equalled that of older men in occupational groups I and II, the problem scores of the former group were three times higher. This was thought to be due in part to the younger group's much higher consumption per drinking day compared to the older group who drank the same total amount, but over more drinking days. It also emerged that younger men were more vulnerable to drinking problems and that the higher occupational status groups were protected. Cartwright *et al.* (1978b) concluded that the increased consumption seen between 1965 and 1974 was largely superimposed on to existing drinking patterns. The apparently fixed relationship between increased consumption and increased problems was thought to be due to the stability of the underlying drinking patterns, which determined the distribution of the increase in consumption.

If increased consumption is associated with increased levels of alcohol related problems, it could be postulated that a decrease in such problems might accompany a reduction in consumption. Such an experiment would be hard to set up. However, a naturalistic study was carried out in Scotland in 1981, to explore the impact of a March 1981 increase in excise duty on beer and other alcoholic beverages. In this study, 463 'regular drinkers' originally interviewed and identified in a population sample in 1978/79 were re-interviewed in 1981/82 after the price of alcohol had increased substantially more than the retail price index (Kendell *et al.*, 1983). Between the two time-points alcohol consumption fell by 18%, from an average of 17.5 units to 14.4 units per week. Associated adverse effects fell by 16%. Heavy drinkers and dependent drinkers both reduced their consumption as much as light or moderate drinkers and experienced fewer adverse effects. The results of this study may be biased because none of the 'occasional drinkers' from the 1978/79 study was re-interviewed, their consumption in 1981/82 was unknown and could not be offset against the 74 respondents who were abstinent at the second time-point.

In the UK, per capita alcohol consumption rose between 1970 and 1979, but fell between 1979 and 1982 by 11%, from 9.79 litres per year in 1979 to 8.67 litres in 1982. This fall in consumption was followed by a 16% fall in drunkenness convictions, a 19% fall in first admissions to hospital for alcohol dependence, a 7% fall in drinking and driving convictions and a 4% fall in cirrhosis mortality. There was a twelve-month time-lag before any adverse effects began to fall. 'Alcoholism' admissions, cirrhosis, pancreatitis and oesophageal mortality continued to rise until 1980. Alcohol admissions and cirrhosis mortality fell in 1981 and 1982, but mortality from pancreatitis and cancer of the oesophagus did not. This was thought to be due to a time-lag effect.

More recently, an ecological analysis using data on 32,333 adults who participated in the 1993 and 1994 health surveys for England assessed whether the average consumption of alcohol was associated with the prevalence of heavy drinking, problem drinking, and abstention in the 14 Regional Health Authority areas in England (Colhoun *et al.*, 1997). Mean consumption of alcohol in light to moderate drinkers was strongly, positively associated with the prevalence of heavy drinking: $r = 0.75$ in men and $r = 0.62$ in women drinking more than 21 and 14 units per week respectively. Median consumption was similarly associated with the prevalence of heavy drinking. Abstention was not significantly associated with mean consumption in drinkers: $r = 0.08$ for men and -0.29 for women. Both the mean and median consumption in drinkers were positively associated with prevalence of problem drinking as defined by the CAGE questionnaire: $r = 0.53$ for men and $r = 0.42$ for women for the association with mean consumption. The authors thus confirmed that the prevalence of heavy drinking is strongly associated with the mean and median consumption of the population across England. This finding held for both men and women.

Regional differences in consumption were identified. For instance, the highest prevalence of drinking more than 21 units per week among men was in the Northern region, 38.5%, where mean consumption was 22.7 units per week; and the lowest prevalence was in the North East Thames region, 23.5%, where the mean was 14.3 units per week. The associations between median consumption and heavy drinking were found to be as strong as those for mean consumption. This is an important finding given the fact that median consumption, unlike mean consumption, does not have an inbuilt correlation with heavy drinking.

Colhoun *et al.* (1997) discussed their findings in the light of the Department of Health's (1995a) recommendations of an increase in sensible drinking benchmarks, concluding that higher average consumption among moderate drinkers is associated with higher rates of heavy drinking, and problem drinking. An intriguing finding in this survey was the weak association between the prevalence of abstention and mean consumption in males, suggesting that the social determinants of abstention may differ from those influencing consumption patterns of heavy and moderate drinkers. Thus, an increase in mean consumption among drinkers cannot be assumed to result in decreased abstention.

International Trends in Per Capita Consumption

Understanding population level risks is a complex and incomplete science. Nevertheless, there is strong evidence that per capita consumption of alcohol – usually calculated as the total volume of absolute alcohol consumed by a country, divided by the population aged 16–60 – is a powerful predictor of alcohol related problems in the community. This very general relationship between per capita consumption and alcohol related problems takes centre stage when debating any national alcohol strategy because per capita consumption can, very crudely, be varied by measures available to government.

Alcohol related problems at the population level are a summation of different individual risks. Problems associated with intoxication, predominantly social in nature, are more loosely related to per capita consumption than health problems. Within the category of health problems, relationships are complex: for example, liver cirrhosis is associated with heavy drinkers, whereas coronary heart disease and all-cause mortality is somewhat diminished in light drinkers. We will argue in Chapter 12 that measures at government level are necessary to contain per capita consumption at levels that are consistent with a 'sensible drinking' culture. An understanding of the population risk of drinking is also a prerequisite of the systems approach that we believe addresses the public health agenda as well as the humanitarian, individual help agenda.

The changing patterns of alcohol consumption in the UK have been discussed in Chapter 3; the question here is, what impact do these changes have for the population as a whole and what accounts for the changes? Per capita alcohol consumption almost doubled in the UK between 1945 and 1979. This increase in consumption reflected a trend in Western Europe and North America, as did the levelling off of consumption evident from the early 1980s. The trend towards harmonisation, which implies a decline in alcohol consumption in some European countries, has been attributed to a combination of factors, including an ageing population, economic factors and changes in dietary, cultural and social habits. In the UK the per capita consumption in 1993 was 7.0 litres of absolute alcohol compared with 5.3 in 1970, 7.3 in 1980 and 7.6 in 1990. Similar levels of consumption were reported in Ireland, New Zealand, Canada and the US (Brewers and Licensed Retailers Association, 1998). In France, Portugal and Spain, corresponding 1993 levels of consumption were somewhat higher at 12.3, 11.4 and 9.7 litres respectively.

Many hypotheses have been proposed to explain trends in alcohol consumption. One explanation is that societies go through cycles of more or less liberal attitudes to alcohol consumption. At any given time there will be interest groups pushing and pulling the use of alcohol in different directions. Where the dominant culture allows individual freedom to drink or not, then it is as if society keeps learning that there is a point beyond which the population level of harm resulting from alcohol is too great and per capita consumption is brought back to a tolerable level which is often in the region of 8–9 litres. The so-called 'long waves' of variation in alcohol consumption describe a regular pattern of rises and falls in a number of industrialised societies, which cannot be explained simply in terms of economic cycles (Mäkelä *et al.*, 1981; Room 1991). These long waves are considered to cover centuries, not just decades, and their periodicity is calculated at approximately three generations (Room, 1991). It is postulated that the long waves described in the International Study on Alcohol Control Experiences (ISACE), covering seven countries, started in the mid-nineteenth century when alcohol intake was high in Europe and North America (Mäkelä *et al.*, 1981). The long wave model describes changes in consumption which cannot be explained by obvious factors, but which reflect a kind of dialectic social learning process (Room, 1991). For many industrialised countries an inflection point in the aggregate alcohol consumption can be found in the 1970s and 1980s. It may be that the post-war trend of increased alcohol consumption is over in these countries. In the US and Canada an attitudinal and cultural change is proposed as the main explanation (Smart, 1989; Clark and Hilton, 1991; Room, 1991).

Drinking and Drinking Problems in the UK: The Overall Picture

Standing back from all the detail, the picture that we have from Part II of this book is of a drinking country which, unsurprisingly, is also a country which is experiencing significant alcohol related problems of many different kinds. International comparisons (Edwards *et al.*, 1994, Simpura, 1995) suggest that the UK is drinking less and experiencing lower rates of alcohol related problems than the majority of European countries, and we are probably also doing rather better than Australia and considerably better than the US, at least as judged by cirrhosis death rates. But before taking too sanguine a view of things we would do well to remember that no national drinking experience is fixed for all time. We need to look not just at the static picture but also at the trends.

Let us first examine drinking itself. Our data show that most people in Britain drink, and among those of working age, about 30% of men and 20% of women are drinking at a level beyond that advised by the Royal Colleges. Men and women, people living in different regions, young people and the older population, the better-off and the worse-off, and people in different jobs, all drink somewhat differently and any averaging will conceal this reality of variation and complexity. The pattern of people's drinking has on it the fingerprints of who they are. However, what gives rise to public health concern is evidence that in the 1990s the per capita level of alcohol consumption in the UK was more than 50% up on 1960. From what is known about the background science we would predict that such an increase in population consumption would have a more than proportionate follow-through in terms of alcohol related harm, although for certain indicators there may be time-lag effects rather than an immediate impact.

Cirrhosis death rates, whether expressed in overall terms or with an attempt to differentiate between alcohol related and other causes, provide a good indicator of trends in alcohol related chronic illness. The data here suggest that for men there has probably been about a threefold increase in alcohol related cirrhosis deaths over a recent 20-year period, with a somewhat lesser rate of increase among women. The English psychiatric hospital admission rates are also compatible with the expectation that more drinking at population level will carry with it more problems.

Regarding the data we have been able to assemble on drinking among younger people, on drinking among special populations such as the homeless or prisoners, on alcohol problems among A & E patients or in general hospital wards or psychiatric hospitals, we would argue that what we have here are only small pieces of a far larger possible mosaic which, if completed, would portray both the extraordinary variations and the pervasiveness of drinking and drinking problems as an issue in, and for, UK society.

Summary of Main Arguments

- The methodology applied to and the statistical analysis of epidemiological research in the alcohol field is complex. The strength of evidence derives from a consistency of findings across different populations by studies using different methodologies.
- At an individual level there is an accumulation of evidence enabling the description of risk functions for alcohol intake and different diseases.

- There is evidence that light drinking – 20 g, or 2 units, daily – has a health benefit. The evidence is subject to academic debate and marginal to policy making.
- There is a strong relationship between per capita alcohol consumption and alcohol related problems in the population as a whole. Constraining whole population alcohol consumption is central to policy making.

Part III

Influences on Drinking and Related Problems

6
Price

Considerable amounts are spent by the British people on alcohol each year: £28,006 million – or £590 per adult – was spent in 1996. Assuming alcohol is on sale for 24 hours every day of the year, this corresponds to an expenditure of £77 million for every day of the year, and £53,000 for every minute. Alcohol consumption accounts for 7.4% of total consumer expenditure, so it is perhaps not surprising that trends in alcohol expenditure, particularly its relative affordabilty, are influenced by the same set of variables as most other consumer goods.

In this chapter, data on trends in prices and the affordability of alcohol are presented along with the evidence on the importance of these factors in influencing overall consumption levels and those of specific groups. In this chapter we discuss:

- theory and models
- price and income trends
- price and income effects at the population level
- price and income effects at the individual or household level
- prices, taxes and revenue.

Theory and Models

People have to make choices about what to consume. These decisions will be influenced by economic factors, namely the prices of goods and the income (and credit) available for the purchases. In general, as prices increase for a particular good, consumption will fall; whereas, as income rises, demand for the good will normally rise. The size of the price and income effects will depend on the type of product; in particular, whether it is seen as essential or as a luxury by consumers. Goods seen as essential usually have low price responsiveness, meaning consumption not changing by large amounts even if there are substantial price falls or rises. In contrast, changes in consumption of luxury goods may be very responsive to price changes. As income increases across the population goods can move along this necessity–luxury spectrum.

Economists usually consider the size of price and income effects in terms of elasticities. A price elasticity can be defined as follows. If prices change by a small amount, with all other variables that influence demand being held constant, then demand will also change: the price elasticity is defined as the ratio of the proportionate change in demand to the proportionate change in price. A price elasticity of –1.0, for example, would imply that a 1% increase in price would result in a 1% fall in demand all other factors remaining fixed. While price elasticities are generally negative, income elasticities are generally positive.

Non-economic factors also have an effect, especially in determining preferences for different goods. Advertising may play a part in influencing these preferences, certainly in terms of brand choice, but also in influencing whether a consumer purchases, say, a can of beer rather than some other good on offer in the supermarket. Time involved in purchasing is also a cost, especially since the availability of alcohol is often restricted.

Economists rarely have experimental data and therefore estimating the effect of any one particular factor involves using statistical techniques, usually some form of multiple regression, to focus upon the effect of interest while controlling for all other factors. Simple correlations between consumption and price, for example, while being of descriptive interest cannot be used to prove or disprove a relationship. Many existing studies use quite complex mathematical and statistical techniques and there is a tendency with such research to take results at face value. However, estimates, their standard errors and statistical significance based on these estimates, will only be meaningful if the model has been correctly specified. There are a range of statistical checks to test the validity of the models but these are still not universally applied.

Another problem involves the number of different theoretical models available. These imply different roles for price or income. The most extensive model of addiction has been proposed by Becker and Murphy (1988). In this model an individual's well-being is assumed to depend on health, the psychological and physiological benefits of consuming the addictive substance and the benefits derived from the consumption of all other goods. Health is expected to depend, amongst other things, on the cumulative past consumption, or stock, of the addictive substance. Greater past consumption is predicted to have a negative effect on the benefits gained from current consumption; that is, tolerance effect. Other aspects of addictive behaviour, such as reinforcement effects, and the avoidance of withdrawal effects are also built into the model. The demand equation derived from the model includes future and past price and consumption terms. This model leads to the prediction that 'addictive' goods will be more price sensitive in the longer run than 'non-addictive' goods. This model has not been fully tested with UK data. Ideally, all new empirical work would estimate new and 'older' models of this kind and carry out full statistical tests to validate the theoretical models proposed. However, this has not been general practice in published work and this hinders the comparison of estimates of price effects.

One reason for different estimates of price or income effects relates to differences in the data employed by the study. Many studies employ population aggregate data over time, and effects from these studies are often considered to give estimates of average shorter-term responses. In contrast estimates derived from considering the differences in consumption across individuals or households are thought to give an estimate of the longer-term effects. However, models with different data will also be considering different influences. Alcohol consumption can also be measured in a number of different ways. Different studies have used alcohol measured in volume as well as value terms. Some economic models are defined in terms of expenditure shares rather than the monetary amounts. In addition, consumption decisions can be considered in a number of different steps; for example, separating the decision to drink from the decision about how much to drink. Further sophistication can be introduced by modelling the type of drinking behaviour; for example, whether binge drinking or otherwise. Results from such studies could be important in estimating both the benefits and the costs from different taxation strategies.

From a public policy perspective the impact of prices on alcohol consumption, patterns of drinking and problems is of primary interest. Studies have indicated that economic and other influences on consumption vary across beverages and therefore it is usual to disaggregate consumption at least into main beverage types. However, the alcohol market is complex and there are many sub-markets within each beverage type. It would be expected, for example, that the effect of price on consumption may be different in the ordinary table wine market compared to that for high-quality wines. The beer market in the UK has also become more complex with lagers taking an increasing share. Marketing strategies for different beers and lagers reflect the anticipated price responses. Some are marketed as luxury goods with a high mark-up on the cost price while others are directed at the mass market. Some brands will also move along the spectrum as they become more popular and gain market share.

Traditionally in the UK most alcohol was consumed away from the home. However, there has been a considerable change in availability and in the quality of beers and lagers available to the home market. Theory would suggest that alcohol consumed in a licensed premise may be priced higher than the 'same' good in a take-home form. This is because the on-licence price includes the amenity value of the premises – the beer in the pub is a different consuming experience than the beer at home. However, this neglects the total market position. Take-home beer has to be packaged and was a smaller market than draught beer. In the 1960s and 1970s, off-licensed prices were on average higher than on-licensed prices for a similar quantity of beer, although wine and spirits prices were lower. Recent technology in canning beers has improved the quality of take-home beer along with a more general move towards lager consumption where there may be less quality difference. There is, however, little data to explore these trends and their implications. In 1996 the government estimated the weight for the retail price index assuming 47% of all alcohol was spent in on-licensed beer and lager sales, 13% on beer or lager off-licensed sales and 40% for wines and spirits total sales (Brewers and Licensed Retailers Association, 1998). These figures compare to 4% of alcohol expenditure being in the form of off-licensed beer consumption in 1973 and 8% in 1986 (Tether and Godfrey, 1990).

Finally, the effects of price and income may be expected to have different effects across different groups of the population. Drinking is a popular pastime among the young although income is often limited. For many goods, therefore, young adults may be expected to be more price responsive than older groups. However, young adults are brand conscious and therefore may be price responsive within a brand group but not prepared to shift consumption to, say, a supermarket own brand. Price sensitivity may also be expected to vary across different drinking patterns. The hypotheses about heavy drinkers are varied. Heavy drinkers may be spending a large proportion of their income on alcohol and therefore may be expected to be price sensitive, whereas light consumers may not change consumption in response to, say, a tax increase. Dependent drinkers, however, have been hypothesised to lack sensitivity to price changes because of their need for alcohol. This is an issue which requires empirical testing.

Price and Income Trends

General inflation has varied considerably over the past 30 years and to make sense of changes in alcohol prices it is necessary to relate these changes to overall inflation rates. In Figure 6.1 the trends of prices for different beverage groups between 1960 and 1996 are presented. The indices are adjusted for general price changes and are all centred on a base of 100 in 1979. Variations from 100 indicate whether the beverage has become cheaper or dearer than other goods. The figures are based on the implicit price deflators used in the National Accounts. Prices will vary with changes in the 'quality' of goods consumed within each beverage category as well as with changes in individual commodities, such as the price of a pint of draught beer.

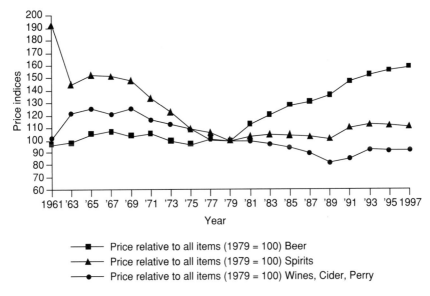

—■— Price relative to all items (1979 = 100) Beer
—▲— Price relative to all items (1979 = 100) Spirits
—●— Price relative to all items (1979 = 100) Wines, Cider, Perry

Source: ONS (various quarters and years).

Figure 6.1   Trends of prices for different beverage groups between 1961 and 1997

The trends in prices have been quite different across the beverages. Prices of beer varied below and above general price rises in the 1960s and 1970s but have risen substantially above the general rate of inflation in the 1980s and 1990s. In contrast the price of spirits fell substantially until the mid-1970s, although the rate varied year by year. Prices then were fairly stable until they began to

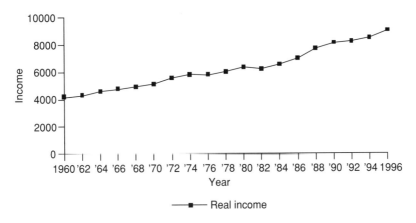

—■— Real income

Source: CSO (various months, years).

Figure 6.2   Trends in real personal income per person, 1960–96

rise again in the 1990s. Wine prices were variable in the 1960s but have since been on a long downward trend until the last few years.

In Figure 6.2 trends in real personal income per person are presented for the period 1960–96. Overall, income has more than doubled over the period although there have been periods when income has fallen.

In Figure 6.3 the prices of different beverages relative to the income changes are presented as an affordability index. This is constructed as a price trend adjusted for increase in real income, a fall in this index in the figure indicates that the price adjusted for income is falling – in other words, alcohol is more affordable. Wines, cider and perry as a group did become less affordable at the start of the period but prices have since fallen below the average for all alcohol. Spirits have shown the most significant falls, being 71% more affordable in 1996 than in 1960. Beer has shown a more variable pattern, although still more affordable at the end of the period than at the beginning.

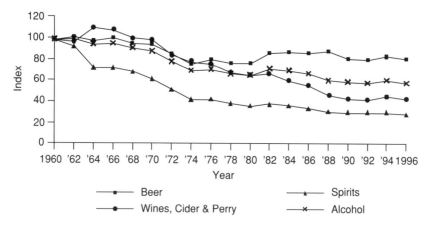

Source: CSO (various months, years); ONS (variuous quarters and years).

Figure 6.3   Prices relative to personal disposable income

Indices are difficult to interpret and it may be easier to consider affordability in terms of the minutes required to earn the price of a typical product. However, these figures will vary with the group and gender income rates examined and with the 'typical' alcohol product which may well change over time. Some examples are given in Table 6.1 – draught beer has become relatively less affordable since 1979, whereas whisky and wine are considerably more affordable.

The data for the whole period suggest that while income has generally been rising, making alcohol overall more affordable, trends between and within beverage type have been more complex. These data relate to averages across the population and the models which have attempted to model these data are reviewed below.

Table 6.1 Time needed (minutes) to earn a typical alcohol product by a male manual worker

Product	1979	1985	1990	1996
Pint of draught beer	11	13	12	14
Bottle of whisky	132	114	108	102
Bottle of table wine	33	32	28	27

Source: Centre for Health Economics Database.

Price and Income Effects at the Population Level

There have been a number of recent reviews which have considered data from different countries, but the purpose of this section is to examine the evidence for the effects of prices and income on population level alcohol consumption in the UK. A literature search was conducted across economic, social science and medical databases to identify studies that had been undertaken since 1990 to update the previous reviews (Godfrey, 1990; Leung and Phelps, 1993; Österberg, 1994). This is a more complex task than undertaking a systematic review of health care intervention effectiveness. As argued above there is no single 'effect' that is being examined; furthermore, the influence of price and income on alcohol consumption may well change over time. In addition, published studies vary in their methodological rigour. Nevertheless, they consistently show that increases in price are associated with decreases in consumption, whilst increases in income tend to be associated with increases in consumption.

Price Elasticities

A summary of price elasticity estimates derived from a number of UK studies is given in Table 6.2. Further details of each model used, and data definitions, are available in the individual studies or in reviews by Ponicki (1990), Österberg (1994), and Leung and Phelps (1993).

The results from these studies are very varied. In general, the price elasticity estimates for beer are lower than those for other beverages, especially for studies using data from the 1960s, 1970s and 1980s. Studies with more recent data have shown greater variation, with two giving higher estimates of price elasticities for beer and one having estimates closer to some of the earlier studies.

Estimates of the wine price elasticities are particularly variable, ranging from −0.23 to −1.14. In general, the wine figures are higher than respective estimated beer elasticities. Estimates of the price elasticities for spirits also have a large range, from –0.24 to –1.45.

Table 6.2   Price elasticity estimates

Authors	Time Period	Beer	Wine	Spirits
Prest (1949)	1870–1938	–0.66	na	–0.57
Wong (1988)	1920–1938	–0.25	–0.99	–0.51
Stone (1945)	1920–1938	–0.73	na	–0.72
Stone (1951)	1920–1948	–0.69	–1.76	–0.57
Walsh (1982)	1955–1975	–0.13	–0.28	–0.47
Clements & Selvanthan (1987)	1955–1975	–0.19	–0.23	–0.24
McGuinness (1983)	1956–1979	–0.30	–0.17	–0.38
Duffy (1983)	1963–1978	na	–1.0	–0.77
Godfrey (1988)	1956–1980	na	–0.76 to –1.14	–0.56 to –0.99
Duffy (1987)	1963–1983	–0.29	–0.77	–0.51
Selvanathan (1988)	1955–1985	–0.13	–0.37	–0.32
Jones (1989)	1964–1983	–0.27, –0.40	–0.77, –0.94	–0.95,–0.79
Selvanathan (1991)	1955–1985	–0.13	–0.40	–0.31
Duffy (1991)	1963–1983	–0.09	–0.75	–0.86
Glen and Carr-Hill (1991)	1965–1989	–0.80	–0.91	–1.45
Duffy (1995)	1963–1992	–0.01 to–0.34	–0.33 to –1.10	–0.64 to –1.13
Salisu & Balasubramanyam (1997)	1963–1992	–0.10,–0.32	–0.66,–1.09	–1.16,–1.28
Blake and Nied (1998)	1952–1991	–1.27,–0.95	–0.82,–0.93	–1.31,–1.32

Sources: Österberg (1994) and original articles.
Note: Elasticity estimates depend on the model. Some are constant throughout the data range, some vary with the data. Ideally, all estimates would be estimated at the same equivalent point in time, but this requires the data from the authors.

An alternative source of information on price elasticities are those used by the Treasury to calculate revenue yields. Unfortunately these figures are not always published. In Table 6.3 some previously published figures are reported. These show some interesting trends, with beer price elasticity being estimated to be increasing over time, partly in line with the relative price increases for beer, while spirits estimates have fallen. The most recent estimates suggest some parity of price effects across different beverage types which contrasts with most of the research studies shown in Table 6.2. However, the general conclusion that can be drawn is that price is an influence on overall population levels of alcohol consumption. Given the changes in the mix of consumption, with more spirits and wine consumption rather than beer, overall responsiveness to average alcohol prices may be higher now than in the 1970s and 1980s.

Table 6.3 Treasury estimates of price elasticities

	Beer	**Wine**	**Spirits**
Treasury (1980)	–0.2	–1.1	–1.6
Treasury (1987)	–0.5	–1.3	–1.3
Treasury (1992)	–1.0	–1.1	–0.9

Source: Godfrey (1994); Duffy (1991).

While most studies have considered broad beverage groups, a few have considered specific beverage categories. For example, Glen and Carr-Hill (1991) examined beer and lager separately, finding lager more price sensitive than beer, and Blake and Nied (1998) separated cider expenditure from the wine, cider and perry total. However, the results for cider in terms of price and income effects varied quite significantly between the two forms of the model estimated. In a previous study Blake and Boyle (1992) considered the demand for cider and found price elasticities of –0.3 and –0.4 for long drink cider and –0.85 for packaged cider. They also found that cider was becoming more price elastic after cider tax was introduced in 1976.

Many of the more recently published demand studies have used models that explicitly explored the links between the consumption of different beverages and the impact of the price of any one beverage on the consumption of others. If alcohol was drunk purely for its alcohol content it might be expected that consumers would change consumption patterns in line with relative price changes. In contrast, if certain beverages act as complements, a price rise in one beverage may also result in a reduction of demand in another beverage. Empirical estimates of these effects have, however, generally been small and there is little consistency between studies. Additionally, many of the studies fail to meet the economic theory restrictions suggested by the model being estimated.

Some studies have considered the interaction of the demand for other goods, particularly tobacco. This is of considerable policy interest given the rates of smoking among heavy drinkers and the combined health effects of such adverse behaviours. Jones (1989) found tobacco to be a complement to all types of alcoholic drink with results suggesting that a 1% rise in tobacco prices would lead to a decrease in beer and wine consumption of 0.2% and a decrease of spirits and cider consumption of 0.5%. Duffy (1991), however, found a degree of substitutability between alcohol and tobacco. Some interaction between the prices of legal and illegal drugs may also be expected, although no UK studies were found that have been able empirically to estimate such effects. Some US studies have considered the effect of different regulatory changes on alcohol and marijuana use among young people which suggest there may be links between markets (DiNardo and Lemieux, 1992; Yamada *et al.*, 1993).

Income Elasticities

Income elasticities have generally been found to be positive and suggest that income is an important determinant of alcohol consumption. In Table 6.4, estimates of income elasticities are presented for the most recent demand studies.

Table 6.4   Estimates of income elasticities from population based studies

	Beer	Wine	Spirits
McGuinness (1983)	0.13	1.11	1.54
Duffy (1983)	0.85 to 1.07	2.22 to 2.54	1.6 to 1.7
Godfrey (1988)	na	1.16 to 1.39	0.22 to 2.76
Duffy (1987)	0.71	2.18	1.78
Selvanathan (1988)	0.41	1.74	2.14
Jones (1989)	0.31	1.15	1.14
Selvanathan (1991)	0.52	1.31	1.83
Duffy (1991)	0.54	1.87	2.07
Glen & Carr-Hill (1991)	0.12	1.73	1.38
Duffy (1995)	0.72 to 1.44	2.07 to 3.36	1.36 to 2.74
Salisu & Balasubramanyam (1997)	0.70, 0.76	1.42, 1.55	1.06, 0.88
Blake & Nied (1998)	0.81, 0.89	1.85, 1.61	1.16, 0.98

Sources: Ponicki (1990) and individual studies.

In general income elasticities for wine and spirits have been above those for beer. Treasury estimates have suggested that wine demand is the most sensitive to income changes but they also confirm other research results show that income is an important determinant of alcohol consumption (see Table 6.5).

Table 6.5   Treasury estimates of income elasticities

	Beer	Wine	Spirits
Treasury (1980)	0.7	2.5	2.2
Treasury (1987)	0.6	2.6	1.8
Treasury (1992)	0.9	1.6	0.9

Source: Godfrey (1994), Duffy (1991)

Other Influences

Many studies have been confined to examining price and income effects. Partly this is because other factors such as population characteristics may not change significantly year by year and therefore their influence could not be measured by population level data. Some studies have included advertising and licensing effects. Studies of advertising effects have shown mixed results, although a number have found small but positive impacts, suggesting that increases in advertising expenditure may result in small rises in consumption. The results for the effects of licensing have also been mixed. Godfrey (1988) found that the number of licensed outlets had a significant impact on both wine and beer consumption: results suggest, for example, that an increase of 1% in the number of licensed outlets would increase wine consumption by nearly 5%. Blake and Nied (1998) found that the number of off-licences significantly, positively influences the demand for beer but negatively influences the demand for wine and cider, although the reason for the negative relationships is unclear. In contrast, Blake and Nied found that the number of on-licensed premises has a positive impact on the demand for wine. These studies have not investigated the impact of the deregulation of hours and conditions of licences.

Blake and Nied (1998) have also examined the impact of demographic and socio-economic factors. They found falling employment in the production sector helped to reduce the demand for beer but increase the demand for cider. Other variables had mixed effects; for example, the proportion in social classes C2 and D, and the proportion of young people, had positive effects on spirits consumption in one specification but no effects in another. The importance of socio-demographic factors in determining overall levels of demand has also been demonstrated for the US. Treno *et al.* (1993) included variables such as female labour participation rates and marital instability, although the results were not always in the direction predicted. In general, however, these effects are better examined with household or individual based data.

Price and Income Effects at the Individual or Household Level

Expenditure decisions are frequently made at a household level and economists have a special interest in explaining changes in household level expenditure patterns. However, unless data are available over time it is difficult to investigate the impact of changes in prices. The UK has a regular annual survey of household expenditure, the Family Expenditure Survey, and a few studies have used these data combined over a number of years to investigate the impact of prices and income. These data are also useful as they allow the investigation of the impact of various social and demographic variables on alcohol consumption, but using such results to guide alcohol policy decisions has to be undertaken with some care. Households are not equivalent to individuals and the same household expenditure could be distributed among individual members in a number of different ways. There is also the problem with all household surveys that the heaviest drinkers are often excluded. Grossing-up expenditure from household surveys usually accounts for less than 70% of that estimated from sales data.

There are far fewer demand studies in the UK which have used household level data. Atkinson *et al.* (1990), drawing on data from the 1970 to 1983 Family Expenditure Surveys, considered the determinants of overall alcohol consumption with a model that specifically took into account that a number of households would have no expenditure on alcohol. Alcohol was found to be price elastic, with estimates of –1.12 and –1.42 depending on the model specification, with the total expenditure elasticities being in the range between 1 and 1.5. The expenditure elasticities are equivalent to income elasticities in the population model. Baker and McKay (1990) used a model disaggregating beer, wine and spirits expenditure using data from the 1970 to 1986 surveys. The price elasticity estimates were –0.88 for beer, –1.37 for wine and –0.94 for spirits with expenditure elasticities being 0.89, 1.61 and 1.00 respectively. Finally, Crawford and Tanner (1995) used data from 1974 to 1993 and a similar model to Baker and McKay. Their estimates of price effects estimated for 1993 were –0.67 for beer, –1.40 for wine and –1.18 for spirits.

While such studies could be used to examine potential differences across household types, the published studies were limited in this respect. Baker and McKay (1990) did attempt to analyse the effects of equalising rates of taxes on the heaviest drinkers, but using a construction from household expenditures of male equivalent consumption. It is difficult to validate this concept. From a public policy perspective it is of more interest to understand the behaviour of individual drinkers rather than households. However, it should also be noted that an individual's drinking patterns may well be influenced by the drinking of others in the household or his or her social network. Most individual data are in the form of surveys and generally cover only one year. Within large jurisdictions such as the US, with state differences in taxation, it is sometimes possible to estimate price effects with a single year's survey. However, it is not always clear how large a variation in prices occurs in any one year, or how accurate the available price data may be. In the UK, tax levels are uniform and although there are considerable local variations in prices, no data are published which could be used in empirical studies. It is therefore necessary to combine data from a number of annual surveys.

Sutton and Godfrey (1995) used data pooled from the General Household Surveys for the years 1978, 1980, 1982, 1984, 1986, 1988 and 1990 when individuals were asked about their alcohol consumption. This study was confined to males aged 18–24, a group of major policy interest accounting for approximately 10% of alcohol consumption in 1994 (author's calculation from GHS data). In this study the alcohol variable being considered was the probability of being in different drinking risk groups based on weekly consumption. The results indicated that the heavier drinkers were more responsive to price. There was also an interaction between price and income, with young males on lower incomes having a higher price responsiveness than those with higher incomes. World-wide studies which have used individually based data to examine either the consumption of particular groups, especially the young, or variations across levels of drinking, are rare. Manning *et al.* (1995) used a regression technique that divides drinkers into quintiles, which is a statistical device to cope with a highly skewed distribution of drinking. As this is a statistical means of dividing consumption, the division of the groups may not have any particular meaning and obviously will vary with each sample of data. The study was based on data for the whole adult population, but only for one year, and the variations in prices across the sample is not stated. The results suggest that light and moderate drinkers are responsive to price changes but heavy drinkers are less price elastic than moderate drinkers. A similar estimation method was used by Kerr (1997) for US data pooled over a number of years. Price effects were found to be significant for the 30% to 90% quintile group with the largest elasticity estimates being for the 80% and 90% group. However, the heaviest group of drinkers in the next highest quintiles had lower estimates of the price effects.

Previous studies in the US, such as that of Grossman *et al.* (1987), have suggested that young people have higher than average price elasticities. A more recent study examined the impact of price on binge drinking (Chaloupka and Wechsler, 1995). This study of college students found an estimated price elasticity of binge drinking of –0.145 compared to an average estimated price elasticity of drinking participation. These estimates differ from those reported above as they are based on probabilities of behaviour rather than percentage changes in consumption. Grossman *et al.* (1998) considered whether the demand for alcohol by young people in the US could be modelled with the rational addiction model. They found long-run price elasticities 60% higher, average –0.65, than short-run price elasticities, –0.41, relating to the number of drinks in a year, which provides some support for the rational addiction model.

The final group of US studies have examined the relationship between prices and problem rates. Two of these focused upon relationships between prices, road traffic deaths and cirrhosis mortality (Cook, 1981; Cook and Tauchen, 1982) and both found significant effects of tax changes on problem rates. Saffer and Grossman (1987) and Chaloupka *et al.* (1991) suggest that an increase of the beer tax would reduce drink driving fatalities. Cook and Moore (1993) and Moore and Cook (1995) have indicated the importance and long-term effects of drinking for the young. As results suggest that young people tend to be price sensitive, a tax policy may well have a lifetime effect. Grossman *et al.* (1993) suggested that an increase in alcohol tax was more economically efficient than raising the drinking age.

While the body of evidence from the US is substantial, it is not clear that it can be automatically translated to other countries, especially as US tax rates are substantially lower than those in the UK. Examining individually based models and examining the relationships between prices and problems is a high priority for further research in the UK.

Prices, Taxes and Revenue

Taxes are the major means by which governments can seek to influence the price of alcohol. The public health arguments for taxation can take a number of different forms. Historically, high taxes on alcohol have been imposed to raise revenue, although there has always been an element of controlling availability. There are two alternative views on how taxes should be set to control alcohol related problems: to ensure revenue covers the social costs of alcohol; or a more directional public health policy designed to minimise the harm of drinking both to the individual and to the rest of society.

The difference between these two approaches depends on the definition of social costs used. The most narrow definition would confine such costs to those that are imposed on third parties, on the 'polluter pays' principle. However, this third party model would achieve an economically efficient solution if consumers are assumed to be fully informed about the risks of consumption and are rational, i.e. not irrationally addicted and not able to change behaviour. The external cost model can be extended to include these effects (Godfrey, 1990) although no estimates have been made for UK data. Current estimates of the social costs of alcohol in the UK are likely to be considerably underestimated both because they cover only the heaviest drinkers (Maynard and Godfrey, 1994) and because loss of life of third parties – through road accidents, for example – has been considerably underestimated (Godfrey, 1997). It is therefore difficult to come to a conclusion as to whether current levels of taxation yield sufficient revenue fully to cover the total social costs of alcohol misuse.

An alternative public health model is one based on minimising harm both to the individual drinker and to third parties. Using this model, a more pragmatic approach would be to estimate the changes in problems and social costs that occur with different tax changes, and the costs associated with the tax policy, and seek the solution which maximises the benefits at the least cost. However, public policy concerns have not been the major factor guiding UK tax policy (Godfrey and Harrison, 1990; Leedham and Godfrey, 1990). Even if a health perspective was accepted by governments it would have to compete with the desire to maintain revenue and with pressure from alcohol trade lobby groups.

Tax on alcohol in the UK is made up of two components: a specific alcohol duty which varies for each beverage, and general Value Added Tax imposed on the final selling price which includes the specific component. Any rise in the specific component is inflated by the imposition of VAT. In Figure 6.4, rates of taxes for different beverages adjusted for general inflation are shown. These figures are in rates per hectolitre of average strength of the beverage, except for spirits, which are shown in terms of tens of litres to ease the visual comparison. Wine tax has shown the most variation and this is due to a number of factors, including changes imposed by European regulations. While the rate in 1996 was slightly higher than in 1973, this hides a dramatic decline from the peak value of 1976. Spirits specific taxes have undergone a gradual decline in real value, partly because they were left unchanged for many years. Duty on cider was not imposed until 1975 and since that date it has increased, but in a ratchet fashion. Beer taxes have been remarkably constant in real terms, which contrast starkly with the increases in on-licensed prices discussed above.

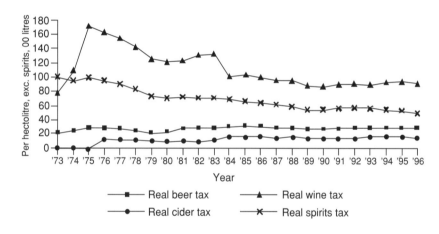

Source: Strachan (various years).

Figure 6.4   Rates excise tax rates 1987 £

Trends in the components of on-licensed beer prices are shown in Figure 6.5. This illustrates that specific taxes are only one component of price and governments are somewhat limited in their ability to influence these prices. The excise tax component of a pint of beer from a pub has been remarkably constant. The amount taken in VAT has risen, but this is due to the increase in the cost and profit element of the price which has risen substantially.

Trends in the total tax component of price are shown in Figure 6.6. This figure indicates that the total tax burden is still far higher for whisky than for other

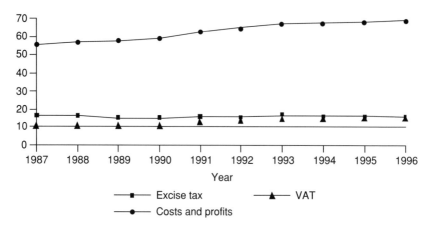

Source: ONS (various quarters and years); Strachan (various years).

Figure 6.5   Trends in components of beer prices, 1987 real

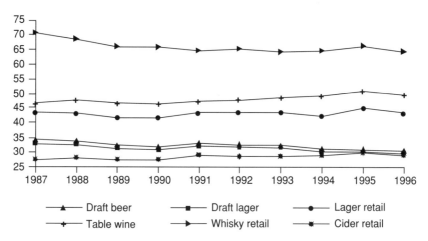

Source: Strachan (various years).

Figure 6.6   Total tax as a proportion of retail price

alcoholic beverages, although it has declined. By 1996 the share in price of total tax burden was similar for retailed cider, lager and draught beer. In contrast, draught lager had a higher tax component than draught beer. The tax component of table wine increased slightly over the ten-year period.

Another way of comparing tax rates is to consider the tax in terms of alcohol content. The tax rates operational from January 1998 convert to the following sums per litre of pure alcohol:

- Beer (average strength) – £11.14
- Table Wine (11% alcohol) – £13.15
- Wine (17% alcohol) – £11.34
- Cider (4% alcohol) – £6.12
- Cider (5% alcohol) – £4.59
- Coolers (3%) – £14.86
- Coolers (5%) – £12.26
- Spirits – £19.96

While the government is constrained by European law to treat beer and wine as like products, the differential rates for other products is less clear cut. Average tax rates also hide considerable variation in the way different alcohol beverages are treated. Beer and lager are taxed directly by alcohol content, whereas wine, cider and coolers are subject to the same rate within quite wide ranges of alcohol content.

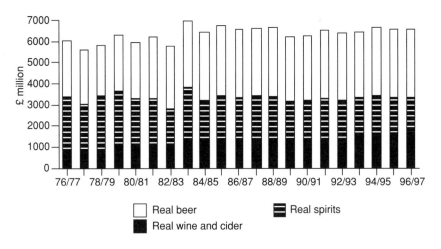

Source: Centre for Health Economics Database.

Figure 6.7   Total alcohol tax yield, 1987 values

Analysis of budget decisions suggests that changes are made or not made for a variety of reasons. Clearly one overriding objective is to maintain the flow of revenue from alcohol. In Figure 6.7, trends in the real value of alcohol revenue, specific taxes and VAT receipts are shown. In the tax years from 1976/77 to 1996/97 the yield has risen slightly, although alcohol as a percentage of total government tax receipts continues to decline. There is no evidence in this graph that the opening of the European borders and increases in legitimate and illegal cross-border trade have impacted on overall yields. A recent government estimate suggested that the revenue loss as a result of the smuggling of alcoholic drinks was £195 million compared to the yield of £10,038 million for 1996/97 in current value terms (Hansard, 10 February 1998). The government suggests that 70–80% of the smuggled alcohol is a substitute for similar purchases in the UK. A larger proportion of legitimate cross-border trade may be additional consumption. Trade estimates suggest that this legitimate consumption accounts for 18% of off-trade sales; however, this is still a small proportion of total alcohol sales whose trends show no obvious impact of the opening of the borders.

Lobbying by the alcohol trade about the effect of smuggling and legitimate cross border sales has been considerable and this may well have impacted on recent budget decisions. However, the impact of cross-border trade on the industry's pricing decisions is not obvious. On-licensed prices have risen substantially, although off-trade prices have been more in line with general price rises. It may have been expected that the opening of markets would have impacted on the trade component of prices if this was considered a major threat to their trade.

Summary of Main Arguments

- The available evidence suggests that price changes affect the level of alcohol consumption, although it may be difficult to get precise estimates at any one point in time.
- There are consistent findings on the influence of income for the UK. This suggests that if there is a desire to control overall alcohol consumption levels, attention needs to be paid to the affordability of alcohol.
- There are still considerable gaps in knowledge of the effects of prices, income and taxes on subgroups of the population of particular policy interest, especially young binge drinkers. There is evidence to support the power of a tax policy to reduce alcohol related problems.
- Tax is only one component of price. The ability of governments to influence prices directly may be limited, especially given the constraints imposed across Europe. Governments are also subject to a number of pressures and the desire to maintain the real alcohol tax revenue yield remains an important goal.

7
Regulation

There are a number of features of alcohol use in the UK which mark out the nation's particular drinking culture. Most often quoted as a symbol of national idiosyncrasy is the particular system of licensing regulations which affect when, where and to whom alcohol is available for sale or consumption. Licensing regimes around the world vary enormously and reflect the prevailing national culture – from the total prohibition in some Muslim countries to the implicit assumption in, say, some Mediterranean countries that certain types of alcoholic drinks are as much a part of daily diet as the staple foodstuffs and should be as readily available. The regulations in force in the UK, it has been argued, reflect an ambivalence in the British attitude towards alcohol whereby it is deeply ingrained in the social and ritual life of the country and yet associated with relatively high levels of social and physical harm. It is the recognition of alcohol's potential for harm which has led to the adoption of measures to limit its availability, in the expectation that such restrictions will bring reductions in excessive drinking and its adverse consequences, particularly disturbances of the peace. Set against this rationale, however, is the popular association of alcohol with leisure and pleasure, bringing about resistance to taking measures which would appear to militate against such pursuits. There is a constantly shifting balance between these two approaches. In this chapter we discuss:

- the rationale for licensing laws
- licensing law reform
- number and type of outlets selling alcohol
- restrictions on purchasing times
- children and young persons
- other regulations
- local action
- enforcement of the law.

The Rationale for Licensing Laws

The British licensing laws in their present form date back to the emergency war-time legislation of 1915. Those arguing for the dismantling of these controls argue that the special circumstances which led to their introduction, coupled with the social changes that have since taken place, undermine their credibility. While few would dispute the need to modernise the licensing laws, it is worth remembering that the present system was introduced after a long and sustained campaign against the social and economic consequences of alcohol misuse dating back to the 1830s (see Chapter 1). The circumstances of 1915 high-lighted problems that were already there and provided an added impetus to tackle them.

While it is undoubtedly true that a great deal has changed in the intervening period, including the nature and circumstances of much drinking, alcohol's association with social, economic and physical harm has remained unaltered and the question as to the role that restrictions on availability can play in minimising that harm remains valid. Of particular relevance must be questions as to whether there are specific patterns of drinking which are more commonly associated with adverse consequences and whether restrictions on availability can play a moderating role.

The rationale for regulating alcohol availability has remained much the same over the years, though the emphasis on particular consequences of alcohol use has shifted, for example, in the last century, the impact on morality seemed to be a greater consideration than in modern times. Current licensing practice is largely founded on the 1964 Licensing Act and in Scotland the 1976 Licensing (Scotland) Act; however these have been subject to a series of sub-stantial amendments designed to serve a diverse range of interests, such as the development of tourism or the principle of deregulation, which are inde-pendent of any policy focus on the degree to which the potential for harm associated with alcohol consumption can be minimised. As a result of this piecemeal approach, licensing legislation has taken on the appearance of an exercise in balancing a range of public, political and commercial interests, rather than that of one designed to influence the level and impact of alcohol consumption through any core purpose or rationale. Reasons for regulating availability include: (i) the protection of children and young people; (ii) the prevention of crime, violence and public disorder; (iii) the prevention of ill-health and premature mortality; (iv) the maintenance of personal and social morality and standards of conduct; (v) the prevention of accidents and injuries; (vi) the protection of commercial interests from excessive competition; (vii) the minimisation of costs to industry; and (viii) the minimisation of costs to health and social care systems.

Economic as well as social reasons have been crucial to the development of regulation in this field. Both the Prohibition campaign in the US and the restrictions imposed in Britain during the First World War were strengthened crucially by concerns about national efficiency. Moreover, there are occasions when it is in the economic interest of the alcohol trade to call for greater regulation, as illustrated in recent years by the demands from these quarters for tighter controls on cross-channel imports.

Focusing primarily on the prevention of social problems, however, there are two main aims behind the regulation of alcohol. First, to restrict consumption – either the consumption of alcohol by the population as a whole, or of a specific subgroup such as children. Second, regulation can aim to shape the environment in which drinking takes place. As will become clear, the failure to clarify these aims has led to a considerable amount of confusion about the purpose of the law regarding availability, thereby undermining its effectiveness.

The licensing laws provide the legal basis for the regulation of alcohol in the UK (Phillips, 1995). Separate legislation exists for each part of the UK. For example, in Scotland the principal statute is the Licensing (Scotland) Act of 1976. In England and Wales, the Licensing Act 1964 remains the principal statute, though it has been amended significantly in recent years, notably by the Licensing Act of 1988, which will be discussed later.

Other statutes also have a bearing on the regulation of alcohol availability. The Road Traffic Acts, for example, seek to regulate alcohol consumption by motorists. The Sporting Events (Alcohol Control) Act 1985 and the Criminal Justice Act 1980 in Scotland govern the availability of alcohol at or on the way to sporting fixtures. The Children and Young Persons Act (1933) sets the legal age for alcohol consumption outside licensed premises. Furthermore, legislation in other fields – such as health and safety at work, planning regulations, the licensing of buildings for entertainment casinos – is often relevant to alcohol and may be used as a basis for regulating availability.

Regulation is shaped further by the interpretation of current legislation. Case law often refines and clarifies existing statutes. However, in some cases, rulings merely add to confusion by making it difficult to enforce the legislation. Governments may introduce fresh legislation to close new loopholes in the law, but they are not compelled to do so. Such amendments must compete with other items on the government's legislative agenda.

Other instruments can also be used to influence the availability of alcohol and this is an area in which there is much scope for local action and variation. By-laws can be implemented as a means of shaping the drinking environment. In addition, local decision makers, such as liquor licensing authorities and the police, may adopt certain policies in an effort to control availability (Tether and Robinson, 1986; Light and O' Brien, 1995). As will become clear, much depends on the way in which the existing legislation is interpreted and enforced at local level. Finally, one should not ignore the capacity of private organisations to regulate their own activities in relation to alcohol availability. Organisations such as schools, youth clubs, workplaces and social clubs may devise their own policies on alcohol. Moreover, the licensed trade has its own rules and regulations governing the conduct of staff on licensed premises. Taken together, these self-regulatory activities have the potential to reinforce the effectiveness of legal regulation to a considerable extent by promoting a consistent approach to availability at the local level, and by improving the enforcement of existing laws.

Having outlined the main aspects of alcohol availability, the remainder of this chapter focuses on two key aspects of regulation: first, the impact of the law relating to availability is examined in the context of recent and possible future reforms; second, the significance of local action and self-regulatory initiatives, in so far as they affect availability, is explored.

Licensing Law Reform

Although one can identify a range of possible reasons why governments might seek to restrict the availability of alcohol, there is nevertheless a great deal of confusion about the purpose of the licensing laws. In particular, there is disagreement over the aims of the legislation: some emphasising that licensing laws are potentially an instrument for regulating overall consumption; others stressing the role of licensing law in shaping the context in which drinking takes place (Hope, 1986). As suggested earlier, there are elements of truth in both these perspectives, but little attempt is made to combine them into a coherent philosophy of alcohol regulation.

The lack of a clearly stated rationale has undoubtedly weakened the impact of the licensing laws and fuelled the case for relaxing the legislation. Since the early 1960s the trend has been in this direction, beginning with the 1960 Act which, among other things, extended the hours of off-licences, introduced new forms of retail licence for hotels and restaurants, and reduced the absolute control of the licensing justices over the granting of licences. Further efforts to reform the law occurred in the 1970s with the establishment of two committees of inquiry – the Clayson Committee in Scotland (Scottish Home and Health Department, 1973) and the Erroll Committee (Home Office, 1972) south of the border. Many of Clayson's recommendations to relax the law were incorporated in the Licensing (Scotland) Act of 1976 which, among other things, introduced extended hours and permitted all-day opening. In contrast, the Erroll Report gathered dust as backbench MPs sought unsuccessfully to extend hours in England and Wales through private members' legislation. Further impetus was added to this campaign by the zeal for deregulation demonstrated by the Thatcher and Major governments. The 1987 Licensing (Restaurant

Meals) Act enabled restaurants to serve alcohol during the afternoons, while the Licensing Act 1988 abolished the afternoon break for pubs and clubs. The latter also extended closing times, added an extra hour on Sundays and increased permitted hours for off-licences. Subsequent legislation further extended opening hours, abolished the afternoon break on Sundays (Licensing (Sunday Hours) Act, 1995) and introduced – under the Deregulation and Contracting Out Act, 1994 – children's certificates, which permit the holder to admit children under the age of 14 into the bar of licensed premises.

Not all recent changes have led to relaxations in the law. For example, a new provision in the 1988 Licensing Act means that it is no longer necessary to prove that a person knowingly served alcohol to a person under the age of 18 in order to obtain a conviction (18 is the minimum legal drinking age), although the accused can still evade conviction by proving that he or she exercised all due diligence to avoid committing the offence or had no reason to suspect that the person was under 18. The 1988 legislation also strengthened the law in other areas, by giving licensing justices new powers to curtail hours and by disqualifying premises primarily used as a garage from holding a liquor licence.

The evidence regarding the impact of licensing law reform is difficult to interpret for a number of reasons. First, the law on licensing is not a single measure but a collection of restrictions and regulations relating to the purchase, sale and consumption of alcohol by persons, from particular outlets, at certain times (Tether and Godfrey, 1990). It is therefore possible to relax the law in one respect – by extending hours, for example – while at the same time tightening it up in another area, by strengthening the provisions relating to under-age drinking, which creates obvious difficulties for an evaluation of distinct elements within a reform package.

A second difficulty is that licensing laws have a cultural dimension. As the Central Policy Review Staff noted in their report (1982, p. 20), 'the precise effect of these controls on existing customs and habits is uncertain and licensing is so deeply embedded as not to be easily capable of separate analysis'. It is sometimes maintained that the licensing laws have a symbolic value over and above the specific measures embodied in the legislation and that, consequently, a perceived relaxation in these laws may give out the wrong signals about alcohol, inducing excess rather than moderation. This impact is extremely difficult to evaluate.

The variation in drinking cultures between different countries creates additional problems for comparative studies of availability. Measures operating in one country may not have the same effect when applied to another, while drinking cultures may change over time, so that even a comparison of controls in different historical periods within the same country may be of doubtful validity. Comparative studies can, however, illustrate the broader potential impact of controls on availability, and in this respect may be useful.

A third problem encountered by researchers in this field is that enforcement of licensing law varies enormously. Formal changes in the law are meaningless unless they are properly implemented. In some respects the law itself is at the heart of the problem because it does not compel central direction or monitoring and fails to give sufficient powers to authorities implementing and enforcing the legislation. This point will be returned to later.

Finally, as with the evaluation of control measures generally, a variety of indicators may be chosen as a basis for assessing the impact of change. The choice of indicators is crucial and raises a number of methodological questions. Should research focus on the impact of licensing controls on alcohol consumption, or on alcohol related problems? Should it examine trends in the general population or in a specific subgroup believed to be particularly at risk? What measures should be chosen as relevant indicators? Even when these indicators have been agreed upon, one is then faced with a further set of problems regarding the availability of good-quality data and in particular the kind of disaggregated data required for a sophisticated analysis.

Any attempt to evaluate the impact of recent licensing reforms, or to predict the likely effect of future changes, is clearly fraught with difficulty as there are many confounding factors. However, evaluation is not impossible providing one seeks to distinguish between the impact of different dimensions of control, whilst bearing in mind that legislation may well have a synergetic effect. Other factors – such as price, income, unemployment levels and advertising – are likely to affect levels of alcohol consumption and problems. Licensing law can influence some of these factors – notably price, as we shall see later – while others may be independent. Moreover, there is often a complex interplay between these factors, licensing and the drinking culture, as suggested by recent research (Gruenewald *et al.*, 1995). For example, economic constraints can affect choices about where purchase and consumption will take place. This has implications for policies which affect disposable income and prices, which may be counterproductive if they promote purchase or consumption in premises associated with a higher risk of alcohol related problems. In addition, broader economic policy decisions such as changes in interest rates and tax rates, and trade policies such as the encouragement of cross-border alcohol sales, can generate further confounding factors. (See also Chapter 6.)

However, efforts to evaluate licensing reforms have been assisted by the timing of recent reforms in the UK. The relaxation of Scottish law in 1976 left England and Wales unaffected, yielding some comparative evidence on the effects of change. Subsequently, the relaxation of the law south of the border provided a further opportunity to undertake a comparative analysis.

International and comparative studies, reviewed by the World Health Organization (Edwards, *et al.*, 1994), suggest that although availability has a broad impact on alcohol consumption and problems, it is widely accepted that the link is complex and that the consequences of increasing or relaxing controls are often difficult to predict. There is a growing body of evidence regarding the effect of specific measures to control availability. This relates to each of the main dimensions of control contained within the provisions of the Licensing Acts: control over the number and type of outlets, permitted hours and the restrictions on children and young persons.

Number and Type of Outlets Selling Alcohol

According to Stockwell (1997), 'the scientific literature on the relationship between outlet density and alcohol-related harm is perplexing'. Evidence from studies in other countries suggests a positive association between the number of outlets selling alcohol and overall alcohol consumption. This includes research by Gruenewald *et al.* (1993) and Watts and Rabow (1983) in the US, and Österberg (1982) in Finland. Some have also found a significant link between the number of outlets and specific alcohol related problems. Wilkinson (1987) and Blose and Holder (1987) discovered an association between outlets and road accidents in the US. These findings have since been confirmed by other studies from the US (Scribner *et al.*, 1994; Jewell and Brown, 1995). Research from the US also suggests a link between outlets and other alcohol related problems (see Watts and Rabow, 1983), including, for example, assaultive violence (Scribner *et al.*, 1995).

In the UK the rise in the number of outlets selling alcohol has been accompanied by a growth in alcohol consumption. The number of outlets rose from 129,367 to 201,148 between 1960 and 1995, an increase of 55%. Over the same period the number of off-licence outlets alone almost doubled. Meanwhile, average alcohol consumption rose from 5.7 litres of pure alcohol per year for every person aged 15 and over in 1960 to a peak of 9.8 litres by 1979. Since this time average consumption has only once (1982) dropped below 9 litres per head.

A positive association between outlets and alcohol consumption within the UK was supported by research undertaken by McGuinness (1980). However, the methods employed in his work were challenged on the grounds that the measure of alcohol consumption was not disaggregated (Walsh, 1982). Subsequent research by McGuinness (1983) suggested that the number of licences nevertheless had a considerable impact on the demand for beer. Others disagreed, including Duffy (1983), who argued that licensing was itself determined by consumption rather than vice versa. Godfrey (1988) investigated the matter further and found that different alcoholic drinks did indeed require different assumptions about the consumption–licensing relationship. No relationship was found for spirits, but wine consumption was apparently influenced by the number of licences. For beer, however, the situation was much more complex: the number of licences affected demand, but was itself influenced by beer consumption. When the data were re-estimated using a different technique, significant licensing effects were found, though caution was urged in the interpretation of the findings given the limited nature of the data set. Nevertheless, the findings supported Godfrey's comment that it would be 'unwise to ignore licensing effects when modelling the demand for alcohol' (1998, p. 20).

The overall number of outlets can have a series of potential knock-on effects on alcohol consumption and related problems, none of which have so far been examined in detail. A saturation of outlets can reduce the costs of obtaining alcohol by reducing travel time and associated transaction costs. It can also produce competitive pressures that lead to falling prices and increased consumption (Home Office, 1993; Wagenaar and Langley, 1995). 'Happy hours' – times at which drinks are sold at low prices – are a prime example of this. The All Party Group on Alcohol Misuse echoed a wider concern about happy hours and called for this practice to be taken into account when licence renewals were being considered (1995, p. 20). In addition, competitive pressures may force licensees to tolerate activities on their premises which they would not usually condone – including drunkenness and under-age purchasing. Furthermore, a concentration of outlets within a small area is often linked with disorder, although this problem may be ameliorated to some extent by other approaches discussed later in this chapter.

The distribution of specific types of alcohol outlet may be as important a consideration as the overall number of licences issued. Evidence from Australia suggests that different licences are associated with different levels of risk relating to assaults and road accidents, with nightclubs and bars involving a higher level of risk than social clubs and restaurants (Stockwell *et al.*, 1992). In contrast, an American study found that motor vehicle accidents were significantly associated with outlet density for restaurants, liquor stores and mini-markets, but not for bars. Researchers in the US have also revealed important variations in the performance of specific types of outlet with regard to the observance of under-age drinking laws (Wolfson *et al.*, 1996). Grocery stores were more prepared to sell to under-age purchasers than other outlets, while on-licence outlets deriving a larger proportion of their income from alcohol were less likely to do so. licence outlets that were part of a chain were also less likely to break the law, as were on-licence outlets which were members of a trade association, suggesting that organisational and inter-organisational factors have an important role in licensing law enforcement.

Studies have also focused on the impact of the growth of particular types of licence. Wagenaar and Langley (1995) found that a change in the law in New Zealand allowing grocery stores to sell wine was associated with a 17% increase in wine sales between 1983 and 1993. Earlier research by Wagenaar and Holder (1991) into the impact of a similar policy change in Iowa and West Virginia,

USA, during the 1980s also found increases in wine consumption. These findings were challenged (Mulford *et al.*, 1992), but the critics' own methods have been criticised, in particular for failing to control for national trends in alcohol sales (Wagenaar and Holder, 1993). In a further study the introduction of spirits sales in bars, pubs and restaurants led to an increase in consumption of 6–8% and was associated with a significant increase in alcohol related traffic accidents (Blose and Holder, 1987; Holder and Blose, 1987).

In the UK, the growth in the number of off-licensed premises since the 1960s has been particularly dramatic. British research from the mid-1970s provided circumstantial evidence of a specific link between off-licence growth and alcohol problems (Williams, 1975) but no further analysis has since been undertaken. There is circumstantial evidence that certain outlets, off-licensed premises and also clubs, are more difficult to police than others, such as pubs (All Party Group on Alcohol Misuse, 1995, p. 17). In addition, a considerable variation exists in the quality of supervision and management of outlets, both within and between different parts of the retail sector. For example, the high turnover of landlords in some licensed premises is believed to be a factor in poor management and disorder (All Party Group on Alcohol Misuse, 1995, pp. 20–1). Furthermore, small independent outlets in the off-licence trade often do not have access to the information and training resources available to larger enterprises (Standing Conference on Crime Prevention, 1987, p. 23); this is more likely to lead to poor management and supervision of alcohol sales.

Restrictions on Purchasing Times

Evidence from other countries concerning the effects of altering the hours during which alcohol can be sold demonstrates a significant positive relationship, with longer hours leading to increased problems and shorter hours resulting in a reduction in such problems (Edwards *et al.*, 1994). However, some studies suggest a direct link between permitted hours and problems, leaving consumption unaffected (Olsson and Wikstrom, 1982; Nordlund, 1985). This suggests that in some circumstances variations in hours can have a direct impact on alcohol problems.

In the UK, recent licensing reforms have extended permitted hours, and the fact that these reforms were implemented at different times in different parts of the country meant that it was possible to identify the relative effects of change. When Scottish licensing hours were increased in 1976, the rest of the UK acted, in effect, as a control in the experiment. The situation was reversed in 1988 when similar measures were introduced south of the border.

The official evaluation of the Scottish licensing changes by the Office of Population Censuses and Surveys (OPCS) focused primarily on the impact on overall alcohol consumption (OPCS, 1986a). A 13% increase in consumption was reported, although this was mainly attributed to a large increase in female drinking of 35%. In view of the differential impact on the sexes, the report argued that it was unlikely that the law was the crucial factor behind the increase in consumption, though it was accepted that there may have been an underlying increase in male consumption offset by the impact of the recession. In other words, in the absence of the recession male drinking might well have increased more as a result of the licensing changes. The OPCS report did not examine the impact of the new law on indicators of harm, though it did find evidence of a more relaxed attitude to drinking among the public.

Others did explore the impact on alcohol related problems, but arrived at different conclusions. Eagles and Besson (1985) examined general hospital admissions and psychiatric referrals in North East Scotland in the period following the reforms. They discovered a decrease in male general admissions and a small decrease in the admission of males to psychiatric hospitals. However, the authors themselves noted that other factors were present. Unemployment in the region more than tripled in the period 1974–82, while the real price of alcohol rose in 1981. Moreover, during the period of the study, community alcohol services developed rapidly, making it possible that some admissions might have been prevented by diverting problem drinkers to these services. In addition, it was noted that in contrast to men, admissions of women with an alcohol related diagnosis increased during the study period. Contrasting findings were produced by Northridge *et al.* (1986) who detected an increase in self-poisonings in West Fife following the changes, though their research was later criticised for failing to provide control data (Platt, 1987).

Duffy and Plant (1986) examined changes in alcohol misuse in Scotland relative to trends in England and Wales and found that with regard to health, the reforms caused neither harm nor benefit. This study was also challenged on a number of grounds, including its use of liver cirrhosis – which, as a chronic disease, develops over the long term – as a short-term indicator of harm (Eagles and Besson, 1986). Others, however, have argued that the indicator is valid on the grounds that liver cirrhosis deaths are responsive to short-term changes in availability (Saunders, 1985).

Clayson (1984), the architect of the Scottish reforms, examined the impact of the changes. Comparing Scotland's experience with England and Wales, he found that drunkenness, drink driving and alcohol related violent crime all declined relatively in Scotland, while liver cirrhosis rates rose. Saunders (1985) criticised Clayson's methodology, in particular the crude aggregation of the data into six-year blocks, which prevented the measurement of year-on-year trends. Further analysis by Saunders indicated that other factors, such as unemployment, may have exerted downward pressure on consumption and indicators of harm in the period after the reforms were introduced.

It is not easy to draw any firm conclusions from the Scottish experience. As Tether and Godfrey (1990, p. 133) commented in their review, 'the empirical evidence on the link between permitted hours and alcohol-related problems is therefore unclear'. However, this did not prevent government from proposing a relaxation in the permitted hours in England and Wales in 1988. These changes provided a further opportunity to examine the impact of extended hours on alcohol problems, with Scotland this time acting as the control.

Early evidence relating to the reforms south of the border found no significant increase in alcohol consumption. Indeed, the OPCS study of drinking in the late 1980s discovered that average reported alcohol consumption had fallen slightly in England and Wales following the reforms (OPCS, 1991). In view of the fact that the drinks industry reported a small increase in consumption, this was attributed to some extent to under-reporting by respondents. Others pointed out that the OPCS report in fact revealed a rise in immoderate and heavy drinking by some sections of the population: average consumption for male heavy drinkers rose by 4% and by just over 1% for female heavy drinkers (Bennett, 1991). Between 1987 and 1994 consumption above 'sensible drinking' limits by women rose from 9% to13% in England and Wales (calculated from OPCS, 1991 and OPCS, 1996a). Over the same period the percentage of men drinking above these limits rose from 24% to 27% (peaking at 28% in 1990). This suggests a considerable growth in excessive drinking among women in the period following the changes, and a slight increase followed by a decrease during the recession years, among men.

Official surveys into drinking habits before and after the reforms do not provide comparable data on the level of alcohol related problems (OPCS, 1991). Prior to the changes a third of men and a quarter of women had admitted being drunk on two or more occasions in the previous three months, while 6% of men and 4% of women reported having two or more alcohol problem symptoms (OPCS, 1987). In the subsequent survey most of the questions relating to alcohol problems were not put to respondents in the same way, invalidating a direct comparison between the two periods. The only exception was drink driving behaviour, where among men the proportion admitting to drinking and driving over the limit almost halved (from 12% to 7%). This, as the report's author noted, could have been due to a growing reluctance to admit to such behaviour (OPCS, 1991).

The second survey did reveal a significant amount of alcohol related problems in the period following the reform (OPCS, 1991): 54% of men and 42% of women claimed to have experienced the short-term effects of excessive drinking in the previous year (such as 'memory loss' and 'difficulty getting up'), while 9% of men and 5% of women admitted severe and chronic signs of alcohol dependence such as 'drinking first thing', 'shaking hands' and 'secretive drinking'. In spite of the problems of comparison, these figures suggest at the very least that the relaxation of the law had not improved the situation.

Pinot de Moira and Duffy (1995) compared trends in alcohol related mortality in England and Wales with those in Scotland in the period 1980–91 and found that mortality rates for chronic liver disease and cirrhosis, pancreatitis, alcohol dependence or psychosis were unaffected by the extension of opening hours. Deaths from alcohol poisoning did increase, but the authors believed that this was difficult to interpret unequivocally in view of a large decline in this cause of death in Scotland over the same period. They concluded, therefore, that there was no clear evidence of a significant increase in alcohol related mortality since the 1988 changes. Subsequently the same authors compared trends in other alcohol related problems (Duffy and Pinot de Moira, 1996). This second study revealed that only reported non-sexual crimes and slight accidents in the workplace had increased in England and Wales relative to Scotland. They concluded that there was little to support the view that longer licensing hours had a major effect on the prevalence of alcohol related problems, although acknowledging that their use of routinely collected data permitted only a broad-brush approach. The focus of such studies on 'hard' data diverts attention away from other important sources of information, such as self-reported harm. Moreover, although such studies provide a valuable overview, they often fail to detect the impact of changes on specific groups which face a greater risk of developing alcohol problems, including heavy drinkers, women and young people.

Finally, we turn to examine evidence regarding the specific impact of altering the closing times of licensed premises as a means of reducing alcohol related problems. Research undertaken on behalf of the Home Office (Hope, 1986; Tuck, 1989) found that violent incidents tended to cluster around closing time. Thus it has been suggested that closing times might be staggered in order to minimise these problems, although it does not necessarily follow that either later or staggered closing times will in fact reduce problems. Such steps may simply disaggregate the problem, but even this might be an advantage from a policing point of view, if it improves the ability of law enforcement authorities to manage outbreaks of disorder.

Adopting a more flexible approach to closing times would be very much a leap in the dark. However, there is some evidence to suggest that if selectively applied and carefully managed, such a strategy might have an impact on alcohol related disorder. An experiment in extended and staggered closing times in Manchester in September 1993 (Lovatt, 1996) was found to have been associated with a fall in city-centre arrests and a 14 % decline in alcohol related incidents. The initiative was welcomed by the police for its impact on public order, although it should be noted that similar experiments in other cities have been less successful. In Glasgow, for example, the introduction of a later closing time merely delayed disorder because most people remained in licensed premises as long as possible.

A further experiment took place in Manchester in June 1996, when hours were extended during the Euro 1996 soccer tournament. On this occasion alcohol related incidents did increase when compared with the same month in the previous year: criminal damage by 7%, assaults by 12%, street disturbances by 10% and disturbances on licensed premises by 13% (Lovatt, 1996). However, this has to be seen in the context of the special circumstances prevailing during the soccer tournament – 20,000 visiting soccer fans, five times more officers on patrol, more premises open later and more often. Nevertheless, the police were reportedly content with the outcome, believing that flexible hours had minimised the potential problems of alcohol disorder.

A flexible approach to licensing hours is increasingly supported by senior police officers. If this continues to grow, an important political obstacle to later closing times will be removed, making legislation more likely. What is clear from the evidence, however, is that flexibility must crucially be attuned to local circumstances. For example, the impact of later closing times will be far greater on the living environment in residential areas than it will in city centres comprising largely commercial premises. The availability of transport and other facilities – and, in some cases, police officers – will also have a bearing on what happens when people leave pubs at a later time and after a longer period of access to alcohol.

Children and Young Persons

Licensing law, and other legislation, contain several provisions relating to the protection of children and young people. These take the form of age restrictions with regard to the sale, purchase and consumption of alcohol and the presence of children on licensed premises. Hence children under five cannot be given alcohol except on medical orders (Children and Young Persons Act, 1933); must not, under 18 years of age, purchase, be supplied with or consume alcohol in a bar (Licensing Act, 1994); and, under 14 years of age, may not be present in a bar unless there is a children's certificate in force (Licensing Act 1964, as amended by the Deregulation and Contracting Out Act, 1994).

Evidence from other countries suggests that the age restrictions on consumption play an important role in the prevention of alcohol related problems (see Lister-Sharp, 1994). An Australian study found that overall levels of male juvenile crime rose by between a fifth and a quarter after the lowering of the drinking age to 18 in some states during the 1970s (Smith and Burvill, 1987). Similarly, in the US, the reduction of the legal drinking age was linked with an increase in alcohol consumption and alcohol related road accidents involving young people (Wagenaar, 1993a). When drinking ages in the US were subsequently raised, the rate of traffic accidents among young people fell, suggesting a fairly clear relationship between age limits and these problems (US General Accounting Office, 1987).

The main difficulty in measuring the impact of the age limits is that the rules are so widely flouted (see Hawker, 1978; OPCS 1986b; Balding, 1987; Plant, Plant and Morgan-Thomas, 1990). Although levels of under-age drinking are high (between 30% and 40% of those aged 15–16 claim to buy alcohol from a pub or club according to most studies), there is no evidence to suggest that under-age drinking on licensed premises has increased over the last two decades. However, one study found that the amount of alcohol consumed by under-age drinkers in each drinking session had increased in recent years (Newcombe *et al.*, 1995).

Clearly, one way of discouraging both under-age drinking on licensed premises and illegal purchase of alcohol from all types of licensed premises is to enforce the existing law more vigorously. This has been supported by most of the expert committees that have looked at this problem in recent years (see Standing Conference on Crime Prevention, 1987; British Paediatric Association and the Royal College of Physicians, 1995). As noted earlier, the law was amended in 1988 to tilt the balance slightly in favour of the prosecution in cases where licensees were accused of selling alcohol to persons under the age of 18. This led to an increase in convictions for this offence, although the figures remained low relative to the extent to which the law was being broken. Subsequently, the number of convictions has fallen back to the levels of the early 1980s – only 240 people were convicted of selling to persons under age in 1993. Convictions for purchasing alcohol under age also fell, from 2310 in 1989 to 370 in 1993 (Home Office, 1994).

Concern has been expressed recently about the impact of sweet-tasting alcoholic 'designer' drinks, commonly known as 'alcopops'. Critics argue that these are attractive to children and younger teenagers and therefore encourage under-age drinking. Research has confirmed this appeal and the association of these products with drunkenness among children of secondary school age (Health Education Authority, 1996; McKeganey *et al.*, 1996; Hughes *et al.*, 1997). As a result the focus of attention has shifted towards law enforcement in the off-licence sector where it is believed these products can more easily be purchased by those under age. Under-age drinking of alcohol in public has also become a prominent issue of late and the Confiscation of Alcohol (Young Persons) Act was passed in 1997 to give police greater powers to remove alcohol from young people in public places or places where they have gained unlawful access.

The presence of children in licensed premises is regulated by law. However, recent legislation has relaxed these provisions. In England and Wales, licensees may permit children under the age of 14 into the bar of licensed premises providing they are accompanied by an adult and a children's certificate is in force. In order to obtain this certificate, the licensee must satisfy licensing justices that the premises are suitable for children and that meals and non-alcoholic beverages are available. The licensing authorities may add any conditions they see fit to the certificate, including restrictions on the days or hours during which it is operational.

A possible advantage of the new law is that it may encourage a family atmosphere in licensed premises, promoting a more relaxed attitude to drinking. On the other hand, it is possible that children may be inappropriately exposed to alcohol and alcohol related problems (British Paediatric Association and the Royal College of Physicians, 1995). Much depends on the responsibility of licensees, parents, the licensing authorities and the police. So far the reform has been implemented cautiously. By June 1996, 18 months after the scheme was introduced, 3.7% of public houses in England and Wales had been granted certificates (Home Office, 1996). Although 94% of certificate applications in this period were granted, in some areas licensing justices were more keen than others to impose conditions in an effort to promote a safe and appropriate environment for children (*Which?*, May 1995 pp. 28–9). These conditions related to washing, toilet and nappy changing facilities, smoke-free zones and the removal of gambling machines. Magistrates have since come under pressure to adopt a more uniform approach to the granting of certificates.

It is too early to evaluate the impact of the children's certificates, though it is extremely important that their impact be carefully monitored (British Paediatric Association and the Royal College of Physicians, 1995). Much, as ever, depends on enforcement and implementation. At the moment the balance of regulation seems sensible, though this is not a sentiment shared by the licensed trade. An 'automatic' children's licence, granted on the basis of relatively few explicit conditions, which many in the trade see as a less bureaucratic measure, could lead to children being exposed to an inappropriate adult drinking environment.

Other Regulations

The licensing laws regulate activity in a number of other areas. For example, it is an offence to serve someone who is drunk, though prosecutions and convictions are in fact quite rare. Magistrates also have the power to exclude potential troublemakers from licensed premises under the Licensed Premises (Exclusion of Certain Persons Act) 1980. These powers, similarly, are not used as much as they might be (Portman Group, 1993).

Potentially, licensing law could be used to extend and strengthen the regulation of licensed premises. It would be possible to outline licensees' responsibilities more clearly within the legislation, particularly with regard to serving drunks and people under the age of 18. The law could specify minimum periods of training or qualifications for licensees (Light and O'Brien, 1995) and for servers. At present only the age of servers is specified in legislation, although there has been pressure from the trade to reduce this from 18 years. Others, however, believe this age limit should be raised. The British Paediatric Association and the Royal College of Physicians (1995), for example, have called for a trained server aged 21 or over to be on duty at all times. In this context it should be noted that server training has been shown to be an important means of reducing alcohol problems, particularly with regard to under-age drinking (Holder and Wagenaar, 1994; Wagenaar *et al.*, 1996).

More radically, the law could be changed so that irresponsible licensees are exposed to legal liability as a result of their actions, as in some states in the US (Holder *et al.*, 1993). Another possibility would be to clarify the criteria relating to the suitability of people applying for a licence. At present, licensing authorities must assess whether or not the applicant is 'a fit and proper person'. Yet, as Light and O'Brien (1995) have shown, this concept is open to wide interpretation. They argue that it should be reformulated as 'qualified and of suitable character' and that a list of non-exclusive criteria should be drawn up as a means of assessing this in practice. As a more drastic step, persons who have acted irresponsibly in relation to the serving of alcohol, such as those convicted for serving under-age drinkers, could be banned from holding a licence. A compromise would be a penalty-points system similar to that which applies to driving licences. Licensees could receive fines or even lose their licence by accumulating such penalty points, which might be imposed for specific offences such as serving drunks, disorder on the premises and under-age drinking.

Local Action

It is clear that the effectiveness of licensing law depends greatly upon implementation and enforcement. Poor enforcement and inadequate implementation at local level is one reason why the prevention potential of licensing legislation has not been fulfilled (Tether and Robinson, 1986).

Although UK licensing legislation is national law, it is implemented locally. In Scotland the task is undertaken by local authority licensing boards made up of councillors, while in England and Wales, licensing committees comprising local magistrates discharge this function. The advantage of such a decentralised system is that it can be responsive to local conditions. The main disadvantage is that in the absence of a clear framework of decision making, licensing authorities vary in the extent to which they use their role as a means of preventing alcohol related problems.

Central government has little influence over local licensing authorities and can do no more than urge licensing committees in England and Wales to take into account the problem of alcohol misuse; licensing magistrates exercise a quasi-judicial function and have wide discretion when granting licences. In Scotland there is more clarity, in that the specific grounds for refusing a licence are set out in legislation. These include the suitability of premises; potential consequences for public order, nuisance and safety; and whether the granting of a licence would lead to over-provision. As in England and Wales, the licensing boards have a great deal of autonomy, although Scottish ministers have sought to intervene to influence licensing board decisions. In 1988, following controversy over the routine granting of extensions to pubs and clubs, the Scottish Office issued guidance which made it clear that regular extensions should be the exception and when granted should be based on good reasons.

Given the scale of alcohol related problems, most licensing authorities have developed policies to guide their decision making (Light and O'Brien, 1995), as recommended by the Faculty of Public Health Medicine and the Royal College of Physicians (1991). However, in England and Wales, particularly, there are problems with this approach. As quasi-judicial bodies, the licensing committees must examine each case separately and base their decisions on reason and justice (Justices' Clerks Society, 1983). If the adoption of a policy is seen by appeal bodies as prejudicial to an individual case, licensing committee decisions can be overturned. Another problem is that policies have developed in the absence of national standard guidelines and lack uniformity of content and expression (Light and O'Brien, 1995).

Three main ideas to improve the licensing process with regard to the prevention of alcohol related problems have been advanced. The first of these is clarification of the grounds on which a licence can be refused, as is already the case in Scotland. The Home Office is currently consulting on this issue (Home Office, 1993). In addition, new grounds might be added to those already in force north of the border, such as the protection of public health or of school children. The second is to improve the quality of information – relating to crime, public disorder, health and safety – at the disposal of licensing authorities when making licensing decisions. The third is to encourage greater collaboration on licensing issues between the various agencies at local level, such as the police, magistrates, health and local authorities, schools, youth organisations, and so on. In this context, Tether and Robinson's (1986) proposal for a licensing forum comprising representatives from local agencies deserves to be taken up more widely than it has been so far.

The issue of collaboration is also relevant to enforcement and will be discussed further below. Before this, mention must be made of the recent trend among local authorities to introduce their own local legislation with regard to alcohol. Coventry was the first city to introduce a by-law ban on alcohol consumption in certain public areas. Around 40 cities in Britain currently have similar laws and more are expected to follow suit. The general impression is that these schemes have been successful in reducing the fear of crime and disorder related to alcohol (Ramsay, 1989). However, there are a number of problems associated with them. Much depends, yet again, on enforcement of the law and, even if successful, such measures may simply push the problems of crime and disorder to other unregulated areas. As yet there is no systematic evidence regarding their effectiveness. Nevertheless, local authorities and the police seem satisfied with the experience so far, as reflected in the rapid take-up rate. In addition, some local authorities (including Torbay, Rotherham and Maidstone) are exploring the possibilities of new by-laws to shape the drinking environment further, including bans on drinking from the bottle in pubs and nightclubs.

Enforcement of the Law

In their present form the licensing laws represent a formidable collection of regulations governing the sale and serving of alcohol (Davies and Walsh, 1983). As has been shown, however, many important measures are either unenforced or under-enforced, so that the legal provisions fall into disrepute. Principal examples are the under-age drinking laws and the law relating to the serving of drunks, while there have been allegations that, particularly in rural areas, permitted hours are exceeded, although the evidence for this is wholly anecdotal.

The presence of the police is associated with stricter enforcement of the law. In an experiment in Torquay in the late 1970s , high-profile policing of licensed premises, with particular regard to enforcing the laws relating to under-age drinking and drunkenness, was associated with a decrease in the number of arrests and rates of crime (Jeffs and Saunders, 1983). Rigid enforcement of the law relating to drunks and under-age customers by bar staff may be counter-productive, although the data are difficult to interpret – largely because a police presence, whether undercover or overt, may itself influence the reporting of incidents and offences (Stockwell, 1997).

In some localities, the police – sometimes in conjunction with other organisations – have experimented with a variety of techniques in an attempt to improve law enforcement. High-profile operations to counter under-age drinking have been mounted, as in Perth in 1996 (*Glasgow Herald*, 20 September 1996). Some forces, such as North Tyneside (*The Journal*, 30 October 1996), York, Kent and Merseyside, have used undercover operations to gather evidence on retailers suspected of breaking the law. In some cases teenagers have been used as informants or have made 'test purchases' to trap law breakers. Another approach adopted by some forces, such as the Southend police, is to inform the parents and teachers of teenagers who have been found drunk in a public place (*Southend Evening Echo*, 16 July 1996).

Effective implementation requires more than police enforcement: other interested agencies and individuals – publicans and magistrates, for example – need to be involved (All Party Group on Alcohol Misuse, 1995). The community has a vital role to play in tackling alcohol misuse, including problems associated with availability (Ritson, 1996). There are many examples of local collaboration to improve enforcement of existing legislation, of which the following is only a small selection.

In Ipswich a multi-agency group including publicans, shopkeepers, parents, teachers and youth workers has been established to combat under-age drinking (*East Anglian Daily Times*, 27 September 1996). Similar groups have been established in a number of other towns and cities, including Milford Haven (*Western Mail*, 9 September 1996), York (*Yorkshire Evening Press*, 18 July 1996), Leamington Spa and Chichester.

Some local collaborative schemes involve the alcohol industry and the licensed trade, who have a key responsibility to help enforce the law. There are situations where self-regulation has advantages over direct regulation: it can often promote a flexible response to problems and involve lower political costs (Baggott, 1986). However, self-regulatory initiatives tend to work best when reinforcing legislative provisions rather than simply standing alone. It is also unfortunate that these collaborative ventures have not been effectively evaluated.

The drinks industry has a role to play in developing such initiatives, though this is restricted when, as in the case of 'designer drinks', short-term commercial interests and wider social responsibilities appear to be in conflict. The industry, via the Portman Group, has established a number of programmes to examine particular aspects of alcohol misuse, some of which have been relevant to licensing law enforcement. In 1996 a task force on under-age drinking was established to examine this particular issue in depth, including the question of law enforcement. Earlier, in 1993, the Group published a guide to the prevention of alcohol related disorder which set out a range of practices and procedures that could be adopted at local level, including multi-agency coordination, industry initiatives, the law on exclusion, prevention of disorder in town centres, and the design of licensed premises and training (Portman Group, 1993).

The Portman Group has also promoted some schemes in which it has an interest at local level. For example, it has supported improved training schemes for licensees, servers and door staff and promoted its own efforts to tackle under-age drinking. The Proof of Age Scheme, whereby people aged 18 or over can obtain identity cards stating their age, was launched in 1990 and by 1996 had issued over 200,000 cards. This still represents a small proportion of the target age group and does not apply directly to those who are drinking illegally. However, if such a scheme could be taken up to a greater extent, it could assist law enforcement: if most 18- and 19-year-olds carried identification, it would be more difficult for licensees accused of serving under-age drinkers to argue that they had exercised due diligence to avoid committing an offence.

Collaborative arrangements at local level, coupled with active involvement by the licensed trade, has led to effective local action in some areas (All Party Group on Alcohol Misuse, 1995). However, the development of local action has been uneven. One of the main problems is the absence of central coordination and direction. As the All Party Group on Alcohol Misuse observed, there are still too few examples of full-blooded joint working, and local action must be supported by co-ordinated action at central government level (1995, p. 11). There is also considerable scope for reforming the licensing laws, so as to restate their purpose and ensure that local implementation and enforcement authorities are operating within in a clear legislative framework.

Summary of Main Arguments

- Current legislation has been enacted in a piecemeal way and without clear intent. There is scope for reviewing different sections of legislation to form more cohesive and effective laws.
- Legislation is an effective way to control the availability of alcohol. The distribution of outlets and their opening times will have an impact on both public order and consumption. Variations will be most effective as part of a local alcohol plan.
- Increasing the age limit for drinking in public places has been associated with reductions in alcohol related problems.
- Enforcement of legislation, coupled with measures to encourage the public and those selling drink to comply with the law, has been shown to reduce alcohol related incidents. High-profile enforcement also increases public awareness.

8
Mass Media

Belief in the power of the mass media to influence drinking practices has a long history. One of the biggest sponsors of the magic lantern, arguably the first genuine mass media, was the Temperance movement, which produced a great many lantern slides in the late nineteenth and early twentieth centuries. Characteristic images from the early magic lantern shows, like a reformed father watching his offspring sign the pledge, were carried over into the early cinema. As Denzin (1991) found, between 1908 and 1989 over 600 Hollywood films were produced that had an explicit concern with problem drinking. They included some of the most popular and financially successful films of their day: *Lost Weekend, I'll Cry Tomorrow, The Morning After* (Denzin, 1991). Recent studies of Hollywood have drawn attention to the role of film and television studios as cultural institutions, actively engaged in making sense of the social world. The cinema, in particular, played a major role in legitimising the disease concept of alcoholism, and, together with tabloid newspapers, has helped to shape the popular understanding of alcohol and drug problems (Room, 1989; Denzin, 1991; Basic, 1992; Lagerspetz, 1994).

The way in which drinking is portrayed in different cultures, and at different times, and through different media, has far-reaching implications for public health. Cultural representations of drinking mirror society, in a way that shapes and reinforces the public discourse on alcohol related problems. This helps determine whether alcohol related problems are seen as private troubles or as public issues requiring government action. If action is believed to be necessary, the representation of the problem in the mass media helps to shape the policy agenda.

These issues will be explored in greater detail in this chapter, which will then consider the use of the mass media as a means of disseminating public health information, examining the evidence for its effectiveness in doing so. The provision of information and education about alcohol use to school students, although not strictly speaking a mass media exercise, is the final point for discussion. Thus the chapter will cover the following:

- media presentation of alcohol
- alcohol advertising and vulnerable groups
- alcohol advertising and aggregate demand
- the use of the mass media for health education purposes
- school-based alcohol education programmes.

Media Presentation of Alcohol

For many years, public health campaigners have been concerned about the way in which alcohol is portrayed in the mass media, particularly on television. Many feel that drinking is shown too frequently and that the negative consequences of drinking are rarely depicted. In 1977, the Advisory Committee on Alcoholism (DHSS and Welsh Office, 1977, p. 7) called for a 'more balanced representation' of the effects of drinking, particularly in television programmes, and this recommendation was supported by the Labour government in the 1977 White Paper *Prevention and Health* (DHSS, 1977). The government announced in the White Paper that it had taken steps to bring the Advisory Committee's views to the attention of the BBC and ITA (Independent Television Authority; now IBA – Independent Broadcasting Authority), the broadcasting authorities which had responsibility for programme content (DHSS, 1977, p. 46). A Conservative government returned to this issue four years later, in the discussion document *Drinking Sensibly*, and stressed that care taken by broadcasting authorities, programme makers, producers and writers over the presentation of alcohol was an 'important component in any preventive strategy' (DHSS, 1981, pp. 65–6). Similar concerns continued to be voiced throughout the 1980s (see, for example, Royal College of Psychiatrists, 1986; Standing Conference on Crime Prevention, 1987; Ministerial Group on Alcohol Misuse, 1989).

Despite these concerns, drinking continued to be shown frequently in drama and light entertainment, usually in positive or at least non-problematic contexts. In a systematic content analysis of all evening programmes broadcast on British television over a two-week period, Hansen (1986) showed that visual and verbal references to alcohol occurred in approximately two-thirds of all prime-time programmes. There were more frequent references in fictional than non-fictional programmes, with over 70% of fictional characters being seen to consume alcohol. Drinking was rarely associated with harmful effects. While 12% of characters were seen drinking at work, for example, there was no reference to alcohol related work accidents, or impaired efficiency or productivity (Hansen, 1985, p. 23).

Since then, at least one popular soap opera has included alcohol related problems such as dependence and drink driving in the storyline, but the overall representation of drinking on television remains positive. Pendleton *et al.* (1991) produced similar findings to Hansen in a systematic sample of 50 programmes broadcast on British television in 1988, which they compared to a baseline study they had conducted in 1986 (Smith *et al.*, 1988). The frequency of references to drinking fell marginally over the two-year period 1986–88, but remained relatively high. Nearly three-quarters of the programmes sampled in 1988 contained references to alcohol and, on average, drinking was seen or mentioned every six and a half minutes. Based on the costs of advertising on prime-time television, the authors calculated that the presentation of drinking was worth approximately £487 million in free promotion to the alcohol industry each year, at 1988 prices.

However, some have questioned whether the overwhelmingly positive portrayal of drinking on British television has any impact on behaviour. Waxer (1992) compared the depiction of drinking in comedy, soap opera and drama productions on British, American and Canadian television. British television had three times the amount of alcohol consumption seen on either American or Canadian television. In spite of the more frequent portrayal of alcohol consumption in the UK, Waxer argues, all indicators of alcohol related harm are lower than in Canada or the US. Cross-national comparisons of this kind are difficult, however, because of marked variations between countries in drinking patterns and the scale of alcohol related problems, differences in the production and interpretation of official statistics, and in the policy context. Moreover, Waxer may have misconstrued the direction of causality; the self-regulation of television programme content could be stricter in Canada and the US precisely because of their higher levels of alcohol related problems.

Wober (1986) conducted a survey in London for the IBA, using a questionnaire and diary to investigate an audience's perception of the veracity of the presentation of drinking on television. He also investigated whether the viewers' exposure to the depiction of drinking on television was linked to attitudes about alcohol policies, or about the costs and benefits of alcohol consumption. Wober studied 350 respondents in a representative sample of adults from the London region. Respondents believed that fictional programmes under-represented both the positive and the negative consequences of drinking, compared to the frequency with which such effects occurred in real life. Attitudes to alcohol control policies, and assessments of the costs and benefits of alcohol consumption, were correlated to drinking behaviour but not television viewing; that is, those who were heavier drinkers stressed the positive consequences of drinking, and did not favour policies designed to restrict consumption, such as high taxation.

There appeared to be a negative relationship between the number of fictional programmes viewed on television and drinking behaviour in Wober's survey; if anything, drinking was related to watching sports and news broadcasting. There was no evidence that those who viewed television extensively, and were thus exposed to frequent positive portrayals of alcohol consumption, were more likely to drink or to have positive attitudes towards alcohol. This is in line with the findings of surveys in the US, where Signorielli (1987) found that adults who watched more television were *less* likely to report current alcohol consumption.

Laboratory-based studies of the impact of the portrayal of drinking on television have generally employed a design in which exposure to television programmes with alcohol advertisements is manipulated experimentally, while alcohol consumption is measured covertly (McCarty and Ewing, 1983; Kohn *et al.*, 1984; Sobell *et al.*, 1986; Kohn and Smart, 1987). These studies are mostly North American, have used adult subjects, and usually find no effect for advertising. For example, Sobell *et al.* (1986) conducted an experimental study in Canada to assess the influence of television on the drinking behaviour of 96 male college students. Students were assigned at random into groups which viewed video sequences of a popular television programme, which either did or did not depict drinking, and were shown with or without alcohol advertisements. Subjects were subsequently invited to perform a taste rating of different beers, which provided a covert measure of their alcohol consumption. There was no evidence that viewing alcohol advertisements or drinking scenes in television programmes was associated with increased alcohol consumption by the students.

The artificial nature of laboratory tasting trials, which are unlike social drinking occasions, means that it may not be possible to generalise from such experiments to real-life situations. Also, the experiments only measure the immediate and short-term effects of advertising, such as whether it functions as a cue for drinking, whereas many believe that the impact of the media portrayal of drinking is cumulative, and affects social norms or cognitive variables, which in turn affect behaviour. However, the existing evidence does suggest that while drinking is depicted frequently on television, this does not appear to have any direct and immediate effect on the established drinking behaviours of adults of drinking age.

It is possible that media effects take place over a longer time-span, however, influencing not the current adult drinking population but the attitudes and behaviours of children and young people. For many young people, the largely positive representation of drinking on television is their main source of information about alcohol. In a study which included 795 New Zealand children aged eleven, television was nominated as the *principal* source of knowledge about alcohol by 47% of children (Flett *et al.*, 1987).

The volume of references to drinking on television means that children are likely to witness several fictional representations of drinking each day. Moreover, alcohol advertising increases significantly during sports programmes and over holiday periods, like Christmas and New Year, when children are more likely to be watching (Barton and Godfrey, 1988). Young people are also more likely to watch popular music programmes, and a high proportion of the videos shown on such programmes depict band members consuming alcohol, usually in glamorous surroundings (Durant *et al.*, 1997).

No British study has looked at whether the portrayal of alcohol on television has a direct effect on young people's alcohol related attitudes or behaviour, as opposed to those of adults, and the few studies that have been undertaken have all been in the US. Tucker (1985), in a survey of 394 high school boys, found that those who watched most television reported the heaviest alcohol consumption, in contrast to Signorielli's (1987) findings for adults, while Neuendorf (1985) found that television viewing among American children was related to positive attitudes towards alcohol. Neither study provided an adequate account of the methodology, however, and neither study was able to establish the direction of causality: it is just possible that alcohol related attitudes and behaviours affect television viewing, rather than the other way around.

There have been two experimental studies in the US which did attempt to address the question of causality by establishing the temporal sequence of events (Rychtarik *et al.*, 1983; Kotch *et al.*, 1986). In both studies, children were shown video recordings of scenes involving drinking, taken from popular television programmes. In Kotch *et al.*'s (1986) study, children were randomly assigned either to an experimental group, which was exposed to alcohol portrayals, or to a control group, which was shown video sequences that did not feature drinking. The children subsequently completed a questionnaire on their attitudes and beliefs about alcohol. There were no differences for girls; the only significant difference for boys was that those in the experimental group were more likely to believe that the benefits of alcohol consumption outweighed the costs. Rychtarik *et al.*'s (1983) experiment was similar, except that it included a no-television control group, and children were tested on a task which required them to choose glasses of either whisky or water to serve fictional adults and children. Children who were exposed to television drinking were significantly more likely to choose alcoholic beverages for fictional adults, but not for children. Both of these experimental studies provide limited support, therefore, for the hypothesis that the mass media influence children's behaviour, but once again their findings have to be considered in the context of the laboratory setting, which may not generalise to real-life television viewing.

While British research has focused on children and adolescents as a group that might be particularly vulnerable to positive media messages about alcohol,

North American researchers have also considered the impact on adults who have already developed problems with their drinking. Sobell *et al.* (1993) examined the self-reported ability of 96 people with alcohol related problems to resist the urge to drink heavily after seeing a videotape of a popular television programme either with or without alcohol scenes, and with or without advertisements for beer, non-alcoholic beverages, or food. Television programmes containing alcohol cues significantly affected the perceived ability of those with severe alcohol dependence to resist the urge to drink heavily, compared to subjects who watched the same programme with the alcohol cues edited out.

Alcohol Advertising and Vulnerable Groups

While there have been relatively few studies of media presentation, there are rather more which look specifically at the influence of advertising on vulnerable groups within the population. Such studies have used survey or experimental designs, and have sought to establish whether these groups are particularly exposed to, or aware of, alcohol advertisements; whether advertisements promote alcohol use among susceptible groups; and whether they encourage adolescents to commence drinking. Many researchers have operated with a theoretical explanation of mass media influence based on social learning theory (Bandura, 1977), proposing that the frequent depiction of drinking can model behaviour; others emphasise the effect on young people's beliefs and expectations about alcohol (Brown *et al.*, 1980). Alcohol related expectancies are believed to develop in childhood, before there is any significant experience of drinking, and are known to predict future drinking behaviour among young people (Christiansen *et al.*, 1989; Miller *et al.*, 1990; Carey, 1995; Killen *et al.*, 1996). Alcohol advertising could predispose young people to drinking, or lead to earlier experimentation, it is argued, because it produces positive expectancies of drinking (Grube, 1993; Grube and Wallack, 1994).

One American study has found that advertising has no discernible effect on expectancies, however. Lipsitz *et al.* (1993) asked 166 school children to watch 40 television advertisements that included either 5 beer commercials, 5 soft-drink commercials, or 5 beer commercials plus 2 anti-drinking messages. Exposure to different advertisements produced no differences in drinking expectancies, as judged by the Alcohol Expectancy Questionnaire – Adolescent Form.

Such experiments may be operating with a relatively crude model of the way in which children develop alcohol expectancies. On the basis of a cross-sectional survey of 154 pre-adolescents, Austin and Meili (1994), argued that children develop expectancies through an active interpretation process that makes use of both real-life and broadcast sources of information. Further studies by Austin and Nach (1995), Austin and Johnson (1997) and by Slater *et al.*

(1996) suggest that such insights could be utilised to develop training for young people in resisting alcohol advertising messages.

Several UK studies have demonstrated that children and young people are aware of alcohol advertisements, despite the claims of the alcohol industry that their marketing is aimed at older age groups. Alcohol advertisements tend to feature qualities like humour and sociability, which appeal to children and young people (Aitken *et al.*, 1988). Therefore, even when these advertising campaigns are targeted at young adults, they are likely to attract the attention of younger teenagers. Aitken *et al.* (1988) asked 160 Scottish children aged 10–14 to discuss advertisements which they liked or disliked. Awareness of advertisements for alcoholic drinks increased with age, as did the popularity of the advertisements. From the age of 10, children were aware that lager and beer commercials were targeted at men, and they believed that advertising for aperitifs was aimed at sophisticated women. Older children (14–16) tended to see beer commercials as promoting masculinity, sociability and working-class values, while advertisements for vermouth and liqueurs were linked to sociability, style, sophistication and sexual attractiveness.

This is important, as children of this age are often extremely concerned about their social image. In one American study, 156 boys and girls aged 8–16 were asked to rate the appeal of social image-oriented advertisements for alcohol, tobacco, clothing and personal care products (Covell, 1992). There was a marked age effect: a stronger preference for image-oriented alcohol and tobacco advertisements was shown among 14–16-year-olds than 8–10-year-olds.

Considerable care goes into the design of alcohol and tobacco advertising, in an attempt to associate positive social images with alcohol or tobacco products. Schooler *et al.* (1996), analysing 901 advertising posters in California, found that alcohol and cigarette advertisements were more likely to make use of attractive models, to use models of the same race as the target audience, and to use social modelling cues, such as anticipated rewards. This manipulation of positive social images to make drinking seem socially desirable is likely to have a particular impact on younger adolescents, who often seek adult status. There is a risk, therefore, that such advertising promotes alcohol use, reinforces under-age drinking, recruits young people as new drinkers, or leads them to experiment earlier than they might do otherwise.

There is some evidence to support each of these propositions. First, in the US, Atkin and Block (1981) published the results of a major multi-method research programme on the effects of alcohol advertising, based on a large quota sample of 1227 adolescents. Sub-studies showed that exposure to alcohol advertising was correlated with increased alcohol use, with those exposed most being more likely to drink, to drink heavily and to take risks such as drinking while driving (Atkin *et al.*, 1983; Atkin *et al.*,1984). These correlations remained strong after controlling for demographic, media, communication and consumption variables. Like most researchers adopting a survey design, Atkin *et al.* utilised a self-report methodology, which some have criticised on the grounds of unreliability (for example, Strickland, 1984). However, although the reliability of self-report measures can be lower among younger people, whose drinking habits are more subject to change, both younger and older adolescents have been shown to give generally reliable and valid responses in self-report surveys (Harris *et al.*, 1994; Williams *et al.*, 1995).

In contrast, another large survey of 1650 adolescents, by Strickland (1983), found a significant but very small relationship between exposure and consumption, once demographic, peer group and parental variables were controlled for. Strickland excluded non-drinkers, however, which could lead to an underestimation of the effect if advertising encourages experimentation among youth. Also, awareness of advertising was measured indirectly, by counting the frequency of reading magazines or viewing programmes known to contain advertisements. Exposure to advertising does not necessarily mean that consumers are paying attention to the advertising messages.

Second, it is possible that alcohol advertising reinforces existing behaviour, like under-age drinking. Aitken *et al.* (1988) conducted individual interviews with 433 children aged 10–17 in Glasgow, to examine whether there were any differences between non-drinkers and under-age drinkers in their response to alcohol advertising. The under-age drinkers were more able to recognise and identify the brand imagery in photographs of different alcohol advertisements, and were more appreciative of advertisements. Since the under-age drinkers gained pleasure from alcohol advertisements, the authors argued that it could be reinforcing their drinking behaviour. However, Aitken *et al.*'s study does not establish that this is the case; it simply points to the potential of advertisements to act as positive reinforcement.

Third, alcohol advertising which appeals to children and young adolescents may make them more likely to experiment with drinking in later adolescence. In the US, Unger *et al.* (1995) investigated the relationships between adolescents' apparent susceptibility to substance use and their recognition and enjoyment of alcohol and tobacco advertising. They removed any identifying information from 40 alcohol, tobacco and other product advertisements, and asked 386 Californian adolescents to identify each brand name and type of product, and rate how much they liked the advertisements. Respondents were divided into three groups, depending on their substance use: non-susceptible non-users (those who had never used alcohol or tobacco and did not intend to do so); susceptible non-users (who had not used but who had not made a firm commitment not to experiment in the future); and users (those who had tried drinking or smoking). Level of alcohol use was a significant predictor of the popularity of alcohol advertisements: drinkers liked the advertisements most; 'non-susceptible' non-drinkers liked them the least. Three of the six brands were most popular with those who were susceptible to experimentation; only one of them significantly so: a much stronger effect was found for cigarette advertisements, which were as popular with susceptible non-smokers as with smokers.

As this was a cross-sectional study, it is not possible to make any inferences about causality, but the appeal of advertising to those who are susceptible to drinking lends support to the proposition that alcohol advertisements may help recruit new adolescent drinkers, particularly as there is evidence of a relationship between awareness of advertising and behavioural intentions. Grube and Wallack (1994) examined the relationships between television beer advertising and knowledge, beliefs and intentions towards drinking in a random sample of 468 Californian school children. Rather than estimate exposure to advertising, Grube and Wallack studied awareness of advertising, by asking children to identify commercials from which all identifying information had been removed. Awareness of television beer advertising was related to more favourable beliefs about drinking, to greater knowledge of beer brands and slogans, and to increased intentions to drink as an adult. Thus many of the children exposed to alcohol advertising were aware of the products being advertised, and many of those who were aware had formed an intention to try the advertised brands at some point in the future.

Further evidence comes from two longitudinal studies (Connolly *et al.*, 1994; Pierce *et al.*, 1998). The first, conducted in New Zealand by Connolly *et al.* (1994), investigated the associations between alcohol consumption at the age of 18 and the recall at 13 and 15 years of media messages about drinking. Among young women, the frequency and quantity of wine and spirit consumption were positively associated with the time spent viewing television at ages 13 and 15, in contrast to the findings of Signorielli (1987) that adults who watch more television are less likely to report current alcohol consumption. Women were less likely to recall beer advertising than men, and those who recalled the portrayal of beer in entertainment programmes were less likely to drink beer at the age of 18, which may be related to the gender stereotypes noted by children in Aitken *et al.*'s (1988) study. Among young men, recalling more alcohol advertisements at age 15 predicted drinking larger quantities of beer at age 18.

The second longitudinal study was conducted by Pierce *et al.* (1998) in the US. This was also a prospective cohort study with a three-year follow-up. It was designed to examine the influence of tobacco rather than alcohol advertising, but is included here because of its relevance to the discussion over whether advertising can influence the initiation of substance use. In 1993 Pierce *et al.* interviewed a random sample of 1752 Californian adolescents who had never smoked and would not consider experimenting. Respondents were reinterviewed in 1996. Having a favourite cigarette advertisement in 1993 predicted which adolescents would become susceptible to smoking, or would actually experiment with cigarettes, by an odds ratio of 1.82; willingness to use a tobacco company promotional item in 1993 was even more strongly associated with future progression along the 'smoking uptake continuum' (odds ratio = 2.89). Receptivity to cigarette advertising and promotions is associated, therefore, with progression from non-susceptibility to susceptibility, and from susceptibility to experimentation.

It is always going to be difficult to establish a causal link between advertising exposure and alcohol consumption among population subgroups. Experimental designs can be criticised for their lack of generalisability, while cross-sectional surveys can only establish correlation, not causation. The studies cited above do not necessarily mean that awareness of advertising led to increased drinking: it is possible that those who were more likely to drink in adulthood showed more interest in alcohol advertising during early adolescence. The convergence of both cross-sectional and longitudinal studies, however, does suggest that there is a link. Also, most adolescents are exposed to advertising before they begin to drink, so advertising is more likely to be the antecedent variable and therefore the causal agent. Nor can the correlation between advertising exposure and increased behavioural intentions among those who do not yet drink be explained readily by reverse causality.

To summarise, drinking is depicted frequently in the mass media, particularly on television soap operas and drama productions. Although some programme makers in recent years have made efforts to show the costs as well as the benefits of alcohol consumption, drinking is usually shown in a positive context. Research findings suggest that exposure to media portrayals of drinking, and to alcohol advertising in particular, has little effect on adults but may have an effect on children and young people. Few studies have employed a robust methodology, however, and there is a need for more sophisticated survey and experimental studies that take into account a wider range of variables. There is some evidence that the presentation of alcohol in the mass media may encourage young people to begin drinking, by producing positive expectancies of alcohol consumption. There is also evidence from the US that the frequency of alcohol cues in television programmes creates difficulties for those who are already vulnerable to drinking problems.

We now move on to consider whether advertising can increase the aggregate market for alcoholic drinks. If advertising increases total demand, and increases in volume consumption lead to increases in alcohol related harm, there could be a strong case for restrictions on advertising in order to prevent the growth of the alcohol market.

Alcohol Advertising and Aggregate Demand

There has been considerable controversy over whether alcohol advertising stimulates the total demand for alcohol, rather than simply defending the market share of particular brands of alcoholic drink. Research into aggregate demand is best carried out using econometric techniques, which measure how far one economic variable responds to changes in another. The investigation of the relationship between advertising and the aggregate demand for alcohol is complex, however; there are many factors, including price and available income, and the availability of alcohol, that are known to influence alcohol consumption, and these have to be discounted before the advertising effect can be estimated. Also, there may be a correlation between advertising and consumption, if firms set budgets in relation to sales figures, so spurious results are possible unless the possibility of feedback is allowed for.

Econometric studies of the influence of advertising depend on the use of demand modelling (Godfrey, 1990). A common approach is to use a single equation model, which considers the demand for alcohol in isolation, with perhaps an element in the equation to represent demand for other goods. An alternative approach involves demand system modelling. Demand system modelling is used by economists to predict the demand for a group of products analysed as a system, rather than as isolated goods. This is because changes in the demand for one product may affect the demand for others, given that consumers have to prioritise expenditure.

Both approaches have their drawbacks. While single equation models need careful testing because of their lack of theoretical underpinning, the demand systems approach suffers from a lack of agreement over the specification of the demand equations (for example, Johnson, 1985; Selvanathan, 1989). Because of limitations with the available data it is not always possible to test whether demand models are adequate, and inadequate modelling may lead to misleading estimates of the effects of policy changes (Godfrey, 1989). For example, it is not clear whether some demand models are able to deal adequately with goods that have addictive potential, such as alcohol and tobacco.

Given the complexity of demand modelling, and of the alcohol market, it is perhaps not surprising that numerous methodological difficulties have been encountered (Godfrey, 1986, 1989, 1990; Harrison and Godfrey, 1989). First, the data on advertising are not of good quality and are incomplete. The data are derived from private surveys and cover some media, typically television and the press, and not others. They usually exclude the new electronic media, such as cable television or the World Wide Web, and ignore sponsorship, point of sale displays and other forms of promotion, which may be highly effective forms of advertising. Second, there has been some debate over whether to use the volume of advertising messages or advertising expenditure as variables

(McGuinness, 1980; Franke and Wilcox, 1987). Further differences arise over whether advertising should be measured at a national or a local level (Saffer, 1996). There has also been some debate over whether the effects of advertising are cumulative, and therefore need to be studied over a lengthy time-period, although here the empirical evidence appears to show that the effects of alcohol advertising are relatively short-lived (Duffy, 1982; Selvanathan, 1989).

There have been number of UK studies which have included advertising variables (McGuinness, 1980, 1983; Duffy, 1983, 1989; Johnson, 1985; Godfrey, 1988; Selvanathan, 1989; Calfee and Scheraga, 1994), all of which looked at national level data. Calfee and Scheraga considered not only the UK but also France, Germany, the Netherlands and Sweden. Despite differences in methodology, time-periods and data sets, they all estimated the influence of advertising to be negligible, or at best very small, and certainly of much less importance than price as a determinant of total alcohol consumption.

However, studies like these, which use national data, are examining a relatively high level of annual alcohol advertising expenditure that varies little from year to year. Advertising appears to be effective at increasing sales from a low base, but if the economic theory of diminishing marginal product is correct, further expenditure on advertising will not continue to enhance sales at the same rate (Saffer, 1996). The theory of diminishing marginal product predicts that the response of consumers will begin to diminish as the volume of advertising increases; the continued addition of advertising messages will eventually result in smaller and smaller increments of sales. Empirical studies show that the theory of diminishing marginal product holds true for advertising brands of beer (Rao and Miller, 1975), and the likelihood is that it applies to the aggregate demand for alcohol. Therefore, one reason why econometric studies of national advertising data might fail to find a major effect on consumption is because at high and relatively stable levels of advertising expenditure they are observing a marginal effect that is quite small.

Saffer (1996) argues that advertising must be observed over a wider range in order to estimate its effects accurately. Studies that use local level data typically find a wider variation in the level of advertising than national studies, as advertisers often alternate between high and very low levels of expenditure in localities. There have been no UK studies of local advertising, and only a couple in the US (Goel and Morey, 1995; Saffer, 1997). Unlike national studies, however, these local studies found that alcohol advertising significantly increased alcohol consumption.

Another way to observe advertising over a wider range might be to compare countries or localities where alcohol advertising is banned with those where it is permitted. There are a number of difficulties in practice, as prohibitions are difficult both to implement and evaluate in an era of deregulation and technological innovation (Harrison and Godfrey, 1989). Governments find it hard to eliminate advertising from channels broadcast outside of their jurisdiction, such as satellite channels, and this form of advertising would increase in volume if terrestrial advertising was prohibited. Also, any attempt to introduce a ban would probably be countered by a massive advertising campaign opposing restrictions, and this could act as a form of advertising for alcoholic drinks.

There have been several studies of alcohol advertising bans which have been introduced in Canadian provinces (Smart and Cutler, 1976; Ogbourne and Smart, 1980; Makowsky and Whitehead, 1991) and one comparative study of 17 Organization for Economic Co-operation and Development (OECD) countries (Saffer, 1991). None of the Canadian studies found any evidence that full or partial advertising prohibition influenced total alcohol consumption. Smart and Cutler (1976) evaluated a 14-month ban in British Columbia; Ogbourne and Smart (1980) analysed a ban on beer advertising over 8 years in Manitoba; and Makowsky and Whitehead (1991) studied the ending of a 58-year ban in Saskatchewan in 1983, examining monthly sales data for the years 1981–87. The only impact of alcohol advertising on sales was found by Makowsky and Whitehead, where beer sales increased at the expense of spirits.

Saffer's (1991) analysis of data from 17 OECD countries for the period 1970–83 did find that banning broadcast advertising had a significant effect on consumption, however. Countries which prohibited spirits advertising had about 16% lower alcohol consumption than countries that did not, and countries which banned beer and wine advertising had about 11% lower alcohol consumption than countries which banned only spirits advertising. There is a possibility of reverse causality, however, if countries with lower alcohol consumption are more likely to ban advertising.

Despite differences in methodology, all UK econometric studies have estimated the influence of advertising on total alcohol consumption to be very small, and these findings are in line with studies conducted in the US and elsewhere (Smart, 1988). However, the results from such studies cannot be used to predict the effect of a major policy change like a ban on advertising, as the demand models used can only forecast marginal changes with accuracy (McGuinness, 1983; Harrison and Godfrey, 1989; Saffer 1996). Studies of countries or localities which have introduced advertising bans might be able to address this policy question, but there are serious methodological problems and the results from existing studies have been far from conclusive.

Restricting information through partial or complete bans on advertising is only one of the options available to government. Imperfections in the information market can be met by governments sponsoring the provision of information as a public good. There are two main objectives of government intervention: to change behaviour directly, by providing the data which enables consumers to make rational choices; or to change the social climate, thereby preparing the way for other policy measures, such as price controls. The following discussion examines the use of the mass media to disseminate health information.

The Use of the Mass Media for Health Education Purposes

Relationships with the mass media and with advertising agencies have been extremely important to successive British governments. Ministers get to know advertising executives quite well, as government, individual departments of state and the main political parties have close relations with advertising agencies, because of the growing importance attributed to the presentation of policy. It is therefore not surprising that advertising has been growing in importance as a means of disseminating health information. The British government is now one of the largest advertisers in the UK, and the Department of Health is one of the largest advertisers within government, while every reorganisation of health education since the Second World War has involved a greater emphasis on the use of mass media advertising. When the Health Education Council replaced the Central Council for Health Education in 1968, its budget increased fivefold to enable it to make more use of mass advertising (Harrison, 1989, p. 196). The Council's failure to make sufficient use of advertising was given as one of the main reasons for replacing it with the Health Education Authority (HEA) in 1986.

The HEA has made the use of mass media campaigns an important component in its programmes (Hagard *et al.*, 1991). Mass media campaigns are believed to be cost-effective because of their 'reach'; that is, the percentage of the target audience receiving the message. Indeed, many credit the marked decline in smoking prevalence in the UK between the 1960s and 1980s, at a time when tobacco prices were decreasing in real terms, to the use of mass media communication, arguing that brief advice from health professionals, although effective, had a limited impact owing to the low numbers that could be reached. It is because the media are believed to be capable of influencing mass audiences effectively that Reid (1996, p. 108) maintains, in relation to current health promotion on smoking, that 'health professionals can achieve more for their patients through the media than through personal advice.'

However, there is more evidence for the effectiveness of brief advice than there is for mass media communications aimed at general populations (see Chapter 9). Evaluations of mass media education campaigns aimed at influencing the consumption of alcohol, tobacco or illicit drugs show some effects on knowledge and attitudes, but little on behaviour (Dorn and South, 1983). The message which many British alcohol education campaigns have sought to promulgate has been one of 'moderation', and this has often taken the form of advice about the number of 'units of alcohol' which constitute lower risk drinking. Unfortunately, this is a fairly complicated message, and there is evidence not only that the public find it confusing, but also that it is not readily understood by many health professionals (Kemm and Rowe, 1992). Other countries have also found it hard to get the public to attend to, or act on, moderate drinking messages. In Connolly *et al*.s' (1994) longitudinal study of New Zealand adolescents, for example, there was no association between the awareness of moderate drinking messages on television and alcohol consumption three years later.

There is evidence that media campaigns can be successful if they seek to model specific behaviours rather than change attitudes (Barber *et al*., 1989). It may also be more effective to target specific risk groups, or particular risks like drinking and driving (Murray *et al*., 1993) or drinking while pregnant (Casiro *et al*., 1994). In the US, mass media campaigns on drinking and driving seem to be most effective when they support community action rather than operate in isolation (Holder, 1994). They appear to increase public awareness of alcohol related road traffic deaths and to maximise support for prevention policies, such as lower blood alcohol levels, random breath testing or stricter enforcement of the law. Also, media campaigns can heighten the perceived risk of detection for drinking and driving, and raise awareness of the penalties incurred if convicted.

There has been controversy in the past over the use of fear arousal techniques in media campaigns on the dangers of drinking and driving sponsored by the Department of Transport. Television advertisements have depicted young girls with badly lacerated faces resulting from accidents involving drinking drivers, for example, and some believe this to be counterproductive. On the whole, the empirical evidence supports the use of fear arousal, providing that the advertisement includes a reassuring message and specific guidance on the action required to avert risk (Sutton, 1992).

Despite the large sums committed to drink driving campaigns in the UK, expenditure on education campaigns is heavily outweighed by commercial advertising for alcoholic beverages. One option, which has been used in relation to tobacco but not to alcohol advertising in the UK, is to place mandatory warning messages on all advertisements. This has been done in the US, where it is believed to be a potentially important way to communicate information about risk, which can help prevent health messages being overwhelmed by the sheer volume of messages promoting alcohol use (Smith, 1990). Highly conspicuous warnings on alcohol advertisements appear to be noticed, but less conspicuous warnings are no better than having no warnings at all (Barlow and Wogalter, 1993). While prominent messages can attract attention, however, research on the use of warnings on alcohol beverage containers suggests that they have little impact on risk perceptions (Scammon *et al*., 1991).

Although those evaluating mass media campaigns have found it difficult to demonstrate effectiveness in the short term, it is possible that the campaigns have considerable influence in the longer term, through the cumulative impact of news stories, advertising and other mass communications. Thus, the cumulative effect of drink driving publicity over the last 30 years may have been to alter risk perceptions and reduce the social acceptability of drinking and driving. Mass media communication could have an important role in offsetting the effects of advertising and promotion, and the general trend towards the liberalisation of alcohol controls. In New Zealand, for example, a community action programme which included a media campaign focused on reducing the high-risk drinking of young men succeeded, against the national trend, in maintaining support for control policies on alcohol advertising, availability and price (Casswell and Gilmore, 1989).

There is growing interest in using the mass media to gain support for changes in alcohol policy by raising public awareness, through an approach known as *media advocacy*. Media advocacy has been defined as the 'strategic use of mass media to advance public policy initiatives' (Wallack, 1994, p. 420), and as such has been associated in the past with the activities of interest groups like Action on Smoking and Health rather than with health educators. It involves encouraging the mass media to highlight the extent of alcohol related harm in news programmes and documentaries, thereby focusing public attention on specific issues in support of prevention policies (Holder and Treno, 1997). In North America and Australasia, media advocacy has been used successfully to reduce the illegal sale of alcohol or cigarettes to children (Grube, 1997; Altman *et al.*, 1989); to gain support for changes in alcohol availability on university campuses (Alcohol Advocacy Resource Center, 1992); and to mobilise communities in support of alcohol control policies (Casswell and Gilmore, 1989; Barber and Grichting 1990; Holder, 1994; Holder and Treno, 1997). Aggressive approaches like media advocacy may be more effective than mass media advertising as a way of generating support for alcohol control policies.

School-based Alcohol Education Programmes

There have been two major reviews in this field within the last five years and here we rely heavily upon both. The first was completed for the UK Alcohol Education and Research Council (Gorman, 1994); the second was funded by the UK Health Education Authority in conjunction with the NHS Centre for Reviews and Dissemination (Foxcroft *et al.*, 1995).

The evolution of alcohol education has involved three phases (Ellickson and Bell, 1990; Gorman, 1994). The first group of studies focused upon *information-based* approaches designed to provide factual information about the effects of alcohol use and misuse. Gorman (1994, p. 2) concludes that such an approach, which prevailed in the early 1960s to the early 1970s, turned out to be 'at best ineffective and at worst detrimental'.

The second phase (early 1970s to early 1980s) involved *personal development* and typically focused on stress management, decision making and clarification of values. In the third phase (from the early 1980s) the *social influence* model has predominated. This social approach covers resistance skills training as well as more comprehensive approaches which usually include other social and communication skills as well as decision making and problem solving skills.

School-based Personal Development Programmes

These approaches are based on the assumption that young people misuse drugs and alcohol as a consequence of personal problems and that such problems can be solved. The ability to make decisions by weighing up the positive and negative consequences of an action is frequently the focus of attention. Another strategy attempts to influence decision making by asking students to identify conflicts between existing personal values and the consumption of alcohol use (Hansen, 1993). This approach has been labelled *values clarification*.

Gorman (1994) has reviewed 17 programmes which focused on personal development. Fourteen were delivered directly to students and three were designed to help teachers to improve their skills in Effective Classroom Management (ECM), including the ability to foster positive attitudes and self-esteem. Gorman reaches the same conclusion as earlier reviews (for example, Botvin 1990; Hansen 1992). The personal development approach does not appear to be effective in preventing alcohol misuse among adolescents whether the programme is delivered directly to students or delivered to teachers.

School-based Social Influence Programmes

These programmes can be split into those which focus mainly on resistance skills training and those that involve a wider range of social and personal skills. It is often argued that such approaches have been shown to be effective.

Gorman (1994) identified 16 studies of Resistance Skills Training, of which only five reported positive findings. When examined in detail these five studies do not provide sufficiently strong evidence to support this approach, even though Resistance Skills Training has become fashionable with some health educators.

McAlister *et al.* (1980) demonstrated that of those in the Resistance Skills Training group, only 5.6% reported that they had been 'high' or drunk in the previous week, compared to 16.6% in the control group. However, only two schools were compared and there was no assessment prior to the intervention. It is highly likely that the schools were not equivalent prior to the implementation of the programme.

The Alcohol Misuse Prevention Study (Dielman *et al.*, 1986, 1992; Shope *et al.*, 1992) involved 5635 fifth and sixth grade Michigan students (10- and 11-year-olds) who received either the Resistance Skills Training programme or Resistance Skills Training plus booster sessions. These were compared to a randomised control group. No significant differences were identified for the fifth grade students and only a small subsample of the sixth grade students appeared to benefit. Overall, the Alcohol Misuse Prevention Study was effective only for an extremely small minority of students.

Project SMART (Hansen *et al.*, 1988) was conducted at eight junior high schools in Los Angeles and involved 2863 seventh grade students (12-year-olds). The Resistance Skills Training programme did appear to produce a modest beneficial effect, mainly on delaying the onset of drinking amongst those who were non-drinkers prior to the start of the study. Nevertheless, this effect is difficult to interpret since there was significantly less drinking in the Resistance Skills Training group than in the control group, even prior to the intervention.

A World Health Organization Collaborative Study (Perry *et al.*, 1989) involved an evaluation of both an adult-led and a peer-led Resistance Skills Training programme designed to delay onset or reduce alcohol consumption. Five sessions of Resistance Skills Training were delivered to students aged 11–18 in Australia, Chile and Norway (n = 2329). The findings were disappointing. Neither programme was at all effective for those who were already drinking and only Norway found a small effect for those who were not drinking at baseline. Moreover the effect could be described as preventing those who never drink from moving into the 'rarely drink' category. In other words, the effect is of little practical significance.

In Project ALERT (Ellickson *et al.*, 1988; Ellickson and Bell, 1990) 30 junior high schools in Oregon and California were randomly allocated to one of three conditions, namely a 'health educator-led' Resistance Skills Training programme, a 'peer-led' Resistance Skills Training programme and a no-intervention control group. A sample of 6527 seventh grade students (12-year-olds) were followed up at 3, 12 and 15 months, but only 40 per cent were reassessed at this last follow-up point. Although the authors identified 5 significant effects from 68 possible comparisons, both Gorman (1994) and Gerstein and Green (1993) conclude that the ALERT curriculum had virtually no overall effect.

The overall conclusion from these studies is that Resistance Skills Training, although a very popular approach, does not have a strong body of evidence to support widespread use. Some more comprehensive school-based programmes are based upon the fact that social pressure is only one of the many factors which influence alcohol use. Programmes which take these other psychological and social factors into account will now be considered.

Comprehensive School-based Programmes

Gorman (1994) identifies ten different types of comprehensive programmes which focus upon those skills which are required to deal with everyday life stresses and events. For example, the well known Drug Abuse Resistance Education programme (DARE) includes the following components: role modelling, assertiveness, self-esteem enhancement, media influences, decision making, alternative activities, stress management, social supports, information, and resistance training. This programme was developed by the Los Angeles Police Department in collaboration with the Los Angeles Unified School District (see, for example, Clayton *et al.*, 1991). It is taught by uniformed police officers who receive 80 hours of training and comprises 17 sessions, each lasting about 50 minutes. In spite of its popularity there is no evidence that this approach has any impact on hazardous drinking. For example, Rosenbaum *et al.* (1994) reported on a one-year follow-up of a well designed study carried out in Illinois and involving 1584 fifth and sixth grade students (10- and 11-year-olds). Participation in the DARE programme had no statistically significant effect on initiation of alcohol use, decreased use or quitting. Gorman (1994) found that only 3 out of 16 studies of such comprehensive approaches produced any positive effects, and these were small effects of little practical significance.

Policy Implications of the Social Influence Research

Based on available evidence, school-based social skills interventions cannot be supported as a major plank of a prevention policy. Although many researchers and practitioners have concluded that Resistance Skills Training is an effective approach, the overall picture is rather different. As Gorman (1994, p. 34) concludes:

> Resistance Skills Training programmes are not universally effective. The majority of studies reviewed showed that such programmes, while not detrimental, have little or no influence upon participants. In those studies reporting a positive effect, this is limited to sub-groups of the target population and generally involves very trivial levels of alcohol use.

Although more comprehensive approaches are very popular and can be justified by arguing that they focus upon proven risk factors, the evidence is certainly not strong enough to justify large-scale implementation.

Foxcroft *et al.* (1997) carried out a systematic review of school-based interventions and reached the same conclusion as those outlined above. With the exception of one study (Botvin *et al.*, 1995), there was no evidence of long-term effects. Whether interventions focused upon alcohol alone or alcohol as one of a number of drugs was not a key factor. It should be remembered, however, that the studies were carried out mainly in the US where the goal of misuse prevention is usually abstention from any substance use, including alcohol. Alcohol education approaches in the UK usually focus upon harm reduction or sensible drinking. Nevertheless, the clear policy implication is that there is not a solid body of evidence to support a school-based approach.

Foxcroft *et al.* (1997) also make an important policy recommendation if further work is carried out in this field in the UK. They point out that most of the UK research studies were not methodologically sound and could not be included in their review. They propose that a comprehensive guide to carrying out process and outcome evaluations needs to be developed and more widely available through the appropriate agencies. Furthermore, education, health service and research funds should be targeted towards only well designed evaluation studies, with long-term follow-ups and good reasons for believing that the intervention might be more successful than previous school-based approaches.

Summary of Main Arguments

- The positive portrayal of drinking in the mass media may influence the behaviour of children and vulnerable adults. The overall effect on consumption is marginal
- The self regulatory policies governing the advertising of alcohol secure some control.
- There are gaps in current understanding of the influence of mass media advertising. It may be that there is a link between the general availability of alcohol and impact of advertising: high availability results in advertising impacting on choice of beverage rather than itself encouraging drinking.
- There is scope for more effective use of mass media advertising to promote moderate drinking. Health education campaigns might usefully model specific behaviours, rather than attempt to change attitudes, and target specific risk groups or particular risks.
- Encouraging news programmes and documentaries to focus on alcohol-related problems and policy issues through media advocacy tactics may be an effective means of generating support for alcohol control policies.
- Although school-based approaches are popular, there is no strong evidence to support the widespread adoption of such interventions.

9
Generalist Treatment and Minimal Interventions

Treatment for alcohol problems in the United Kingdom can be divided roughly into two classes of activity: generalist and specialist responses to alcohol problems. This chapter will consider the first of these two classes, leaving coverage of specialist treatment to Chapter 10. The distinction is in some ways artificial since there is frequent communication and collaboration in treatment between generalist and specialist workers, and this will be noted where appropriate in both chapters.

Before proceeding, it may be necessary briefly to justify providing problem drinkers with treatment of any kind. Many problem drinkers feel they have lost control of their drinking and of their lives, and need help to recover from their difficulties with alcohol. They behave in ways that damage their health, or risk doing so, and this in itself justifies intervention. This damage may, like the consequences of many forms of self-destructive behaviour, be self-inflicted, but that should not be a barrier to compassion and help in a society that considers itself civilised. Apart from any other consideration, it will be more costly to health and social services in the long run if excessive drinking continues. Thus, in the interests of problem drinkers themselves, in the interests of cost-effective services and in the enlightened self-interest of society in general, the need for help or treatment for problem drinkers is self-evident.

This chapter discusses:

- characteristics of generalist treatment of alcohol problems
- general medical practice and primary health care
- general hospital wards
- Accident and Emergency services
- general psychiatry
- social services
- the criminal justice system.

Characteristics of Generalist Treatment of Alcohol Problems

Generalist treatment involves a range of professionals who routinely encounter problem drinkers in their day-to-day work. In medicine, these include general medical practitioners (GPs), general psychiatrists, hospital physicians, and Accident and Emergency specialists. Professions allied to medicine, mainly nurses, are also involved in this treatment response. Outside the medical profession, social workers, police, probation officers and prison officers can be involved in the attempt to change harmful drinking behaviour. Interventions for alcohol problems can also occur in the workplace. Alcohol treatment policy issues are relevant to the work of all these occupational groups and settings.

The work of generalists in the alcohol area increasingly consists of formal or informal screening for alcohol problems and subsequent minimal intervention to modify drinking behaviour. This kind of activity is usefully called *opportunistic*: advantage is taken of opportunities that arise when people present to a facility or service for reasons unconnected with a possible alcohol problem to identify hazardous or harmful drinkers and offer minimal interventions, usually aimed at reducing drinking to low-risk levels. These minimal interventions are normally restricted to individuals with only low levels of alcohol dependence or alcohol related problems, those more seriously impaired being referred on to specialist services. However, this is not always the case and some generalists feel able to offer intensive treatment to more serious cases. The nature of the relationship between generalist and specialist services, especially with regard to the concept of 'shared care', is a particular topic for treatment policy.

Opportunistic screening and minimal intervention for excessive – that is, hazardous and harmful – drinking are often justified as a means of early intervention and secondary prevention of alcohol problems. The attempt is made to help the drinker reduce consumption or abstain before seriously adverse consequences arise and before alcohol dependence and life problems have reached levels that make intensive treatment difficult. However, minimal interventions can also be seen as making an important contribution to the public health approach to reducing alcohol related harm at the population level (Heather, 1996) – for example, as contributing to the achievement of *Health of the Nation* targets for reducing proportions of men and women in the population drinking over medically recommended levels by the year 2005 (DoH, 1992). As public health measures, there is no incompatibility between the widespread implementation of minimal interventions by generalists and the adoption of fiscal, legislative and other control policies discussed in other chapters (see Chapters 6 and 7). These two strategies can be seen as mutually reinforcing and as acting synergistically in reducing and preventing alcohol related harm.

General Medical Practice and Primary Health Care

Among the various generalist professions with an interest in alcohol problems, by far the greatest amount of attention has been paid to general medical practitioners. This is for very good reasons. Over 98% of the population of the UK is registered with a GP; there are over a million GP consultations every day; two-thirds of a practice population visit their GP within a one-year period; and 90% do so within a five-year period (Fraser, 1992). Moreover, heavy drinkers visit their GP roughly twice as often as light drinkers (Anderson, 1989). GPs and other primary health care staff still enjoy a high status and credibility within the local community, there is often an opportunity for the family contact that can be an important element in helping problem drinkers, and the primary health care setting largely avoids the labelling process and consequent stigma that often arise in mental health or specialist alcohol services (Babor *et al.*, 1986). While similar opportunities may exist in other countries to some extent, the unique British system of primary health care and its role in the National Health Service represent an engine of enormous potential for the reduction of alcohol related harm.

In the UK, efforts have been made since the 1940s to increase the involvement of GPs in the treatment of alcohol problems and to provide training for them in this area (Glatt, 1997). Prevalence studies by Parr (1957) and by Moss and Beresford-Davies (1967) suggested that GPs were aware of only a fraction of the problem drinkers on their lists. In a landmark study over a one-year period, Wilkins (1974) gave questionnaires to a selected sample of 546 patients of GPs in Manchester. On the basis of responses to this questionnaire, Wilkins developed an At Risk Register to assist GPs with the detection of alcohol related problems. The Maudsley Alcohol Pilot Project (Shaw *et al.*, 1978) was also highly influential in focusing attention on the GPs' response to alcohol problems. Reflecting this attention, the Royal College of General Practitioners (1986) produced a special report on alcohol. Among many recommendations, the report urged GPs 'to review urgently their working methods so that questions about alcohol consumption and records of that consumption become a normal part of the health care process'(p. 1).

Effectiveness of Minimal Interventions in Primary Health Care

Recent attempts to involve primary health care teams in the response to alcohol problems have mainly concerned opportunistic minimal interventions. The case for increasing this involvement has been considerably strengthened by a series of randomised controlled trials that have demonstrated minimal interventions in the primary health care setting to be highly effective. Two major studies in the UK have firmly established that minimal intervention leads to reduced alcohol consumption among excessive drinkers. Wallace *et al.* (1988)

used 47 group practices throughout the UK selected from the Medical Research Council's General Practitioner Research Framework. Patients in the intervention group received an assessment interview about alcohol consumption, problems and dependence and were then given advice and information about how to cut down drinking, plus a drinking diary. Up to five repeat consultations were scheduled. Patients in the control group received assessment and the usual care. At one-year follow-up, the proportion of men with excessive alcohol consumption had fallen by 44% in the treatment group compared with 26% in the controls, with corresponding proportions among women of 48% and 29%. The mean value for the gamma glutamyl transferase enzyme (a 'marker' of recent alcohol consumption) dropped more in treated men than in controls, but there were no significant differences in women.

Evaluating a similar kind of intervention, Anderson and Scott (1992) reported that heavy drinking men who had received advice from their GP had reduced their drinking in excess of 65 g of pure alcohol per week at one-year follow-up, compared with controls. Among women, both intervention and control groups showed large reductions in consumption and there were no significant differences between the groups (Scott and Anderson, 1991).

The public health potential of minimal interventions in primary health care was highlighted by Wallace *et al.* (1988) when they calculated on the basis of their findings that consistent implementation of their intervention programme by GPs throughout the UK would result in a reduction from excessive to low-risk levels of the drinking of 250,000 men and 67,500 women each year. Such a policy would clearly make a major contribution to *Health of the Nation* targets for reducing excessive drinking in the population at large. It must be pointed out, however, that both British trials of brief intervention were, in terms of Flay's (1986) distinction, *efficacy* rather than *effectiveness* trials – they provided a test of minimal interventions under optimum conditions rather than real-life conditions of routine primary health care. For example, patients entering the study were identified and recruited by the research team rather than by the busy physician in the normal course of his or her practice, and this may have resulted in more motivated patients being selected for study. In a project in which minimal interventions were evaluated in naturalistic general practice settings in Australia (Richmond *et al.*, 1995), far fewer patients returned for consultation following assessment, and the beneficial effects of minimal intervention were less obvious. Accepting that the beneficial effects of minimal interventions among excessive drinkers found in primary health care settings has been demonstrated in efficacy trials, we now need to focus research on effectiveness trials concerning the real-life circumstances under which excessive drinkers are recognised and offered minimal interventions.

However, it should be stressed that subsequent international research has fully confirmed the potential of minimal interventions in primary health care to reduce alcohol related harm on a widespread scale. The most influential study was the World Health Organization's clinical trial of minimal intervention in primary health care (Babor and Grant, 1992), an international collaboration involving 10 countries and 1655 heavy drinkers recruited from a combination of various, mostly medical, settings. This clearly established that, among male excessive drinkers at least, a minimal intervention delivered at the primary care level and consisting of 5 minutes' simple advice based on 15 minutes of structured assessment is effective in reducing alcohol consumption, with concomitant improvements in health. More recently, large studies by Israel *et al.* (1996) in Canada and Fleming *et al.* (1997) in the US have added to this body of positive evidence.

There is, as ever, a need for more research on minimal interventions, particularly regarding the longer-terms effects of intervention. We also need a better understanding of which kind of excessive drinker responds best to which kind of intervention, and why.

Cost-benefits from Brief Interventions

One of the chief arguments in favour of the implementation of minimal interventions is that they can save money for the health care system in the long run. Evidence to support this proposition is beginning to accumulate.

In the Malmö study in Sweden, Kristenson *et al.* (1983) reported outcomes from minimal interventions of direct relevance to cost savings. Thus, compared to a non-intervention control group, excessive drinkers who had received a brief intervention showed an 80% reduction in sick absenteeism from work in the four years following the intervention, a 60% reduction in hospital days over five years and a 50% reduction in mortality from all causes over six years following intervention. In their American study, Fleming *et al.* (1997) found that men in the minimal intervention group reported less than half the total number of hospital days in the twelve months following intervention than men in the control group. In Canada, Israel *et al.* (1996) reported that intervention group patients showed significantly reduced physician visits in the year following counselling, compared to controls.

In a review of relevant evidence prepared in the context of the introduction of the managed care system in the US, Holder *et al.* (1995) estimated that, for every US$10,000 spent on minimal alcohol or drug abuse intervention, US$13,500 25,000 would be saved in medical spending for the managed care provider. Fremantle *et al.* (1993) calculated that the direct cost of a minimal intervention delivered to an excessive drinker in the UK was less than £20.

Implementation of Minimal Interventions

Despite the attention paid over the years to integrating alcohol interventions in primary health care, and despite the promising research findings reviewed above, studies of GPs' behaviour in relation to alcohol suggest that there has generally been a wide gap between actual and recommended good practice. Wallace and Haines (1984) showed that 80% of patients believed that their GP should be interested in their alcohol related problems, but only 20% thought that their GP was actually interested. Studies by Anderson (1984) and Clement (1986) in the UK and by Reid *et al.* (1986) and McLean (1988) in Australia have all reported low levels of activity among GPs in screening and intervention with heavy drinkers. A recent household survey in England by the Office of Population Censuses and Surveys found that, of current and former drinkers who had spoken to a medical practitioner or other health professional in the last year, only 7% (men = 12%; women = 5%) reported having discussed alcohol consumption with their GP at the practice surgery (ONS, 1996).

Two recent surveys of GPs have confirmed this picture of low-level brief intervention activity. In a nation-wide survey of GPs in England and Wales (Deehan *et al.*, 1996), data were collected by a postal questionnaire survey from a 20% random sample of GPs (n = 2377), with a response rate of 44%. Of the respondent GPs, 15% reported seeing no patients at all for excessive drinking within the last month. Of those who did report seeing patients because of consumption over recommended guidelines, the average number of patients seen in the last month was 3.8.

The other survey was conducted in the English Midlands as part of Phase III of the WHO International Collaborative Project on the Identification and Management of Alcohol-related Problems in Primary Health Care (Kaner *et al.*, 1997). This took the form of a postal questionnaire survey of a random sample of 430 GPs, with a response rate of 68%. A striking finding was that GPs appear not to make routine enquiries about alcohol, with 67% enquiring only 'some of the time'. In addition, 57% of GPs had requested 5 or less blood tests in the last year because of a concern about alcohol consumption. The fact that 65% of GPs managed only 1–6 patients for excessive drinking in the last year is also striking in view of evidence that approximately 20% of patients presenting to primary health care are likely to be at least hazardous drinkers (Anderson, 1993). Given that the average list size per GP is 1820 (Royal College of General Practitioners, 1996), it seems that each GP sees on average 364 hazardous or harmful drinkers per year, suggesting that a majority of GPs may be missing as many as 98% of the excessive drinkers presenting to primary health care.

Thus there is little evidence that GPs have increased their levels of enquiry, identification and intervention regarding excessive drinking since the start of concerted efforts to involve them in this area of work over 20 years ago. It is true, however, that GPs are more likely than they were to see alcohol work as a legitimate part of their practice and evidence for this will be presented below. There is also little doubt that changes are taking place within the medical profession with respect to preventive work in general and prevention of alcohol problems in particular, although these changes will inevitably take time to reach full potential. Meanwhile, efforts to ensure a more effective response to alcohol problems in primary health care need to be sustained.

Why are GPs Reluctant to Intervene to Promote Safer Drinking?

An early and influential piece of work that attempted to answer this question was the Maudsley Alcohol Pilot Project (MAPP) which began in 1973 (Shaw *et al.*, 1978), although this study also considered the work of other professions such as social workers and probation officers (see below). In a population study of 286 adults, MAPP found that those who were drinking excessively and problematically made three times as many contacts with generalist community services as other respondents, yet none had been helped specifically with their drinking. The MAPP investigators concluded that this inadequate response was explained by three major and related anxieties on the part of helping agents: (i) 'role legitimacy' (uncertainty as to whether it was their job to deal with alcohol problems); (ii) 'role adequacy' (lack of the information and skills necessary to recognise and respond to problem drinkers); and (iii) 'role support' (having nowhere to turn for help and advice when unsure how to respond). These three key factors will be used to structure the following discussion.

Role Legitimacy

The recent nation-wide GP survey provides an opportunity to compare the MAPP results with GPs' present-day attitudes to working with problem drinkers (Deehan *et al.*, 1996). Despite the fact that most respondents saw excessive drinkers as difficult to work with, the majority (87%) agreed that primary health care was an appropriate setting in which to detect and manage alcohol problems. Over half believed that GP advice was an effective way of reducing harmful alcohol consumption in the general population, and few saw their role as confined only to treating the medical complications of heavy drinking. Similar findings were obtained by the English Midlands survey (Kaner *et al.*, 1997). It would therefore appear that, in the 20 years since the MAPP findings were published, there has been an increase in GPs' perception of their role legitimacy in dealing with alcohol problems, no doubt due to the increased emphasis on preventive medicine and health promotion in medical training and practice.

Role Adequacy

Despite the high level of role legitimacy among GPs, only 42% of respondents in the Deehan *et al.* survey felt they were adequately trained to detect alcohol problems, and even fewer (24%) felt adequately trained in treating them. Probably as a result, less than 30% felt confident in treating alcohol problems. In the English Midlands survey (Kaner *et al.*, 1997), 34% of the sample reported receiving between 4 and 10 hours of post-graduate training, continuing medical education or clinical supervision on alcohol and alcohol related problems, while 31% had received less than 4 hours. A further 10% indicated they had received no post-graduate training at all. Importantly, 58% of GPs felt that they would be effective in helping to reduce consumption if they were given appropriate information and training.

There is also evidence that primary health care staff make less use of training opportunities on alcohol than other occupational groups. From a survey of alcohol trainers, Albery *et al.* (1997) concluded that this was not because primary health care practitioners are necessarily unmotivated to improve their knowledge and skills in this area, but because trainers' beliefs about what was required in training did not match GPs' needs. It was also concluded that training across all addictive substances was not necessarily the optimal approach.

Role Support

Viewing support from a broad perspective, there are five characteristics of a supportive environment for primary health care that could be seen as encouraging brief alcohol interventions.

(i) *Working practices that allow time for tackling a difficult topic and for uncovering hidden problems.* Both GPs (Pollack, 1989) and their patients (Thom *et al.*, 1992) believe doctors do not have time to deal with alcohol problems. Kaner *et al.* (1997) found that 'Doctors are just too busy dealing with the problems people present with' was the most frequently endorsed (72%) barrier to minimal intervention among GPs. Even the five minutes of brief advice found to be effective in research (for example, Babor and Grant, 1992) seems time-consuming when the consultation will probably have been about a set of presenting symptoms that also need attention within the same appointment. The Kaner *et al.* survey found that English GPs reported higher workloads than found in all but one of the nine countries included in the project, with the majority of English respondents reportedly seeing over 150 patients per week.

(ii) *Community-based specialist services for consultancy or referral purposes in which the GP has confidence.* The nation-wide GP survey found that only 35% of GPs thought they were adequately supported by specialist services. In the English Midlands survey, 'If support services were readily available to refer patients to' was the most frequently endorsed (85%) potential incentive to minimal intervention work, suggesting that an obstacle to intervention is the fear of uncovering more difficult cases with no readily available means of dealing with them. Thus it appears that the majority of GPs feel unsupported by specialist services, both in terms of advice and consultancy concerning their own interventions, and in terms of appropriate onward referral. It is relevant here that the English Midlands survey found that most GPs could efficiently discriminate between vignettes of a case involving low alcohol dependence, in which they might legitimately intervene, and one of higher dependence which would probably require onward referral.

Two trials have investigated whether a facilitator with a specific alcohol brief can appropriately support primary health care activity (John, 1992; Butcher, n.d.). Findings suggested that an alcohol facilitator did improve rates of recording of patients' alcohol consumption and led to increased referral rates to the local specialist alcohol agency. The training element of the alcohol facilitator's role resulted in small improvements in attitudes.

Another strategy is to give specialist alcohol service providers an additional role in supporting primary health care professionals. There are two main streams to this strategy: community alcohol teams and practice-attached counsellors. In the last decade, both community alcohol teams and alcohol advisory services have tended to combine the role of providing services for problem drinkers with that of training and supporting primary level workers to achieve early recognition of alcohol problems and minimal interventions to promote safer drinking. One of Thom and Tellez's (1986) proposals, following their qualitative study of GPs' attitudes to alcohol problems, was to bring specialist alcohol services physically into general practice. They suggested this would: (i) allow patients to receive expert help for alcohol problems in a familiar, non-stigmatising setting; (ii) enable practice staff to extend their knowledge of management techniques and stay in touch with the patient's care; (iii) enable incoming specialists to benefit from the GPs' knowledge of the patient and gain a better understanding of the work done in general practice; and (iv) promote better links between primary care and specialist workers. Over recent years, following the increase in provision of generic counselling in general practice, there have been initiatives to offer alcohol counselling, sometimes with an additional remit of providing training, consultancy and support for health promotion work. Alcohol Concern published a list of 13 alcohol counselling agencies known to be working closely with Health Authorities in England (Alcohol Concern, 1994a). Few of these services have been formally evaluated.

One such project in Birmingham found that, compared to changes in a control practice over the same period, the presence of an alcohol counsellor in three general practices significantly increased rates of identification of at-risk drinkers, of recordings in the notes of the provision of brief advice and of referrals for counselling (Mason, 1997a, 1997b). There are several other examples from around the country of local initiatives aimed at bringing specialist services and primary care closer together.

(iii) *Clear and acceptable guidelines and protocols for brief intervention work.* One strategy that has been tried is to develop a package of materials complete with instructions on how to use the screening tools and patient booklets, and to distribute this to GPs. A number of packages have now been developed for this purpose, including packages for national use from the Health Education Authority and the Scottish Health Education Group (now the Health Education Board for Scotland), as well as various local initiatives.

Having produced materials, projects have tried different means of dissemination (Mason and Williams, 1990). A further strand of the WHO International Collaborative Project on the Identification and Management of Alcohol-related Problems in Primary Health Care was a randomised, controlled comparison of three methods of disseminating a brief intervention package to GPs in the northern region of England: mail only, telemarketing, and personal contact. Findings showed that telemarketing was the most cost-effective strategy for the dissemination of minimal intervention to GPs (Kaner *et al.*, 1998). A second component of this study randomised GPs taking part in the trial to one of four levels of training and support. At a three-month follow-up, it was found that practice-based training plus support telephone calls was the most cost-effective way of encouraging the implementation of brief alcohol intervention by GPs (Kaner *et al.*, 1998).

However, it may be that the interventions most likely to be taken up by primary health care professionals are not being promoted. Richmond and Anderson (1994) reconsidered the logic that, because of time constraints, GPs are most likely to use the shortest possible intervention. In relation to smoking, it has been proposed that it is better to intervene with a large number of patients, even if only with a low – 5%, say – success rate, than to work with a small number of patients with a higher – say, 30% – success rate (Chapman, 1993). The public health benefits that could ensue from the mass implementation of very brief advice for excessive drinking have been emphasised (for example, Heather, 1998). However, promoting the briefest interventions assumes that GPs are more concerned about the time the work takes them than its effectiveness. In the smoking field in the US, low success rates and repeated failure to change patients' behaviour have been shown to be major factors affecting doctors' attitudes to intervening (Ockene, 1987) and the 'Smokescreen' Project in Australia found that some doctors wanted to be convinced of a high abstinence rate before they were prepared to use a minimal intervention (Richmond and Heather,1990). Richmond and Anderson (1994) therefore suggest that GPs may, in the long term, make more use of 'longer' minimal interventions that have a better success rate than of very minimal interventions that produce low success rates. Another possibility is that the minimal interventions work best for the small number of excessive drinkers who are ready to change drinking behaviour (that is, in Prochaska and DiClemente's (1992) Action stage) and that more complex motivational interventions are needed for those who are unsure or unwilling to change (i.e., Precontemplation and Contemplation stages). Studies of minimal interventions have not yet been conducted over a sufficiently long period to determine whether or not there are diminishing returns over time within a given practice population, and it is not known which interventions doctors are most likely to continue using over a period of several years.

(iv) *Support for sensible drinking from government policies.* Anderson (1990) described four major, controllable factors that influence how much a society drinks: price, availability as determined by licensing laws, advertising and health education (see also Edwards *et al.*, 1994). It can be argued that GPs in the UK have been exhorted to deliver the fourth of these strategies without much support from implementation of the other three. In the English Midlands survey, the statement that 'Government health policies in general do not support doctors who want to practice preventive medicine' was the third most commonly endorsed (56%) barrier to minimal alcohol intervention (Kaner *et al.*, 1997).

(v) *Changing the economic and policy context of general practice to encourage minimal interventions and alcohol health promotion work in general.* The General Medical Contract introduced in April 1990 (DoH, 1989) was an attempt formally to confirm general practice as an ideal setting for health promotion and the prevention of illness. The 1993 revised contract, in the wider context of the *Health of the Nation* public health strategy, might have been expected to generate more activity around the promotion of safer drinking. In practice, the data collection exercise that formed part of the contract, which included collecting data on patients' reported alcohol consumption, came to be given more emphasis than quality of care issues and in 1996 the contract was changed again. The new arrangements involve GPs having to apply to Health Authority Health Promotion Committees for approval of their individual practice health promotion programmes, although it is not obligatory to include alcohol work in these programmes. Informal discussions with the National Health Service Executive in one region suggest that plans currently submitted by practices for funding tend not to include alcohol work. It would seem that there are still few structural incentives for general practitioners' involvement in brief intervention and health promotion in the alcohol field.

The Role of Primary Health Care Nurses

If GPs are too busy or unwilling for other reasons to engage in alcohol work, then it is sensible to suggest that primary health care nurses might be a suitable alternative, particularly since nurses are by far the largest workforce in the health care services (Heather, 1997). Using practice nurses for health promotion work has, in some surgeries, led to 15-minute appointments being available for alcohol intervention, but there have been no evaluations to date of this type of intervention.

Unfortunately, nurse training does not necessarily prepare nurses any better than their medical colleagues for alcohol work (Hartz and Anderson, 1990;

John 1992; Cooper 1994). For example, Cooper's (1994) study of 347 registered nurses found that only 42% had received any input on alcohol problems during basic training and only 35% had received post-registration training on the subject – 29% had received no education on alcohol misuse at all. A training scheme in the West Midlands (Mason and Williams, 1990) reported improved activity and attitudes to alcohol work among community-based nurses following training.

GP Treatment of More Severe Alcohol Dependence and Problems

In research relevant to treatment of more serious alcohol problems in general practice, Drummond *et al.* (1990) consecutively assigned 40 patients with established alcohol problems either to a specialist alcohol clinic or to treatment by their GP. All problem drinkers included in the study received initial assessment and brief counselling in the specialist clinic before referral back to their own GP. At a six-month follow-up, statistically significant reductions in consumption and alcohol-related problems were found in both groups and there were no differences between the groups in this respect. Despite the small numbers of subjects in this study and the consequently low statistical power for detecting a difference between the two groups, these findings suggest that this kind of shared care model has merit. However, the average level of alcohol dependence in the sample was relatively low and the patients in question probably had only moderate degrees of dependence, although the subjects for this study had been referred to a specialist clinic for treatment. Nevertheless, conclusions might have been different if a somewhat more severely dependent sample of problem drinkers had been studied.

There is, of course, no reason why GPs who take a special interest in the treatment of alcohol problems should not be encouraged and supported in treating more serious cases. It is also the case that the model of shared care examined by Drummond *et al.* (1990) has interesting possibilities. But if most GPs are apparently too busy or lack the necessary skills for minimal intervention among those with mild problems and dependence, it would surely be unwise to locate the main thrust of treatment for alcohol problems in primary health care rather than specialist services.

General Hospital Wards

In some ways, the general hospital ward offers a setting more conducive to minimal interventions than primary health care, mainly because patients have more time available for screening and counselling. Nevertheless, familiar problems have been described in persuading medical and nursing staff to carry out screening and offer advice to patients in this setting.

Screening in the General Hospital

The prevalence of alcohol problems has already been addressed in Chapter 3. A number of studies indicate that just over a quarter of male in-patients have a current or a previous alcohol problem; the rates for women are lower and more variable.

On the basis of their results, Barrison *et al.* (1982) concluded that, with the aid of a simple questionnaire and some encouragement, junior medical staff can become quite adept at detecting abnormal drinkers in the course of their routine practice. However, in a study designed to establish whether housemen took an adequate drinking history from their patients, Barrison *et al.*, (1980) noted a failure to record alcohol consumption in 39% of cases; furthermore, in only 37% of the medical notes studied was an accurate history of consumption obtained, while in the remainder only an inaccurate descriptive estimate was recorded. In the light of these findings, the authors pointed to 'a serious defect in medical education' (p. 1040).

The difficulties of screening for alcohol problems in the general hospital were pointed out by Lloyd *et al.* (1986). In a study of 161 problem drinkers found among male medical in-patients, they found that over half had been admitted with an illness not typically related to alcohol, and a similar proportion reported levels of consumption that had previously been considered safe. Classical symptoms of dependence were uncommon but specific enquiry revealed a broad range of social problems related to alcohol. The authors concluded that recognition of this profile was necessary if problem drinkers were to be identified at an early stage and to benefit from counselling. In its report on alcohol, the Royal College of Physicians (1987) commented:

> In their daily work they (physicians) must become better able to detect alcohol-related problems, and to detect them at an earlier stage. At the moment their role is too often concerned with managing serious physical damage. Earlier detection should lead to more preventive work and more effective treatment. (p. 102)

The report also stressed the need for better education on alcohol problems for medical students and young doctors (p. 107).

With regard to the most cost-effective form of screening, Tolley and Rowland (1991) compared screening by doctors, nurses and a specialist worker among medical and orthopaedic admissions to a district hospital over a 21-month period. Results suggested a greater positive case identification rate could be achieved by employing a specialist worker, but at greater cost. There is also evidence that, on the hospital ward at least, limited time itself is not a barrier to screening. Rowland *et al.* (1988) found that even when doctors worked on several different wards with different regimes and pressures, the screening rates of individual doctors remained the same. Some doctors screened for alcohol regularly whichever ward they were on, and others had a consistently low rate of screening.

Effectiveness of Minimal Interventions in the General Hospital

Chick *et al.* (1985) allocated 156 male problem drinkers identified on wards of an Edinburgh hospital either to a single session of counselling from a nurse lasting up to one hour or to routine medical care only. At twelve-month follow-up, both groups reported a reduction in alcohol consumption and there was no significant difference between the groups in this respect. However, counselled patients showed improved outcome on a composite measure involving alcohol related problems, level of consumption and the results of blood tests or a relative's report.

In research conducted in New Zealand, Elvy *et al.* (1988) showed that the offer of referral for counselling to problem drinkers identified by screening on hospital wards led to significantly greater improvements in self-reported alcohol problems at twelve-month follow-up compared with a group not offered counselling. In Australia, Heather *et al.* (1996) reported that male heavy drinkers given brief counselling at the bedside showed a significantly greater reduction in consumption at six-month follow-up than a non-intervention control group. Moreover, in a finding relevant to matching patients to appropriate forms of minimal intervention, patients who were deemed 'not ready to change' in terms of Prochaska and DiClemente's (1992) stages of change model did better if they had received brief motivational interviewing than if they had received skills-based counselling, as would be predicted from the model.

These findings suggest that screening and counselling hazardous and harmful drinkers on hospital wards could be an important strategy for early intervention in alcohol problems and should be practised more widely in Britain. When Saunders *et al.* (1985) interviewed 156 patients with newly diagnosed liver disease, 35% claimed they had never been advised to reduce or stop drinking before their presentation with disease and only 22% had been referred to a hospital clinic for specific management of an alcohol problem. This gives an indication of the gains that might be expected from routine screening and counselling of heavy drinkers on hospital wards.

Accident and Emergency Services

It is well established that excessive drinkers are over-represented among attenders of A & E departments. Holt *et al.* (1980) found that 40% of casualty patients had consumed alcohol before attending and 32% had a blood alcohol concentration over the legal limit for driving (80 mg%). In a study of emergency general admissions, Lockhart *et al.* (1986) found that 27% of 104 admissions and 17% of bed occupancy could be attributed to alcohol consumption.

Despite the inherent difficulties in carrying out opportunistic screening in this setting, it seems that it is possible to detect excessive drinkers in A & E departments (Lockhart *et al.*, 1986). In a study in the A & E departments of two central London teaching hospitals, Green *et al.* (1993) found that almost half the patients they identified as having an alcohol problem accepted an invitation to return to the department the following day for advice on drinking, suggesting that A & E departments can be appropriate settings in which to offer help to reduce consumption. A practical and effective screening questionnaire for use by A & E staff has been developed by Smith *et al.* (1996).

Effectiveness of Brief Interventions in Accident and Emergency Departments

There are no published studies of the effectiveness of brief interventions in A & E departments in the UK. However, in Finland, Antti-Poika (1988) randomised 120 heavy drinking men attending an emergency service because of injuries to an intervention or control (usual care) group. The intervention group received up to three sessions of counselling from a trained assistant nurse. Results were encouraging: at six-month follow-up, 45% of patients in the intervention group had either moderated their drinking or abstained, compared with 20% in the control group; a statistically significant difference supported by changes in liver enzyme values. This study suggests that minimal intervention can be effective in the A & E setting, but more research on this possibility is needed. The potential benefits from alcohol interventions in trauma centres have been discussed by Gentilello *et al.* (1995), and guidelines for carrying out this work are provided by Dunn *et al.* (1997).

General Psychiatry

Within the last 20 years, the Royal College of Psychiatrists (1979, 1986) has produced two reports on alcohol, but these were aimed at improving the treatment and prevention of alcohol problems in the community as a whole. Unfortunately, there are signs that general psychiatrists are increasingly reluctant to become involved in treating alcohol problems, preferring to see them as a matter for specialists and not their concern. There are, however, three respects in which general psychiatrists can be involved in the treatment of alcohol problems.

Treatment of Alcohol Problems as an Integral Part of General Psychiatry

Parallel with the development of specialist services for alcohol problems over the past 50 years, there has been a tradition that sees the treatment of alcohol dependence as a proper and necessary part of general psychiatry based on the assumption that addictions are a subclass of mental illness (Meyer, 1996; O'Brien and McLellan, 1996). The fact that specialist services for alcohol problems were pioneered in the UK by psychiatrists meant that there was initially an inbuilt connection between the alcohol treatment and general psychiatry, although this was considerably weakened with the advent of non-statutory services and the closer involvement of professions other than medicine.

The existence of delirium and hallucinations associated with severe alcohol withdrawal, of paranoid states such as morbid jealousy and of severe forms of alcohol related cognitive impairment, such as Korsakov's syndrome, strengthens the need for psychiatrists' contributions to treatment in this area. At the same time, alcohol dependence can both cause and be caused by anxiety states (Stockwell and Bolderstone, 1987; Schuckit and Monteiro, 1988) or depressive disorders (Davidson and Ritson, 1993; Madden, 1993). In a survey of all new admissions to in-patient wards of a· general hospital in the US, Moore *et al.* (1989) found the highest prevalence of 'alcoholism' in psychiatric wards. In a study of the prevalence of alcohol problems and psychiatric disorders in two linked psychiatric hospitals in London over a twelve-year period, Glass and Jackson (1988) reported that a steady 9–11% of all diagnoses were alcohol related, pointing to the significant contribution of drinking problems to the workload of the psychiatric hospital.

Once again, however, despite evidence that up to a fifth of admissions to psychiatric hospitals may be heavy drinkers (Bernadt and Murray, 1986), other evidence shows that psychiatric registrars fail to take a proper drinking history from their patients (Farrell and David, 1988). Psychiatric registrars were only slightly better in commenting on alcohol consumption than junior hospital doctors and were poorer in regard to the quantitative assessment of drinking. Further, in a study involving the random allocation of case vignettes to a sample of consultant psychiatrists, Farrell and Lewis (1990) found that psychiatrists rating vignettes with a diagnosis of alcohol dependence were more likely to rate the patient as difficult, annoying, less in need of admission, uncompliant, having a poor prognosis and more liable to be discharged from follow-up. Negative attitudes such as these are clearly inimical to the proper treatment of alcohol dependent individuals within the setting of general psychiatry.

The UK Alcohol Forum (1997) has recently produced guidelines for the management of alcohol problems in primary care and general psychiatry. The main aim of the guidelines is to address differences in the availability and quality of care for individuals with alcohol related problems in various parts of the UK. An integrated approach to treatment is recommended that includes the support of family and friends, counselling, self-help groups, psychothera-pies and pharmacotherapy, as appropriate. The particular point is stressed that, since alcohol dependence is essentially a relapsing condition, relapse should provoke not withdrawal of treatment, but rather a continuation or modification of the treatment programme. Chick (1996) has provided guidance to general psychiatrists on the use of medication in the treatment of alcohol dependence.

Consultation and Liaison Psychiatry

The role of the psychiatrist in providing consultation and liaison with general hospital services has been discussed by Beresford (1979). With respect to alcohol problems, consultation usually involves responding to alcohol related emergencies, such as the appearance of delirium tremens, and advising on the complications that the patient's drinking causes to his or her hospital care and the outcome of treatment for the organic condition. The liaison role is more proactive and entails establishing relationships with medical, nursing and social work staff to develop an effective method of detecting and responding to alcohol problems in hospital patients, including the provision of single-session interventions for excessive drinkers.

Laugharne *et al.* (1997) recently reported the prevalence of alcohol problems among in-patients referred to a liaison psychiatrist. Of a sample of 100 consecutive referrals, one-third were found to be positive for 'alcoholism' on the CAGE questionnaire and 14% were found to warrant a diagnosis of alcohol dependence syndrome. The authors conclude that it would be advantageous for liaison services to work closely with alcohol services.

Comorbidity of Alcohol Problems and Psychiatric Disorders

Although issues related to this form of comorbidity, or dual diagnosis, have been neglected in the UK until recently, there are signs that they are now being taken more seriously. In 1996, the Department of Health established a Working Party on Substance Misuse and Psychiatric Comorbidity and commissioned a review of the evidence on this topic (Crome, 1996). In the same year, the Centre for Research on Drugs and Health Behaviour produced a report on dual diagnosis for use by local services (Franey, 1996). A national network for treatment providers interested in dual diagnosis has also been established.

Regarding the prevalence of alcohol problems among people with psychiatric disorders, Menezes *et al* (1996), in a community survey of 121 psychotic patients in South London, found that the one-year prevalence rate for alcohol problems was 32%. Smith and Hucker (1993, p. 653) assert that 'given the extent of the problem, substance misuse among severely mentally ill patients should be considered usual rather than exceptional'. Psychiatrists should suspect dual diagnosis when working with young male patients presenting with problems such as violence, poor treatment compliance and poor outcome.

As implied above, the existence of these comorbid conditions makes a strong argument for increased attention to the treatment of alcohol problems as part of general psychiatry. The potential significance of comorbidity for service provision has been well described by Krausz (1996, p. 2): '[The] coincidence of severe mental illness and addiction is and will be one of the most important clinical challenges in psychiatry in the coming years which will also point out structural weaknesses in the treatment system between psychiatric and addiction treatment.' There is also a pressing need for more and better training in this area so that psychiatrists and other mental health workers can acquire the knowledge and skills to deal with alcohol related problems and other addictive behaviours. The implications of comorbidity for the provision and coordination of services will be returned to in Chapter 10 on specialist treatment services.

Social Services

Since the beginnings of the profession, social workers have always been confronted with the personal and social problems caused by the misuse of alcohol and by alcohol dependence. This aspect of social services was increased in importance by the National Health Service and Community Care Act (1990) which required local authorities to plan for social care aspects of services for problem drinkers. Evidence suggests that alcohol is a significant component in between 20% and 40% of all social work caseloads (McGarva, 1979; Isaacs and Moon, 1985) and is likely to exceed these estimates in child abuse cases (Oliver, 1985). Studies have shown that parental alcohol misuse is the most important contributory factor to the reception of children into local authority care (Alaszewski and Harrison, 1992).

The literature on alcohol and social work has been reviewed by Alaszewski and Harrison (1992) who reveal problems similar to those encountered among GPs and other generalist workers. Among the findings of Shaw *et al.* (1978) from the Maudsley Alcohol Pilot Project was the observation that social workers were able to identify very few of the problem drinkers on their caseloads and showed the same lack of role legitimacy, adequacy and support as had been found among GPs. Subsequent research and comment by Goodman (1981), Abel (1987), Fanti (1986), McLaughlin (1988), Smith (1989), Thornton and Holding (1990) and Lawson (1994) has shown that these problems have continued to exist in the social work profession. In an American study of four social work agencies, Kagle (1987) found that only 15% of alcohol and other drug problems were correctly identified by social workers; there is no reason to believe that the situation in Britain is any better. As in the medical field, social workers respond to manifest difficulties of their clients, typically in the financial, marital or child care domains, but rarely attempt to identify or address the underlying causes of these difficulties in problem drinking.

Social Work Training in Alcohol Problems

There is widespread agreement that professional education and training is a major factor in the neglect of the alcohol component in the delivery of social services (see Chapter 11) and that the qualifying training of social workers fails to prepare them for work with the large number of problem drinkers they encounter in routine practice (see, for example, Thornton and Holding, 1990). Despite a number of recent advances, Alaszewski and Harrison (1992) advocate a continuing strategy for enhancing social work education on alcohol by addressing both the supply and demand sides of the equation; that is, the need for trainers to have access to up-to-date training packages and the parallel need to ensure widespread acceptance by training bodies of the indispensability of an alcohol component in professional qualifying courses.

Alcohol Interventions in Social Work

There is no shortage of advice on how social workers should carry out interventions for problem drinkers among their caseloads (see, for example, Leckie, 1990). In particular, Barber (1994) has provided valuable guidance on social work practice with addictions based on Prochaska and DiClemente's (1992) stages of change model. Attention has also been paid to the needs of specific groups of clients with drinking difficulties: young people (Jenson *et al.*, 1995; Fossey *et al.*, 1996); the elderly (Barnea and Teichman, 1994; Simpson *et al.*, 1994; Harrison, Manthorpe and Carr-Hill, 1996); people with learning disabilities (Manthorpe, 1996); homeless individuals (Harrison and Luck, 1996), people from black communities (Harrison, Harrison and Adebowale, 1996), pregnant women (Anderson and Grant, 1984; Andrews, 1995) and women in general (Thom and Green, 1996; Waterson, 1996). The Social Services Inspectorate of the Department of Health (DoH, 1997) has recently issued standards and criteria for the inspection of social services for people who misuse alcohol and other drugs. This report is also concerned to ensure the description of the network of services currently being provided in an area, the evaluation of their quality and the identification of any development work that is necessary.

With specific regard to minimal interventions, Shawcross *et al.* (1996) conducted a pilot project in the Lothian area to investigate whether minimal interventions could be appropriately placed and effectively used in a social work context. A minimal intervention package, consisting of information and screening, assessment, brief counselling and evaluation, was developed for the project. However, despite training and joint planning initiatives, it was found that the majority of social workers were unable to incorporate minimal interventions for alcohol problems into their normal practice; objections to comprehensive screening of all clients on a caseload appeared to be a particular obstacle to implementation. On a more positive note, those clients who did receive the brief intervention were found to have benefited from it on the whole, although this observation was based on small numbers. The author concluded that recording systems in social work departments should be reviewed to ensure that data collection methods were more alcohol-sensitive, that competency-based training should be introduced recognising the special skills needed to work with alcohol issues, and that research should be commissioned to build on the preliminary finding that brief alcohol interventions were of benefit to families attending social work centres.

Despite its somewhat discouraging findings and limited scope, the Lothian pilot project is a good example of a kind of research that is much needed if attention to alcohol related issues in social work practice is to achieve its proper recognition and implementation. More generally, there is a complete dearth of research aiming to evaluate the effectiveness of alcohol intervention by social workers and how it might be improved. Such research could help to demonstrate that alcohol focused interventions are effective in reducing clients' problems in a range of domains and to show that the implementation of these interventions in normal practice is a realistic aim.

The Criminal Justice System

The close association between excessive drinking and crime, especially violent crime, is well known. The All Party Group on Alcohol Misuse (1995) has published a report with the aim of breaking the link between alcohol and crime. The report quotes estimates by the British Medical Association (1989) that 60–70% of homicides, 75% of stabbings, 70% of beatings and 50% of fights or domestic assaults are associated with alcohol. A survey by the West Midlands Police in 1987 found that alcohol consumption was a factor in 82% of cases of disorder and 43% of assaults, with most of these offences taking place at weekends around closing times of licensed premises.

The All Party Group report also found that services for individuals with alcohol problems were very poor throughout the criminal justice system, and that access to and coordination with services provided outside the criminal justice system were also inadequate. Costs of alcohol related crime could be reduced by an investment in alcohol services, and increased access to services could also reduce custodial costs. While recognising the valuable contribution already made to the treatment and rehabilitation of problem drinking offenders by the voluntary sector, the All Party Group recommended the establishment of specialist alcohol criminal justice services, urged that special funding be made available for this purpose and made specific suggestions as to how such funding could be found. In conjunction with the All Party Group report, Alcohol Concern has published a guide for alcohol services on partnership with the police, probation and prison services (Webster and Chappell, 1995). In addition, the Mental Health Foundation has recently published a report on the care and treatment of persistent street drinkers (Mental Health Foundation, 1996).

In addition to causing harm to others, the many problem drinkers in contact with the criminal justice system also harm themselves by their drinking, and the various sectors of the criminal justice system represent settings in which problem drinkers can be identified and offered help. McMurran and Hollin (1993) provide a guide to practitioners in the criminal justice system, based mainly on cognitive-behavioural principles and methods, on how to help young offenders with alcohol related problems. There is no reason why the same methods should not also be applied to older offenders.

Police

Webster and Chappell (1995) describe various ways in which the police can contribute to the treatment and rehabilitation of offenders with drinking problems. In the first place, there is a growing tendency for police to consider alternatives to prosecution for minor drunkenness offenders and this has led to the setting-up of various types of referral schemes between police stations and local alcohol agencies. Second, police officers on street duty in urban areas with established homeless and heavy drinker communities can use their extensive knowledge of the community to become unofficial referral sources for alcohol agencies and can assist agencies with information about their clients.

Third, officers at the police station can display posters and promotional material for alcohol treatment agencies, hand out referral cards to appropriate detainees and encourage the detainee to follow up the services on offer. More formally, arrest referral schemes can be established in which, following a caution at the police station, offenders are offered the option of referral to a specialised treatment project. Webster and Chappell (1995) describe various models for these schemes. Research on alcohol and drug referral schemes (Dorn and Maynard, 1994) suggests that the uptake of referral offers is sometimes disappointingly low due to difficulties experienced by police officers in identifying suitable referrals and detainees being unwilling to admit to a problem, among other factors. However, there is ample opportunity for schemes to be improved to overcome these obstacles.

Probation

The crucial relevance of problem drinking to probation work is shown by the fact that in 1994 probation officers reported 30% of their caseloads as having severe problems with alcohol. For over seven in ten offenders in this category, an alcohol problem was directly related to the most recent offence (All Party Group on Alcohol Misuse, 1995). Nevertheless, the familiar deficiencies in the training of probation officers in responding to the alcohol problems of their clients have been noted many times, and most of the comments above on the training of social workers apply equally to the training of probation officers. However, there may be some grounds for optimism about the therapeutic role of probation officers because of the stages of change model, which gives a rationale for the use of motivational interviewing principles and techniques with unmotivated problem drinking offenders (see Harrison, 1996). Additionally, there have been recent changes to the qualifying training of social workers and probation officers designed to improve their alcohol related knowledge and skills (Harrison, 1992a, 1992b; Scottish Office, 1993).

One of the main modes of intervention for problem drinking used in probation work is the so-called Alcohol Education Course, although education in this context refers more to skills training and attitude change than merely to the provision of information (Baldwin, 1990). These courses are run in group format, consist of a maximum of six weekly sessions and are normally directed at young offenders with alcohol problems. They may be provided either as a condition of probation or on the basis of a deferred sentence, with some evidence that the latter mechanism is becoming more widely used. Alcohol Education Courses are delivered either by probation services funding voluntary organisations to carry them out or by providing them in-house. Trends suggest that the latter option is becoming more popular owing to budgetary restraints within probation services (Webster and Chappell, 1995).

The Prison Service

The first attempts to provide treatment for alcohol problems among serving prisoners in the UK were carried out by Dr Max Glatt in Wandsworth Prison in the 1950s (see Glatt, 1977). Using various definitions of problem drinking, a number of studies have reported high proportions of serving prisoners with identifiable alcohol problems (McMurran and Baldwin, 1989; McMurran and Hollin, 1989) and even higher proportions claiming that their offences were associated with heavy drinking. However, many prisoners recognise the connection between their crimes and their drinking and state a wish to abstain or to cut down. McMurran and Baldwin (1989) carried out a postal survey to enquire about the extent of alcohol related intervention in UK prisons, with a response rate of 83%. Of all responding establishments, 91% claimed to provide services for prisoners and 58% gave details. Services were provided mainly by probation officers, social workers, prison officers and Alcoholics Anonymous, and were offered on either an individual or a group basis. However, service development was found to be haphazard, lacking in central coordination and not subject to evaluation. McMurran and Baldwin make a case for the appointment in each prison of a central facilitator responsible for staff training on alcohol issues, establishing a communications network, encouraging new interventions to match prisoners' needs, encouraging closer links with community workers and guiding evaluative research.

Little is known about whether these recommendations or any other developments in the prison setting have subsequently taken place. The report of the All Party Group on Alcohol Misuse (1995) concluded that services were reaching far too few problem drinkers in prison and that the availability of services in prisons was extremely variable. Among various recommendations, the report urged the development of a coherent policy for the care and treatment of prisoners with alcohol problems at every stage of their sentence and a mechanism for ensuring that this was included in individual sentence planning. The Alcohol Education Course model referred to above is also applied to serving prisoners (Baldwin, 1990). However, it is obviously essential that this type of intervention continues after the prisoner's release if there is to be any chance of achieving long-term gains.

Summary of Main Arguments

- Specialist services are intended to reach only a fraction of people whose lives are adversely affected by alcohol or whose excessive use of alcohol adversely affects others. The involvement of generalists in prevention and treatment is essential.
- Specialist services are required to deal with the more severe problems, as well as to provide ongoing support, training and consultation to generalists in the field. A balance between specialist and generalist activity must be struck if treatment is to be widely effective.
- Collaborations between generalist agencies from different sectors as well as cooperation between generalist and specialist agencies increases treatment cost-effectiveness. There is an important role for specialists in the planning and coordination of such collaborative work.
- Across all sectors of generalist activity, there is a lack of training and scant use of basic skills, notably minimal interventions.
- There is enormous potential within primary health care to have a significant impact on alcohol related harm at the population level. It is likely that improvements in education and training will not be sufficient in themselves to routinise alcohol interventions.

10
Specialist Treatment

This chapter is concerned with specialist treatments for alcohol problems. These treatments are seen as existing along a continuum with the interventions described in the previous chapter rather than belonging to an entirely separate domain. *Specialist* treatment here is used in two different senses. First, it refers to treatment by personnel who have received some form of training in the area of alcohol problems or addictive disorders in general and in the treatment of these conditions. It also refers to treatment delivered by services that are specialist in the sense that they deal exclusively with alcohol problems or, at least, with addictive disorders. These services may employ staff who are not specialists in the first sense. Also, 'treatment' as used here has a wide meaning and includes 'counselling' or what some would prefer to call merely 'help' for problem drinkers, provided that help is based on some special training and expertise; treatment does not here imply a specifically medical procedure.

Why, given the evidence reviewed in Chapter 9 on the effectiveness or potential effectiveness of generalist treatment, is specialist treatment for alcohol problems needed at all? The most obvious answer to this question is that specialist treatment is essential to address the needs of those problem drinkers with especially severe problems. Problem drinkers are often very troubled individuals indeed and show complex and longstanding difficulties with alcohol combined with serious problems in many other areas of life. These problems need careful and experienced assessment and the treatment designed to address them needs to be based on special training and skills if it is to stand any chance of success. This level of experience is simply beyond the capacities of the busy generalist who will rightly resent being expected to respond to these very difficult cases.

Beyond that, specialist services are essential as a repository of high-level knowledge and expertise in the alcohol problems field. It was made clear in Chapter 9 that, in order to deal effectively with alcohol problems encountered in their day-to-day practice, generalist workers must be able to call on the services of specialists for advice, training and consultation. Without such specialist input, the generalist response to alcohol problems and the high hopes this has engendered are doomed to failure and disappointment. On a broader level still, an adequate national response to alcohol problems must be able to call upon the special expertise required to be alert to changes in the nature of alcohol problems in society, to keep up with innovations in treatment technology and to integrate theory, research and practice, treatment and prevention and local and national imperatives. This expertise can only be found in specialist alcohol or addiction services and it is essential that it is preserved. In this chapter we discuss:

- effectiveness of treatment for the individual
- benefits of treatment to society
- the economic benefit of treatment
- combined or alcohol only services
- alcohol problems and psychiatric comorbidity
- treatment for different population subgroups
- mutual aid for alcohol problems
- the current state of alcohol treatment services.

Effectiveness of Treatment for the Individual

The first question that must be answered is whether treatment is effective among those who receive it. As a result of receiving treatment, are clients' alcohol problems eliminated or reduced, and are their lives improved? This question has received much attention over the years (see, for example, Clare, 1977; Edwards and Grant, 1980; Heather *et al.*, 1985), especially following the publication of Orford and Edwards' (1977) comparison of treatment and advice, which appeared to show no superiority for the former. It is, of course, a very difficult question to answer definitively, partly because of the impossibility of forming no-treatment control groups by withholding treatment from those who request or appear to need it; partly because of the complexities involved in drawing conclusions from all the relevant evidence, and partly because of uncertainties about what is meant by treatment and by natural recovery. Nevertheless, there is now some agreement among therapists and researchers alike that treatment for alcohol problems is better than no treatment. A rough estimate is that the rate of spontaneous remission or, at least, naturally occurring improvement in populations comparable to those receiving treatment is one-third, whereas roughly two-thirds of individuals receiving treatment show some improvement over their pre-treatment condition (Babor, 1995).

We have not discussed the relative effectiveness of different types or modalities of treatment for alcohol problems. The evidence on this topic has been reviewed extensively in recent years (for example, Mattick and Jarvis, 1993; Heather, 1995a; Miller *et al.,* 1998; Raistrick and Heather, forthcoming) and, in any event, we are more concerned here with policy issues relating to alcohol treatment *as a whole* rather than with any specific form that treatment might take.

Benefits of Treatment to Society

Treatment for alcohol problems need only be justified on humanitarian grounds, as providing assistance to those who are suffering from and whose lives are adversely affected by the harmful consequences of their drinking. The National Health Service costs of some late interventions are often high; for instance, the treatment of hepatic cirrhosis, pancreatitis or alcohol related brain damage. Only a fraction of those treated for the health consequences of their drinking receive specific treatment focused on their drinking behaviour. Assuming that this treatment is effective on an individual level, it might be expected that such treatment would also have the effect of reducing to some extent the aggregate level of alcohol related harm in a society. This proposition is very difficult to test, mainly because the data needed to examine it are mostly absent in the UK. There is, however, some relevant evidence from research conducted in North America.

Mann *et al.* (1988) began with the observations that liver cirrhosis mortality and morbidity in the province of Ontario, Canada, had decreased substantially in years prior to their study and that, over the corresponding period, substantial increases had occurred in the number of people receiving treatment for an alcohol problem. The potential contributions of both changes in treatment usage and changes in per capita alcohol consumption to declines in hospital discharges for liver cirrhosis were examined. Results showed that, with the exception of one area of the province, increases in treatment were closely related to decreases in cirrhosis discharges.

In a further study, Smart *et al.* (1989) looked at the impact of changes in rates of Alcoholics Anonymous membership and per capita consumption of alcohol on changes in rates of cirrhosis, drink driving charges and 'liquor act charges' for the ten provinces of Canada over the period 1974–83. In this analysis, neither Alcoholics Anonymous membership nor consumption changes were significantly related to changes in cirrhosis rates. However, both measures were associated, in an interactive manner, with changes in drink driving and liquor act charges. Mann *et al.* (1991) examined changes in cirrhosis death rates in the 50 US states and the District of Columbia between 1974 and 1983 and compared these rates with changes in per capita consumption, Alcoholics Anonymous membership and alcohol problems treatment over roughly the same period. No significant relationship between treatment and cirrhosis rates was observed, but the authors suggested that the measure of change in treatment they used may not have reflected the full extent of changes that occurred during the 1974–83 period. As predicted, however, decreases in per capita consumption and increases in Alcoholics Anonymous membership were significantly associated with decreases in cirrhosis rates.

Holder and Parker (1992) examined the hypothesis that an increase in the provision of treatment for alcoholism in the US had resulted in a break in the established relationship between level of alcohol consumption and the rate of cirrhosis deaths. This hypothesis was tested using data from the US state of North Carolina. The results indicated that, with the treatment factor controlled, changes in cirrhosis mortality were independent of changes in alcohol consumption. Furthermore, treatment had a short-term lagged effect on cirrhosis mortality, suggesting that the impact of treatment on chronic problem drinkers may be one of delaying the harmful consequences of heavy drinking.

While there may be some doubt regarding the validity of the relationship between treatment or other individually directed interventions and acute alcohol related problems, the relationship with chronic problems seems well founded and a finding of considerable potential significance for national alcohol policy. Taken together, the implication of the relevant findings is that *both* decreases in per capita consumption and increases in treatment availability independently reduce liver cirrhosis mortality and other chronic problems. Thus, combining population-based, environmental measures and individually based interventions can work together to achieve a large-scale reduction in alcohol related harm. However, these implications from North American research need to be tested in the different cultural context and unique treatment system of the UK.

Other Population Benefits of Treatment

The question of the potential contribution of treatment to reducing aggregate harm is not exhausted by the kind of research described above. For example, the following might also be considered as beneficial contributions of treatment (Edwards *et al.*, 1994):

a)   Active and effective treatment programmes, together with mutual aid activities (see below), can help to increase public awareness of alcohol problems and thus influence agenda setting by policy makers and politicians. While empirical evidence to support this claim may be hard to find, it is reasonable to conclude that treatment can affect the climate of opinion regarding alcohol problems in a country.

b)   Treatment is directed primarily at helping the problem drinking individual but can also have the effect of protecting society or saving immediate societal costs. Obvious examples here are drink driver intervention programmes, workplace treatment programmes and alcohol interventions among pregnant women.

c) Interventions can also be aimed directly at helping the person on whom the drinker's behaviour adversely impacts. This has long been practised by the mutual aid group Al-Anon, but formal treatment programmes are increasingly catering for people harmed by a problem drinker's behaviour.

Underlying these possibilities is a more general change in the field of alcohol problems – the breakdown of any clear distinction between treatment and prevention. If the varieties of alcohol problem are seen as lying on a number of continua, as they should be seen, then treatment and preventive activity are inevitably merged at both national and community levels. Moreover, the distinction between individual level treatment activities and population level preventive measures must ultimately be a false dichotomy, if for no other reason than because the population is made up of individuals. A practical consequence of this is that all treatment agencies, as part of their remit, should attempt to engage in local preventive activity (Tether and Robinson, 1986). Many specialist treatment agencies therefore have a potential or actual role in prevention and health promotion. It is misleading and potentially wasteful to categorise treatment and prevention as separate activities.

The Economic Benefit of Treatment

Aside from any societal benefits of treatment that may be observable in a reduction of alcohol related harm, there is the question of whether it produces economic benefits for society as a whole. The total cost of alcohol problems in the UK has been estimated as approaching £3 billion (Maynard and Godfrey, 1994) and this is probably an underestimate. But to what extent do the beneficial effects of treatment on problem drinkers compensate for these costs? In the previous chapter, mention was made of the cost savings to be expected from minimal, early intervention by generalists for hazardous and harmful drinking. Here we are concerned with the economics of specialist treatment for mostly more severe problems. There is a body of research that is relevant to this issue, again mostly from outside the UK.

Cost Offsets of Alcohol Treatment

There can be no doubt that harmful use of alcohol and alcohol dependence are associated with high medical costs arising from alcohol related organic damage, accidents and injuries. Moreover, it is known that problem drinkers and their families consume health care resources at a rate two or three times higher than non-problem drinkers (Holder and Hallan, 1986), but is alcohol problems treatment effective in reducing these medical costs? Can it be shown to pay for itself in later health care savings or even produce a net benefit for the health care system? In short, does treatment result in cost offsets for the health care system?

In a pioneering review in the US, Jones and Vischi (1979) examined twelve studies that had considered the impact of treatment on the use of medical care. The authors concluded that all these studies demonstrated a reduction in health care utilisation, either by direct measures such as in-patient days and out-patient visits, or by more indirect measures such as sick days and sickness benefits. Using more sophisticated methods, Saxe *et al.* (1983) re-examined four of the studies previously reviewed by Jones and Vischi, together with two newer studies. They cautiously concluded that there was some evidence to support the hypothesis that treatment was cost beneficial and that the benefits of treatment exceeded the costs of providing it. They also pointed out that many treatment services available in the US – mainly in-patient, medically based treatment – were clearly cost ineffective, there being less expensive ways of reaching the same outcomes.

Holder (1987) reviewed research published since Jones and Vischi's analysis and claimed these studies had fewer methodological limitations than those in the older literature. Holder concluded that, taken as a group, the studies reviewed confirmed the potential of alcohol problems treatment to contribute to sustained reductions in the total use of health care resources and in associated costs. Reductions in post-treatment costs were found to continue into the fourth and fifth year after the start of treatment.

Interpretation of this line of evidence is not without its difficulties. One problem is debatable evidence for cost offsets among economically and socially disadvantaged groups who use publicly funded programmes in the US. It is possible that, compared with the relatively more privileged groups among whom cost offsets have been shown to exist, the poorer population has more severe medical problems before treatment for alcohol problems is taken up and fewer personal and social resources for the maintenance of recovery after treatment (Luckey, 1987). However, in a study of recipients of Medicaid in the US, Reutzel *et al.* (1987) found a decrease in non-alcohol treatment costs in the six months following treatment and a somewhat smaller decrease in total health care costs. A rather more complicated conclusion was arrived at by Booth *et al.* (1990) from their study of low socio-economic status problem drinkers who had received treatment in Veterans' Administration hospitals. These authors described two distinct groups among treatment recipients – one that had experienced very little hospitalisation either before or after treatment, and another, associated with higher levels of consumption over a longer period of time, with frequent hospital care.

Two more recent American studies have used data from employers' health insurance schemes to study cost offsets. Blose and Holder (1991) looked at health care utilisation among severe problem drinkers and compared different age and gender groups with the normal population. The two younger groups of problem drinkers, aged 30 or younger and 31–50, showed health care costs twice as high as the normal population during ten years before treatment, but also showed falls in total health care costs after treatment, with a trend suggesting a return to age and gender norms. For those over 50, however, there was an increasing trend following the immediate post-treatment fall in health care costs. Holder and Blose (1992) compared costs among problem drinkers who had received treatment with costs among individuals with severe alcohol related medical conditions who had not received treatment. Health care costs were estimated to be 24% lower in the treated than the non-treated group.

In the context of the shift towards managed health care in the US, Holder *et al.* (1995) amalgamated data from three studies (Holder and Blose, 1986, 1991, 1992) to arrive at an estimate of return for investment on funding of treatment for alcohol dependence from the payer's perspective. They calculated that, for every US$10,000 invested, treatment saves about US$30,000 in medical spending for the managed care provider. They also concluded that medical costs typically spike in the year before a crisis requiring alcohol treatment and that low-cost identification methods that had the effect of moving problem drinkers into treatment earlier could prevent those costs. This again points to the need to integrate identification of alcohol problems at the primary health care level with specialist treatment.

It is clear that more research is needed in the area of cost offsets and there is an especially urgent need for research into the British health care system. Meanwhile, despite complexities of interpretation and despite the possibility of differences between subgroups of problem drinkers, the American findings make a *prima facie* case for the proposition that treatment for alcohol problems as a whole produces net gains for the health care system and is therefore a worthwhile and efficient use of financial resources.

Recent Research in the UK

Recent British research has examined the costs and consequences of treatment for alcohol problems. The SECCAT (Socio-economic Costs and Consequences of Alcoholism Treatment) survey looked at demographic, health service resource use and quality of life data among clients at an alcohol problems clinic in Edinburgh (McKenna *et al.*, 1996). Since this was a cross-sectional study based on retrospective interviews and a review of records, firm conclusions regarding cost offsets in the use of health services were not possible. Conclusions were also limited by a low interview response rate.

Nevertheless, the SECCAT survey found clear evidence of high rates of adverse socio-economic events and accidents among the cohort studied, as well as striking evidence of poor quality of life overall. In terms of drinking outcomes following treatment, both extremes of high and low abstinence were associated with lower costs than medium-level degrees of abstinence. The relatively high cost of the abstainers in the sample was due to the specialist treatment they had received during the six-month period. Those problem drinkers diagnosed as 'alcohol dependent' made greater use of health care resources and showed health care costs roughly double those labelled 'alcohol abusers'. The authors also concluded that, while effective treatment might be unlikely to have a dramatic impact on total health service costs of problem drinkers in the short term, there was substantial scope for improvements in quality of life and adverse socio-economic consequences which might be revealed by longer-term follow-up. In subsequent findings from the SECCAT survey, Patience *et al.* (1997) offered evidence that a measure of alcohol related problems could serve as a proxy for health services resource use and quality of life among problem drinkers receiving treatment. Potamianos and others (1986) showed that comparable benefits were conferred on patients allocated to a day centre treatment and standard specialist in-patient and out-patient care. The former was significantly less costly.

Wider Economic Benefits of Treatment

Benefits to the health care system in terms of cost offsets are only one aspect of possible economic advantages that treatment might bring. It could also result in reduced criminal activity and criminal justice costs, reduced social care and housing demands, reduced accidents and productivity and training gains for employers. Added to these third party benefits are possible benefits to individual problem drinkers and their families in improved employment prospects and earnings, improvements to social functioning, reduced risk of arrests for drunkenness, drink driving, and so on, and reduced expenditure on alcohol, all of which can be considered as economic gains (Godfrey, 1994). Thus, an important area of research is whether treatment for alcohol problems results in greater benefits than costs from what economists refer to as a societal perspective. Once more, the research that has addressed this question comes from the US.

In a complex analysis of data from five cohorts of clients referred to a mental health centre, Cicchinelli *et al.* (1978) estimated an overall average return of nearly US$10 for every US$1 spent on alcohol treatment. In a more conventional economic study, Rundell *et al.* (1981) undertook a cost-benefit analysis of a treatment programme in Oklahoma and included possible benefits for the national economy in terms of health, productivity, road traffic accidents and arrests, and criminal justice costs, but not quality of life. They reported favourable cost-benefit ratios for the treatment programme and for the state-wide alcohol treatment services. Finally, Lessard *et al.* (1985) provided a rough and conservative estimate of societal benefits from changes in welfare payments, health care costs and criminal activity following treatment. They calculated that the pay-back of treatment costs within the first six months was 49%. All these studies can be criticised on methodological grounds (see Godfrey, 1994) but, again, provide *prima facie* confirmation of wider benefits of treatment to society.

Cost-effectiveness of Treatment

Although treatment for alcohol problems can be considered to bring economic benefits to the health care system and to society as a whole, there is clearly much that can be done to make treatment more cost-effective. Indeed, in a situation of increasingly scarce health service resources and fierce competition for these resources from many fields of health care, it is imperative that alcohol treatment providers take seriously the need to make services more cost-effective and, furthermore, produce evidence that the treatment they provide gives value for money.

It will not be possible here to discuss the many factors that bear upon this issue. Suffice it to say that there are several aspects of treatment that have important implications for cost-effectiveness: group versus individual approaches, treatment setting – in-patient, day-patient or out-patient, duration and intensity of treatment, as well as treatment modality (Heather, 1992). The cost-effectiveness of different types of treatment service and modality has been reviewed by Holder *et al.* (1991), Godfrey (1994) and Finney and Monahan (1996).

It is also clear that much more attention needs to be paid to issues of cost-effectiveness, and to economic evaluation in general, in research into the treatment of alcohol problems conducted in the UK. An assessment of cost-effectiveness should now be a routine part of all treatment evaluation studies.

Combined or Alcohol only Services

There has been, in recent years, a move towards establishing combined alcohol and other drug services. The main impetus for combined services is the increase in poly-drug use over the last 20 years or so. It is commonly accepted that many individuals making contact with treatment agencies in the UK present with problems associated with alcohol use compounded by harmful use of other substances. Without a combined service, it is reasoned, the problems of poly-drug users would either be shuttled back and forth between different agencies, involving significant logistical and therapeutic difficulties, or might be partly or wholly ignored. In addition, a combined service is said to represent an economy of scale, making savings in terms of administrative and other costs.

It also seems logical to bring together training and acquired experience in one service, since broadly similar models of assessment and treatment are employed on different addictive substances. A combined service therefore integrates theory and practice and, in addition, makes more efficient and arguably more effective use of available resources (Raistrick, 1988). While there is no detailed information available on the number or distribution of such combined services, it seems reasonable to assert that commissioning agencies now appear more favourably disposed towards their purchase, no doubt because of the increasing emphasis on cost-effectiveness in the context of scarce resources.

The potential disadvantages of combined alcohol and drug services require careful consideration, particularly in the absence of research comparing the two models. It is argued that problem drinkers differ from those who have primary drug problems in some important ways, the most obvious example being age range. The mean age of problem drinkers lies between 35 and 45 and that for drug users between 25 and 35. It has also been argued that, despite a common explanation for addictive behaviour, drug users are more likely to require services sensitive to their particular subcultural backgrounds. The two groups will, it is claimed, have very different lifestyles and there is a danger that the more 'conventional' problem drinkers will be put off by the more 'deviant' lifestyles and possible criminal involvement of the illicit drug takers. In Prochaska and DiClemente's (1986) terms, precontemplators using illicit drugs, who might best be described as 'drug-seekers', receive substitute prescriptions and contribute to a significant proportion of a combined agency's client group; in contrast, problem drinkers taken on for treatment are generally not precontemplators but rather 'help-seekers' in the action stage of change. This may worsen the existing culture clash between the two client groups.

Another argument is that, despite a common explanation for addictive behaviours, the service needs of illicit drug users are very different, the prescribing of methadone being the obvious example. Finally, some argue that, in a combined service, the media publicity given to illicit drugs, coupled with external pressures from various sources, tends to skew service priorities away from alcohol problems and to swamp attention to problem drinkers and the purchasing arrangements that affect them.

While arguments both for and against combined services have some force, it is likely that, where there are sufficient commonalities to justify combined services in a commissioning area, they can be seen to work on an organisational level. The key concept is 'totality of care'; that is, it must be ensured in combined services that an adequate response is made to the individual needs of all clients, no matter what particular form of dependence they show. Thus, while combined services make sense from managerial and training viewpoints, there should be no attempt to force clients 'through the same door' and the specific needs of those with alcohol problems should be catered for at the local level. Age and readiness to make change are probably more important matching variables than substance.

Alcohol Problems and Psychiatric Comorbidity

This topic was discussed briefly in Chapter 3, and in Chapter 9 on generalist treatment for alcohol problems. It was pointed out there that the existence of psychiatric comorbidity among problem drinkers had been neglected in the UK but that there had been an increase of interest in recent years. This occurred mainly because of pressures from those commissioning services to differentiate more clearly the roles of secondary or tertiary providers from primary health care teams.

Comorbidity is important to a consideration of alcohol treatment services for two reasons. First, people who have an alcohol problem and one or more additional psychological or mental health problems have a less favourable prognosis than those people with an 'uncomplicated' drinking problem (McLellan *et al.*,1983; Project MATCH Research Group, 1997). Second, people with a comorbid problem use many more health and social care resources than those without comorbidity. Typically, treatment agencies find that a small proportion of service users, of the order of 10%, use a disproportionate amount of resources and many of these people have comorbidity problems: Coyle *et al.* (1997) found that 10% of one service's patients used 54% of the agency's treatment resources.

It is clear that clients in this category show a high utilisation of services and impose considerable costs on health and social care. This takes place in a political climate of increasing public and government concern regarding the personal and wider social consequences of comorbidity following the shift to community care. Dual diagnosis patients are some of the most vulnerable and needy individuals in society, with homelessness, poor physical health and arrests for violence or other criminal behaviour adding to their adjustment problems. Yet the indications are that comorbid individuals are more likely than others to be excluded from mainstream services, chiefly because of the lack of adequate service provision for this group (Rorstad and Checinski, 1996).

There is a growing view that separate mental health and addiction services, whether adopting a serial approach to dual problems or treating them in parallel, are ineffective (Johnson 1997). This is because patients are often shunted between services that are inadequate to meet their special needs or because treatment approaches used by many modern addiction services place an emphasis on client motivation and personal responsibility for change that is often too stressful and insufficiently supportive for them. Although some National Health Service Trusts have developed liaison posts between psychiatry and substance misuse services, there are no accepted models of treatment or service provision in the UK. However, a number of combined and integrated services are described in the American literature (see, for example, Mintoff and Drake, 1991; Galanter *et al.*, 1994). These do not necessarily involve the creation of entirely new services but a more efficient and targeted reorganisation of existing psychiatric structures. Some alcohol treatment agencies are developing special programmes to respond to this patient group (Franey, 1996) and this is to be strongly recommended.

Treatment for Different Population Subgroups

Some of the populations that come into consideration for special services have already been mentioned in the previous chapter on generalist treatment for alcohol problems (and also in Chapter 3); for example, young offenders, drink drivers, problem-drinking offenders in general, and problem-drinking employees. Many others might be proposed but we will confine attention here to four groups – problem-drinking women, young people with alcohol problems, elderly problem drinkers, problem drinkers from ethnic minorities and people with alcohol related brain damage.

From time to time there has been a call for separate services for women and for people of different ethnic allegiance which is usually based on the themes that people in these groups are under-represented in agency attendances and that agencies, because they cater predominantly for white men, are not equipped to cater for women and people of different ethnic or religious origins. Similar concern has been voiced about services for older people with alcohol problems whose problems are often overlooked because of stereotypical assumptions about the elderly.

On the subject of women, the calculation of representative proportion is often based upon population figures, namely something approximating to 50%, whereas the prevalence of alcohol problems in women is quite out of proportion to the ratio of men to women in the general population. Fillmore *et al* (1997, p. 42) note that 'within the same nation and age group, women are generally less likely than men to drink heavily, frequently, or with problems'. The actual differences will vary from country to country and from culture to culture as well as between different age groups, but the consistent pattern is of a ratio different from 1:1. Therefore simple headcounts are insufficient grounds for making the calculation of representativeness.

More important, however, is the question of appropriateness of service. We have knowledge of only one study demonstrating a preference for single-sex agency attendance and this study was based upon the likelihood of continuing to attend a single or mixed-sex agency in Australia. The finding was that where women had sexually segregated lifestyles and a history of sexual abuse they were more likely to continue to attend a single-sex agency. Otherwise women showed no preference (Copeland and Hall, 1992). The 'evidence' for separate services for different ethnic groups is anecdotal and sometimes based upon evidence of lower rates of detection of alcohol problems amongst some groups (Cochrane and Sukhwant, 1990).

It is difficult to make a case for sexual or ethnic stereotypes in the provision of services, nor would it be easy to justify. The likely result would be diminished funding for that which is perceived to be a minority group, the consequence of which is lower quality of service provision. The preferable route would be to ensure privacy, some choice and individually tailored treatments for the whole gamut of gender, ethnic and cultural groups within mainstream services. This does not detract from the need to ensure equity and ease of access to appropriate services for individuals from minority ethnic groups.

Homeless individuals have an increased prevalence of alcohol dependence: 16% amongst hostel residents, 44% amongst those sleeping in night shelters and 50% of those who are roofless (Jenkins *et al.*, 1998). These disadvantaged groups require special consideration in obtaining appropriate treatment. Access and proper engagement in help is often a major problem. It is also very difficult to detoxify from alcohol and regain sobriety in a drinking environment. Specialist residential care is commonly required as a step towards longer-term rehabilitation. Accessible and suitably supported housing is also an essential feature of the network of support that is needed. The needs of problem drinkers should be part of plans to meet the needs of homeless people. Young homeless individuals are increasing in number and may need additional services specifically designed for their age group.

Substance misuse services for children and young people were the focus of a recent report from the Health Advisory Service (1996). Collaboration between relevant agencies is the key to providing proper services to this group who often combine alcohol and drug misuse and also have a higher prevalence of other psychiatric disorders. The report (Health Advisory Service, 1996, p. 13) identifies certain linchpins to proper care for this group, including a commissioning strategy that takes account of local needs, with trained staff to undertake careful assessment, coupled with interventions that are targeted in ways that recognise 'younger people who are at particular risk and the differing needs of children and adolescents at different points in their development'. There are few properly integrated services for young people in existence in the UK. This is a major area of need which requires urgent attention.

One of the most distressing consequences of long-term alcohol misuse is the development of varying degrees of brain damage, which include Korsakoff's psychosis. There has been recent concern that the prevalence of this condition is increasing (Ramayya and Jauhar, 1997). Vigorous treatment with vitamin therapy, detoxification and rehabilitation can lead to a striking improvement in some cases. None the less, there remain a significant number of individuals with chronic alcohol-induced brain damage who will require residential care for prolonged periods of time and in some cases for the remainder of their lives. The development of care plans that will maximise the likelihood of recovery for this group of individuals is urgently needed.

Mutual Aid for Alcohol Problems

A major source of what can reasonably be described as specialist treatment for alcohol problems within the non-statutory sector is often omitted from discussions of treatment because it lies outside the formal planning and funding framework. This is the mutual help that problem drinkers offer to each other in the attempt to recover from their problems. Although often termed 'self-help groups', 'mutual aid' is a more accurate term for these groups' activities.

Alcoholics Anonymous

By far the most prominent of these mutual-aid groups is Alcoholics Anonymous (AA) which began in the US in 1935 and reached Britain in 1948. The AA Fellowship is completely self-financing and places no financial burden whatever on the national exchequer. AA offers in the region of 2900 meetings in England and Wales (averaging 15 meetings per week for each Health District). Data from AA Headquarters in York indicates an active membership in the UK of some 60,000 people.

While obviously a significant resource in the effort to reduce alcohol related harm, for longstanding philosophical reasons AA chooses not to be represented on planning groups or committees and operates in a relatively autonomous way. Two offshoots of AA are Al-Anon for relatives of 'alcoholics' and Al-Ateen for teenage children. No data are available to estimate the numbers in these offshoot groups.

It has proved extremely difficult to conduct research on the effectiveness of AA, mainly because of the anonymity the Fellowship properly insists on and because of the problems in forming randomised control groups. The Fellowship itself has no doubt as to its effectiveness, with success rates of over 75% having been put forward. Rates such as this may apply to the small group of total converts who persevere with regular AA attendance over a number of years but as a general statement of outcome among all those who attend or are referred to AA, they must be regarded with considerable scepticism. Nevertheless, from the point of view of many individual problem drinkers, AA is highly accessible and offers help on a continuous, 24-hour basis. It is likely that the spiritual teaching of AA, encapsulated in the famous Twelve Steps, is responsible for its success in many cases. However, there is little doubt that the social organisation of AA, which provides strong support for a new life without alcohol and an entirely new self-concept and social identity, is also crucial. As implied above, no formal treatment service can match AA for the continuity of support it offers to its new adherents and there is also no question that it is an extremely valuable resource in any country's effort against alcohol related harm. Further description and comment on AA can be found in Robinson (1979) and McCrady and Delaney (1995).

In the UK census data (see Appendix 2), AA was the most frequently used additional form of 'treatment', with 9% of clients on the Census Day recorded as also attending AA meetings. Although this figure is likely to be, if anything, an underestimate of those simultaneously attending AA meetings, it is clear that it would be much larger in some other countries, most notably in the US. In the UK, the figure reflects a departure from the days when many hospital treatment programmes for 'alcoholism' consisted of little more than a formalised version of AA's principles or made attendance at AA meetings a compulsory part of the treatment regime. Among the general public, AA is still likely to be thought of as the leading 'treatment' for alcohol problems, but among many of those engaged in formal alcohol treatment programmes the AA model of alcoholism has clearly waned considerably in influence, no doubt owing to criticisms of the disease concept of alcoholism in professional and scientific circles (Heather and Robertson, 1997).

Other Mutual-aid Groups

Although the only requirement for membership of AA is a desire to stop drinking, there are good reasons to believe it is helpful to particular kinds of individual (Emrick, 1987) and unhelpful to others. Of all those who initially attend AA or are referred to it by a professional worker, it is likely that only a small proportion will attend regularly (McCrady and Delaney, 1995), the rest either attending on a spasmodic basis or else dropping out completely. Particularly in secular societies like modern Britain, many problem drinkers are discouraged by the spiritual aspects of AA teaching and others have difficulty in revealing the details of their personal lives to others. There are probably many reasons why AA is not appropriate for all problem drinkers, in the same way that no specific formal treatment approach is suitable for all clients. This argues the need for a range of alternative treatment and mutual-aid approaches to be made available.

Over the last 15 or 20 years a number of mutual-aid groups have developed in the US that eschew the Twelve Steps and other AA principles and propose a different basis for mutual-aid for problem drinkers. The first of these was Rational Recovery which is based upon the principles of rational-emotive behaviour therapy (Trimpey, 1991). Rational Recovery's approach challenges assumptions about the permanence of the disease status and the need for continued attendance at meetings that is part of AA teaching. There is no sign that Rational Recovery has reached the UK, but it is possible it may gain a foothold in the future.

A group called Women for Sobriety does, however, exist in Britain. As the name suggests, Women for Sobriety was founded primarily as a feminist alternative to AA and admits only women. It was inspired by a perception of AA meetings as male-dominated and frequently chauvinistic in content. Furthermore, AA's emphasis on powerlessness, lifetime dependence on the group and the endless re-processing of past traumas was thought to be inimical to women's best interests and counter-therapeutic. Instead, Women for Sobriety stresses personal control, the development of an identity as a competent woman, putting the past behind oneself and the belief that once a woman can cope with life without alcohol, she no longer needs the group (Kirkpatrick, 1978).

Another alternative to AA which has reached the UK, and which is intended for all those who are uncomfortable with the spiritual context of the Twelve Steps, is Secular Organisations for Sobriety. This group avoids what it sees as the indoctrination of the Twelve Steps and substitutes six 'suggested guidelines' for sobriety. These guidelines view the attainment of sobriety as quite separate from religion and spirituality and aim to promote 'non-destructive, non-delusional and rational approaches to living sober, rewarding lives' (Christopher, 1997 p. 397). Although rejecting the AA form of sponsorship, Secular Organisations for Sobriety recognises the importance of supportive family and friends, targeting a lot of its activity at enabling them to understand and cope better with the problem drinker's behaviour.

Even more recently in the USA, there has emerged a mutual-aid group aimed specifically at moderate drinking (Kishline, 1994). Moderation Management provides a detailed, nine-step programme of change for people who feel they may be drinking more than is good for them and who wish to reduce their intake of alcohol. It is explicitly not intended for problem drinkers with a significant degree of dependence on alcohol, but only for people who have experienced mild to moderate degrees of alcohol related problems. More than any of the mutual-aid groups considered here, Moderation Management is based on current theory and research into the treatment of problem drinking.

Perhaps the most interesting aspect of the mutual-aid groups briefly described above is that they may be able to retain the obvious advantages of AA – the understanding and acceptance of a drinking problem by fellow sufferers, the group cohesion and social support for a new lifestyle, the availability of help in a crisis and the high cost-effectiveness as a way of combating alcohol problems – while abandoning the spiritual content that many people find off-putting. Indeed, these groups seem to have interesting possibilities; they should receive encouragement and, when requested, support from the alcohol treatment community.

The Current State of Alcohol Treatment Services

In attempting to provide a description of specialist treatment at a national level, it is evident that there is very little reliable and up-to-date information on service provision. The insecurity of funding for many services has increased the complexity of the situation because treatment agencies tend to appear and disappear or reconfigure the services they offer in response to changes in funding arrangements. Thus, generalisations regarding the treatment situation in Britain are increasingly hazardous. In an effort to remedy this state of affairs, a national census of alcohol treatment agencies was carried out specifically for the purposes of the Tackling Alcohol Together project. The census findings are presented in Appendix 2.

The contention that no one agency can meet all the needs of people experiencing alcohol problems is one on which there is likely to be wide agreement. To deal effectively with the diversity of alcohol problems requires the combined and coordinated efforts of a wide range of organisations and professional groups that encounter such problems in their day-to-day work (see Chapter 9). In addressing this issue, Heather (1995a) points out that it is better to speak of a treatment *system* rather than merely a collection of treatment services. This is reinforced by Edwards and Unnithan (1992) who describe a comprehensive and integrated approach to alcohol service provision which emphasises the need for collaborative working relationships across different services and organisations, guided by a clear set of strategic objectives and pulled together within a coherent and agreed framework. The concept of a treatment system emphasising the interdependence of the component parts highlights the needs for effective coordination and common purpose.

Given the need for inter-agency collaboration and joint working, it is unfortunate that there is no national agreement regarding who should be responsible for the planning, funding, development and coordination of an alcohol treatment system which would meet the needs of people experiencing alcohol related problems. The absence of a national alcohol strategy, along the lines of the drugs strategy set out in *Tackling Drugs Together* (DoH, 1995a) and its successor, *Tackling Drugs to Build a Better Britain* (Home Office, 1998), and the current absence of agreement on minimum purchasing and commissioning guidelines for specialist alcohol services, have contributed to a highly variable patchwork of treatment provision across the UK. Treatment services are often poorly coordinated and afforded a low level of priority in planning systems.

At national government level, a major stumbling block to strategic action in this area is the fact that there are at least 18 different government departments involved in one way or another in alcohol-relevant policy. The fact that so many different government departments have different priorities, which at times pull in different directions, means that a piecemeal and generally uncoordinated approach has been taken. This situation is replicated to a greater or lesser extent at a local level.

This is not, of course, to argue that treatment of alcohol problems has not progressed over the years; indeed, Anderson (1990) identified four major policy shifts across the last 20 years or so, namely a positive change in the attitude of the medical profession, the provision of community care and an increased willingness among policy makers to concur with the demands for greater service provision, coupled with the recognition of the harm caused by alcohol related problems in the UK. All these things have led to improvements in the range of treatment responses to alcohol problems. But while these factors have enriched the service network and added to options, in the absence of a well formulated and clearly articulated national strategy and, for the most part, locally agreed strategic policy and plans, significant problems emerge when different institutions attempt to devise and agree upon shared priorities and, in particular, divert funds to enable developments to take place. These problems are due in part to differences in ethos, organisational structure and core objectives, coupled with the pressing issue of the relative priority given to the perception of alcohol related problems in a climate of inadequate resources.

Local funding of specialist alcohol services, particularly within the non-statutory sector, has been resourced through ad hoc monies, gained from central initiatives and time-limited project funds such as joint finance schemes, as well as voluntary donations and subventions from Social Work and Health budgets. This has led to local service developments being driven by the availability of specific project funds, rather than on the basis of objective needs assessment. In the statutory sector, Regional Units have become smaller with a more local focus, have lost key functions such as training and research and development due to lack of a critical mass and, in some cases, have closed.

A particularly pressing problem for statutory services is the provision of specialist beds within dedicated Alcoholism Treatment Units. With the apparent demise of Regional Addiction Services, a wide range of models has been adopted in order to re-provide bed spaces for those in need of in-patient care. Whilst some District Health Authorities have sought to achieve economies of scale by contracting in-patient services across several districts, other services have earmarked beds on general psychiatry wards and, in some cases, medical wards.

Major changes in service provision were promised at the time of the new Community Care legislation in 1993. In the case of people presenting to alcohol services, concern had been expressed that a system designed to meet mainstream social needs might be ineffective. For example, it was suggested that many social services staff lacked background knowledge of alcohol or, indeed, drug issues; they certainly lacked specialist assessment skills and possessed a poor understanding of specialist alcohol services.

A study of local authorities' preparedness for Community Care in respect of those with alcohol and drug problems was undertaken in 1992 (Croft-White and Raynor, 1993). This indicated that local authorities had afforded a very low priority to assessment of those needs associated with drug or alcohol use. While the new approach to assessment and care management was intended to produce benefits for clients, almost all specialist drug and alcohol agencies surveyed felt that the new procedure would be more time consuming, or act as a disincentive to a client's motivation to seek help. In the context of diminishing budgets, it was feared that this might lead to service closure. A report by Alcohol Concern (1997b), entitled *Alcohol in the System*, gave the results of a survey which aimed to establish what changes had followed the implementation of Community Care. The key finding indicated that local planning mechanisms were often 'lacking in strategic direction and excluded many service providers' p. 7. There was evidence of division and competition between service providers and purchasing organisations which tended to hamper effective joint working arrangements. However, the new legislation did make provision for the production of Community Care Plans by local authorities in consultation with local communities. This system required joint planning teams to be established, drawing in the expertise and experience of local professionals and other groups, including the non-statutory sector.

With the launch of *Tackling Drugs Together* in 1995, and the establishment of Drug Action Teams, concern was expressed that alcohol issues might be afforded an even lower place in the hierarchy of competing priorities, with illicit drugs trumping alcohol by virtue of the central imperative spelled out in *Tackling Drugs Together* and the public perception that drugs present the greater risk to society (Alcohol Concern, 1997b). Whilst as many as one-third of Drug Action Teams have included alcohol within their remit, this does not remove the danger that alcohol will run a poor second to drugs in terms of service development; in fact, it might be argued that there is a greater risk that mere lip-service to alcohol issues will be paid.

At the end of 1997 plans were launched which will restructure the NHS in Britain. The detailed proposals differ significantly between England, Scotland and Wales, but all placed an emphasis on the role of consortia of primary health care teams in consultation with users and guided by evidence determining the needs and services within that community (DoH, 1997; Scottish Office and DoH, 1997; Welsh Office and DoH, 1998). In England, Mental Health Services will be provided by a single Trust, while Scottish Mental Health Services will be incorporated within Primary Care Trusts.

The place of the specialist alcohol service in these new arrangements remains to be clarified. There should be enhanced opportunities for joint planning across social work, health and the non-statutory sector. The concern will be that alcohol services will have a low priority within these new structures and not receive a clearly identified budget to ensure that an adequate range of services is provided. The creation of Drug Action Teams with requirements to plan jointly at the highest level within local areas may become a model taken up by alcohol services. The need for an alcohol strategy was identified in government initiatives (DoH, 1998; Scottish Office and DoH, 1998) which initiated a debate on broad strategies to improve the public health. Both in England and Scotland, the need for a national alcohol strategy has been identified and the time seems opportune for a serious commitment to tackling alcohol related problems at a community and national level. The extent to which this ambition becomes reality will become clear in the next two or three years.

Summary of Main Arguments

- Despite difficulties in evaluating the evidence on treatment effectiveness, there are firm grounds for concluding that treatment is effective among those who receive it.
- Research suggests that treatment reduces the harmful impact of alcohol misuse at the population level, particularly with respect to more chronic alcohol problems. This makes a *prima facie* case for the aggregate benefits of alcohol treatment.
- There is evidence that alcohol treatment produces cost-offsets for the health care system; that is, savings that cover the cost of the treatment itself and more. Treatment also produces wider economic benefits for society as a whole.
- Combined services for addiction problems can be justified at an organisational level and on efficiency grounds, provided adequate provision is made for totality of care and the particular needs of problem drinkers within a combined service. Misuse of illicit drugs has dominated the political agenda and there is a risk that combined services may become overwhelmed with illicit drug users.
- Certain sub-populations have special service needs, notably young people, the homeless and those with co-existing psychiatric disturbances. The objective is to ensure equity and accessibility to services for all of the population.
- The special expertise and role of specialist National Health Service addiction units needs to be strengthened. Specialist services are required to support policy implementation at a local level, to support primary health care teams and alcohol counselling teams, and as a focus for training and research.

11
Training Professionals

We have already referred to the need for improved training of both generic staff (see Chapter 9) and specialists (see Chapter 10). Paradoxically, the development of specialist services often encourages generalists to refer on rather than deal with alcohol problems themselves. Attitudinal studies on the question of treating alcohol misuse in the primary health care setting (Thom and Tellez, 1986; Deehan *et al.*, 1996) and the hospital setting (Rowland *et al.*, 1988) have demonstrated a lack of enthusiasm to treat people with alcohol problems on the part of medical practitioners. This finding is common though not universal among health care professionals, and a notable exception, distinguishing community psychiatric nurses from social workers, was found by Lightfoot and Orford (1986). Whether this is attributable to the confusion surrounding the nature of the problem or to the absence of knowledge and skills to deal with it has been the subject of many debates. Some investigators have suggested that the absence of professional and post-basic or post-graduate training in the subject has accounted for an unwillingness to respond (Shaw *et al.*, 1978), while others have focused on the presence of organisational constraints (Lightfoot and Orford, 1986) and the ordering of organisational priorities. A consistent finding has been that there exists a relationship between the provision of education and training at the qualifying and post-qualifying stages of professional careers and the willingness to become involved in treatment (Anderson, 1985; Clement, 1986). Theories attempting to explain this relationship have been proposed (see Cartwright, 1980; Tober and Raistrick, 1990; Gorman, 1993).

In this chapter we discuss:

- training strategy
- occupation-specific training
- specialist training
- evaluation of training

Training Strategy

In 1978, the government made recommendations for the provision of training in the identification and management of alcohol problems (DHSS and Welsh Office, 1978).

> Doctors, nurses, health visitors, social workers and probation officers all need to have received a minimum basic education and training about problem drinking so that they can carry out the appropriate treatment and care of problem drinkers at the primary level ... Those who will form part of the secondary services require a more extensive education and training ... (p. 27)

The report proposed that post-qualifying training should 'supplement the specific training occasioned by the special professional responsibilities of their own discipline' (p. 27). Furthermore, it proposed that this training should be made available in-service by Health Authorities and Local Authorities on an interdisciplinary basis to facilitate discussion of common problems.

The report went on to make recommendations for the training of voluntary counsellors and that they should be offered participation in the locally organised in-service training to be provided by health and local authorities. In the event, the organisation and delivery of training was slow to get off the ground; those specialist organisations employing volunteers found themselves to be in a particularly difficult situation where their staff may have had no professional training of any kind and they therefore adopted the Volunteer Alcohol Counsellors Training Scheme (VACTS) developed by Alcohol Concern (Alcohol Concern, 1989) for the purpose of ensuring minimum standards of provision in the non-statutory sector. Much of the training required for this scheme was provided in-house or purchased from education providers, thus the agencies were bearing the cost of training their voluntary staff themselves at significant cost.

It could be argued, on the basis of the available evidence, that the report did not influence the designers of core professional training curricula. Not until some 15 years later were curriculum proposals made by the English National Board (ENB) for Nursing, Midwifery and Health Visiting (ENB, 1996b) and the Central Council for Education and Training in Social Work (Harrison, 1992a); similar recommendations for medical training were made by the Medical Council on Alcoholism. However, the Council is only able to make recommendations to the Deans of undergraduate and post-graduate medical education; it does not have the power to enforce them. The medical Royal Colleges are responsible for stipulating the amount and nature of training in specialist as well as generalist post-graduate medical education and make recommendations to the Joint Planning Advisory Committee on the number of training posts that should be available; recently a recommendation was adopted that made eight additional senior-level training posts available, but consultants who are specialists in the field would argue that insufficient resource is available to provide training for the required number of specialists.

In 1990, Tober and Raistrick reported on the development of a district training strategy which, they claimed, could profitably be adopted at the regional and the national levels. The training strategy was based upon a number of fundamental principles, including the following.

- Different professional groups had a different role to play in the prevention and treatment of alcohol problems. The enthusiasm for 'multi-disciplinary' training had somewhat obscured this basic truth in the quest for breaking down barriers between the professions.
- Role legitimacy is conferred through introduction of the topic at an early stage in professional training rather than as a 'bolt-on extra' after the core, and by implication, therefore, essential subjects have been taught.
- Attitudes to treating problems of alcohol misuse will be determined to a large extent by the question of whether the professional is confident that he or she has the knowledge and skills to tackle the problem.

This training strategy argued for the routine inclusion of addiction training in core curricula at each career stage, for the standardisation of training within professional groups and for the provision of training by staff with specialist knowledge and competence to practise in the field. The strategy acknowledged different levels of training based upon needs for occupation-specific or specialist knowledge and skills.

One of the points of particular emphasis in this strategy approach is the recognition that those professional staff who have contact with problem drinking, namely medical practitioners, nurses, social workers, probation officers, occupational therapists, the police, teachers and health promotion officers, have their own very specific role in the prevention and treatment of alcohol misuse. On the basis of defining this role, specific competencies can be described and their acquisition form the content of training.

Specialists in the field would receive training which is provided by recognised education and training providers, validated by award-making bodies, normally universities, and teaching a standard set of core addiction competencies supplemented by higher-level super-specialist knowledge and skills. Examples would be the management of care for pregnant problem drinkers, dual-diagnosis patients or the under-16s.

The strategy was able to be implemented in Leeds and in the districts covered by the then Regional Health Authority, namely the Yorkshire Regional Health Authority. Training was incorporated into the core curricula of undergraduate medical students, social work – including probation – students, student nurses, youth and community workers and health promotion officers. It was also incorporated at the post-graduate training level in the relevant medical specialisms, while university-validated specialist courses were offered for those professionals seeking to take their occupation-specific training to a more specialist level. It remained the case that the subject of addiction had to compete with other important subjects in increasingly pressurised professional curricula and in the training of clinical psychologists: in Leeds, for example, the subject was dropped for this reason. However, the Regional Health Authority and subsequently a number of the District Health Authorities began to require specified levels of training for specialist agency staff in their contractual agreements in line with policy recommendations.

At the same time as the publication of the Leeds strategy, the Advisory Council on the Misuse of Drugs published their report on training (1990) and recommended somewhat different levels of training which incorporated the need to train managers, presumably the sort that purchase services rather than provide them. Although the government of the day separated its deliberations on drug problems from those on alcohol problems, giving far greater prominence to the former, many agencies and purchasers who combined services for these subgroups used recommendations from this report to inform their local strategy.

The national body in England, Alcohol Concern, has taken a number of initiatives to develop a training strategy (Alcohol Concern, 1994b) and to improve standards of practice through training (Alcohol Concern, 1987, 1989). A somewhat similar function is undertaken by the Scottish Council on Alcohol in promoting and standardising counsellor training in Scotland. In 1991 a working group, under the chairmanship of Professor Cary Cooper of the University of Manchester, was set up to review the need for a national alcohol training strategy. It duly made recommendations for the setting up of such a strategy. The report contained an overview, citing some of the available research literature on the training of the variety of professionals on the subject of alcohol and alcohol misuse. There was a description of what exists and identification of the professional bodies responsible for the development of curricula and those making specific recommendations to training institutions on the inclusion of alcohol and its attendant problems. Finally, it made recommendations for training in line with a tiered four-stage training design similar to that described in the report of the Advisory Council on the Misuse of Drugs (1990). These recommendations were based upon a description of what professionals might be expected to do with alcohol problems at each career stage, including the adoption of a specialist role. It also made recommendations for the adoption of National Vocational Qualifications (NVQs) for voluntary counsellors and untrained staff and proposed that consideration should be given to requiring NVQs for professionally trained staff in the field as well.

The report of this working party was arguably the most wide-ranging in its coverage of the variety of professional groups and their training. The section on recommendations for alcohol specialists, however, belies one of the problems in the report: there are recommendations for using therapeutic approaches which have no proven benefit for patients with problems of alcohol misuse; indeed, the authors state that 'the end product is to help counsellors increase their range of skills in helping clients to express feelings' (Alcohol Concern, n.d., p. 58). Moreover, there was more detail on the amount of time to be spent in training than on listing the competencies staff might be required to demonstrate that are associated with an outcome of reduced consumption and alcohol related problems in their clients. In an era when treatments are required to be evidence based, such recommendations are unlikely to be able to be adopted.

A further problem with the report was the lack of consultation with the professional, vocational and academic award-making bodies and the question of whether the parent body, Alcohol Concern, was likely to have any influence on the future selection of topics for inclusion in the core curricula of professional training via these groups.

In 1993 the Health Education Authority published a report entitled *Training for Alcohol Practitioners*, written by the head of the first diploma course to be established for alcohol counselling (Kent, 1993). This report contained a review of training in the field up to that point, though it focused upon specialist training as opposed to components of the curricula of professional training courses and made recommendations for future directions. It is not clear at whom this report was aimed, nor was it widely disseminated. It did identify key points in the requirements for the adequate provision of services for problem drinkers and highlighted the route to ensure such provision was made through the training of staff at all levels. The proposed content of training included some basic universal, in the sense of cross-professional, skills followed by the learning of occupationally and professionally determined skills. This report, like other reports, called for a national body, a 'Specialist Training Group ... to facilitate discussion and consultation across the disciplines ... [and] form part of a national drug training agency overseeing education and training in the field as a whole' (Kent, 1993, p. 39). The report called for policies at the national level which are agreed by 'policy makers at all levels in health and social care' (p. 39) and for the development of local strategies which are 'carefully negotiated and their performance strictly monitored' (p. 39). It recommended that the Specialist Training Group be charged with the responsibility for ensuring the geographical distribution of training, the provision of adequate funding, the establishment of criteria for the validation of training and of individual practitioners, and for providing a central focus for research initiatives and a database for training initiatives. It was not made clear at what national level this group would operate and who would be in a position to grant it these powers; none the less, the detail contained in the recommendations regarding practice-based training needs, professional differentiation, quality assurance and the maintenance of standards of practice gave clear direction on some of the essential components of a national training policy.

Occupation-specific Training

Social Workers

Procedures for the organisation and validation of professional training in the UK have made it difficult to report on the provision of any particular subject in training institutions. In the early part of the 1990s, Harrison conducted a survey of social work training which aimed to establish the quantity and content of social workers' training on alcohol and drug misuse (Harrison, 1992b). A survey of all Certificate of Qualification in Social Work (CQSW) courses yielded a response of 74%, of which 11% of courses provided no formal substance misuse training. Those that did offer training provided a median of 8 hours of study, with over 70% of students receiving less than 11 hours. The survey revealed that 24% of courses did not attempt to train students in treatment or management and 42% of courses did not include any teaching on prevention. Of the social work courses in the sample, 19% claimed to provide training in the prevention, detection and management of alcohol and drug related problems, and yet they allocated on average less than 11 hours to the subject. The median for alcohol teaching was 5 hours and the mode was 1 hour. Harrison compared his findings to the US picture and to those of other professional groups. He found that US social workers received far greater levels of routine training in the subject, a UK equivalent of approximately 30 hours per annum. He also found that social workers received slightly less training than medical students when comparing his results with those of a survey by Glass (1989).

Harrison's concerns focused upon the lack of preparation of social workers to deal with the alcohol and drug problems they would encounter in the everyday practice of social work; furthermore, he was concerned at the extent to which guidelines of the Central Council on Education and Training in Social Work (CCETSW) (1992) on minimum requirements for social workers at the point of qualification, namely the ability to demonstrate knowledge of substance misuse, were being disregarded.

The need to ensure the inclusion of core knowledge and skills in the social work curriculum was given new impetus by the publication of the above findings and by an initiative from the Inter-Ministerial Group on Alcohol Misuse. Somewhat earlier, the British Association of Social Workers reported on pressure from within the profession which favoured giving priority to alcohol training (1988). In 1990, the CCETSW launched a two-year curriculum development programme to be directed by a small team at the University of Hull (Harrison, 1995). The project produced guidance notes which the CCETSW used to specify the minimum knowledge and skills that qualifying practitioners need in relation to substance problems (Harrison, 1992a). This document specified the knowledge, values and skills required by social workers at the point of qualifying and went some way towards referring to specific, validated and standardised methods. Unfortunately, the authors stopped short of citing a comprehensive list of specific interventions, thus reducing the probability of standardisation across training centres, nor were assessment of skills or evaluation of training mentioned. Given the nature of the CCETSW, with its reluctance to dictate specific methods to social workers combined with an aversion to examining knowledge and competence, this document did make significant progress in identifying the general nature of practice and knowledge deemed necessary for working with drug and alcohol misusing clients. A resource directory (Harrison, 1993a) and a guide to teaching materials and specialist training courses (Harrison, 1993b) were produced as part of the same project.

1991 saw the introduction of a new and more rigorously assessed social work qualification, the Diploma in Social Work (DipSW). This was seen to be an opportunity to implement the core social work competencies in alcohol and substance misuse problems management which had been developed by a CCETSW working party and published as part of a series of Guidance Notes on the new social work curriculum (Harrison, 1992a).

Harrison (1993b) has described the way that the CCETSW *Guidance Notes on Substance Misuse* have been incorporated into social work qualifying training at the University of Hull at both undergraduate and post-graduate level. One of the problems in adopting this approach universally has been that the CCETSW regarded its guidance as purely advisory, and did not normally refuse to validate a qualifying programme which failed to include training on responding to alcohol problems. At the time of writing, plans are being made to replace the CCETSW as the validating body for social work education. Whether its successor organisation is prepared to take a more proactive approach to training on alcohol problems remains to be seen.

Nursing

In 1994, the English National Board for Nursing, Midwifery and Health Visiting funded a two-year Substance Misuse Education and Training Project whose aims were to:

i) identify the needs of nurses, midwives and health visitors for pre- and post-registration education and training on substance misuse and

ii) develop and implement a strategy for meeting those needs (ENB, 1996a; 1996b).

The first aim of the project was achieved through a training needs analysis which revealed wide variation in the standard and quality of education and training on substance misuse, in the extent to which the subject was covered in the core curriculum, in how closely the curriculum reflected the nature and extent of the problem, and in the accessibility and quality of learning opportunities. The report recommended that substance misuse should be included in all pre- and post-registration nursing, midwifery and health visiting curricular guidelines, at a standard appropriate to each particular programme (ENB, 1995). As a result, two sets of guidelines were produced: *Creating Lifelong Learners: partnerships for care* (ENB, 1996a) contains guidelines for pre-registration training, and *Substance Use and Misuse: guidelines for good practice in education and training of nurses, midwives and health visitors* (ENB, 1996b) contains the guidelines for post-registration training. In Scotland there are no equivalent modules, but there are some specific courses arranged by individual Health Boards as part of a professional studies module. All of these professional studies modules will become part of the specialist practice qualification.

While the ENB, like the CCETSW, has dispersed validating centres which are determined on a geographical basis, the procedures for validation are determined nationally and certain of the criteria are subject to national guidelines. For example, it stipulates that agencies and workplaces which are to be used for the purpose of supervised practice and the assessment of practice will be subject to annual audit and appraised as to their suitability both for the general task of training students and for the specific task of training them in a particular specialism. Audit questions examine the availability of staff time for supervision as well as the availability of adequate opportunities for practice and sufficient work space for the student. The institution providing the training which has been validated by the ENB is required to submit an annual report which will normally include the results of the audit of practice sites. The Education Officers of the ENB are subsequently required to produce a report to the ENB on how the institutions have performed.

To what extent the institutions of pre-registration nurse training have adopted the guidelines to date is uncertain. At the post-registration level, the ENB has six programmes of study on substance misuse in its portfolio:

- ENB 612   Drug and Alcohol Dependency Nursing
- ENB 616   Drug Dependency Nursing
- ENB 620   Alcohol Dependency Nursing

- ENB 962   Recognition and Management of Substance abuse
- ENB 963   Short Course on the Recognition of and Nursing Response to the Problem Drinker
- ENB N79   The Promotion and Instruction of Harm Reduction Techniques to Injecting Drug Users

In addition to validation by the ENB, these courses are franchised to universities and often jointly validated by the university local to the agency providing the course, or they may be provided by a university department, in which case university validation will be essential. The name of the course does not predetermine the level at which it is provided either in the Universities Awards system or in the Credit Accumulation and Transfer Scheme. Each institution providing one of these programmes will decide at which level they wish to do so and will then be required to ensure that teaching and assessment standards are consistent with those required by the specific award or level. With the publication of the guidelines for pre- and post-registration training, the ENB has been more prescriptive than previously on the question of specific content of programmes. However, the guidelines do not contain the curricula for each of the above named courses and the content of each programme will vary according to the local perspectives and preferences of the providers. While there is consensus in general terms on the need to develop practice in evidence-based interventions, the reading of the 'evidence' may vary from institution to institution. There remains considerable scope for variation in emphasis and on the inclusion of such topics as public policy and research methods.

Medicine

During the 1980s, a number of studies investigated the attitudes of GPs and hospital doctors to their patients with alcohol dependence and related problems. Both Anderson (1985) and Clement (1986) were able to demonstrate that GPs who had received alcohol education during their undergraduate medical training had more positive attitudes to problem drinkers and were more likely to perform alcohol related tasks, such as bringing up the subject, ordering liver function tests and giving advice on moderate drinking goals or abstinence. The attitudes of GPs were re-examined in the 1990s when a 20% random sample of all GPs in England and Wales was surveyed using a postal questionnaire. Of a 44% response rate, over half the respondents believed general practice was an appropriate setting for the detection of alcohol misuse and the vast majority saw the GP's role as extending beyond the treatment of medical complications arising from alcohol misuse. However, around 66% saw this patient group as presenting major management problems and only 24% felt adequately trained in the treatment of alcohol misuse. (Deehan *et al.*, 1998).

Glass (1989) reported on a survey of all medical schools in the UK in which she demonstrated the relatively low priority given to the subject of alcohol misuse in undergraduate medical curricula. The survey was repeated ten years later by Crome in an attempt to examine whether changes that had occurred in the addiction field and in the knowledge and attitudes about addiction problems had any impact on the priority afforded the subject in medical training curricula. Specifically, the changes Crome cites in the background to the study are the increases in knowledge about the subject of addiction and its prevalence in young people, *Health of the Nation* targets specifying addiction related problems and expansion in academic posts, including the introduction of new Chairs in Addiction (Crome, 1999). Crome reports a disappointing response to her survey questionnaire with an overall response rate from all heads of departments of 14%, but 66% of Deans and 75% of heads of departments of psychiatry responded. However, only 33% of heads of departments of public health and 20% of heads of departments of primary care responded. Psychiatry was pinpointed as the key department in all medical schools, thus demonstrating a combination of a lack of interest and a lack of perception of the relevance of the subject in the other specialisms. Crome's conclusions are that there has been a modest increase in the establishment of academic posts matched by limited improvements in some training programmes. She has found that exemplary programmes are associated with a close alliance between service and academic developments. In a quarter of medical schools – the 25% where even the department of psychiatry did not respond to the questionnaire – it is possible that very little training is being offered, while in another quarter the provision of training is very good. The absence of involvement of primary health and public health departments is likely to perpetuate the absence of training by these departments. This is in spite of three Royal College reports (Royal College of General Practitioners, 1986; Royal College of Psychiatrists, 1986; Royal College of Physicians, 1987) describing the gravity of alcohol problems in the population and the responsibility of medical practitioners in all branches of medicine to make a contribution to the response at both the individual and the public health levels.

In the absence of a consensus regarding the methods and content of training for medical practitioners on the subject of managing alcohol misuse, it is hardly surprising that the evaluation of such training, where it exists, is even less evident. Conclusions from American studies which are more commonly conducted may, however, be relevant. Rohrbach *et al.* (1997) showed that three hours of teaching medical students the knowledge and skills to deliver minimal interventions for alcohol problems was insufficient for the purpose of achieving good clinical performance, although significant improvement was achieved. The method of teaching, whether traditional didactic or interactive with practice and feedback, made no difference to the outcome.

Seale *et al.* (1995) reported positive results of a study of the attitudes of ten psychiatric residents who had completed an addiction rotation in their training. Positive attitudes and addiction knowledge increased significantly and were shown to be associated with their perception of responsibility and clinical behaviour towards people who use drugs. It was the view of the investigators that an addiction rotation can have a positive measurable impact.

Findings on the relative efficacy of medical practitioner advice compared to that given by nurses in the UK (Rowland *et al.*, 1988) and on the efficacy more generally of giving brief advice in the general practice setting (Wallace *et al.*, 1988; Anderson, 1993) were received with enthusiasm during the 1980s when there was a search for evidence to back the need for more training of medical practitioners. More recently these results have been treated with caution (Drummond, 1997) in the fear that such enthusiastic interpretation of relatively modest findings, in an era of major health service cuts, will result in the demise of specialist treatments. None the less, there appears to be a consensus regarding the importance of the contribution to be made by GPs in screening and advice to low-dependence at-risk drinkers for the purpose of reducing their consumption and the attendant harms (Heather, 1995b). The role of the specialist sector equally will suffer in the future from the lack of undergraduate and post-graduate medical training, as few young doctors are likely to select this unpopular specialism (Deehan *et al.*, 1996) when choosing their career path.

A recent study of alcohol trainers in the UK yielded a new perspective on the problem of lack of uptake of training by GPs (Albery *et al.*, 1997). The investigators in this study examined the beliefs of alcohol trainers about training different primary health care groups, including GPs, and the frequency of training in alcohol related issues in these groups, in an attempt to explain observed discrepancies in training exposure. They found that the take-up of training by GPs was the lowest of all members of primary health care teams, and while this finding is consistent with past findings (Clement, 1986), the authors in this case postulated that the reason may not lie in the lack of motivation to learn (Tober and Raistrick, 1990) but rather in the attitudes held by the trainers themselves and the ways in which training is offered to GPs. The investigators found that trainers believed that GPs were the most important members of the primary health care team to intervene with patients' alcohol problems, and yet it would appear that the training offered was least well suited to their needs. Examination of the professional background of trainers revealed that none had a medical training themselves, suggesting that training was being offered to GPs by staff with non-medical backgrounds. This is no more a problem for the medical profession than it is for any other profession and was the basis of the training strategy principle asserted by Tober and Raistrick (1990), that trainers should include at least one practitioner from the same professional group as that being trained. It is argued that putting this principle into practice will confer legitimacy on the trainers and the content of training will be assumed to be based upon an understanding of the professional role in question. This avoids the not uncommon allegation that people with no under-standing of professional roles and constraints are attempting to tell others what to do. Multi-disciplinary training may be perceived as offering skills which are outside the scope of the GP's role.

The problems in training uptake by GPs reported by Albery *et al.* (1997) may have been due in part to the methods of teaching and the focus on attitudi-nal change. It is more likely that GPs will attend for training if it will teach them something they need to know, rather than what they should be thinking about a subject or a group of patients. The preferred methods of training identified by respondents in the sample surveyed were experiential and didactic for GPs, whereas they were experiential for nurses. The need to train people in the usual venues and their usual styles of learning was emphasised by the authors, but it was unclear whether this approach was used to inform the respondents' answers to questions of preferred training method.

The experience of uptake of training for GPs would appear to be quite varied. In Leeds, where the principles of the strategy described by Tober and Raistrick (1990) are put into practice, greater success in the uptake of training is reported. GP training is offered as post-graduate *medical* training in line with the principles of a training strategy which promotes the teaching of skills designed to solve the profession's own problems, not someone else's. Teaching medical practi-tioners commences in their undergraduate medical training, is continued in their GP registrar training, and followed by in-service training. It is validated by the medical school Department of Continuing Medical Education, offered outside surgery hours and taught by trainers of whom one is always a medical practitioner. Training is based upon theory, research of general practice inter-ventions and a problem solving approach to participants' own cases. Emphasis is on medical interventions for problem drinkers appropriate to the general practice setting.

Specialist Training

Specialist training spans a broad spectrum of both validated and non-validated programmes of study. A recent survey of treatment agencies in the drug field (Boys *et al.*, 1997) comprising a one-day postal census of agency staff, found that nearly half the sample – 489 workers who comprised 95% of the workforce from 91 UK drug agencies, with a response rate of 76% – had entered the drug field with no professional qualifications, and almost a quarter of the sample were still unqualified. Of the sample, 8% stated that they had no professional qualifications nor any additional training after entering the field. There were 68 positive responses to the question of specialist qualifications, covering the

ENB courses cited above (32), Diploma courses in Addiction, Alcohol Counselling and Drug Dependence and Substance Misuse (29), and Masters degrees in Addiction (7). It is not unreasonable to suppose that the results of a survey for the alcohol field would have been similar, given that so many agencies serve both alcohol and drug-misusing clients. However, the existence of the Volunteer Alcohol Counsellors Training Scheme (Alcohol Concern, 1989) may have resulted in the greater implementation of minimum standards of practice in the alcohol agencies. The scheme carries with it the requirement to attend training albeit at the basic level. Courses taken as part of the scheme's requirements will not necessarily be validated programmes of study.

The national bodies, Alcohol Concern and the Standing Conference on Drug Abuse (SCODA), maintain a register of training courses whether or not validated by a recognised educational establishment. The list of programmes of study includes whole awards in Addiction Studies, or similar, at either the Diploma or the Master's degree level; modules of study that may be undertaken as part of another award – a degree in Health Sciences, for example – and courses that are neither validated nor credit rated, but which may be recognised by purchasers of services as being appropriate courses for the training of specialist staff in the field. A major concern among education and training providers regarding the courses in this latter category is that where students are not examined at the end of a course it is not possible to ascertain what they have learned. Evaluation is a matter which will be addressed at the end of the chapter.

The major validating bodies are the universities at both the undergraduate and post-graduate level and, for internal and external courses, the English National Board and the Central Council on Education and Training in Social Work. It is notable that even where a national training and validating body exists, as in the case of the ENB, there are no standard criteria for course content in either knowledge or skills. Rather, the ENB will give the course a name and a code, shared by other courses whose subject area is the same, and determine only the level – that is, the credit rating – which the course should carry. Given that the ENB is organised on a regional basis with power to validate courses devolved to the regional level, as the CCETSW has recently done, it becomes an even stronger imperative to adhere to the recommended curriculum guidelines if consistency is to be achieved. The case of the CCETSW is even more complicated as the power of validation has been devolved to consortia which vary considerably in their contributing membership.

In 1998 there were some 25 validated training courses in substance misuse offered at different universities and colleges around the country. To date there is no central validation, no universally accepted entrance criteria, learning outcomes or even consensus over what the requisite knowledge and skills should be at the certificate, diploma, degree or master's level. There is no obvious barrier except the willingness to cooperate, as there is evidence from other fields of training – midwifery supervision at the Universities of Leeds, Sheffield and York, for example – where collaboration has resulted in validation of the same course at different universities.

A recommendation for the future would be to establish a consensus regarding the content and outcomes of training at each level, that these should be centred on evidence-based practice in education, prevention and treatment and should include the research evidence and theoretical backgrounds that inform them. Determined jointly between the treatment and training fields, universally agreed knowledge and skills should be curriculum requirements for the validation of training for all educational and training providers.

The Royal College of Psychiatrists requires that doctors wishing to become Addiction Psychiatrists must complete a three-year training at Specialist Registrar grade to qualify for a Certificate of Completion of Specialist Training (CCST). The Addiction Psychiatrist is assessed for competence in the management of mental illness, psychosocial and pharmacotherapies for the treatment of dependence, training skills, research and audit skills. There is a shortage of training posts for Addiction Psychiatrists, suggesting that addiction is an unpopular speciality within psychiatry (see Royal College of Psychiatrists, 1997).

In addition to the training required for those who will specialise in the field, there is a need for training in the recognition of alcohol related problems and their management. Those requiring such experience would include workers in education, police officers, marriage and other counsellors, occupational therapists, prison staff and a variety of other professions who encounter individuals whose problems may have been engendered by their own or others' drinking. Occupational Health and Alcohol in Employment policies are a further area where training is essential. A number of attempts have also been made to train bar managers and other staff in the hospitality industry who are particularly well placed to advise about sensible drinking habits and to deal with and reduce the harm caused by intoxication. The extent to which the attainment of specific competencies is required in the training of these groups varies enormously. It would be beneficial if relevant standards could be established for both the qualifying and post-qualifying training in these areas.

It is now much more likely that specialist agencies will require applicants for employment to have specialist qualifications and purchasers may demand these as part of their contracts. Standardisation of specialist training would enable employers and purchasers of training to stipulate the level and nature of qualification with a far greater degree of confidence in what they would be getting.

Evaluation of Training

Evaluation of training methods and programmes in the UK addiction field is not often reported in the literature. There has been a dearth of funds to conduct such evaluations and until the recent requirements of validation and accreditation, few purchasers of training seemed concerned with stipulating any requirements of programme evaluation.

Award-making bodies require institutions providing training to evaluate their training in a number of ways. At the most basic level there is a requirement to evaluate the delivery of training; this process is perhaps more akin to an audit process than a true evaluation. It will commence with asking about the publicity of the course, whether it contained sufficient information and was adequate to the task of enabling a decision on the suitability of the training, whether entry requirements, expectations of participants such as time commitments and private study requirements were made clear, and whether venue and provision of resources were adequately described.

A component of the delivery of training will be a customer satisfaction survey which will focus upon questions of whether participants felt that the training met their expectations and needs; whether the learning resources, including the teaching staff, were adequate, and whether they felt they had learnt anything. Despite numerous studies questioning the validity of such self-report (Yancey and Kelly, 1990), it appears to remain one of the more common forms of evaluation. For example, it is routinely required by Post-graduate Medical Education departments where examination of post-qualification trainees is not the norm.

At the next level, evaluation focuses on the question of whether students have learnt the material they have been taught. This level of evaluation requires examination of the students' knowledge and/or skills, but it also requires audit of the methods by which they have been taught and examined. Review of the composite outcomes for students reveals whether the examination is appropriate to the level and material taught as well as demonstrating for each student whether he or she has become a competent and knowledgable practitioner.

At the most sophisticated level, evaluation asks whether the training has resulted in any benefit for the patient or client. As the responsibility for this level of evaluation often rests with the employing agencies in that the evaluation of client outcomes would be in their domain, it is more difficult to require it as a component of training. An example of this level of evaluation is demonstrated in a recent multi-centre trial of alcohol treatment in the US (Project MATCH Research Group, 1997). In preliminary reports, the unusually good outcomes reported are attributed to the quality of the treatments and their delivery. This in turn is attributable to the methods used in the design of the treatments, the selection and training of therapists and the maintenance of standards of treatment delivery. The monitoring of therapists throughout their training and the delivery of the treatments ensured that the treatments were delivered as designed and individual differences between therapists' behaviours were minimised. Treatments were precisely specified for number and duration of sessions, likely effective components and nature of delivery. Protocols were provided in manual form. The therapists were allowed to practise only when they had completed the initial training and demonstrated their competence by video-recorded practice. They were required to continue to demonstrate their competence throughout the trial by the continuing video-recorded assessment of their practice, so that by the end of the study it was possible to say that the treatments had been delivered as prescribed and that the therapists were competent in the treatment they had been taught. The client outcomes were then assessed. The Project MATCH results are evidence that methods described for therapist selection, centralised therapist training and continuing monitoring of treatment delivery (Carroll, 1994) are effective in minimising therapist variability and enhance the generalisability of results.

There is a marked absence of reports in the literature on the routine evaluation of training, and it would be difficult to describe the methods used in the Project MATCH study as suitable for routine use. Much of the evaluation of training emanates from the findings of specifically funded studies and demonstrates a depressingly consistent finding on the outcomes of brief training courses in alcohol misuse, namely that many courses had little effect on attitudes and behaviour, although in some cases an increase in knowledge was able to be demonstrated (Gorman, 1993). A study conducted by Rychtarik (1990) of alcohol training in South East England showed that while there was little evidence of change in knowledge and attitudes during a Diploma course in Alcohol Counselling, there was evidence of a number of changes in behaviour and a perceived growth in student maturity, confidence and role security.

The reason postulated by Gorman (1993) for the failure of evaluation initiatives to identify positive outcomes for training is that the implementation and evaluation of training (and therefore the scope for its development and evolution) has, in the main, not been theory driven. Rather than pursue the simple input/output method normally associated with summative assessment, he advocates examination of the processes involved at each stage of a sequential and interactive relationship between theory, research and implementation. Citing the model developed by Tober and Raistrick (1990) as an example of the way in which theory might generate some hypotheses regarding predisposing therapist characteristics to be measured, and his own work with Cartwright (Cartwright and Gorman, 1993) which explores the processes of developing therapeutic commitment, he proposes a method of evaluation which takes account of all the variables contributing to the outcome. Findings regarding the outcomes of training will be used to develop the theory further. In this way, argues Gorman, the repeated testing of the same model is avoided. Simply put, progress is made in the design and delivery of training so that improvements may be achieved.

The evaluation of training and the assessment of students varies markedly from one course to the next, not least because even the national validating bodies do not require the same assessment methods to be used. Different universities require different assessments. Thus, some universities require assessment by unseen paper as well as other methods, some require only one form of assessment such as the long essay or dissertation. Not all require students' practice to be examined by a panel of examiners in the way that written work might be. These broad discrepancies, coupled with a lack of universal specification of competencies at the outset, result in a situation where it is difficult to assume the nature of the competencies which have been achieved as a result of gaining a particular qualification.

The Requirement for Trained Practitioners

In the study conducted by Rychtarik (1990), a survey of senior administrators in Health and Social Services in London and the South East of England demonstrated the belief that the majority of clients with alcohol problems were not detected, and a lack of resources to provide satisfactory training schemes was among the principal reasons cited. Only a minority of agencies provided secondary-level training of any sort, and the majority placed alcohol problems at the bottom of their list of priorities for training and, by implication, for services overall.

It is hard to know if this situation was universal, and it may have changed as a result of recent developments. The *Health of the Nation* targets and the government White Paper *Tackling Drugs Together* (DoH, 1995a) gave addiction problems a higher profile and a greater sense of priority. Training purchasers began to write into contracts the requirement for employing staff with recognised qualifications. The Royal College of Psychiatrists has established a Faculty of Substance Misuse giving credibility and training criteria to the specialism. Specialist senior registrar posts will ensure a higher standard of training for psychiatrists at the outset of their addiction careers. It is possible that training in the management of alcohol problems has been given greater prominence by the expression of a need for training in the management of drug problems; it is equally possible that, once again, the former has been sidelined by the latter.

Summary of Main Arguments

- There has been a lack of consensus over the required knowledge and skills to be taught both to different professional groups and to specialist practitioners. There is now sufficient evidence for skills and practices to be agreed.

- There is a lack of coordination of curriculum input on alcohol problems at national level; professional bodies exist at the national level to instigate such coordination.
- The outcomes of training are currently not subject to any universally agreed evaluation criteria; it is difficult to know whether training has resulted in new behaviour where it has occurred. Established methods of assessment of trainees' knowledge and practice give a good indication of the quality of training and the meaning of qualifications.
- To date, training strategy initiatives have remained uncoordinated and unadopted. Best practice in strategy development requires a broad base of authority for its adoption. The power to influence purchasing bodies and professional validating bodies needs to be identified for the adoption of a consistent training strategy.

Part IV

A Systems Approach to Policy

12
The Policy Mix

The preceding chapters have made clear that the need for a coherent alcohol policy is not solely an academic question, it is something that is of vital concern to all of us. Alcohol related problems are a drain on the human and economic resources of the country and impoverish the quality of the environment. As frequently mentioned throughout this book, alcohol also has positive benefits in these domains. It is, therefore, a question of balance and weight, but, for the reasons explained in the opening chapters, policy cannot be left to *laissez-faire* commercialism alone when the economy and public health are so clearly implicated.

We have also seen that government, both local and national, plays a crucial part in weighing the balance for good or ill. This is determined by the emphasis which they place on relevant legislation, taxation, trade, education, treatment and rehabilitation. All of these areas involve choices, investment and commitment. The debate about policy needs to be joined by those who have special interests or concerns but it also needs to be influenced by the scientific evidence which has been collected in this book. Although the emphasis here has been on science and, where possible, the presentation of statistical data, this must not allow the debate to become detached from the images of everyday experience. It is important to bear in mind the human face as well as the community interest: the lifetime facial scars of a drunken attack, the years of nursing and homecare devoted to the victim of a drink driving accident, family lives ruined by excessive drinking, and so on. The efforts of families, communities and other agencies to minimise alcohol related harm are profoundly affected by policy decisions made by government at a national level.

We recognise that these solutions to local policy issues may seem easy when the problem is tackled from a single narrow viewpoint. In the real world, social policy is about balancing conflicting costs and benefits in society as a whole. The main purpose of this chapter is to define the key elements that should comprise a national alcohol policy. The policy mix will be considered under the following headings:

- the rationale of the policy mix
- policy objectives and strategies
- policy organisation and monitoring
- putting it all together.

The Rationale of the Policy Mix

Simple and Cohesive

In Chapter 2 we noted that the drinks producers and distributors, alcohol researchers, and those people working in treatment or prevention areas all represent vested interests. All of these parties have responsibilities which we believe should be made explicit and we consider a national alcohol policy as the most effective way to achieve this goal. We consider a national policy to be the preferred vehicle to reconcile the inevitable tension between the aspirations of the drinks industry to increase profits with the aspirations of the health and social care lobby to minimise alcohol related harms. It may be that a policy is insufficient to achieve the desired regulation but we believe that a clear statement on the perceived benefits and costs of alcohol in society today is, of itself, a powerful influence and a prerequisite to any supplementary legal controls that might be deemed necessary at a later date.

In Chapter 2 we also made reference to the national drugs strategy. There may be good reason for cynicism regarding the enthusiasm of the public and professionals alike to welcome an increasingly restrictive drugs policy while maintaining ambivalence towards an alcohol policy, but there is much that can be borrowed from the drugs strategy. For example, the six strategy principles described in *Tackling Drugs to Build a Better Britain* (Home Office, 1998, p. 11) apply equally well to alcohol policy:

- integration of social policy issues
- evidence-based measures
- joint action
- consistency of action
- effective communication of policy
- accountability.

Government thinking in the late 1990s has been conducive to setting up a national alcohol policy. It has been a time when the broad thrust of social policy is about balancing rights and responsibilities. *Commissioning in the New*

NHS (National Health Service Executive, 1998) emphasises delivering quality care from the health service and an insistence on effective clinical governance: presumably these same principles should also be welcomed in social care services and the criminal justice system. An implication of this new thinking is a refocusing of effort on building and strengthening local communities. Once again, much can be borrowed from the illicit drugs field where ideas about the prevention of problems at a community level are already well advanced. The report *Drug Misuse and the Environment* (Advisory Council on the Misuse of Drugs, 1998) brings together a comprehensive range of community actions, some of which are specific to illicit drugs and many of which have a more general application to problems related to alcohol or other drugs. One aspect of joint action, therefore, is for the 'drugs' and 'alcohol' fields to learn from each other.

Our preferred model is the Community Systems approach to alcohol prevention described in Chapter 2 which at one and the same time captures the enormous complexity of the use and misuse of alcohol within society and reduces this to a relatively simple and comprehensible model (see Fig 2.1). Of course, a model is an oversimplified view of reality, but an evidence-based representation of a community, such as the dynamic computer modelling capability of SimCom (Holder, 1998, pp. 147–53) provides a framework within which to formulate policy. Furthermore, a tool such as SimCom frees policy makers from attempting to familiarise themselves with technical research reports on a whole range of prevention and treatment subjects and allows the policy maker to anticipate at community level some of the consequences of following particular policy pathways.

Consistency

It is inevitable that the emphasis on different elements of policy will change as the political landscape changes, but we believe that the long-term view should be applied to some key benchmarks. Equally, information systems should be controlled by independent advisory groups and not politicians or others with vested interests. We believe that per capita consumption and safe limits are of such importance that they merit careful and consistent presentations.

First, we have argued in Chapter 5 that per capita consumption of alcohol is a valid surrogate measure of a variety of health and social alcohol related harms. It follows that the significance of per capita consumption should be given sufficient expression in national policy promotion. Resources need to be allocated to ensure the accurate estimation and independent reporting of annual per capita consumption figures. Marked variations in per capita consumption can occur over a short time-span, following the ups and downs of the economy, but the trends that occur over decades say more of cultural shifts.

The importance attached to monitoring per capita consumption does not imply that regulation of per capita consumption should be the only, or principal strategy for preventing alcohol related problems; none the less, the importance of population level measures needs to be understood by policy makers.

Second, the matter of what are regarded to be safe drinking levels needs to be clearly and authoritatively disseminated. The idea of safe limits allows for a simple and helpful health promotion message which has achieved some limited recognition, at least among social drinkers. Individual level risks from drinking are discussed in Chapter 5; suffice it to say that a joint review of safe limits by the Royal Colleges of Psychiatrists, Physicians and General Practitioners (1995) concluded that the weekly alcohol intake of 21 units for men and 14 units for women should remain unchanged. The report *Sensible Drinking* (DoH, 1995b, p. 32) states that 'a regular consumption of between 3 and 4 units a day by men and 2 and 3 units by women will not accrue any significant health risk'. These recommendations appear to increase the safe limits to 28 units for men and 21 units for women when multiplied up to weekly amounts, and this interpretation was widely disseminated in the media. Confusingly, the report goes on to say that consistently drinking 4 or more units a day by men and 3 or more units a day by women is not advised as this carries a 'progressive health risk'. In reality, many social drinkers consume all their weekly units of alcohol on one or two drinking occasions and the daily allowance of units is seen to be more prescriptive than a weekly allowance. We have concluded that *Sensible Drinking* is a sophisticated analysis of the evidence but that the interpretation of the evidence and the switch to daily safe limits has been unhelpful. The use of weekly safe limits does not preclude the use of messages targeted at high-risk behaviours, such as drinking and driving, drinking and outdoor sports, or drinking during pregnancy.

Policy Objectives and Strategies

The overarching aim of a national policy is to minimise the harmful consequences of alcohol use while preserving the beneficial aspects of drinking. For a national alcohol policy to capture the imagination of policy makers, professionals and the general public it must have a manageable number of clearly stated, achievable objectives. We have selected just four, albeit that each has quite broad scope. We have proposed that each policy objective be driven by strategies, each of which is sufficiently cohesive that lead responsibility can be allocated to a single government department, national agency or more locally based authority. Examples of policy measures put into practice are detailed in Chapter 13.

Policy Objective One – To Increase Public Information and Debate about Alcohol

There are four key proposals to support this objective.

i) Create a national and local structure to coordinate action on alcohol. The chosen structure needs to be led at ministerial level.
ii) Funding to ensure the availability of statistical information, surveys and research. Research needs to meet the Culyer Committee requirements of producing definitive answers within planned programmes of investigation.
iii) Promulgate a simple safe limits message supported by labelling of alcohol content of drinks.
iv) Designated people at national and local levels to develop the skills of media advocacy and build positive media relations.

Strategy One – Public health Promotion Campaigns Linked to Encouragement of Local Action

Agencies such as the Health Education Authority, Health Education Board in Scotland or Health Promotion Wales would be expected to take a lead role on this strategy, but it would be important to build partnerships that can deliver local action to coincide with centrally coordinated mass media campaigns.

Strategy Two – Working with the Media to Ensure Accurate Reporting of Alcohol Issues and Encourage Public Debate

A central Alcohol Policy Coordinating Unit would probably claim the right to own this strategy, but an independent agency such as Alcohol Concern might be more proactive and adhere more innovatively to the spirit of the strategy. The regional network of Alcohol Concern lends itself to coordinating active public debate.

Policy Objective Two – To Encourage the Drinks and Leisure Industries to Introduce Innovative Schemes to Discourage 'Drunkenness'

There are four key proposals to support this objective.

i) Extend the role of drug action teams to include alcohol and be responsible for community action.
ii) Evidence-based reform of the licensing regulations to harmonise national and local controls. Licensing should include criteria of need and monitoring of untoward incidents associated with licensed premises.
iii) Licensing should require server training and seek to agree a fair system of server liability with the drinks trade.

iv) Set priorities for local enforcement schemes including those based on incident monitoring.

Strategy Three – Innovation to Encourage Safer Drinking Environments

The drinks and leisure industries are well able to develop their business, but what is needed is encouragement and commitment to developments within the intentions of the alcohol strategy, perhaps through formal controls. Providing family areas in pubs or ensuring public transport to service pubs in the late evening are two examples.

Strategy Four – Enforcement of Legislation and Agreements with Automatic Sanctions for Transgressions

Local police action in partnership with licensing magistrates, town planners and representatives of the trade would be one way of leading on this strategy.

Policy Objective Three – To Maximise Community and Domestic Safety

There are four key proposals to support this objective.

i)   Zero tolerance of domestic violence. This requires local schemes that enable the immediate removal of violent drinkers from the home into treatment programmes backed by legal sanctions.
ii) Reduce prescribed limit for drinking and driving to a blood alcohol level of 50 mg%. There should be harmonisation of drink driving laws across Europe. Appraisal of vehicle immobilisers should be undertaken as a medium-term strategy.
iii) Increase the age limit for selected drinking related activities.
iv) Incentives and support for employers to develop workplace policies and employee assistance programmes.

Strategy Five – Take Action to Prevent and Reduce Accidents and Other Untoward Incidents Related to Drinking

National campaigns would be the backdrop to action which would be mainly local and coordinated through the Drug Action Teams or their alcohol equivalents. Public support against drinking and driving needs to be extended to other behaviours where drinking causes unacceptable risks or nuisance.

Strategy Six – Take Action to Prevent and Reduce Violence or Nuisance Related to Drinking

The national legislation required to implement this strategy is already in place. What is needed is collaboration between local police, social services and probation services backed by a commitment from the Drug Action Teams or their alcohol equivalent to take action. Intolerance of intoxication leading to violence needs to permeate our culture.

Policy Objective Four – To Reduce Alcohol Related Health Problems Below 1990 Indicator Levels

There are four key proposals to support this objective.

i) Fiscal measures to maintain per capita consumption below 8 litres of absolute alcohol. These measures should be declared in the Chancellor's annual budget statement.
ii) Establish a network of addiction training centres and accredited courses. Training is a prerequisite if services are to match their potential as described in this review of treatment outcome research.
iii) Create incentives for generic services to become effective at delivering minimal interventions. Efforts need to extend beyond primary health care into social services, probation and others.
iv) Ensure that equal access to specialist NHS units is available in all health authority districts. Specialist services need to be of a standard not only to deliver more complex treatment, but also to undertake research and contribute to training and policy initiatives.

Strategy Seven – Maintain Per Capita Consumption at or Below 1990 levels

Once commitment is achieved, implementation of this strategy is ultimately a technical, Treasury exercise. If other measures to contain consumption fail then government can deploy fiscal measures to bring per capita consumption down to predetermined levels. Also implied is concurrent public education to create a climate of understanding that would make such measures practical and acceptable.

Strategy Eight – Implement a Comprehensive Health Service Response to Alcohol Problems

It is expected that the Department of Health, which already has mechanisms for influencing and monitoring treatment services, would continue to take the lead role for this strategy. It is important that funding arrangements reflect the broad remit of specialist services within a health district.

Policy Organisation and Monitoring

National and Local Coordination

There is no evidence base to inform the organisational requirements for implementing a national alcohol policy. We have argued that there are sufficient commonalities between drinking, cigarette smoking, and the use of illicit drugs for there to be similar policies relating to all psychoactive drugs. Equally, we recognise that in the medium term alcohol will be considered as a social policy issue which is seen to be separate from other drugs. It is the business of government to reflect its values in the institutions it creates and it makes sense that the structures for implementing alcohol policy should mirror those that already exist for implementing illicit drugs policy. In the absence of an evidence base to inform decisions about structure we commend five principles which in turn imply five tiers of organisation:

1. *Central coordination.* A national alcohol policy requires cooperation across government departments. There is no one department that should obviously take the lead role and we believe, therefore, that a Central Alcohol Coordinating Unit should be established. The Central Alcohol Coordinating Unit would need to have the status of a Cabinet Office base or the equivalent and be headed by someone from outside the civil service in like manner to the appointment of the UK Anti-Drugs Coordinator, commonly known as the 'Drugs Czar'. An Alcohol Policy Coordinator would have responsibility for drawing up a ten-year strategy and monitoring progress on the implementation of strategy.

2. *Quality assurance.* A Central Alcohol Coordinating Unit would not be in a position to define quality standards or the audit requirements of agencies involved in delivering a national policy. There would need to be a two-way interaction between the office handling central coordination and a variety of quality-setting organisations. For example, in England, the National Institute of Clinical Excellence will need to be involved in setting clinical health care standards; the Substance Misuse Advisory Service will need to be involved in standards of commissioning, and Alcohol Concern is likely to continue to set standards for non-statutory service providers. It is not clear how quality in social care and the criminal justice system will be determined in the future. The need for training has been identified repeatedly: again, there needs to be a two-way discussion between the Alcohol Policy Coordinator, the Royal Colleges and other accredited training organisations.

3. *An independent advisory group.* There is value in having an independent advisory group which can bring together a range of expertise and tackle new problems in an informed and dispassionate way. The Advisory Council on the Misuse of Drugs fulfils this role for illicit drugs. An Advisory Council on Alcohol could formally be constituted to advise ministers, but in so doing would also advise the Central Alcohol Coordinating Unit and thereby impose checks and balances on the Unit.

4. *Local coordination.* The network of Drug Action Teams is now well established. The idea of having teams that are empowered to make executive

decisions is a good one and to be commended as a means of coordinating alcohol strategy. The effectiveness of Drug Action Teams has not been formally investigated, but anecdotally some are said to function extremely well while others struggle against inertia or internal political hostilities. It makes perfect sense that Drug Action Teams should become Drug and Alcohol Action Teams as they are in Wales, and in order to ensure that the balance between the needs of the alcohol and drugs strategies were maintained, the Teams would need to be supported by separate local alcohol and drugs coordinators.

5. *Local representation.* There is a difficulty that the people making up Drug Action Teams and other commissioning groups are not necessarily knowledgeable about alcohol or other drug problems. We believe, therefore, that, in addition to receiving strong guidance from the Substance Misuse Advisory Service or an equivalent body, a Drug and Alcohol Action Team should be required to meet at least annually with local providers and discuss broad strategy issues. The existing drug reference groups can readily adapt to become Drug and Alcohol Reference Groups. Equally, a local Alcohol Action Group could avoid dominance by professionals and play a crucial role in making city centre and community initiatives work.

Putting it all Together

A national alcohol policy is not so much about introducing new ideas that will dramatically change how we deal with alcohol and alcohol related problems, but it is to do with setting out some clear direction and engaging all the key stakeholders in achieving policy objectives. Experience from the national drugs policy suggests that even a well publicised and well supported policy document does not necessarily bring about change; for example, there has been minimal change in prescribing practice for drug users (Strang and Sheridan, 1998) following publication of the policy. In this chapter we have suggested four primary objectives, sixteen key measures and eight strategies to support those objectives. It is difficult to see that there could be serious objection to either the objectives or the strategies; rather, it will be implementation of policy that is the more controversial.

Many of the ingredients that will be needed to make the policy happen are already in place. Our cultural ambivalence towards alcohol, which has been mentioned many times throughout this book, may, however, have the capacity to dissipate the energy generated by a national policy. In order to protect against this we have proposed a lead agency or government department for each of the eight proposed strategies and in order to drive the strategies forward we have proposed a lead Cabinet Minister or, alternatively, an 'Alcohol Czar'.

A new challenge is to find ways of keeping frontline agencies enthused: there is a need to include, but also go beyond, financial incentives.

In this book we have drawn together evidence to inform a national alcohol policy. The alcohol and alcohol problems knowledge base is enormous and unequivocal on many important policy issues. Absorbing and interpreting this knowledge is not a task that can be expected from commissioners and it follows that commissioners should be provided with suitable guidance, which may take the form of expert opinion or may be centrally prepared documentation. We believe that the alcohol field is informed by a very strong evidence base on what works, and, in many areas, can show not only what is effective but also what is cost-effective.

13
Policy in Practice

In this final chapter we bring together some examples of the specific actions that can be taken in support of policy. It would be impractical and unduly prescriptive to attempt a comprehensive listing of the specific measures required to achieve the primary policy objectives, and the evidence base to inform ideas for action is contained in previous sections. The policy 'tools' that we describe here are intended to give a flavour of the diversity of action envisaged: each tool has a very different history and has been written as an exemplar of thinking around a subject area. Each tool is accompanied by comments on acceptability, resources required, and methods of audit.

We have argued that the implementation of a national alcohol policy is everyone's business and policy tools are therefore a mixed bag: a minister needs different tools from the magistrate, a policeman needs different tools from the publican. For reasons of clarity we have regarded each policy tool as having its main, direct effect on one sub-system within the Community Systems Model (see Fig 13.1) but, of course, the secondary effects on other sub-systems are all important. The examples of policy in practice that we discuss are divided in accordance with the subsystems of the Community Systems Model:

- Consumption subsystem
- Social Norms subsystem
- Alcohol Sales and Production subsystem
- Formal Controls subsystem
- Legal Sanctions subsystem.

Consumption Subsystem

Taxation

UK taxes are levied at different rates and in different forms for different beverages, but the specific element of the tax is in the form of a monetary

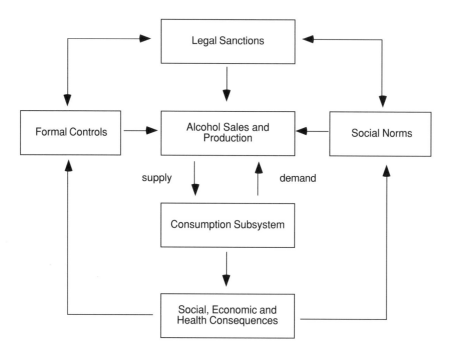

Source: Adapted from Holder (1998, p. 22).

Figure 13.1   Conceptual Community Systems Model for alcohol use

amount for a given quantity. With inflation the real value of these specific duties falls over time and, in consequence, consumption and problems increase.

The government has an opportunity to change duty rates in each annual budget. However, these changes have to be within the current EU policy of minimum rates, agreed structures and comparability of rates between like products such as beer and wine. The UK government has stated that health arguments are one of the factors taken into consideration when setting alcohol duties. These arguments should be strengthened to underpin a more active policy, revisited at each budget, which also acknowledges the wider social harms associated with alcohol.

Acceptability? Using taxes to control smoking has gained broad acceptability from both non-smokers and smokers. The case for alcohol is potentially stronger in that alcohol causes considerable problems to third parties as well as to the drinker themselves. Industrial lobbying has campaigned for tax cuts to reduce smuggling and cross-border shopping. However, cutting taxes can have a number of adverse effects including an overall further loss in revenue. As with smoking, the policy response should include tightened controls on organised smuggling and lobbying within Europe to reconsider the current indicative limits on personal alcohol use.

Resources? Given the annual budget mechanisms there is little additional cost to the government of changing tax rates. Clearly there are some resources required in the retail trade to change prices of goods on the shelves, but such changes regularly occur for other reasons. Additional controls to discourage smuggling will require resources, but these may be recouped from revenue gain.

Audit? The impact of tax changes can be monitored by the type of economic analysis described in Chapter 6. The data on taxes, price, income and alcohol consumption are readily available through government sources.

Price Controls

Taxes are only one component of price; tax levels are low enough for manufacturers and retailers to have considerable influence on the prices faced by consumers. For beer the action of the industry has raised prices far above those generated by any tax change. No doubt these price increases were designed to maximise profit, but they will also have had the effect of curtailing consumption. However, some trade practices on prices have the potential to cause damaging consequences. In particular, 'happy hour' reductions or reduced prices for some groups of the population may encourage binge drinking. It is important to monitor the conditions of sale of alcohol in a local context and these aspects of price control may need to be part of broader licensing controls.

Acceptability? Clearly, manufacturers and retailers are competing for business and price is one mechanism for attracting customers. However, there is a need for responsibility among retailers in marketing what is a potentially dangerous product.

Resources? Some resources are required to monitor local practices and to ensure that these adhere to local alcohol policy.

Audit? Local action groups could monitor the marketing of alcohol, including price, in their district. These data could be combined with crime audits to pinpoint areas which may cause concern.

Harmonisation in Europe

The EU has influenced UK tax policy and does limit the government in devising policies. For example, even where a product can be shown to be producing specific harm, individual governments cannot impose specific health related tax as this is considered to be contravening European competition policy. Currently there is no policy to move towards further harmonisation of tax duties across Europe, although this issue is raised periodically by European commentators. Changes in tax policy require unanimous agreement of the member states. It is important, therefore, that the significant role of tax changes in changing levels of alcohol problems is recognised at both national and

European level. Some increase in competence of the EU to consider public health impacts of policy is part of the Amsterdam Treaty.

Acceptability? Harmonisation within Europe is increasingly acceptable to the general public. The usefulness to a UK national policy depends upon maintaining the real cost of alcohol.

Resources? There are no resource implications as the mechanism for this already exists.

Audit? The price of different beverages should be monitored across EU member states.

Social Norms Subsystem

Media Advocacy

The development of realistic socially acceptable norms is a key factor in reducing alcohol related harm. Particularly important are strict norms for drinking in certain contexts, such as when using equipment, when diving or swimming, or when driving. A media advocacy approach, described by Wallack (1994, p. 420) as the 'strategic use of mass media to advance public policy initiatives' can be taken at the local level in order to establish community awareness, norms and support for local prevention strategies.

Successful media advocacy requires the existence of a particular policy objective as well as awareness of and support for this objective within the community and on the part of key decision makers. This may be achieved by providing local data which highlight the extent of alcohol related problems – figures on drink driving casualties, for example – and encouraging the media to make use of this in creating local news programmes or documentaries. As well as having an influence on public opinion and on community leaders, this can also serve as a lightning conductor for enthusiasm; the associated publicity may help to motivate community coalitions as well as key decision makers, and provide local project staff with a sense of efficacy and the potential for change

Such media campaigns may also be used to increase public perception of the risk of detection if a law is broken – by selling alcohol to minors, by serving intoxicated customers or by driving whilst intoxicated, for example.

Acceptability? High. The media are generally keen to publicise local data and innovative ideas.

Resources? The main investment would be the cost of training in media advocacy.

Audit? Levels of media coverage of particular issues can be readily measured; Holder and Treno (1997) have developed a very useful composite news score for this purpose. The impact of such coverage on behaviour change is notoriously difficult to measure, although trends in data relating to policy objectives might be monitored and compared with data on levels of media coverage.

School-based Education

In developing a school-based prevention initiative a number of considerations need to be taken into account. First, there is no strong evidence that any particular approach effectively reduces alcohol consumption or risk drinking. Second, young drinkers are the ones most likely to be absent from school and less likely to pay attention to alcohol education messages; those who could benefit the most are the least likely to be influenced. Third, an alcohol education programme can only take up a small amount of classroom time, so exposure will be limited. Finally, an environment which encourages excessive or risk drinking will, to a large extent, counteract any beneficial effects of an alcohol education programme. New school-based initiatives therefore need to be evaluated and only relatively brief interventions should be implemented unless and until longer programmes are proved to be effective.

One of the ethical principles of the *European Charter on Alcohol* is: 'All people have the right to valid, impartial information and education, starting early in life, on the consequences of alcohol consumption on health, the family and society' (WHO, 1995a). Until we have clear evidence that behaviour can be changed by a more intensive psychosocial programme, the objective should be to ensure that information on the effects of alcohol is communicated in a brief but memorable way.

Acceptability? School-based programmes are not only acceptable but are often implemented with enthusiasm, even when there is no evidence of effectiveness.

Resources? Resources are not needed for lengthy school-based programmes. Rather, the many programmes being initiated by teachers and health promotion departments need to be integrated within the curriculum. There needs to be regular updating of teachers' resource packs.

Audit? Since we need more evidence relating to the effectiveness of school-based initiatives, any new developments should be linked to a national, coordinated research programme.

Workplace Policies

Certain occupational groups are more at risk of alcohol problems than others and particular efforts need to be made in these settings to minimise access to alcohol and harmful consequences. The workplace is also an excellent location for the delivery of alcohol prevention programmes and early intervention to help the drinking employee before his or her problems cause accidents or disruption to him- or herself and others.

In high-risk occupations, where other employees or the public may be put in danger, there is a case for compulsory checks to ensure that employees are fit to work. There is also a case for all work environments to be supportive of abstinence from alcohol, and other drugs, in and around the workplace. Health and Safety legislation alone is insufficient to create a non-drinking ethos; rather, there is a need for regular education programmes backed by supportive measures such as alcohol-free canteens or removing alcohol from workplace hospitality. Workplace policies can have a powerful effect on reducing accidents and preventing excessive drinking.

Several studies have shown that light social drinkers have some protection against workplace stresses such as poor relationships with supervisors, a poor working environment, and excessive workload – both abstainers and heavier drinkers are more likely to take sickness absence (Vasse *et al.*, 1998). There is therefore a direct incentive for employers to minimise stress at work. Some organisations have Employee Assistance Programmes available but most smaller companies will need to contract out. Agencies undertaking workplace counselling should have very clear guidelines in forming the relationship with the employer and employee.

Acceptability? High. Most people prefer not to work with colleagues who are regularly intoxicated, and particularly so if this results in a reduction in the effectiveness of a team or in putting others at risk.

Resources? There are costs to the employer of maintaining a healthy workplace, but investment in this area would be repaid by work performance. The costs of individual treatment by any outside agency may be high, but the number of cases should be low.

Audit? Uptake of training opportunities and the use of Employee Assistance Programmes can be monitored and evaluated. All serious incidents and sickness absences can be similarly monitored. Specially agreed arrangements should be in place for checks on employees in high-risk occupations.

Public Information

Public information is an essential element in any strategy which aims to influence the behaviours which lead to alcohol related harm. Evidence suggests that there are major gaps in public knowledge about safe drinking levels and the consequences of misuse. Confusion as to the impact of alcohol has sometimes in the past been fed by complex and apparently shifting health promotion messages. These have struggled to make an impression alongside the uncomplicated wholly positive images of alcohol in which the alcohol industry invests its advertising budget. General media portrayals of drinking also tend to focus on positive aspects (Ministerial Group on Alcohol Misuse,1989).

Publicity campaigns will be a key tool in addressing social norms. Evaluations of health education campaigns have shown that, on their own, they are more successful in building knowledge than in changing behaviour; however, they are shown to be effective when allied to specific actions designed to target particular types of behaviour. Conversely, campaigns of action to address specific situations such as drink driving require the back-up of publicity to render them effective. A consistent message about safe or sensible drinking levels, promulgated in associated with campaigns providing information about the health and antisocial consequences of misuse and about action to reduce harm, might be the aim of a national mass media campaign.

Acceptability? High. If seen to provide the basis for informed choice rather than to attempt to dictate behaviour, except in areas where there is demonstrable risk of harm to others, such as drink driving, domestic violence, and so on.

Resources? Significant resources are required to mount a mass media campaign including the back-up of locally useable materials. Some degree of national and local coordination is needed to ensure that campaigns achieve maximum impact.

Audit? The impact of campaigns can be measured against their individual objectives, whether in terms of knowledge or behaviour. Limited baseline data currently exist and these could be collected in advance of and following any new campaigns.

Safe Limits and Labelling

Over the last decade the UK generally accepted that enhanced public information and knowledge about alcohol requires some form of benchmark against which individuals can set their own drinking in order to assess their level of risk and regulate their intake. This takes the form of identifying safe, or sensible, levels for individual consumption in terms of units of alcohol. This approach requires an awareness by the public not just of the recommended levels, but also of the risks associated with exceeding them on a regular basis. It also, crucially, relies on an understanding of the alcohol content of drinks as measured in units. Whereas this information can be included in general messages about sensible drinking, the calculation required is increasingly complicated by the proliferation of different drinks available and the range and variety of their strengths measured in alcohol by volume (abv). An important element therefore of the safe or sensible drinking approach has to be the provision of information at the point of sale about the number of units contained in the given measure of that particular drink.

Acceptability? High. There is broad consensus on the acceptability of the safe levels approach, although not necessarily on the details of its expression. Most of the key players in the alcohol industry have recently agreed to adopt a voluntary system of unit labelling, and the introduction of such labelling in Australia gained public and political support (see Stockwell, 1993).

Resources? The only resources required are those identified as part of a public information campaign. While there may be some transitional costs for the industry in adjusting the labelling of products, in the long-term these measures are cost-neutral.

Audit? These measures in themselves do not offer themselves for audit, rather being subject to the audit of the impact of public information campaigns and the resources invested in them. There could be occasional surveys of public knowledge about the units of alcohol contained in different drinks.

Alcohol Sales and Production Subsystem

Community Action

Community action engages different elements of community life in responding to alcohol related issues at a local level. It has the advantage of being based on local evidence and experience, but is often most effective when local action is allied with a national or regional alcohol strategy. Problems associated with the use of alcohol manifest themselves in many different spheres of community life. The very breadth of these problems shows clearly that many sectors will already be dealing with them knowingly or otherwise. One primary objective of a community alcohol action plan is to identify those sectors of community life which are currently working with problem drinkers or experiencing the social and economic cost due to alcohol problems and to help them collaborate in a concerted plan of action.

One promising approach to advancing an action plan is to form an Alcohol Action Group. This involves gaining interest and commitment from many partners including health, social welfare, education and youth services, the media, the police and criminal justice system, licensing authorities, recreation, tourism and commercial organisations, voluntary agencies, and employers and employee groups. One of their first tasks will be to raise awareness about the role alcohol plays in the community and to build a network of understanding between groups and individuals involved with and concerned about alcohol policy at the local level. It helps if the group is formally assigned responsibility and authority by local government and the alcohol action plan has a place within municipal planning structures. Political support is important and wherever possible should be reinforced by resolutions committing the local authority to enacting and evaluating the alcohol action plan. Examples of the approach described above are to be found in the WHO regional publication *Community and Municipal Action on Alcohol* (Ritson, 1996).

Acceptability? High. It is directly within the spirit of communitarianism and has the advantage of focusing on local concerns. Problems may arise from the competing interests of, for instance, licensees and those concerned with public order.

Resources? Local coordination of existing resources. Individual projects will require specific funding which will normally be non-recurrent.

Audit? Indicators should be locally based and collected, and sensitive to local alcohol problem 'hot spots' – for example, public order offences related to drunkenness and under-age drinking. Police might monitor the percentage of their work time that is devoted to alcohol related problems, and A & E departments could monitor alcohol related attendances. For examples of programme evaluation in Europe, see Holmila (1997) or Hannibal *et al.* (1995).

Server Training

Many of the controls and preventative measures adopted to reduce alcohol related harm place a burden of responsibility on those whose job it is to serve drinks in bars and off-licences. Important skills are required in order to preserve a peaceful and safe environment when, for example, refusing service to those who, by virtue of age or intoxication, are not legally entitled to purchase alcohol; or when defusing, or preferably pre-empting, situations which could lead to aggression or other forms of potentially harmful behaviour. These skills need to be backed up by an awareness and understanding of the ways in which alcohol acts upon the mind and the body.

Training for staff in licensed premises can be delivered locally to a nationally identified curriculum and guidelines by a range of providers. Given the traditionally high turnover of bar staff and the costs to the licensee of releasing staff for training, it would be advantageous if such training were to form part of a broader framework of accreditation in order to encourage both participation and the development of greater quality and experience by locating the role in some form of wider career structure.

Acceptability? High amongst those responsible for dealing with disorder and its consequences, such as the police and magistrates; low amongst licensees and managers with the responsibility and cost burden of organising and funding staff training. Acceptability would undoubtedly be high among the latter group if resources were to be attached to any requirement to arrange training.

Resources? Training schemes might be subsidised but would probably be a cost to employers. In order to implement a nation-wide scheme, however, it is likely that some form of training subsidy would be required. Some initial investment in establishing accreditation for training providers would be needed.

Audit? Implementation of a training scheme would be audited via the issuing of training certificates by accredited providers and the requirement for the production of such certification to the licensing authority as part of the licence renewal proceedings.

Safer Pubs

Concerns about pub safety have a long history (see Greenaway, 1998). Several studies have considered the relationship between the setting in which drinking takes place and the existence of a range of alcohol related problems and concluded that preventing alcohol related harm requires measures to reduce intoxication on licensed premises (Casswell *et al.* 1993; Stockwell *et al.*, 1993; Lang *et al.* 1995). Such measures would include server training, stricter enforcement of existing law on serving intoxicated patrons, and attention to the design of bar areas.

One consequence of intoxication is violence in and around licensed premises which very often involves the use of glass. Home Office estimates suggest an annual figure of 3400–5400 offences in which glass is used as a weapon. Surveys of assault victims conducted in A & E departments in Bristol and London found bar glasses to be the most commonly used sharp weapon (Shepherd, 1994b). Violence aside, two-thirds of injuries to bar staff, mainly to the hands, are the result of glasses being broken while collecting, stacking and washing: 40% of bar workers in one survey had sustained such injuries. The level of accidental and non-accidental injuries sustained in pubs might be reduced by restricting the type of glass which is allowed to be used for serving alcohol. Tempered glass, which is already employed in car windscreens, has the advantage of being more than six times more resistant to impact than non-tempered, and, when it does break, of shattering into small cuboid fragments, rather than into large jagged pieces.

Acceptability? High. The majority of pub users would prefer to drink in a safe environment. The most effective method of implementation might be to require all glassware purchased from a future date to be tempered – in this way there would be minimal cost implications.

Resources? Short-term costs will be borne by owners and landlords and these will necessarily be passed on to the customer in the form of higher prices. The introduction of tempered glass, which can last up to 25 times longer than non-tempered, should, however, result in long-term financial gains for landlords.

Audit? The number of establishments switching to safer glass could be monitored locally. Resulting benefits could be assessed by recording the location and nature of incidents resulting in attendance at an A & E department.

Formal Controls Subsystem

Advertising Regulation

The evidence relating to alcohol advertising is difficult to unravel. It seems likely that any change in the regulations regarding the advertisement of alcohol drinks would have minimal impact on drinking behaviour since advertising is most effective in changing brand loyalties. The existing advertising code for alcoholic drinks has merit on common-sense grounds.

It is possible that cultural attitudes towards alcohol are influenced, from childhood, by repeated daily exposure to enticing images, but the research is not sufficiently strong to support an evidence-based policy. Advertising has a much more powerful effect on commodities which are not generally available. In this sense health promotion messages are a commodity, and investment in targeted harm prevention campaigns is worth while when combined with local action, such as the Christmas drink driving campaigns.

Acceptability? Low for banning alcohol advertising but high for enforcing guidelines.

Resources? Few additional resources would be required. There are already procedures in place to monitor alcohol advertising, but this would need to be strengthened.

Audit? Easily monitored by regular time-sampling of all the appropriate media.

Sporting Events and Outdoor Concerts

The success of a major event depends upon close cooperation between the local community, the local council, the police, and the event's organisers. 'Alcohol management' is one of several issues that needs specifically to be considered. The nature of the expected crowd will be an important determinant of the rules governing a particular event, and only in exceptional circumstances – notably the probability of football hooliganism – have total bans been found necessary (see Alcohol Advisory Council of New Zealand, 1997).

Acceptability? Moderate. Most major events involve significant restrictions on the way alcohol is used: there may be personal searches and confiscation of alcohol brought to an event.

Resources? The presence of alcohol at a major event implies the requirement for additional security and medical resources.

Audit? Monitoring of untoward incidents where alcohol was a factor.

City-centre Initiatives

The police and local councils will often have a variety of measures in place to improve public safety in town and city centres. Specific alcohol control measures have been shown to make an important contribution to public safety. Flexible licensing arrangements were introduced in Scotland following the Licensing (Scotland) Act 1976. Since 1993, extensions have been granted on a regular basis to licensed premises in central Edinburgh within an identified zone. The aim of this restriction was to reduce extended drinking in areas where there was a high density of residential accommodation. Extensions led to concern about public order, noise and particularly violent incidents. The Licensing Committee of the City of Edinburgh Council, supported by Lothian and Borders Police, decided to introduce a uniform closing time in the city. From March 1996, all public houses, hotels and restaurants were required to close by 1.00 a.m., although clubs and places which had entertainment licences could remain open somewhat longer.

The police monitored the average number of crimes of violence in the area and found a 74% reduction in the level of such crimes between 1995 and 1996 when the new practice was implemented. This improvement has been maintained (although at a lower level) and there is a continuing debate about relaxing these restrictions on extended licensing hours.

Acceptability? Publicans have objected to zoning on the grounds that licensees outside the permitted late opening zone are disadvantaged. On the other hand, late-night drinking is not desirable in residential areas and zoning eases the organisation of police resources.

Resources? There are minimal costs involved in the introduction, monitoring and review of by-laws.

Audit? This could form part of more general monitoring of violent and other incidents.

Enforcement Schemes

Many laws and local by-laws governing drinking practices are poorly enforced. This is evident in areas such as under-age drinking, adhering to permitted hours, refusing to serve customers who are already intoxicated, drinking on private coaches, and drinking and driving. The reasons for the lack of adherence to these regulations are various, including lack of police availability and time, lack of public support for that particular law, and lack of awareness. When attempts have been made to ensure that laws concerning drinking are enforced, there has often been a dramatic reduction in the level of problems, particularly in relation to public order. The introduction of random breath testing is one example which greatly increased the likelihood of detection and reduced the level of alcohol related road traffic accidents. Another example was a study (Jeffs and Saunders, 1983) undertaken in a South Coast seaside town in England where licensees initially were reminded of their responsibilities to observe under-age drinking and excessive intoxication. The local police then arranged for uniformed officers to visit the premises in a random but conspicuous way at regular intervals during the summer season and check that the laws were being respected. This level of enforcement resulted in a 20 per cent reduction in recorded offences compared with an adjacent and comparable town where no such measures were introduced. It is also noteworthy that when this policing practice was withdrawn, the levels of offending rose once more.

There is a concern about the prevalence of under-age drinking in public houses and the ease of purchase of alcoholic beverages by minors from off-licences and supermarkets (Sutherland and Willner, 1998). Storekeepers and publicans both stress that it is very hard to identify those who are under-age. Some voluntary identification schemes have been introduced to combat this but these are of uncertain benefit. Proper enforcement of these laws remains elusive and it is doubtful whether the industry's attempt to self-regulate and monitor in this area is proving effective. Currently, research projects are exploring the ease with which under-age purchases can be made.

There has also been concern in Britain recently about smuggling of duty-free alcohol into the country, but it is expensive to monitor and enforce regulations. Similarly, the presence of alcohol on coaches going to sporting events is common and may contribute to public disorder. When resources have been used to enforce regulations in this area, numerous evasions have been detected. There is a need, therefore, to evaluate the benefits of rigorous enforcement, while at the same time considering the costs, both financial and in terms of public support.

Acceptability? With the exception of those individuals who were unaware that they were breaking a law, enforcement is likely to meet with some resistance. As with other aspects of policy, the acceptability of enforcement will depend upon public education and public support.

Resources? The costs of enforcement are likely to be high but should not rest solely with the police. Some should be met by those providing alcohol: this might be a very direct charge – at major events, for example.

Audit? Routine data collection is generally unhelpful since the effectiveness of enforcement depends on the priority it is given.

Legal Sanctions Subsystem

Drink Driving

Drink driving legislation can be seen as the flagship of targeted measures against alcohol related harm. Reducing the permitted blood alcohol level from 80 mg% to 50 mg% can be argued on two counts. First, the majority of EC countries have settled for the 50 mg% level and so, in the interests of harmonisation, the UK should adopt the same law. Second, there is an increased risk of accidents, particularly for young people, when driving with blood alcohol levels between 50 mg% and the present limit of 80 mg%.

There is a danger in placing too much reliance on setting prescribed blood alcohol levels as a means of accident prevention. A significant number of accidents are caused by people drinking significantly in excess of currently prescribed limits; equally, the combination of alcohol and other drugs is an increasing problem. People living in rural areas and more experienced drivers may see themselves to be unduly disadvantaged by regulations designed to eliminate all risk.

Additional measures to prevent drink driving accidents might include a new range of sanctions against drink drivers, such as impounding the vehicle registered to the driver or requiring motor manufacturers to install vehicle immobilisation systems (see Clayton, 1997, pp. 28–31). Vehicle immobilisation devices have the advantage of targeting the problem behaviour – that is, an incapacity to drive – and are therefore effective whether the cause of the incapacity is alcohol, other drugs, or disability due to illness.

Acceptability? Variable. The public are unlikely to accept that there is a scientific basis to a further reduction in acceptable blood alcohol levels. On the one hand, people may wish to see drink driving limits implemented but, on the other hand, may not welcome restrictions of their own personal freedoms to achieve this.

Resources? Considerable additional police resource would be required to enforce the law on the existing or a reduced prescribed drink driving limit. Vehicle immobilisation systems would have a short-term cost for motor manufacturers but would be relatively cheap in the long term.

Audit? The police have routine procedures for collecting statistics on accidents, drink driving offences and blood alcohol level.

Server Liability

In the UK there is not a strong tradition of placing a legal liability upon those who have contributed, via the service of alcoholic drinks, for example, to the behaviour and actions of a third party who has gone on to inflict harm upon themselves or others. However, the principle of server liability has been established in other countries, notably the US, while in New Zealand the Sale of Liquor Act has been supported by a major campaign focused on host responsibility.

In the UK the focus on the responsibility of the individual drinker has been such that the law prohibiting the sale of alcohol to someone who is already intoxicated is rarely enforced. The introduction of a legal presumption of liability upon those who, in an irresponsible way, serve alcohol to those who later come to, or cause, harm would have some clear benefits. It would undoubtedly serve to encourage licensees and others in private situations to take their responsibilities even more seriously and would undoubtedly go hand in hand with the development of a comprehensive and well subscribed training programme for bar staff.

Acceptability? Relatively low. These measures do not conform to a traditional British approach to litigation and individual responsibility. Acceptability would clearly be very low amongst alcohol producers and retailers, albeit high within the insurance industry. Enthusiasm among health professionals and others concerned with social welfare is unlikely to be matched by the general public.

Resources? Probable significant costs to alcohol retailers in insurance premiums and in providing training in order to build a defence against claims.

Audit? True effectiveness is likely to be measured via a decrease in accidents and related injuries rather than in numbers of cases brought before the courts. However, these could be related to incidents occurring in or around particular establishments.

Age Limits

Young people require particular consideration not only because injudicious drinking in this age group carries a significant risk of health, social and educational problems, but also because drinking at this age forms the foundation of subsequent drinking careers. It is also recognised that there is a close relationship between alcohol, other drug use including tobacco, and future mental health and behavioural problems. There is a duty to identify ways of helping those most at risk. Amongst other approaches this will include strategies to limit access. The age at which young people in the UK can legally purchase alcohol, in a public house or from an off-licence, has been set at 18 since the early twentieth century. The reasons for this particular age limit are unclear, but the possibility of changing it in either direction has rarely been considered.

Raising the minimum legal drinking age in order to reduce alcohol consumption may have the potential to reduce many of the negative consequences of drinking among young people. Lister Sharp (1994) reports on evidence from the US which suggested that lowering the minimum age of 21 to 18 resulted in an increase in both alcohol consumption and alcohol related traffic accidents involving young drivers, while subsequent reversal of the law was accompanied by a reduction in road accidents and related fatalities and a significant decline in single-vehicle night-time fatal crashes in drivers under the age of 21. Such measures might also have an effect upon criminal activity. Following a reduction of the minimum age to 18, in two Australian states overall levels of male juvenile crime rose between one-fifth and one-quarter, although it was not clear how much of this crime was alcohol related (see Lister Sharp, 1994).

Acceptability? Low. The restriction of 'rights' is never a popular policy option. A reduction in the minimum legal drinking age would be unpopular with the young people affected currently or in the near future. Nor would such a measure be likely to gain the support of the industry for whom it would result in a substantial financial loss. In addition, all the evidence suggests that current legislation is widely flouted. In a survey carried out for the Health Education Authority (1996), 22% of 13–14-year-olds, 47% of 15–16-year-olds and 80% of 17-year-olds who drank at least once a month reported purchasing alcohol themselves. Given this, raising the minimum age may be a less effective means of tackling the problems associated with young people's drinking than measures to ensure stricter enforcement of existing legislation.

Resources? There would be no obvious, direct costs of implementing the measure apart from the potential loss of revenue to the industry and the Exchequer. Possible added costs of enforcement would be offset by reductions in public order offences and accidents.

Audit? Suitable indicators would be provided by monitoring A & E department figures, police statistics on alcohol related crime and road traffic accidents, and Department of Transport data.

Social, Economic and Health Consequences Subsystem

Professional Training

People who work in the addictions field come from a variety of professional backgrounds including psychiatry, psychology, nursing, social work, counselling, and so on. Equally, there are many alcohol and drugs workers who have no relevant professional training. One difficulty of having such diversity of academic attainment is the absence of any consensus on the required competencies for working in the addiction field. The principles of clinical governance applied within the National Health Service (Scally and Donaldson, 1998) need to be applied across the addictions field and to underpin training.

The need to define competencies is widely agreed, but who should undertake this task is more problematic. There is evidence to support some general principles of training (see, for example, Tober and Raistrick, 1990) and there have been attempts to define broadly the scope of training (see Alcohol Concern and Standing Conference on Drug Abuse, 1998; the Advisory Council on the Misuse of Drugs, 1990). The various professions represented in the addiction field have bodies that are responsible for setting professional standards and accrediting training. Only addiction psychiatry defines a specialist professional role which could be used as a blueprint for other professions.

It may now be timely to recognise a new professional group, addiction therapists or addiction counsellors, whose professional development might be defined by a new educational wing of an existing national body or the establishment of a new national training centre. Accredited and standardised training needs to be available to all professionals in the alcohol field. This might be achieved by having a network of regional training centres. Training should be accessible in both face-to-face and distance-learning formats (see Franey and Tober, 1999).

Acceptability? Practitioners usually welcome training. Managers are more circumspect and need to be persuaded of the benefits of training.

Resources? Training is expensive. Substantial costs are involved in the accreditation of courses and the maintenance of academic procedures. However, investment in training will be repaid in treatment effectiveness.

Audit? Competence can be measured crudely by monitoring therapist activity and client non-attendance rates. Supervision of video-recorded therapy sessions is the best method of judging competence.

Non-specialist Services

Generic services have the major treatment and prevention role in that the whole population have a high degree of exposure to people such as GPs, health visitors, housing workers, social workers, probation officers, and so on. It has been estimated that some two-thirds of people belonging to a general practice will visit their doctor within a twelve-month period. It is also clear that, under optimum conditions, GPs are effective at delivering minimal interventions; that is, interventions that can be contained within the resource constraints of primary health care. The evidence base on the effectiveness of other generic services is limited, but it can be supposed that other professionals will also be effective. The key issue here is that huge numbers of people who are at risk of becoming problem drinkers or are simply drinking in a risky way can be given information and advice that will prevent progression to excessive drinking or prevent risk drinking. The so-called prevention paradox refers to the fact that for many alcohol related problems more harm is prevented by focusing on the large number of people drinking in a risky way than on the smaller number of people who could be called 'alcoholics'.

In addition to direct intervention, generic workers have a role in coordinating the delivery of care plans for people with more severe problems and alerting authorities to problems such as domestic violence and child abuse. There are a variety of models of shared care that can act as a bridge between generic teams and specialist services for dealing with those people who have more complex alcohol related problems. Edinburgh, for example, has established specialist alcohol nurses in a general hospital with the role of providing education and support to staff in general medical wards, facilitating the early recognition of alcohol problems. They are further supported by a specialist team to whom they can make referrals and consult as required (Chick *et al.*, 1985).

Acceptability? High. Generic services are already established and most people build a good relationship with generic professionals, and particularly so with primary health care teams where the relationship will often have been long-standing. Generic services are generally accessible and more familiar to users than specialist services.

Resources? The principal cost would be the training of generic professionals to deal with their existing caseload in a more effective, which also means time-effective, way. Other costs would include time set aside for clinical supervision, and consumables such as information leaflets and drinking diaries.

Audit? Where some form of computerised records are kept it may be possible routinely to output reports of workload which is alcohol related. What is more important is to ensure that professionals are delivering the intervention according to a protocol and this is best checked by occasional video recordings of clinical sessions. Auditing might also include the uptake of training opportunities.

Specialist Services

The shift in the UK to a primary care led National Health Service requires some redefinition of the role of the specialist. Primary health care teams have different levels of exposure to people using alcohol and other drugs, different levels of commitment to dealing with these problems, and different levels of knowledge and skills to offer treatments suited to the primary care setting. There is merit in having clinical services integrated so that a stepped care approach (Sobell and Sobell, 1999) can be made consistent across primary and secondary-level services. Specialist services can be developed, first, to work alongside generalists using one of the shared care models; second, to provide primary level services for people who do not have a GP or prefer to be seen by the specialist service; and, third, to deliver specialist treatments requiring particular knowledge, skills and resources, such as dual-diagnosis work, treatment of people who are socially disorganised, and specialist detoxification.

In addition to having a clinical role, specialist services can be developed as a focus for research and development, training, and evaluating new treatments. In most instances the primary care teams will be unable to supervise and manage addiction therapists; specialist centres can be developed to take the lead role on clinical governance.

Acceptability? High. Within the health service, primary care teams expect to be able to refer to a consultant-led specialist service. Links with non-statutory sector services can usually be built on at local level and are integral to the range of services that should be available.

Resources? The range of specialist services available up and down the country varies considerably. It is likely that there is a need for considerable investment in specialist services in line with guidance from the Department of Health and Substance Misuse Advisory Service.

Audit? Specialist services are likely to have in place audits for specific treatment programmes. Furthermore, there should be resources for routine outcome evaluation. A detailed procedure for performance review should be agreed between the specialist agency and commissioners.

Joint Services

Patients with dual diagnosis ably illustrate the need for collaboration between services. In the US there has been a tendency to combine intensive case management of patients with dual diagnosis, augmenting the care of mental illness with addiction techniques such as relapse prevention and motivational interviewing. Each team member has usually been trained in these techniques. Staff in these teams work specifically with people with dual diagnosis for whom they have 24-hour responsibility. Each case manager typically will have a small caseload of approximately twelve-patients. The character and efficacy of these specialist dual-diagnosis services was reviewed by Johnson (1997). In Britain this group is often treated in a serial way so that the treatment for severe mental illness is followed by a treatment from a specialist addiction service. There are doubts about the efficacy of this approach and more collaborative approaches are being developed and studied. At present, this seems the most likely way forward for UK services and is receiving ongoing evaluation.

Acceptability? A joint approach seems likely to be the most acceptable and will avoid the creation of another cadre of specialists in both areas.

Resources? Collaborative work will avoid the cost of establishing specialist teams working independently of other resources and would facilitate mutual learning. Training costs need to be taken into account. Workers in this area will require reduced caseloads which has staffing implications.

Audit? The principal audit tool would be a measure of compliance with the treatment, the prediction being that patients with dual diagnosis cared for in this way would be more likely to take medication required, attend clinics regularly and relapse less frequently than had been the case in the past.

Appendix 1: Alcohol Policy Landmarks, 1950 to 1998

Not all documents listed in this appendix are 'official', national, policy documents; items range from Acts of Parliament through professional position statements to advice leaflets. Inclusion has been based on the impact each is felt to have had on the nation's drinking, on existing policy responses to that, and on our beliefs about and attitudes to our own and others' drinking. Compilation has involved subjective judgements being made about the relative importance of those things included and excluded. To that extent the list is neither definitive nor exhaustive. In a number of cases it was not possible to consult the document itself – these are marked '[not seen]'.

1959 Licensing (Scotland) Act

Consolidated previous licensing measures and was the principal source of licensing law and practice for Scotland until 1976. Included measures relating to:

- Licensing courts and the granting of licenses of all types
- Permitted hours (On weekdays only, 11.30–5.00 and 5.30–10.00, or as set by licensing court, up to a maximum of 8 hours, broken by a period of at least 2 hours)
- Provisions regulating sales and supply, including sale to intoxicated persons and age restrictions. (Supply of intoxicating liquor to a person under the age of 18 but over the age of 14 was not an offence unless supplied or sold for consumption on the premises.)

1960 Road Safety Act

This was the first post-war Act that mentioned alcohol and other drugs in relation to driving, although not the earliest legislation. The 1930 Road Traffic

Act was the first time that legislative measures were put in place, and even that replaced Section 12 of the 1872 Licensing Act, under which an individual could be charged with *'the offence of being drunk while in charge, on a highway or other public place, of a carriage'*.

1961 Joint Memorandum on Alcoholism

(British Medical Association and the Magistrates' Association (1961) *Alcoholism: a memorandum by a joint committee of the British Medical Association and the Magistrates' Association* (London, BMA). Reprinted (with additions and corrections) from the Supplement to the *British Medical Journal*, 22 April 1961, vol. i, pp. 190–5.)

The memorandum was prepared in recognition of the increasing numbers of patients and offenders presenting with alcohol problems and was intended to assist magistrates and GPs in *'distinguishing between the true alcoholic and the occasional hard drinker'* and provide information on such treatment facilities that existed . Aspects discussed included the definition and recognition of 'alcoholism', education, prevention and rehabilitation, treatment and other services, and the possibility of *'legislation against alcoholism'*, a subject debated by the BMA in 1960.

Conclusions:

- 'Alcoholism' is a serious problem but one which generally responds well to treatment
- There is an 'urgent need' for:

    a) Further research, on the nature and size of the problem and on methods of treatment.
    b) Better undergraduate and post-graduate training of doctors, and public education *'to encourage earlier recourse to medical treatment'*.
    c) More in- and out-patient hospital facilities.

- Legislation to permit compulsory treatment should be considered.

1962 Road Traffic Act

Defined unfitness to drive through drink:

- *'a person shall be taken to be unfit to drive if his ability to drive properly is for the time being impaired'*.

1962 Licensing (Scotland) Act

A number of changes were made to the 1959 Act, including the following:

- Permitted hours were increased, but not significantly (by 30 minutes; now set at 11.00–2.30 and 5.00–10.00)
- Sale or supply of intoxicating liquor to a person under the age of 18, for consumption off the premises, was made an offence.

1962 Penalties for Drunkenness Act

Penalties for drunkenness offences were increased to:

- Maximum fine of £5 for *'offences of being drunk in public places or licensed premises or refusing to leave or attempting to enter a refreshment house or ship when drunk or disorderly'*.
- Maximum fine of £10 or maximum prison sentence of one month for *'offences of drunkenness in aggravating circumstances or violent or indecent behaviour at police stations'*.

1963 Ministry of Health Memorandum: *Hospital Treatment of Alcoholism*

(Ministry of Health (1963) *Hospital Treatment of Alcoholism*, HM (62/43) (London, Ministry of Health) [not seen])

Recommendations were made to Regional Health Authorities on:

- The creation of special in-patient treatment units (8–16 beds).
- These should have out-patient facilities.
- Group therapy was emphasised.
- Cooperation with Alcoholics Anonymous was encouraged.

1964 Licensing Act

Consolidated previous legislation and remains the principal source of licensing law and practice for England and Wales. Includes measures relating to:

- Granting of licences of all types.
- Sale and supply.
- Permitted hours (11.00–3.00 and 5.30–10.30 on weekdays; 12.00–2.00 and 7.00–10.00 on Sundays, Christmas Day and Good Friday).
- Age restrictions.
- Provisions relating to conduct.

1965 Road Safety White Paper

(Department of Transport (1965) *Road Safety Legislation, 1965–6,* Cmnd. 2859 (London, HMSO).)

Considered the relationship between alcohol and road accidents and noted:

- That average risk of accident increases as blood alcohol level rises above 40 mg/100 ml and that *all* drivers are seriously affected above 80 mg/100 ml (based on studies in Canada, the US and Czechoslovakia).
- That the winter (1964/65) campaign 'Don't Ask a Man to Drink and Drive' *'had a good effect on attitudes [but] there is little evidence that it affected ... behaviour'* – legal measures were felt to be necessary.
- Shortcomings of the 1960 and 1962 Road Traffic Acts.

Proposals:

- The introduction of a drink-driving limit of 80 mg/100 ml blood.
- Roadside breath tests by random spot-check.
- Continuation of blood/urine tests for evidential purposes.

1967 Road Safety Act

'An Act to make further provision with respect to persons driving or being in charge of motor vehicles after consuming alcohol or taking drugs and with respect to goods vehicles and to empower constables to arrest persons suspected of driving or attempting to drive while disqualified.'

- Under the terms of the Act it is an offence to drive, attempt to drive, or be in charge of a motor vehicle in a public place if blood/alcohol exceeds 80 mg/100 ml of blood.
- Police officers were given power to administer a breath test to any motorist who commits a moving traffic offence or is involved in a traffic accident. The Act also empowered police officers to stop and test a motorist if there is 'reasonable cause' to believe that there is alcohol in the body (i.e., not the random spot-checks proposed in the White Paper).

1967 Criminal Justice Act

- Removed the penalty of imprisonment for the offence of being drunk
- Increased the maximum fine to £50.

- These provisions would not come into force *'unless the Secretary of State is satisfied that sufficient suitable accommodation is available for the care and treatment of persons convicted of being drunk and disorderly'*.

1968 Ministry of Health Memorandum: *Treatment of Alcoholism*

(Ministry of Health (1968) *Treatment of Alcoholism,* HM (68/37) (London, Ministry of Health) [not seen])

- Inpatient treatment should remain the priority, but as part of a comprehensive service including prevention, assessment, treatment and aftercare.
- More emphasis should be placed on the role of environment, community and family.

1969 Monopolies Commission Report on the Supply of Beer

(Monopolies Commission (1969) *Report on the Supply of Beer,* Cmnd. 21 (London, HMSO) [not seen])

- Concluded that the tied-house system operated against the public interest.
- Recommended a substantial relaxation of existing licensing laws.

1971 Home Office Working Party on Habitual Drunken Offenders

(Home Office Working Party on Habitual Drunker Offenders (1971) *Habitual Drunken Offenders: report of the working party* (London, HMSO).)

The report of a committee appointed in 1967 (in the light of the Criminal Justice Act of that year) to assess the need for treatment of offenders who habitually commit offences involving drunkenness, and to review the hostel accommodation available to this group.

Conclusions and recommendations included:

- Although habitual drunken offenders are not an homogenous group, such individuals are likely to come from a deprived socio-economic background, and many suffer from alcoholism.
- A coordinated system of treatment is required, including facilities to deal with both social and medical problems, and focused on major centres of population.

- The nature of the problem is not essentially different for men and women, therefore treatment facilities should be mixed.
- Treatment should aim to reach clients at an earlier stage than previously, and preventive measures should play a role. Fostering and maintenance of motivation not to drink should be a central concern.
- More hostel accommodation should be provided; a variety of types should be developed and a comparative study undertaken of their effectiveness.
- A variety of community facilities other than hostels should be part of the overall system.
- Special detoxification centres should be set up as an alternative to arrest for public drunkenness. These should combine medical and social work facilities, and have a *'clearly therapeutic purpose'*.

Responsibility for implementing the recommendations was accepted by the DHSS.

1972 Erroll Committee Report on Liquor Licensing

(Home Office (1972) *Report of the Departmental Committee on Liquor Licensing,* Cmnd. 5154 (London, HMSO).)

A committee established to review the liquor licensing laws of England and Wales (the first such review since the Royal Commission on Licensing of 1929–31) in the light of the changes recommended by the Monopolies Commission Report of 1969. With regard to the relationship between the law and 'the social context', the committee concluded that '*[t]he licensing law should concern itself principally with the physical standards and conduct of premises, the character of licensees, the ages for access, purchase and consumption, and hours of opening. Other issues are subordinate.*'

Recommendations included:

- The licensing function should remain the responsibility of licensing justices, but their absolute discretion should be replaced by specified grounds on which applications for the grant or renewal of on- and off-licences may be refused.
- A new system of licensing should be introduced, replacing the present single licence with two types, a personal licence and a premises licence, the latter simplifying the existing system of classification of types of licence by category of premises/liquor.
- Permitted hours of opening should be increased (10.00 a.m.–12 midnight for on-consumption; 8.30 a.m.–12 midnight for off-sales). Licensing

justices should be able to restrict these in some circumstances and grant (or not) applications for extensions.
- The present age limit of 18 should be reduced to 17.
- The employment of persons aged 16 years in bars should be permitted, subject to registration and approved training.

No changes were made until the Licensing Act of 1988 .

1972 Criminal Justice Act

Included provisions to empower police officers to take certain offenders to '*any place approved by the Secretary of State ... as a medical treatment centre for alcoholics*'. These offenders are:

- Persons guilty, while drunk, of riotous or disorderly behaviour.
- Persons who are drunk and incapable.
- Persons guilty, while drunk, of disorderly behaviour in a public place.

1973 DHSS Circular: *Community Services for Alcoholics*

Department of Health and Social Security (1973) *Community Services for Alcoholics*, Circular 21/73 (London, DHSS).

Circulated to all local authorities by the Department of Health and Social Security, to encourage the development of community services as a complement to hospital treatment for 'alcoholics'. Cooperation between relevant agencies was encouraged.

- Discussed the role of 'shop front' information and health education services, detoxification centres as an alternative to custody, and the particular importance of hostels.
- A five year grant scheme – central funding to supplement local authority grant provision to voluntary organisations – was implemented, on the understanding that local authorities would take over funding thereafter. Funds were also made available, via the National Council on Alcoholism, to encourage provision of shop front services.

1973 Clayson Report on Scottish Licensing Law

(Scottish Home and Health Department (1973) *Report of the Departmental Committee on Scottish Licensing Law*, Cmnd. 5354 (Edinburgh, HMSO).)

The committee was appointed in 1971 *'to review the liquor licensing law of Scotland and to make recommendations on what changes, if any, might be made in the public interest'*. Inadequate social controls were felt by the committee to have a significant impact on the extent of alcohol misuse; the role of the licensee in setting and maintaining standards of conduct was argued to be of particular relevance.

Recommendations included:

- Licensing courts should be replaced by **licensing boards**, appointed by district councils.
    - The existing five types of certificate should be retained, and supplemented by the introduction of 'entertainment', 'refreshment house' and 'residential' certificates.
    - The replacement of licensing authorities' absolute discretion to refuse the grant or renewal of certificates should be replaced by specified grounds for refusal; absolute discretion *should* exist in relation to extensions.
- **Permitted hours** should be set at 11.00 a.m. to 11.00 p.m., public houses should be allowed to open on Sundays from 12.30 p.m. to 11.00 p.m. and off-sales should be permitted on Sundays from 12.30 p.m. to 11.00 p.m. Off-sales premises' trading hours should be 8.00 a.m. to 11.00 p.m. (12.30–11.00 on Sundays).
    - Licensing boards should have the power to place restrictions on particular establishments in the interests of public order or safety.
- Conditions for the **conduct of licensed premises** should be set out in statute and certificate-holders held criminally liable for breach of certificate (including by members of staff). Courts should have the power to disqualify anyone so convicted from holding a certificate for a maximum of five years.
    - The Secretary of State should have the power to set additional conditions through statutory instruments and licensing authorities should be able to impose further conditions by means of by-laws.
- **'Children's certificates'**, granted on application to licensing boards, should be introduced to allow the presence of persons under 14 years of age on licensed premises where there is no public interest requiring their exclusion and where the licensing board is satisfied as to the suitability of the premises.
- A **research** organisation should be established in Scotland, to investigate the wider social aspects of alcohol misuse, its extent, possible causes and potential methods of prevention.

1975 White Paper: *Better Services for the Mentally Ill*

(Department of Health and Social Security (1975) *Better Services for the Mentally Ill*, Cm. 6233 (London, HMSO).)

'*A long-term strategic document indicating the general direction in which we should move.*' Broad policy objectives for the future were:

- An expansion of local authority social services.
- The relocation of specialist services in local settings.
- The establishment of organisational links (between administrative and practice levels).
- A significant improvement in staffing.

Included a separate chapter on 'Alcohol and Drug Dependence and Misuse'. Under '*Alcohol*' it noted the need for a multi-disciplinary approach and the frequency of relapse .

Recommendations (in relation to alcohol):

- For *prevention* – both primary and secondary health education initiatives.
- For *treatment and rehabilitation* – an expansion of community services.
- More and better coordination of a network of services.
- Better awareness training for staff.
- Area Health Authorities should assess need and plan appropriate strategies.
- Emphasis in provision should move towards more locally based services.

Appointed an Advisory Committee on Alcoholism (with a special subgroup to promote the development of services for homeless alcoholics). This Committee was wound up in 1978, prior to which it produced reports on *Prevention* (1977, below), *The Pattern and Range of Services for Problem Drinkers* (1978, below) and *Education and Training of Staff* (1979, below).

1976 Consultative Document: *Prevention and Health: Everybody's Business*

(Department of Health and Social Security (1976) *Prevention and Health: Everybody's Business: a reassessment of public and personal health*, (London, HMSO).)

A document prepared by the Health Departments of Great Britain and Northern Ireland to stimulate discussion about the role of prevention within the health and related services.

- A brief overview of alcohol related medical and social problems was included.
- The link between overall level of alcohol consumption and level of alcohol related problems was acknowledged.
- Long-term preventive strategies were seen as potentially including fiscal, legal and social controls; public debate about the nature of these should take place.
- The short-term need to help the problem drinker was recognised. Greater public awareness (to facilitate earlier help-seeking) was identified as a need.

1976 Blennerhassett Committee Report on Drinking and Driving

(Department of the Environment (1976) *Drinking and Driving: report of the departmental (Blennerhassett) committee* (London, HMSO).)

Set up because, despite initial success, the Road Safety Act (1967) did not have the desired impact on alcohol related death and injury, which continued to rise.

Proposals:

- That the existing blood alcohol limit of 80 mg/100 ml should be unchanged (with the recommendation that Parliamentary power to vary the limit should be retained).
- That BACs should be determined for forensic purposes by breath testing within police stations; blood analysis as a fall back option might continue, but urine analysis should be discontinued.
- That existing limits on the powers of police to stop and test should be removed so that a person who is or *who has been* driving or attempting to drive, or *in charge of* a motor vehicle, can be required *at the discretion of* a police officer to take a breath test.
- That some loopholes in the existing law, resulting in acquittals on technicalities relating to deviations from prescribed procedures for administering tests, should be removed: '*proof of an offence should not be unreasonably dependent on compliance with procedural requirements*'.
- That the main penalty for offenders should remain one year's disqualification. Those identified as 'high risk' (repeat offenders; offenders with

very high BACs) should have an additional condition that licences are not restored until the court is satisfied they no longer constitute a major risk.

- That there should be a continuing programme of publicity, particularly aimed at young drivers.

1976 Licensing (Scotland) Act

- Permitted Sunday opening of public houses.
- Extended permitted opening hours – bars could close at 11.00 p.m. instead of 10.00 p.m.
- Allowed licensees to obtain permanent extensions to normal permitted hours.

1977 Consultative Document: *Priorities for Health and Social Services*

(Department of Health and Social Security (1977) *Priorities for Health and Personal Social Services in England: a consultative document* (London, HMSO).)

An attempt to establish agreed priorities throughout the health and personal social services in the light of the White Paper on Public Expenditure to 1979/80 (which set out the need for reduced, though continuing, growth in expenditure). Capital expenditure would be cut back in order to maintain services and local authorities were advised to be guided in their planning decisions by an 'order of priorities' which emphasised low-cost projects, the role of primary and community care and preventive services.

Alcohol was considered under *Services for the Mentally Ill* as follows:

- Acknowledgement was made of the growing numbers of people with drink problems, particularly young people and women.
- The development of more locally based services was recommended, focused on out-patient, day-patient or community facilities and the use of multi-disciplinary teams.
- The need for hostels and specialised services in areas with high levels of 'homeless alcoholics' was recognised.

1977 Expenditure Committee Report: *Preventive Medicine*

(House of Commons Expenditure Committee (1977) *Preventive Medicine: first report from the Expenditure Committee, Social Services and Employment Subcommittee, Session 1976–77* (London, HMSO).)

The report of an inquiry carried out in response to concern over the cost of running the NHS. The committee concluded that greater emphasis should be placed on prevention in order to make savings not only in financial but in human terms – *'it is, literally, a matter of life and death'*. Individual responsibility for health was stressed, but the need for information to support this was highlighted. Emphasis was placed also on the need to target young people and 'at risk' groups.

Fifty-eight specific **recommendations** were made. Those concerning alcohol were:

- A larger proportion of monies raised through alcohol duty and taxation should be devoted to alcohol education. (Recommendation 16)
- The money remaining in the Licensing Compensation Fund should be released for health education purposes. (Recommendation 17)
- Research should be instigated into identifying those drinkers most at risk. (Recommendation 18)
- More use should be made of television advertising to provide information about the dangers of alcohol abuse. (Recommendation 19)
- The age at which alcohol can be legally purchased should not be lowered. (Recommendation 20)
- Preventive work in relation to alcohol should be coordinated by one umbrella organisation. (Recommendation 21)
- The price of alcohol relative to average incomes should remain at current levels. (Recommendation 22)

1977 White Paper: *Prevention and Health*

(Department of Health and Social Security (1977) *Prevention and Health,* Cmnd. 7047(London, HMSO).)

The government's formal response to the Report of the Expenditure Committee (1977, above), outlining their current and proposed measures for preventive action. Their response to the recommendations on alcohol was as follows:

- Recommendation 16: This would be a major departure from current principles governing the distribution of tax revenue and would reduce the government's ability to allocate resources in the light of changing needs and priorities.
- Recommendation 17: Consultations on this are already underway on the basis of the Erroll Committee Report. No decisions will be taken until that process is complete.

- Recommendation 18: '*The Health Departments are conscious of the need to stimulate research in this area and this is likely to form a central part of the research effort on alcohol in the next few years.*'
- Recommendation 19: Television advertising has been used and evaluation shows favourable results. However, the HEC and SHEU must have regard to cost-effectiveness when deciding how to allocate limited resources.
- Recommendation 20: The government has no plans for legislation on this issue. Full weight will be given to the Committee's views when considering the Erroll Committee Report.
- Recommendation 21: The voluntary organisations must decide themselves how best to work together.

1977 Advisory Committee Report on Prevention

(Department of Health and Social Security and the Welsh Office (1977) *Prevention: report of the Advisory Committee on Alcoholism* (London, HMSO).)

A report which acknowledged that the effects of alcohol misuse impact on society as a whole. The Committee concluded that moderate drinking should be encouraged and harmful drinking habits discouraged through a programme of primary prevention (aimed at demand for and availability of alcohol) and secondary prevention (early identification of individuals with problems). Five main 'ingredients' of a prevention strategy were recommended:

- More health education to discourage excessive drinking.
- A change in the way in which alcohol is portrayed in the media in general and by advertising in particular.
- The use of fiscal measures to maintain the price of alcohol.
- Rigorous enforcement of legal restrictions on availability and no reform of these without evidence that reform would not lead to increased harm.
- Encouragement to individuals to recognise and seek help for possible drinking problems.

1978 Advisory Committee Report on Services

(Department of Health and Social Security and the Welsh Office (1978) *The Pattern and Range of Services for Problem Drinkers: report of the Advisory Committee on Alcoholism* (London, HMSO).)

A report on the extent and nature of problem drinking in England and Wales, which concluded that much of this is unrecognised and/or untreated within generic services, while specialist services are unevenly distributed and not well

coordinated. The variety of problems presented, including the special difficulties faced by homeless problem drinkers, was felt to require:

- A flexible, comprehensive, and coordinated range of services provided
  by statutory and voluntary agencies. These should include preventive
  measures, earlier treatment interventions and more long-term support.
- Greater emphasis on the role of generic primary care workers, with
  knowledge, advice and support being provided where necessary from
  specialist workers at the secondary level.
- A change in attitude towards problem drinkers.

1979 Advisory Committee Report on Education and Training

(Department of Health and Social Security and the Welsh Office (1979)
*Education and Training for Professional Staff and Voluntary Workers in the Field:
report of the Advisory Committee on Alcoholism* (London, HMSO).)

A report which '*attempted to define the necessary knowledge and skills required by
the various professional and voluntary staff who come into contact with problem
drinkers*'. This was seen as being of particular importance in the context of the
committee's report on services for problem drinkers and the increased demands
on staff that would be likely to ensue.

Specific **recommendations** were made on:

- Basic education and training of doctors, nurses and social workers.
- Post-basic qualification training of medical staff.
- In-service training of qualified and unqualified social workers.
- The training needs of volunteer counsellors and residential staff.
- The provision of specialist advisors to senior staff in statutory authori-
  ties.

1979 Royal College of Psychiatrists Report: *Alcohol and Alcoholism*

(Royal College of Psychiatrists (1979) *Alcohol and Alcoholism: the report of a
special committee of the Royal College of Psychiatrists* (London, Tavistock).)

A report which summarised contemporary evidence on the extent and nature
of alcohol problems in the UK, examined existing treatment, and made a range
of **recommendations** for future national strategies on both prevention and
treatment. These included the following:

- A greater emphasis in health policy on prevention, with a commitment to ensure that neither per capita consumption nor indices of alcohol-related harms rose beyond existing levels. A number of specific recommendations were made in relation to prevention at government policy, community and personal levels.
- Greater consultation and cooperation between government departments to allow for an integrated response to alcohol problems.
- Greater commitment to the provision of public education and information on the harms associated with alcohol. (The concept that alcohol is a drug, the relationship between per capita consumption and the extent of problems, public disapproval of intoxication and the need for clear guidelines on safe and dangerous levels of consumption were stressed.)
- No further relaxation of licensing laws should be considered.
- A number of recommendations on treatment services, professional education, and research.

1979 'Think Tank Report'

(Central Policy Review Staff (1982) *Alcohol Policies in United Kingdom* (Stockholm, Stockholms Universitet).)

A confidential report which was never published in the UK and was not, therefore, made available to either professionals or the public until 1982, when it was published by the University of Stockholm as part of a research project on Swedish alcohol policy.

The report constituted a review of alcohol policies in the UK at the time, including taxation, licensing, alcohol and work, drinking and driving, the presentation of alcohol (advertising, the media, education) and treatment. Particular emphasis was placed on the large number of public sector bodies with an interest in alcohol policy, including 16 government departments, local health and social service authorities, and the criminal justice system. Broad conclusions were:

- Further and better integrated initiatives are required to halt current trends in misuse.
- Measures to affect change in public attitudes are needed to support any initiatives.
- Action must balance economic and social interests.
- Immediate action is possible in a number of areas.

Detailed recommendations were made for each area of public policy considered. The main elements of these were presented as a *'7 point programme for early action'*, described as being likely to gain public support, not detrimental to employment or exports, similar to those of other reports (for example, that of the Royal College of Psychiatrists) and potentially cost-effective. The seven points are reproduced below:

Item 1   the Government should announce a positive commitment on countering the rise in consumption levels and on the reduction of alcohol-related disabilities;

Item 2   this approach should be interpreted widely. It should pay particular regard to public attitudes and should involve reviewing the impact of pressures in the media and health education on drinking habits, particularly amongst the young and women. And it should influence alcohol policies generally, not just those concerned with the health consequences of misuse;

Item 3   the trends towards making drink cheaper as a result of the lag of revenue duties should be arrested: as a minimum, duty levels should be kept in line with the RPI;

Item 4   liquor licensing should not be further relaxed, its purpose should be clarified and in respect of under age drinking its enforcement improved;

Item 5   a programme should be adopted on alcohol and work; it would involve the Health and Safety Executive taking a firm lead to clarify issues, assemble facts and experience and to disseminate them; and the Government setting an example as a major employer;

Item 6   the momentum on drinking and driving should be renewed and legislation prepared;

Item 7   an Advisory Council on Alcohol Policies should be set up with an activist role, not only to advise and comment but to encourage and monitor action; the activities of national bodies should be rationalised and responsibilities at a local level clarified.

1980 Scottish Home and Health Department Guidance to Doctors

(Scottish Home and Health Department (1980) *Slàinte Mhath? (Good Health):the medical problems of excessive drinking* (Edinburgh, SHHD).)

A memorandum prepared by a working party of the National Medical Consultative Committee, offering guidance to all doctors in clinical practice on dealing with patients who present with alcohol related problems. Evidence of the extent and nature of such problems was presented, along with advice on early identification and treatment of excessive drinking. The emphasis in the document departed significantly from the working group's original remit, which was to prepare a memorandum of guidance on 'aspects of alcoholism', on the basis that *'it seemed more profitable to focus attention on those who are more than social drinkers and whose mental, physical and social functioning is being endangered by excessive drinking'*.

1980 Home Office Research Study: *Alcoholism and Social Policy*

(Tuck, M. (1980) *Alcoholism and Social Policy: are we on the right lines?* Home Office Research Study No. 65 (London, HMSO).)

This study acknowledged the need for policies to decrease or prevent an increase in 'alcoholism or alcoholic problems', but argued that the *'consensus view* [that control of per capita consumption is the best means of doing so] *is neither necessarily correct nor helpful'*. However, arguments about the link between per capita consumption and broader alcohol problems were ignored and the recommendations of reports such as that of the Royal College of Psychiatrists (above) were represented as being intended to minimise 'alcoholism' through restrictions on national consumption.

A discussion of 'weak' and 'strong' versions of 'consumption theory' was presented; the weak version was argued not to imply the need for policy, while the 'strong' version was held not be supported by empirical evidence. The author concluded that *'the need must be to find ways of encouraging safer drinking as safer driving is encouraged'* and made a number of suggestions for research and policies aimed at identifying and dealing with heavy drinkers with 'alcoholic problems'.

1980 Criminal Justice (Scotland) Act

Included provisions similar to those of the Criminal Justice Act 1972 (above) to empower police officers to take drunken offenders to *'any place designated ... as a place suitable for the care of drunken persons'*. In addition, Section V made provision for the control of alcohol at sporting events. Within the terms of the Act the 'period of a designated sporting event' includes two hours prior to and one hour after the event itself.

Offences include:

- Possession of alcohol, or being drunk, on a public service vehicle whose 'principal purpose' is to convey people to or from a designated sporting event.
- Permitting alcohol to be carried on such a vehicle.

- Possession of alcohol or of a 'controlled container' (such as a bottle or can), or being drunk at a sporting event.
- Provisions were also made to allow police officers to search vehicles or individuals and to seize and detain containers.

1980 Licensed Premises (Exclusion of Certain Persons) Act

Empowered courts to grant orders excluding certain categories of convicted persons to enter licensed premises. An exclusion order:

- Can be applied to any person convicted of an offence on licensed premises which involved either violence or the threat of violence.
- Can apply to the premises where the offence was committed, or to *any* licensed premise.
- Must run for a minimum of three months and a maximum of two years.

1981 DHSS Guidelines: *The Problem Drinker at Work*

(Department of Health and Social Security (1981) *The Problem Drinker at Work: guidance on joint management and trade union cooperation to assist the problem drinker* (London, HMSO).)

A booklet offering advice and information on why and how to develop and operate a policy to assist problem drinkers in the workplace.

1981 DHSS Discussion Document: *Drinking Sensibly*

(Department of Health and Social Security (1981) *Prevention and Health: drinking sensibly* (London, HMSO) [not seen].)

A discussion document issued by the UK Health Departments as part of their 'Prevention and Health' series. The booklet summarised the evidence on alcohol misuse and discussed the scope for Government action, and the role of other organisations, in preventing such misuse. Individual responsibility was emphasised; one of the stated aims of the document was *'to encourage sensible attitudes towards the use of alcohol'*.

- Alcohol misuse was defined as *'drinking to excess or drinking in situations which are not appropriate, when the effect in either case is to put the drinker or others at risk of harm'*.
- Public education about *'sensible levels of alcohol consumption'* was described as an important component of a preventive strategy, but 'sensible levels' were not defined.

1981 Scottish Council on Alcoholism Report: *Alcohol and Employment*

(Scottish Council on Alcoholism (1981) *Alcohol and Employment: a problem and an opportunity*, report of the Working Party on Alcohol in Employment (Glasgow, SCA).)

The Working Party on Alcohol in Employment was set up in 1978 to explore effective means of dealing with alcohol related problems in the workplace, which were believed to be greater in Scotland than in other parts of the UK. The results of a survey of Scottish employers on their approach to 'alcoholism' were discussed in the Report.

Conclusions included:

- An existing SCA document '*A Joint Union/Management Approach to Alcoholism Recovery Programmes (1977) represents the best practice in the field of Employment and does not require any modification*'.
- The network of local Councils on Alcohol should be the forum for developments in this area, but the Scottish Council will need to be provided with resources to support this work.
- The Secretary of State should provide a grant of £36,500 per annum to develop a consultancy service for employers and unions.

1981 Office of Health Economics Paper on Alcohol

(Office of Health Economics (1981) *Alcohol: reducing the harm* (London, OHE).)

A paper (published as one of a series on current health problems) which sought to clarify some of the issues around UK alcohol consumption and the ongoing policy debate, with particular emphasis on economic factors. Its aim was to '*stimulate and inform public discussion*' and identify areas for further research. Among the authors' conclusions the following points were made:

- Analysis '*tends to support the contention that, in theory, there is no categorically fixed directional relationship between alcohol consumption and alcohol harm in a community*'.
- Nevertheless, alcohol related distress is a widespread problem and will probably become more prevalent over the next decade.
- Coherent government policy is therefore required to '*maximise the overall benefits over costs from drinking*'.

- The most effective strategy is likely to be the control of per capita consumption through the price mechanism.
- Some relaxation of licensing law (to encourage socially desirable drinking habits and gain public support) might also be considered.
- Harm reduction measures should be based either on primary prevention and/or on measures to identify and help those at risk.
- Continued research will allow polices to be based on evidence.

1981 Licensing (Alcohol Education and Research) Act

Abolished the functions of compensation authorities under the Licensing Act 1964 and provided for the transfer of assets to fund *'education about and research into the misuse of alcohol'*.

Established:

- The Alcohol Education and Research Council (members appointed by the Secretary of State).
- The Alcohol Education and Research Fund, to be applied for charitable purposes in the UK in relation to: public education to prevent 'excessive consumption'; care and rehabilitation of drunkenness offenders; treatment; research.

1981 Transport Act

- Introduced evidential breath testing *(recommended by Blennerhasset)*.
- Introduced procedures to identify and manage high risk offenders *(recommended by Blennerhasset)*.

1982 Joint Committee of Enquiry Report

(National Council for Voluntary Organisations and Department of Health and Social Security (1982) *National Voluntary Organisations and Alcohol Misuse* (London, NCVO).)

The report of a study commissioned by the Department of Health and Social Security, the remit of which was to examine the roles of the four national voluntary organisations in the alcohol misuse field in receipt of DHSS funds not spent directly on services, to ensure that the most effective use was being made of government resources. The four organisations were the Alcohol Education Centre (AEC), the Federation of Alcoholic Rehabilitation Establishments (FARE), the Medical Council on Alcoholism (MCA) and the

National Council on Alcoholism (NCA). It was concluded that, due to lack of cooperation and areas of duplication, the Government was getting a poor return for its grants and that rationalisation and reorganisation were required. The report writers identified five main groups of tasks required in the field of alcohol misuse, of which it suggested that those most effectively carried out at national level were *'public education, public campaigning, advice and support for local services and for training and a national forum for debate'*.

Recommendations:

- These identified tasks should be divided between four national bodies – two new and two existing.
- A new national voluntary organisation should be formed to provide information and advice, undertake planning and development, provide grants for training, and work with industry. This body should also take on the research role previously carried out by the MCA.
- DHSS funding should be made available to the new organisation, in certain circumstances, to maintain and develop services offered by local voluntary organisations.
- A small, public campaigning agency should be formed. This body might take over the prevention work of the NCA.
- The Health Education Council should be encouraged to expand its work in the area of the prevention.

1984 Health Education Council: *That's the Limit*

(Health Education Council (1984) *That's the Limit: a guide to sensible drinking* (London, HEC).)

A booklet aimed at the general public containing advice and information on alcohol and alcohol consumption.

- Advised on sensible drinking within safe limits.
- Defined safe limits as 18 standard drinks per week for men and 9 for women.
- Defined 'too much' as 56 standard drinks per week for men and 35 for women.

1985 Transport Select Committee Review on Road Safety

(House of Commons (1985) *Transport Committee, Road Safety, Vols.1, 2 and 3 with Minutes of Evidence and Appendices,* HC 103 (London, HMSO).)

The report of an inquiry initially begun in January 1983, but uncompleted due to the dissolution of Parliament in 1984. The committee was charged with *'reviewing and examining those aspects of road safety which appear to offer opportunities for achieving further reductions in the number of road casualties'*. In relation to drinking and driving the following measures were considered:

- Extension of police powers to stop and test drivers/random breath testing. Existing powers were felt to be adequate, although resources available for enforcement of current law were described as inadequate.
- Reduction of the 200 mg blood alcohol threshold for identification of high-risk offenders. Recommended that the government should consider this *'at a fairly early stage'*.
- Publicity and education campaigns. Noted the effectiveness of Christmas campaigns and recommended that further campaigns be conducted at other times.

1985 Scottish Health Education Report on Prevention

(Scottish Health Education Co-ordinating Committee (1985) *Health Education in the Prevention of Alcohol-related Problems* (Edinburgh, Scottish Health Education Group).)

A report which sought to inform a broad range of agencies of the extent and nature of alcohol related problems in Scotland and of their potential role in preventing these. In addition the report aimed to encourage cooperation between agencies and individuals and to provide a basis for discussion and the creation of a climate of opinion which allowed for effective action. Specific guidance was provided for statutory and voluntary agencies on the role of each in preventing alcohol problems and recommendations for action to be taken presented.

1985 The Sporting Events (Alcohol Control) Act

Like the Criminal Justice (Scotland) Act 1980 (above), this made provision for dealing with drunkenness offences related to (non-amateur) sporting events at designated sporting grounds. Within the terms of the Act, a 'sporting event' includes a period of two hours prior to and one hour after the event itself , while the outer limit of a 'designated sporting ground' may be determined.

Offences include:

- Permitting alcohol to be carried on public transport going to or from sporting events.

- Possession of alcohol or articles (such as bottles) capable of causing injury at sporting grounds.
- Drunkenness on public transport going to or from sporting events, or at designated sporting grounds.

Provisions were also made to:

- Regulate the sale and supply of intoxicating liquor at licensed premises at designated sporting grounds. Permitted hours cannot include the period of a sporting event, except by magistrates order.
- Allow police officers to close licensed premises at designated sporting grounds if concerns exist about public order.
- Allow police officers to search public vehicles, or individuals.

1986 Working Group Report on Violence/Licensed Premises

(Home Office Standing Conference on Crime Prevention (1986) *Report of the Working Group on the Prevention of Violence Associated with Licensed Premises* (London, Home Office).)

The report of an independent working group established to examine the issue of violence associated with licensed premises and make recommendations for preventive measures.

Recommendations included:

- Educational measures aimed at potential perpetrators and improved training for licensees and staff.
- That consideration should be given, in any review of licensing hours, to the influence of these on levels of violence.

1986 Consultation Paper: *Licensing (Scotland) Act 1976*

(Scottish Home and Health Department (1986) *Licensing (Scotland) Act 1976: a consultation paper*, JAB23405 (Edinburgh, HMSO).)

This paper presented a discussion of attitudes to the 1976 legislation as ascertained by an OPCS survey of 1984 which found that the general public and licensees both 'generally welcomed' the longer hours, although some concerns were expressed about increased consumption levels. The main purpose of the consultation paper, however, was to seek views on the possibility of:

- The introduction of all-day (11.00 a.m.–11.00 p.m.) opening.
- No longer dealing separately with applications for Sunday opening.
- Permitting off-sales on Sundays.
- Relaxing the law to allow parents to bring children into bars at lunch times, either as a general relaxation or as something which would require establishments to hold a 'children's certificate'.

1986 Royal College of General Practitioners Report on Alcohol

(Royal College of General Practitioners (1986) *Alcohol: a balanced view* (London, RCGP).)

A report which acknowledged that the risk of alcohol related harms is linked to the overall level of alcohol consumption, that 'moderate' drinkers account for the greater part of total harm in the community, and that GPs can play a major role in prevention.

Recommendations:

- That the Royal College include alcohol within the agenda for prevention, recognise the limitations of viewing alcoholism and the alcoholic as the core of the problem, and encourage and assist GPs in preventive work.
- That GPs review their approach and working methods in this area, work cooperatively with other groups in the field, and integrate alcohol into preventive policies.

1986 Royal College of Psychiatrists Report on Alcohol

(Royal College of Psychiatrists (1986) *Alcohol: Our Favourite Drug: new report of a special committee of the Royal College of Psychiatrists* (London, Tavistock).)

A report which revised and updated the College's previous report, *Alcohol and Alcoholism* (1979, above) in the light of the mass of data which continued to demonstrate the extent of the nation's alcohol related problems. This edition reflected and discussed developments in thinking in the field, as well as policy changes which had occurred in the intervening period. In addition, new areas of concern, such as workplace problems and women and alcohol, were examined. Existing recommendations remained, although some were expanded upon. In addition, it was advised that the recommendation of the Blennerhasset committee on discretionary testing of drivers be implemented.

1987 Health Education Authority: *That's the Limit* (2nd edition)

(Health Education Authority (1987) *That's the Limit: a guide to sensible drinking* (2nd edition) (London, HEA).)

A new edition of the previous (1984) Health Education Council booklet, similarly containing advice and information on alcohol and alcohol consumption.

- Introduced the concept of 'units' of alcohol.
- Sensible limit was set at 21 units per week for men and 14 for women.
- Too much was defined as 36 units per week for men and 22 for women.

1987 Working Group Report on Young People and Alcohol

(Home Office Standing Conference on Crime Prevention (1986) *Report of the Working Group on Young People and Alcohol* (London, Home Office).)

This independent working group was formed to consider the part played by alcohol in the commission of crime by young people, and review the issue of under-age drinking.

Conclusions:

- Although no causal link can be established between alcohol consumption and crime in general, a strong relationship exists between intoxication and certain crimes of violence and disorder.
- Young people (especially young men) are particularly implicated in these types of crime.
- The law on under-age drinking is *'complicated, anomalous, and widely flouted'*.

Recommendations included:

- A review of educational measures aimed at young people, teachers and parents should be undertaken, and health and social education should be included in the proposed national curriculum.
- Controls on advertising should be extended and the introduction of health warnings on drink containers considered by government.
- Tax on stronger beers and high-strength ciders should be increased.
- Consideration should be given to changes in the licensing law to remove inconsistencies and make enforcement more practical; the consumption

of alcohol by people under 18, in all parts of licensed premises, and in public places, should be made illegal.

1987 Scottish Health Education Guide: *Drink and Drugs at Work*

(Scottish Health Education Group (1987) *Drink and Drugs at Work: a manager's guide* (Edinburgh, Scottish Health Education Group and Institute of Supervisory Management).)

A booklet providing guidance on dealing with problems related to all drugs, although stating that *'alcohol is by a very long way the biggest problem drug in the UK'*. In relation to employment, *'any drinking which adversely affects a person's health or reduces his work performance in the areas of efficiency, safety or attendance'* was defined as problematic. Chapters on 'defining', 'recognising', 'approaching' and 'handling' the problem were included, as was advice on sensible drinking, and on employment law and disciplinary procedures as a last resort. The Scottish Council on Alcohol 'draft policy on alcohol related problems for employing organisations' was reproduced as an appendix.

1987 Royal College of Physicians Report on Alcohol

(Royal College of Physicians (1987) *A Great and Growing Evil: the medical consequences of alcohol abuse* (London: Tavistock).)

A report which gave a detailed account of the physical effects of alcohol on the individual drinker, discussed drinking in relation to the workplace, to accidents and within the family, and examined the role of the physician in identifying and responding to alcohol problems.

Recommendations were made on:

- *Sensible limits of drinking*: not more than 21 units a week for men and 14 units a week for women, including 2 or 3 alcohol-free days.
- *What doctors must do to reduce 'alcohol abuse'*: improve early detection of people at risk, determine the extent of drinking, educate the public to drink within sensible limits and improve medical training.
- *What government can do to reduce 'alcohol abuse'*: reduce overall consumption levels through price control and maintenance of licensing law, control advertising, introduce a 'much tougher drinking-and-driving policy', support relevant research and education and establish a government body to coordinate all areas of policy.

1988 First Report of the Ministerial Group on Alcohol Misuse

(Ministerial Group on Alcohol Misuse (1988) *First Annual Report* (London, HMSO).)

The Ministerial Group was established in 1987 by the Home Secretary and the Secretary of State for Social Services, to review and develop the Government's strategy on alcohol misuse; it was converted to a Cabinet Committee in 1990. The report summarised action taken by the Government, in conjunction with other agencies, in the period since the Group's inception. 17 initiatives were reported to have been taken and a further 11 were said to be 'in hand'.

1988 Road Traffic Law Review Report

(Department of Transport and the Home Office (1988) *Road Traffic Law Review Report* (London, HMSO).)

The Road Traffic Law Review was established in 1985 – as a result of the Transport Select Committee Review – to look at possible improvements to traffic law in terms of simplification, effectiveness and acceptability. Their remit did not include high risk offenders, random breath testing or blood/alcohol levels, although some other policy issues in relation to drink driving were considered.

Recommendations:

- A new offence of bad driving causing death, in the case of motorists over the legal limit for alcohol or unfit to drive because of alcohol or drugs, should be introduced.
- An experiment should be carried out to examine the effectiveness of retraining first time drink driving offenders.
- When considering licence renewal applications, licensing authorities should be allowed to take into account evidence that the licensee had '*regularly or persistently served alcohol to customers who went on to commit drink driving offences*'.
- The government '*should monitor the development of devices to prevent drivers drinking when under the influence of alcohol*' and consider their compulsory inclusion in new vehicles once they are found to be effective, are available and relatively inexpensive.

1988 The Licensing Act

Some amendments of note were made to the principal Act:

- Permitted hours were extended on weekdays to 11.00 p.m., with no compulsory break. On Sundays the break was shortened by one hour.
- The word 'knowingly' was removed from a subsection concerning sale of intoxicating liquor to persons under 18 (although anyone charged can cite the fact that he or she exercised 'due diligence' and had 'no reason to suspect' that the person was under 18).
- Provision was made to exclude a person under 18 from being employed to sell intoxicating liquor off-sale.

1989 Department of Employment Guide: *Alcohol in the Workplace*

(Department of Employment (1989) *Alcohol in the Workplace: a guide for employees* (London. DoE) [not seen].)

A booklet distributed to 77,000 small to medium-sized firms throughout the UK. It advised that alcohol policies should include preventive measures as well as help for individuals, and offered guidelines on policy formation, implementation and monitoring.

1989 Standing Medical Advisory Committee Advice to Doctors

(The Standing Medical Advisory Committee to the Secretaries of State for Health and for Wales (1989) *Drinking Problems: a challenge for every doctor* (London, SMAC).)

A booklet (replacing an earlier version issued in 1973) prepared by the Standing Medical Advisory Committee to provide guidelines to doctors on the prevention and treatment of alcohol problems. Among advice offered was the suggestion that questions about drinking should be asked of patients as a matter of routine. In addition, the booklet gave guidance on assessing the likelihood of alcohol related harm and on appropriate action to be taken to address identified problems.

1989 Scottish Council on Alcohol National Strategy

(Scottish Council on Alcohol (1989) *A National Strategy on Alcohol with Special Reference to Scotland* (Glasgow, SCA).)

A discussion paper produced by the Professional Advisory Committee on Alcohol of the Scottish Council on Alcohol as a contribution to the debate on national alcohol policy in the light of a World Health Assembly resolution of 1983 which stated that, *'an effective strategy to the alcohol related problems necessitates comprehensive national alcohol policies'*. The report outlined the problem, discussed a wide range of potential measures to address it and concluded by strongly urging central government to commit itself to a strategy for prevention and service provision in Scotland. In addition, five 'best buys' from the range of possible measures were suggested:

- Encouragement of written alcohol policies in all major industries and workplaces.
- The introduction of truly random, non-discriminatory breath testing for drivers and a lowering of the legal limit for blood alcohol to 50 mg/100 ml.
- A major evaluation of minimal intervention strategies, concentrating on primary care but including secondary prevention.
- A major programme of promotion of low-alcohol and alcohol-free beverages.
- The promotion of a programme of 'designated places' throughout Scotland.

1989 Interdepartmental Circulars on Alcohol Misuse

(Ministerial Group on Alcohol Misuse (1989) *Alcohol Misuse* (London, DHSS).) (One for England and Wales in February; one for Scotland in August.))

Advice circulated to a range of statutory organisations to encourage inter-agency collaboration in identifying local needs and deciding how these might best be met. The purpose of the Circular was *'to encourage more efficient and better targeted use of existing resources to prevent and tackle alcohol misuse'* although 'substantial extra resources' were referred to as being available to the Health Education Authority to support Regional Health Authorities in developing multi-agency work.

Subsequently:

- 14 Alcohol Misuse Coordinator posts were created in England (one for each RHA).
- Local Coordinating Committees were established in Scotland.
- A Welsh Committee on Alcohol Misuse and Alcohol Advisory Committees for each Welsh county were established.

1989 White Paper: *The Road User and The Law*

(Department of Transport, the Home Office and the Scottish Office (1989) *The Road User and the Law: the Government's proposals for reform of road traffic law* (London, HMSO).)

The government's response to the *Road Traffic Law Review Report* (1988, above), the White Paper set out impending policy changes including further measures to deal with drink driving:

- The introduction of a new offence of causing death by careless driving while unfit through drink (or drugs) or over the legal limit for alcohol.
- The extension of the High Risk Offenders scheme to include all those disqualified while two and a half times or more over the limit – at the time this had to happen more than once in ten years – and any driver disqualified twice in ten years.
- The establishment of an experiment in the use of retraining offenders in order to influence attitudes towards drinking and driving.

1991 Lord President's Report: *Action Against Alcohol Misuse*

(Ministerial Group on Alcohol Misuse (1991) *The Lord President's Report on Action Against Alcohol Misuse* (London, HMSO).)

A report which reviewed contemporary alcohol use and alcohol problems, set out the government's policies, and provided information about a range of initiatives on aspects of alcohol use with some specific examples of good practice.

1991 Road Traffic Act

- Created a new offence of *'causing death by careless driving while under the influence of drink or drugs'*.
- Provided for an experiment in the use of rehabilitation courses for drink drive offenders disqualified for not less than twelve months. Courts may reduce the period of disqualification (by at least three months) on successful completion of an approved course, the fees for which are payable by the offender.

1991 Criminal Justice Act

Included, under Schedule 1A, conditions that may be applied by the court as part of a probation order where an offender is dependent on drugs or alcohol, and (a) the dependence has contributed to the offence and (b) it *'requires and may be susceptible to treatment'*. Such probation orders can include the requirement that the offender submits to treatment, which may be residential or non-residential and last for the duration of part, or all, of the probationary period.

1992 White Paper: *Health of the Nation*

(Department of Health (1992) *The Health of the Nation: a strategy for health in England,* Cm. 1986 (London, HMSO).)

A statement of the government's strategy for health in England which selected 5 'Key Areas' for action and set national objectives and targets for improvements in health within these.

The first Key Area – coronary heart disease and stroke – included the following target in relation to alcohol:

- *'To reduce the proportion of men drinking more than 21 units of alcohol per week from 28% in 1990 to 18% by 2005, and the proportion of women drinking more than 14 units of alcohol per week from 11% in 1990 to 7% by 2005.'*

No specific proposals relating to the achievement of this target were included.

1992 Transport and Works Act

Relates to the safety of railways, trams, inland waterways, etc., and includes provision for dealing with offences involving alcohol or drugs. These are:

- Anyone working in any capacity *'in which he can control or affect the movement of a vehicle'*, or in which he is responsible for the maintenance of a vehicle commits an offence if:
  - ▲ He is unfit to carry out work through drink or drugs (*'if his ability to carry out that work properly is for the time being impaired'*).
  - ▲ His blood or breath or urine alcohol level exceeds the prescribed limit.
- The 'responsible operator' is also deemed guilty, unless 'all due diligence' to prevent the offence has been exercised.

1993 Consultation Paper on Licensing Reform

(Home Office (1993) *Possible Reforms of the Liquor Licensing System in England and Wales: a consultation paper* (London, Home Office).)

This paper set out three proposals for reform of the licensing law in England and Wales, in each case describing the existing law and exploring the advantages and disadvantages of change, including a discussion of how each potential reform operates in Scotland. Comments were sought on a range of questions relating to the three proposals, which were:

- The current absolute discretion of licensing justices to refuse applications for on- or off-licences should be replaced by legally specified grounds for refusal.
- A system of children's certificates should be introduced, which would allow accompanied children under 14 to be admitted to certificated premises.
- A new category of licence for 'continental café-style premises' should be introduced. Accompanied children under 14 could be admitted to such premises.

Comment was also sought on a proposal to introduce legislation to abolish the Welsh Sunday Opening polls.

1993 Consultation Paper on Training in Scotland

(Scottish Home and Health Department (1993) *Scotland's Health, a Challenge to Us All: towards a national strategy for substance misuse training in Scotland* (Edinburgh, The Scottish Office).)

A consultation paper which, in Part I, outlined the existing arrangements for substance misuse training in Scotland and the need for a national strategy, set out a number of options for how this might be organised, and invited comments. Suggested options for the future were:

- The establishment of one centralised training agency within an academic institution.
- The establishment of a new, independent institution.
- The introduction of mechanisms to formalise collaborative working between the two bodies which currently provide training (the Centre for Alcohol and Drug Studies, University of Paisley; the Drugs Training Project, University of Stirling).

Part II of the document consisted of detailed discussion of the training strategy itself: aims and objectives; target groups; type, content and method of delivery of training.

1993 Department of Health Guidelines on Community Care

(Department of Health (1993) *Alcohol and Drug Services within Community Care*, LAC93/2 (London, DoH).)

A circular providing guidance to local authorities on their responsibility to provide services for 'adults who misuse alcohol and/or drugs' under the terms of the National Health Service and Community Care Act 1990 (in force from April 1993). Specific LA responsibilities are:

- Needs assessment of the local population in relation to alcohol and drugs related problems.
- Inclusion of alcohol and drugs services in community care plans.
- Social care needs assessment of individual alcohol and drug misusers.
- Arrangement of appropriate care packages.

Information on grant monies was included, alongside encouragement to purchase services from the private and voluntary sectors. Advice was also offered on assessment procedures, including fast track assessment, and on the 'special circumstances of alcohol and drug misusers'.

1995 Working Group Report: *Sensible Drinking*

(Department of Health (1995) *Sensible Drinking: the report of an inter-departmental working group* (London, DoH).)

The report of a group set up to review the Government's 'sensible drinking' message in the light of evidence which suggested that alcohol may afford some protection from coronary heart disease.

Conclusions:

- Drinking moderate amounts of alcohol (1–2 units a day) is beneficial in terms of reduced CHD mortality and morbidity in men over 40 and post-menopausal women.
- Drinking more than 2 units a day confers no additional benefit.
- Consumption by men of more than 3–4 units a day and women of more than 2–3 units a day brings significant risk of a range of other conditions.
- Advice presented in the form of 'daily benchmarks' is more appropriate than 'a rigid limit' of units per week.

1995 Report of Enquiry into Alcohol and Crime

(The All Party Group on Alcohol Misuse (1995) *Alcohol and Crime: breaking the link* (London, Alcohol Concern).)

The All Party Group on Alcohol Misuse took evidence from a broad range of agencies and professionals in an enquiry which sought to examine the link between alcohol and crime. The link was seen to be strong between alcohol and (especially violent) crime. In addition, '*a high proportion of offenders and re-offenders misuse alcohol*'. The Group also found a consensus on the need for a more coherent response to the problem. Thus 43 recommendations on practical steps to be taken were made, of which the following ten were '*considered to be of paramount importance*':

- All criminal justice agencies should be required to collect routine statistics on alcohol-related crime.
- The Government should consider re-establishing the Ministerial Group on Alcohol Misuse to coordinate interdepartmental policy in response to alcohol related crime.
- Permanent inter-agency groups should be established in each Local Authority to develop responses to alcohol related crime.
- All community safety initiatives should include alcohol misuse programmes.
- A national campaign to increase public awareness and encourage safer drinking should be launched.
- Random breath testing should be introduced and the legal limit reduced to 50 mg/100 ml.
- Drink driving rehabilitation training should be available nation-wide.
- A comprehensive range of alcohol services and information should be available throughout the criminal justice system.
- Care and treatment should be made available to prisoners with alcohol problems.
- A nation-wide network of specialist criminal justice alcohol work projects should be established.

1995 Joint Report on Alcohol and Young People

(Royal College of Physicians and the British Paediatric Association (1995) *Alcohol and the Young: report of a joint working party of the Royal College of Physicians and the British Paediatric Association* (London, RCP).)

A report written to '*assist parents and young people to make good choices, to provide government with information concerning policies that makes those choices easier, and to help professionals in their tasks of prevention and treatment*'. The document examines problems arising from drinking by parents as well as the prevalence and problems of young people's own drinking.

Recommendations on national policy included:

- Annual consumption should not be allowed to rise above its present level (equivalent to 2.5 units per day per person over 15) and action should be taken to reduce this to 1.5 units over the next 10 years.
- Tighter regulation of advertising should be imposed, marketing codes of practice should be reviewed, and labelling of alcoholic drinks should be introduced.
- A review of legislation should be carried out and current legislation concerning the minimum age should be fully enforced.
- The legal limit of blood alcohol should be reduced to 20 mg% for learner drivers and those with less than two years' post-licence experience.

A wide range of additional recommendations were addressed to a range of bodies – for example commissioners and providers of health, education and social services, organisations involved in professional training, recreation and sports clubs for young people, major funding bodies, and the alcohol industry – and to parents, children and young people. These included a call to commissioners of health services to ensure access to a multi-disciplinary specialist centre – a 'Young People's Drug and Alcohol Service'.

1995 DfE Circular: *Drug Prevention and Schools*

(Department for Education (1995) *Drug Prevention and Schools*, Circular number 4/95 (London, DfE).)

Guidance circulated to local education authorities and to the heads and governors of all schools in England in relation to drugs education, including tobacco, alcohol and volatile substances as well as illegal drugs. The circular:

- Explained the statutory position regarding drug education in schools under the National Curriculum Science Order which came into force in August 1995.
- Offered guidance on the principles which should inform such education, the development and implementation of appropriate teaching

programmes and the management of drug related incidents within schools.

1995 DfE/SCAA Guidance for Teachers on Drug Education

(Department for Education and the School Curriculum and Assessment Authority (1995) *Drug Proof: drug education: curriculum guidance for schools* (London, DfE).)

Curriculum guidance developed in consultation with teachers and other professionals. Drug Proof reflected the principles of the DfE circular, *Drug Prevention and Schools* (1995, above) and covered similar ground, but offered more detailed advice on the possible content of a programme of drug education, and on resources to support this.

1995 Licensing (Sunday Hours) Act

An act to make provision for change to the permitted Sunday opening hours.

- The requirement to close for a period during the afternoon was removed, except on Christmas Day and Good Friday. On these days the break was shortened from five to four hours.
- Permitted off-sales hours were extended to Sundays, except Christmas Day.

1996 Mental Health Foundation Report on Street Drinking

(Mental Health Foundation (1996) *Too Many for the Road: report of the Mental Health Foundation Expert Working Group on persistent street drinkers* (London, Mental Health Foundation).)

While acknowledging that the public may feel disturbed and intimidated by the presence of street drinkers, this report focused on the needs of the drinkers, who '*are among the most vulnerable people in society*'. Services to meet these needs were felt to be the most appropriate means of addressing the issue.

Conclusions:

- Accommodation is essential in order to provide stability and tackle health and social problems of this group.
- Coordination between services is needed to enable a 'continuum of care'. Joint planning and the development of working partnerships between

local authorities, health services and voluntary organisations is the best way of achieving this.

• Harm minimisation may be a more realistic goal than abstinence for many street drinkers.

Recommendations included:

• The use of Community Care plans to specify how the relevant services will be coordinated to provide a continuum of care.
• The development of partnerships between local authority social services and specialist services.
• The establishment of local arrangements to facilitate referral by the police of persistent street drinkers to appropriate facilities.
• Nurses should be attached to police stations where large numbers of detainees are held on drunkenness charges.

1996 HAS Guidance on Services for Children and Young People

(NHS Health Advisory Service (1996) *Children and Young People, Substance Misuse Services: the substance of young needs: commissioning and providing services for children and young people who use and misuse substances* (London, HMSO).)

A comprehensive review of existing services for children and young people who misuse alcohol, illicit and prescribed drugs and volatile substances, and information and guidance to commissioners, purchasers and providers of such services. The review uncovered a '*gloomy picture of current service provision*' and identified a number of issues that need to be addressed in order to improve the situation. In addition, suggestions were made for the development of effective service provision, which the review recommended be separate from adult services.

1996 Welsh Office Strategy to Combat Drug and Alcohol Misuse

(Welsh Office (1996) *Forward Together: a strategy to combat drug and alcohol misuse in Wales* (Cardiff, Welsh Office).)

The Welsh strategy on the prevention and treatment of substance misuse was intended to be complementary to that for the rest of the UK (Tackling Drugs Together), although it differed from that document in including alcohol within the range of substances encompassed. Its statement of purpose declared that 'vigorous action' would be taken to prevent the misuse of alcohol and drugs, particularly amongst younger people, and to provide treatment, support and rehabilitation. The document set out aims and objectives stemming from the statement of purpose; for each objective, key tasks, key participants and targets were outlined.

Emphasis was placed on the importance of inter-agency collaboration in the successful pursuance of the strategy. All organisations identified as having a role in this were advised to come together to form Drug and Alcohol Action Teams (DAATs) in the five health authority areas, which were required to submit local strategies to the Secretary of State. At national level, a Welsh Advisory Committee on Drug and Alcohol misuse was established to oversee and advise on the implementation of the strategy, assisted by a Welsh Drug and Alcohol Unit, whose remit also included the provision of practical and administrative support to DAATs.

1997 Confiscation of Alcohol (Young Persons) Act

'*An Act to permit the confiscation of intoxicating liquor held by or for use by young persons in public and certain other places.*' A police constable may require someone in a public place to surrender alcohol and state his or her name and address if:

- The person is under 18.
- The person intends to give the alcohol to someone under 18.
- The person is, or has recently been, in the company of someone under 18 consuming alcohol.

It is an arrestable offence not to comply with such a requirement without reasonable excuse.

1997 Prisons (Alcohol Testing) Act

An Act to enable prisoners in England and Wales to be tested for alcohol. Where a prison officer has reasonable suspicion that a prisoner has consumed alcohol he or she may require the prisoner to provide a sample of breath, urine or other specified non-intimate sample.

1997 Crime and Punishment (Scotland) Act

Contains similar provisions to the Confiscation of Alcohol (Young Persons) Act 1997 (above) and the Prisons (Alcohol Testing) Act 1997 (above).

1998 Alcohol Conference Action Plan Working Group Report

(1997 Alcohol Conference Action Plan Working Group (1998) *Report to the Scottish Office Department of Health* (Edinburgh, The Stationery Office).)

An action plan of recommendations produced by the 1997 Alcohol Conference Action Plan Working Group (ACAP) for the consideration of the Scottish Office Department of Health. ACAP was established to examine and build on the recommendations which came out of a conference held in October 1997, the aim of which was to contribute to the development of a national framework for alcohol policy for Scotland. The recommendations included in the report covered coordination, funding, prevalence and trends, prevention and promotion, provision of services, and licensing, local by-laws, criminal justice and enforcement.

Under 'coordination' the recommendation was that a new Scottish advisory committee on alcohol misuse should be established.

Appendix 2: A National Census of Alcohol Treatment Agencies

The first national census of alcohol treatment agencies in the UK was funded by a grant from the Society for the Study of Addiction to Alcohol and Other Drugs and benefited from the active cooperation of Alcohol Concern in England and the Scottish Council on Alcohol. The method and results of the census will be described here in abbreviated form, but a fuller account is available elsewhere (Luce *et al.*, 1998).

The methods used in the census were adapted from an Australian project (Webster *et al.* 1992; Torres *et al.*, 1995). The central aim was to obtain a record of treatment activity in specialist alcohol agencies throughout Britain on a specific day (Wednesday, 4 December 1996), with particular attention to client demographics and broad characteristics of treatment received. In contrast to the Australian census which was concerned with alcohol and other drug problems, the British study focused on clients whose main reason for attending a treatment agency on the day in question was related to problems with alcohol. A total of 728 agencies across the UK were eligible for the Census.

Main Findings

a) The overall response rate to the Census (42%) was disappointing but it was possible to examine the effects of response bias by using information on type of agency in the Alcohol Concern Services Directory for England and Wales. This revealed that, among responding agencies, there was a substantial under-representation of private (for profit) agencies and over-representations of charities and independent (non-profit) agencies. However, correcting for these under- and over-representations made very little difference to the findings of the Census.

b) The average number of clients seen by each of the 302 responding agencies on Census Day was 13 and the average number of non-attendances was 2, although there were wide variations in these figures. The highest number of clients seen on Census Day was 74. A rough estimate is that 10,000 individuals were seen for treatment or advice regarding an alcohol problem on Census Day in the UK; obviously only a small fraction of those individuals in the UK suffering from alcohol related problems.

c) The non-statutory sector (voluntary, non-profit organisations, charities and independent, non-profit agencies) accounted for almost two-thirds of all clients seen on Census Day. Most of the remaining clients (30%) were seen by National Health Service Trust services.

d) Despite demographic changes in drinking patterns over the last 10–20 years, the 'typical' client attending treatment services in the UK is still a middle-aged man. The client group as a whole showed evidence of major social disadvantage and dislocation, with high rates of marital breakdown, unemployment, homelessness, sickness and invalidity.

e) Compared with national figures, the client sample showed an over-representation of Irish clients seen in English agencies, but there appeared to be no under-representation of other ethnic groups.

f) The most common category of staff providing treatment on Census Day was counsellors, who saw 45% of clients recorded. It is not possible to comment on the amount of training these counsellors had received. Nurses saw 24% of clients and 16% were seen by other professional staff: social workers, medical doctors, psychologists and occupational therapists. Only 10% of clients were seen by unpaid staff. There were significant differences in categories of contact staff between types of agency in England and Wales and between the countries of the UK.

g) Clients' most common presenting complaint was concern about their psychological well-being which was attributed to nearly half the clients in the sample. Very few were apparently worried about occupational, financial or legal problems related to drinking.

h) Surprisingly, in view of evidence on the superior cost-effectiveness of non-residential forms of treatment (Miller and Hester, 1986a; Annis, 1987; Mattick and Jarvis, 1993), 28% of clients in the sample were recorded as being in residential treatment. Among agency types, the highest proportion of clients in residential treatment (79%) was shown in private (for profit) agencies, while agencies with a statutory component, National Health Service Trusts and voluntary/statutory partnerships, showed the lowest proportions.

j) The most common form of treatment received on Census Day was therapy or counselling conducted on a one-to-one basis which accounted for two-thirds of clients receiving some form of psychosocial treatment and nearly two-fifths of all clients in the sample. Group therapy was relatively little used.

k) Among the 7% of clients who received some kind of detoxification service on Census Day, the majority (60%) received it as in-patients. This is surprising in view of evidence on the superior cost-effectiveness of community-based and home detoxification services (Stockwell, 1987; Hayashida *et al.* 1989; Stockwell *et al.* 1990).

l) Of clients seen on Census Day, 42% were estimated to have been in treatment for more than three months, and for 18% treatment had continued for over a year. While interpretation of these figures is difficult, they do suggest that evidence on the cost-effectiveness of briefer approaches to treatment (Miller and Hester, 1986b; Hodgson, 1989) has had no major impact as yet on the duration of treatment in the UK.

m) The most commonly cited other service used in addition to the agency completing the Census Form was Alcoholics Anonymous, albeit mentioned in relation to only 9% of all clients.

n) Of clients seen on Census Day, 85% were recorded as having no illicit drug use. This may be an overestimate of the true proportion, but it is clear that there is a very large of number of people in treatment for alcohol problems in the UK who do not use illicit drugs. While many illicit drug users have problems with alcohol, the converse does not appear to be true.

Appendix 3: Membership of the Tackling Alcohol Together Steering Group

The Tackling Alcohol Together Steering Group was convened under the auspices of the Society for the Study of Addiction:

Eric Appleby	Alcohol Concern, London
Griffith Edwards	National Addiction Centre, London
Christine Godfrey	Centre for Health Economics, York
Larry Harrison	School of Community and Health Studies, University of Hull
Nick Heather	Centre for Alcohol and Drug Studies, Newcastle
Ray Hodgson	Centre for Applied Public Health Medicine, Cardiff
Robert Kendell	President, Royal College of Psychiatrists, London
Jane Marshall	National Addiction Centre, London
Duncan Raistrick	Leeds Addiction Unit, Leeds
Bruce Ritson	Royal Edinburgh Hospital, Edinburgh
Gillian Tober	Leeds Addiction Unit, Leeds

The Steering Group received expert administrative and editing support from Annie Ogletree. Additional secretarial support was provided by Gail Crossley.

Bibliography

Abel, E.L. and Sokol, R.J. (1991) A revised conservative estimate of the incidence of FAS and its economic impact, *Alcoholism: Clinical and Experimental Research*, 15, 514–24.

Abel, P. (1987) How social workers can help to break the vicious circle, *Social Work Today*, 18, 12–13.

Advisory Council on the Misuse of Drugs (1990) *Problem Drug Misuse: a review of training* (London, HMSO).

Advisory Council on the Misuse of Drugs (1998) *Drug Misuse and the Environment* (London, The Stationery Office).

Aitken, P.P., Eadie, D.R., Leathar, D.S., McNeill, R.E. and Scott, A.C. (1988) Television advertisements for alcoholic drinks do reinforce under-age drinking, *British Journal of Addiction*, 83, 1399–1419.

Aitken, P.P., Leathar, D.S. and Scott, A.C. (1988) Ten- to sixteen-year-olds' perceptions of advertisements for alcoholic drinks, *Alcohol and Alcoholism*, 23, 491–500.

Alasuutan, P. (1992) *A Cultural Theory Of Alcoholism* (New York, State University of New York Press).

Alaszewski, A. and Harrison, L. (1992) Alcohol and social work: a literature review, *British Journal of Social Work*, 22, 331–43.

Albery, I.P., Durand, M.A., Heuston, J., Groves, P., Gossop, M. and Strang, J. (1997) Training primary health care staff about alcohol: a study of alcohol trainers in the UK, *Drugs: Education, Prevention and Policy*, 4, 173–86.

Alcohol Advisory Council of New Zealand (1997) *The Management of Alcohol at Sporting Events and Outdoor Concerts*. Conference Outcomes, Dunedin, New Zealand.

Alcohol Advocacy Resource Center (1992) *Tackling Alcohol Problems on Campus: tools for media advocacy* (Washington, DC, The Advocacy Institute).

Alcohol Concern (n.d.) *A National Alcohol Training Strategy* (London, Alcohol Concern).

Alcohol Concern (1987) *Teaching about Alcohol Problems: tutor's manual and student handouts* (London, Alcohol Concern).

Alcohol Concern (1989) *Training Volunteer Alcohol Counsellors: the minimum standards*, (London, Alcohol Concern).

Alcohol Concern (1994a) *Alcohol Services Development Unit Briefing: primary health care and family health Service Authorities* (London, Alcohol Concern).

Alcohol Concern (1994b) *A National Alcohol Training Strategy* (London, Alcohol Concern).

Alcohol Concern (1995) Measure of Concern, *Personnel Today Magazine*, June, p. 32.

Alcohol Concern (1997a) Spending on alcohol, *Acquire: Alcohol Concern's Quarterly Information and Research Bulletin*, 19, 8.

Alcohol Concern (1997b) *Alcohol in the System? How Community Care Has Changed the Work of Alcohol Agencies: results of Alcohol Concern's community care survey* (London, Alcohol Concern).

Alcohol Concern (1998a) Information Unit Factsheets 22–24 (London, Alcohol Concern).

Alcohol Concern (1998b) Alcohol related deaths up, *Acquire: Alcohol Concern's Quarterly Information and Research Bulletin*, 20, 8.

Alcohol Concern and Standing Conference on Drug Abuse (1998) *Quality in Alcohol and Drug Services: draft quality standards manual for alcohol and drug treatment services* (London, Alcohol Concern and SCODA).

All Party Group on Alcohol Misuse (1995) *Alcohol and Crime: breaking the link* (London, Alcohol Concern).

Altman, D.G., Foster, V., Rasenick, D.L. and Tye, J.B. (1989) Reducing the illegal sale of cigarettes to minors, *Journal of the American Medical Association*, 261, 80–3.

Anderson, K., Plant, M.A., Baillie, R., Nevison, C., Plant, M.L. and Ritson, B. (1995) *Alcohol, Tobacco, Illicit Drug Use and Sex Education amongst Teenagers*, report to the Western Isles Health Board (Edinburgh, Alcohol Research Group).

Anderson, P. (1985) Managing alcohol problems in general practice, *British Medical Journal*, 290, 1873–5.

Anderson, P. (1989) Health Authority policies for the prevention of alcohol problems, *British Journal of Addiction*, 84, 203–9.

Anderson, P. (1990) *Management of Drinking Problems*, WHO Regional Publications, European Series 32 (Copenhagen, World Health Organization Regional Office for Europe).

Anderson, P. (1993) Effectiveness of general practice interventions for patients with harmful alcohol consumption, *British Journal of General Practice*, 43, 386–9.

Anderson, P. (1995) Alcohol and the risk of physical harm, in Holder, H.D. and Edwards, G. (eds) *Alcohol and Public Policy: evidence and issues*, pp. 82-113 (Oxford, Oxford University Press).

Anderson, P., Cremona, A., Paton, A., Turner, C. and Wallace, P. (1993) The risk of alcohol, *Addiction*, 88, 1493–1508.

Anderson, P. and Scott, E. (1992) The effect of general practitioners' advice to heavy drinking men, *British Journal of Addiction*, 87, 891–900.

Anderson, S.C. and Grant, J.F. (1984) Pregnant women and alcohol: implications for social work, *Social Casework*, 65, 3–10.

Andreasson, S., Allebeck, P. and Romelsjö, A. (1991) No U-shaped curve for young men, *British Journal of Addiction*, 86, 379–82.

Andrews, M. (1995) Searching for solutions to alcohol and other drug abuse during pregnancy: ethics, values and constitutional principles, *Social Work*, 40, 55–64.

Annis, H.M. (1987) Is inpatient rehabilitation of the alcoholic cost-effective? Con position, *Advances in Alcohol and Substance Abuse*, 5, 175–90.

Antti-Poika, I. (1988) *Alcohol Intoxication and Abuse in Injured Patients*, Dissertationes 19, Commentationes Physico-Mathematicae (Helsinki, Finnish Society of Sciences and Letters).

Atkin, C.K. and Block, M. (1981) *Contents and Effects of Alcohol Advertising*, pub. no. PB123142 (Springfield, National Technical Information Service).

Atkin, C.K., Hocking, J. and Block, M. (1984) Teenage drinking: does advertising make a difference? *Journal of Communication*, 34, 157–67.

Atkin, C.K., Neuendorf, K. and McDermott, S. (1983) The role of alcohol advertising in excessive and hazardous drinking, *Journal of Drug Education*, 13, 313–25.

Atkinson, A.B., Gomulka, J. and Stern, N.H. (1990) Spending on alcohol: evidence from the Family Expenditure Survey 1970–1983, *Economic Journal*, 100, 808–27.

Austin, E.W. and Johnson, K.K. (1997) Immediate and delayed effects of media literacy training on third graders' decision making for alcohol, *Health Communication*, 9, 323–49.

Austin, E.W. and Meili, H.K. (1994) Effects of interpretations of televised alcohol portrayals on children's alcohol beliefs, *Journal of Broadcasting and Electronic Media*, 38, 417–35.

Austin, E.W. and Nach, F.B. (1995) Sources and influences of young school-age children's general and brand-specific knowledge about alcohol, *Health Communication*, 7, 1–20.

Avis, S.P. (1996) Homicide in Newfoundland: a 9-year review, *Journal of Forensic Sciences*, 41, 101–5.

Babor, T.F. (1995) The social and public health significance of individually directed interventions, in Holder, H.D. and Edwards, G. (eds) *Alcohol and Public Policy: evidence and issues* (Oxford, Oxford University Press).

Babor, T.F. and Grant, M. (eds) (1992) *Project on Identification and Management of Alcohol-related Problems. Report on Phase II: a randomized clinical trial of brief interventions in primary health care* (Geneva, WHO).

Babor, T., Ritson, E. and Hodgson, R. (1986) Alcohol-related problems in the primary health care setting: a review of early intervention strategies, *British Journal of Addiction*, 81, 23–46.

Backett, S.A. (1987) Suicide in Scottish prisons, *British Journal of Psychiatry*, 151, 218–21.

Baggott, R. (1986) *The Politics of Alcohol: two periods compared*, Occasional Paper No. 8 (London, Institute for Alcohol Studies).

Bagnall, G. and Plant, M.A. (1991) HIV/AIDS risks, alcohol and illicit drug use among young adults in areas of high and low rates of infection, *AIDS Care*, 3, 355–61.

Baker, P. and McKay, S. (1990) *The structure of alcohol taxes: a hangover from the past*, IFS Commentary No. 21 (London, Institute for Fiscal Studies).

Balding, J. (1987) *Alcohol Consumption and Alcohol-related Problems in Young People: what should be the focus of health education?* (Exeter, Schools Health Education Unit).

Balding J. (1996) *Young People in 1995* (Exeter, University of Exeter).

Baldwin, S. (1987) Old wine in old bottles: why community alcohol teams will not work, in Stockwell, T. and Clement, S. (eds) *Helping the Problem Drinker: new initiatives in community care* (London, Croom Helm).

Baldwin, S. (ed.) (1990) *Alcohol Education and Offenders* (London, B.T. Batsford).

Bales, R.F. (1962) Attitudes towards drinking in the Irish culture, in Pittman, D.J. and Snyder, C.R. (eds) *Society, Culture and Drinking Patterns* (New York, John Wiley and Sons).

Bandura, A. (1977) *Social Learning Theory* (Englewood Cliffs, NJ, Prentice-Hall).

Barber, J. (1994) *Social Work with Addictions* (New York, New York University Press).

Barber, J.G., Bradshaw, R. and Walsh, C. (1989) Reducing alcohol consumption through television advertising, *Journal of Consulting and Clinical Psychology*, 57, 613–18.

Barber, J.G. and Grichting, W.L. (1990) Australia's media campaign against drug abuse, *International Journal of the Addictions*, 25, 693–708.

Barlow, T. and Wogalter, M.S. (1993) Alcoholic beverage warnings in magazine and television advertisements, *Journal of Consumer Research*, 20, 147–56.

Barnea, Z. and Teichman, M. (1994) Substance misuse among the elderly: implications for social work intervention, *Journal of Gerontological Social Work*, 3, 133–48.

Baron, R.A. and Richardson, D.R. (1994) *Human Aggression* (2nd edition) (London, Plenum Press).

Barrison, I.G., Viola, L., Mumford, J., Murray, R.M., Gordon, M. and Murray-Lyon, I.M. (1982) Detecting excessive drinking among admissions to a general hospital, *Health Trends*, 14, 80–3.

Barrison, I.G., Viola, L. and Murray-Lyon, I.M. (1980) Do housemen take an adequate drinking history? *British Medical Journal*, 281, 1040.

Barton, R. and Godfrey, S. (1988) Un-health promotion: results of a survey of alcohol promotion on television, *British Medical Journal*, 296, 1593–4.

Basic, M.M. (1992) Reading the alcoholic film: analysis of 'The Country Girl', *Sociological Quarterly*, 33, 211–27.

Beaglehole, R. and Jackson, R. (1992) Alcohol, cardiovascular diseases and all causes of death: a review of the epidemiological evidence, *Drug and Alcohol Review*, 11, 275–90.

Becker, G. and Murphy, K. (1988) A theory of rational addiction, *Journal of Political Economy*, 96, 675–701.

Bennett, M. (1991) Licensing laws and drinking, *British Medical Journal*, 303, 472.

Bennett, T. and Wright, R. (1984) The relationships between alcohol use and burglary, *British Journal of Addiction*, 79, 431–7.

Beresford, T.P. (1979) Alcoholism consultation and general psychiatry, *General Hospital Psychiatry*, 1, 293–300.

Bernadt, M.W. and Murray, R.M. (1986) Psychiatric disorder, drinking and alcoholism: what are the links? *British Journal of Psychiatry*, 148, 393–400.

Blake, D. and Boyle, S. (1992) The demand for cider in the United Kingdom, *Oxford Bulletin of Economics and Statistics*, 54, 73–86.

Blake, D. and Nied, A. (1998) The demand for alcohol in the United Kingdom, *Applied Economics*, 29, 1655–72.

Blose, J. and Holder, M. (1987) Liquor by the drink and alcohol-related traffic crashes: a natural experiment using time series analysis, *Journal of Studies on Alcohol*, 48, 52–60.

Blose, J.O. and Holder, H.D. (1991) The utilization of medical care by treated alcoholics: longitudinal patterns by age, gender and type of care, *Journal of Substance Abuse*, 3, 13–27.

Booth, B.M., Yates, W.R., Petty, F. and Brown, K. (1990) Longitudinal characteristics of hospital use before and after treatment, *American Journal of Drug and Alcohol Abuse*, 16, 161–79.

Booth, W. (1890) *In Darkest England and the Way Out* (London, International Headquarters of the Salvation Army).

Botvin, G. (1990) Substance abuse prevention: theory, practice and effectiveness, in Tonry, M. and Wilson, J.Q. (eds) *Drugs and Crime*, pp. 461–519 (Chicago, IL, University of Chicago Press).

Botvin, G.J., Baker, E., Dusenbury, L., Botvin, E.M. and Diaz, T. (1995) Long-term follow-up results of a randomised drug abuse prevention trial, *Journal of the American Medical Association*, 273, 1106–12.

Boys, A., Strang, J. and Homan, C. (1997) Have drug workers in England received appropriate training?: 1995 baseline data from a national survey, *Drugs: Education, Prevention and Policy*, 4, 297–304.

Bradbury, A. (1991) Pattern and severity of injury sustained by pedestrians in road traffic accidents with particular reference to the effect of alcohol, *Injury*, 22, 132–4.

Brewers and Licensed Retailers Association (1998) *Statistical Handbook* (London, Brewing Publications Ltd).

British Association of Social Workers (1988) *Policy Guidelines: report of the Addictions (Alcohol) Working Group* (London, BASW).

British Medical Association (1989) *Alcohol and Accidents* (London, BMA).

British Paediatric Association and the Royal College of Physicians (1995) *Alcohol and the Young* (London, Royal College of Physicians).

Brook, J.S., Whiteman, M., Finch, S.J. and Cohen, P. (1996) Young adult drug use and delinquency: childhood antecedents, *Journal of the American Academy of Child and Adolescent Psychiatry*, 35, 1584–92.

Brooke, D., Taylor, C., Gunn, J. and Maden, A. (1996) Point prevalence of mental disorder in unconvicted male prisoners in England and Wales, *British Medical Journal*, 313, 1524–7.

Brown, S.A., Goldman, M.S., Inn, A. and Anderson, L.R. (1980) Expectations of reinforcement from alcohol: their domain and relation to drinking patterns, *Journal of Consulting and Clinical Psychology*, 43, 419–26.

Brown, S.A. and Irwin, M. (1991) Changes in anxiety among abstinent male alcoholics, *Journal of Studies on Alcohol*, 52, 55–61.

Bruun, K., Edwards, G., Lumio, M., Mäkelä, K., Pan, L., Popham, R.E., Room, R., Schmidt, W., Skog, O., Sulkunen, P. and Österberg, E. (1975) Alcohol Control Policies in Public Health Perspective, *The Finnish Foundation for Alcohol Studies*, Vol. 25 (Helsinki, Forssa).

Burton, R. (1621) *Anatomy of Melancholy* (Oxford, John Lichfield and James Short for Henry Cripps).

Butcher, P. (n.d.) *Health Outcomes Project on Alcohol* (Norwich, East Norfolk Health Commission).

Cahalan, D. and Room, R. (1974) *Problem Drinking Among American Men* (New Brunswick, NJ, Rutgers Center of Alcohol Studies).

Calfee, J. and Scheraga, C. (1994) The influence of advertising on alcohol consumption, *International Journal of Advertising*, 13, 287–313.

Carey, K.B. (1995) Alcohol-related expectancies predict quantity and frequency of heavy drinking among college students, *Psychology of Addictive Behaviors*, 9, 236–41.

Carpenter, C., Glassner, B., Johnson, B.D. and Loughlin, J. (1988) *Kids, Drugs, and Crime* (Lexington, MA, Lexington Books).

Carroll, K.M. (1994) Treatment selection, treatment implementation and process assessment in matching research, *Journal of Studies on Alcohol*, Supplement No. 12, 137–38.

Cartwright, A.K. (1980) The attitudes of helping agents towards the alcoholic client: the influence of experience, support, training and self esteem, *British Journal of Addiction*, 75, 413–31.

Cartwright, A.K. and Gorman, D.M. (1993) Processes involved in changing the therapeutic attitudes of clinicians toward working with drinking clients, *Psychotherapy Research*, 3, pp. 95–104.

Cartwright, A.K., Shaw, S.J. and Spratley, T.A. (1978a) The relationships between per capita consumption, drinking patterns and alcohol-related problems in a population sample, 1965–1974. Part I: increased consumption and changes in drinking patterns, *British Journal of Addiction*, 73, 237–46.

Cartwright, A.K., Shaw, S.J. and Spratley, T.A. (1978b) The relationships between per capita consumption, drinking patterns and alcohol-related problems in a population sample, 1965–1974. Part II: implications for alcohol control policy, *British Journal of Addiction*, 73, 247–58.

Casiro, O.G., Stanwick, R.S., Pelech, A., Taylor, V. and the Child Health Committee of the Manitoba Medical Association (1994) Public awareness of the risks of drinking alcohol during pregnancy: the effects of a television campaign, *Canadian Journal of Public Health*, 85, 23–7.

Casswell, S. (1995) Public discourse on alcohol: implications for public policy, in Holder, H.D. and Edwards, G. (eds) *Alcohol and Public Policy: evidence and issues* (Oxford, Oxford University Press).

Casswell, S. and Gilmore, L. (1989) An evaluated community action project on alcohol, *Journal of Studies on Alcohol*, 50 (4), 339–46.

Casswell, S., Gilmore, L., Maguire, V. and Ransom, R. (1989) Changes in public support for alcohol policies following a community-based campaign, *British Journal of Addiction*, 84, 515–22.

Casswell, S., Zhang, J.F. and Wyllie, A. (1993) The importance of amount and location of drinking for the experience of alcohol-related problems, *Addiction*, 88, 1527–34.

Cavan, S. (1966) *Liquor Licence* (Chicago, IL, Aldine).

Central Council for Education and Training in Social Work (CCETSW) (1992) *Substance Misuse: guidance notes for the diploma in social work* (London, CCETSW).

Central Policy Review Staff (1982) *Alcohol Policies in the UK* (Stockholm, Stockholms Universitet).

Central Statistical Office (CSO) (various months and years) *Monthly Digest of Statistics* (London, HMSO).

Chaloupka, F.J., Saffer, H. and Grossman, M. (1991) *Alcohol Control Policies and Motor Vehicle Fatalities*, NBER Working Paper 3831 (Cambridge, MA, National Bureau of Economic Research).

Chaloupka, F.J. and Wechsler, H. (1995) *The Impact of Price, Availability, and Alcohol Control Policies on Binge Drinking in College*, NBER Working Paper No. 5319 (Cambridge, MA, National Bureau of Economic Research).

Chapman, S. (1993) The role of doctors in promoting smoking cessation, *British Medical Journal*, 307, 518–19.

Cherpitel, C. J. (1996) Regional differences in alcohol and fatal injury: a comparison of data from two county coroners, *Journal of Studies on Alcohol*, 57, 244–8.

Chick, J. (1994) Alcohol problems in the general hospital, in Edwards, G. and Peters, T.J. (eds) *Alcohol and Alcohol Problems*, British Medical Bulletin 50, pp. 200–10 (London, Churchill Livingstone).

Chick, J. (1996) Medication in the treatment of alcohol dependence, *Advances in Psychiatric Treatment*, 2, 249–57.

Chick, J., Lloyd, G. and Crombie, E. (1985) Counselling problem drinkers in medical wards: a controlled study, *British Medical Journal*, 290, 965–7.

Choquet, M., Menke, H. and Manfredi, R. (1991) Interpersonal aggressive behavior and alcohol consumption among young urban adolescents in France, *Alcohol and Alcoholism*, 26, 381–90.

Christiansen, B.A., Roehling, P.V., Smith, G.T. and Goldman, M.S. (1989) Using alcohol expectancies to predict adolescent drinking behavior after one year, *Journal of Consulting and Clinical Psychology*, 57, 93–9.

Christopher, J. (1997) Secular organisations for sobriety, in Lowinson, J.H., Ruiz, P., Millman, R.B. and Langrod, J.G. (eds) *Substance Abuse: A Comprehensive Textbook* (3rd Edition) (Baltimore MD Williams and Wilkins).

Cicchinelli, L.F., Binner, P.R. and Halpern, J. (1978) Output value analysis of an alcohol treatment program, *Journal of Studies on Alcohol*, 39, 435–47.

Clare, A. (1977) How good is treatment?, in Edwards, G. and Grant, M. (eds) *Alcoholism: new knowledge and new response* (London, Croom Helm).

Clark, W.G. and Hilton, M.E. (eds) (1991) *Alcohol in America* (Albany, State University of New York).

Clayson, C. (1984) Licensing law and health: the Scottish experience, in *Action on Alcohol Abuse Licensing Law and Health* (London, Action on Alcohol Abuse).

Clayton, A. (1997) *Which Way Forward? A review of drink driving countermeasures in selected countries world-wide* (London, Portman Group).

Clayton, R.R., Cattarello, A. and Walden, K.P. (1991) Sensation seeking as a potential mediating variable for school based prevention intervention: a two year follow-up of DARE, *Health Communication*, 3, 229–39.

Clement, S. (1986) The identification of alcohol-related problems by general practitioners, *British Journal of Addiction*, 81, 257–64.

Clements, K. and Selvanathan, C. (1987) Alcohol consumption, in Theil, H. and Clements, K. *Applied Demand Analysis: results from system-wide approaches* (Cambridge, MA, Ballinger).

Cochrane, R. and Sukhwant, B. (1990) The drinking habits of Sikh, Muslim and white men in the West Midlands: a community survey, *British Journal of Addiction*, 85, 759–69.

Coggans, N. and McKellar, S. (1995) *The Facts about Alcohol, Aggression and Adolescence* (London, Cassell).

Cole-Harding, S. and Wilson, J.R. (1987) Ethanol metabolism in men and women, *Journal of Studies on Alcohol*, 48, 380–87.

Colhoun, H., Ben-Shlomo, Y., Dong, W., Bost, L. and Marmot, M. (1997) Ecological analysis of collectivity of alcohol consumption in England: importance of average drinker, *British Medical Journal*, 314, 1164–8.

Colhoun, H. and Prescott-Clarke, P. (1994) *Health survey for England 1994, Volume 1: findings* (London, HMSO).

Collier, D.J. and Beales, I.L.P (1989) Drinking among medical students: a questionnaire survey, *British Medical Journal*, 299, 19–22.

Connolly, G.M., Casswell, S., Zhang, J.F. and Silva, P.A. (1994) Alcohol in the mass media and drinking by adolescents: a longitudinal study, *Addiction*, 89 (10), 1255–63.

Cook, C.C.H. (1997a) Alcohol and aviation, *Addiction*, 92, 539–56.

Cook, C.C.H. (1997b) Alcohol policy and aviation safety, *Addiction*, 92, 793–804.

Cook, P. (1981) The effect of liquor taxes on drinking cirrhosis and auto fatalities, in Moore, M. and Gerstein, D. (eds) *Alcohol and Public Policy: beyond the shadow of prohibition*, pp. 255–85 (Washington, DC, National Academy of Sciences).

Cook, P. and Moore, M. (1993) Drinking and schooling, *Journal of Health Economics*, 12, 411–29.

Cook, P. and Tauchen, G. (1982) The effect of taxes on heavy drinking, *Bell Journal of Economics*, 13, 379–90.

Cook, T. (1975) *Vagrant Alcoholics* (London, Routledge and Kegan Paul).

Cookson, H. (1992) Alcohol use and offence type in young male offenders, *British Journal of Criminology*, 32, 352–60.

Cooper, D. (1994) Problem drinking, *Nursing Times*, 90, 36–9.

Copeland, J. and Hall, W. (1992) A comparison of predictors of treatment drop-out of women seeking drug and alcohol treatment in a specialist women's and two traditional mixed-sex treatment services, *British Journal of Addiction*, 87, 883–90.

Covell, K. (1992) The appeal of image advertisements: age, gender, and product differences, *Journal of Early Adolescence*, 12, 46–60.

Coyle, D., Godrey, C., Hardman, G. and Raistrick, D. (1997) Costing substance misuse services, *Addiction*, 92, 1007–15.

Crawford, I. and Tanner, S. (1995) Bringing it all back home: alcohol taxation and cross border shopping, *Fiscal Studies*, 16, 94–114.

Critchlow, B. (1983) Blaming the booze: the attribution of responsibility for drunken behaviour, *Personal Social Psychology Bulletin*, 9, 451–73.

Croft-White, C. and Rayner, G. (1993) *Assessment and Care Management for People with Drug and Alcohol Problems: a national study* (London, Alcohol Concern and SCODA).

Crome, I.B. (1996) *Psychiatric Disorder and Psychoactive Substance Use Disorder: towards improved service provision*, report prepared for Department of Health Working Party on Substance Misuse and Psychiatric Comorbidity (London, Centre for Research into Drugs and Health Behaviour).

Crome, I.B. (1999) The Trouble with Training: substance misuse education in British medical schools revisited. What are the issues? *Drugs: education, prevention and policy*, 6, pp. 111–23.

Davidson, K.M. and Ritson, E.B. (1993) The relationship between alcohol dependence and depression, *Alcohol and Alcoholism*, 28, 147–55.

Davies, J.B. (1978) *The Psychology of Music* (London, Hutchinson).

Davies, J.B. (1992) *The Myth of Addiction* (London, Harwood).

Davies, P. and Walsh, D. (1983) *Alcohol Problems and Alcohol Control in Europe* (London, Croom Helm).

Dawson, D.A. (1992) The effect of parental alcohol dependence on perceived children's behaviour, *Journal of Substance Abuse*, 4, 329–40.

Dean, A. (1995) Alcohol in Hebridean culture: 16th–20th century, *Addiction*, 90, 277–88.

Deehan, A., Templeton, L., Drummond, C., Taylor, C. and Strang, J. (1996) *The Detection and Management of Alcohol Misuse Patients in Primary Care: general practitioners' behaviour and attitudes*, a report to the Department of Health (London, Institute of Psychiatry).

Deehan, A., Templeton, L., Taylor, C., Drummond, C. and Strang, J. (1998) How do GPs manage alcohol misusing patients? Results from a national survey of GPs in England and Wales, *Drug and Alcohol Review*, 17, pp. 259–66.

Deery, H.A. and Love, A.W. (1996) The effect of a moderate dose of alcohol on the traffic hazard perception profile of young drink drivers, *Addiction*, 91, 815–27.

Delaney, W., Grube, J.W. and Genevieve, M.A. (1998) Predicting likelihood of seeking help through the employee assistance programme among salaried and union hourly employees, *Addiction*, 93, 399–410.

deLucia, J. (ed.) (1981) *Fourth Special Report to the US Congress on Alcohol and Health* , pp. 83–4 (Rockville, MD, National Institute on Alcohol and Alcoholism).

Denzin, N. (1991) *Hollywood Shot by Shot: alcoholism in the American cinema* (New York, Aldine De Gruyter).

Department of the Environment, Transport and the Regions (DETR) (1998) *Road Accidents, Great Britain 1997: the casualty report* (London, The Stationery Office).

Department of Health (DoH) (1989) *Terms of Service for Doctors in General Practice* (London, HMSO).

Department of Health (1992) *The Health of the Nation: a strategy for health in England and Wales* (London, HMSO).

Department of Health (1995a) *Tackling Drugs Together: a strategy for England 1995–1998* (London, HMSO).

Department of Health (1995b) *Sensible Drinking: the report of an inter-departmental working group* (London, DoH).

Department of Health (1995c) *Hospital Episode Statistics, Volume 1: England: financial year 1993–4* (London, Government Statistical Service).

Department of Health (1996) *Primary Care: delivering the future* (London, HMSO).

Department of Health (1997) *The New NHS: modern, dependable*, Cm. 3807 (London, HMSO).

Department of Health (1998) *Our Healthier Nation: a contract for health* (London, The Stationery Office).

Department of Health and Social Security (DHSS) (1977) *Prevention and Health*, Cmnd. 7047 (London, HMSO).

Department of Health and Social Security (1981) *Prevention and Health: drinking sensibly* (London, HMSO).

Department of Health and Social Security and the Welsh Office (1977) *Prevention: report of the Advisory Committee on Alcoholism* (London, HMSO).

Department of Health and Social Security and the Welsh Office (1978) *The Pattern and Range of Service for Problem Drinkers: report by the Advisory Committee on Alcoholism* (London, HMSO).

Dielman, T.E., Kloska, D.D., Leech, S.L., Schulenberg, J.E. and Shope, J.T. (1992) Susceptibility to peer pressure as an explanatory variable for the differential effectiveness of an alcohol misuse prevention program in elementary schools, *Journal of School Health*, 62, 233–7.

Dielman, T.E., Shope, J.T., Butchart, A.T. and Campanelli, P.C. (1986) Prevention of adolescent alcohol misuse: an elementary school program, *Journal of Pediatric Psychology*, 1, 259–82.

Dielman T.E., Shope, J.T., Leech, S.L. and Butchart, A.T. (1989) Differential effectiveness of an elementary school-based alcohol misuse prevention program, *Health Education Quarterly*, 16, 113–30.

DiNardo, J. and Lemieux, T. (1992) *Alcohol, Marijuana, and American Youth: the unintended effects of government regulation*, Working Paper No. 4212 (Cambridge, MA, National Bureau of Economic Research).

Doll, R., Forman, D., LaVecchi, A. and Wouterson, F. (1993) Alcoholic beverages and cancers of the digestive tract, in P.M. Verschuren (ed.) *Health Issues Related to Human Alcohol Consumption*, a report for the Amsterdam Group, pp. 125–66 (Brussels, International Life Sciences).

Doll, R., Peto, R., Hall, E., Wheatley, K. and Gray, R. (1994) Mortality in relation to consumption of alcohol: 13 years' observations on male British doctors, *British Medical Journal*, 309, 911–18.

Donovan, C. and McEwan, R. (1995) A review of the literature examining the relationship between alcohol use and HIV-related sexual risk-taking in young people, *Addiction*, 90, 319–28.

Dorn, N. and Maynard, A. (1994) *An Analysis of Drug Referral Schemes* (London, Prison Reform Group).

Dorn, N. and South, N. (1983) *Message in a Bottle: a theoretical overview and annotated bibliography on the mass media and alcohol* (Aldershot, Gower).

Downs, W.R. and Miller, B.A. (1996) Intergenerational links between childhood abuse and alcohol-related problems, in Harrison, L. (ed.) *Alcohol Problems in the Community*, pp. 14–51 (London, Routledge).

Drake, M., O'Brian, M. and Biebuyck, T. (1981) *Single and Homeless* (London, HMSO).

Drummond, D.C. (1997) Alcohol interventions: do the best things come in small packages? *Addiction*, 92, 375–9.

Drummond, D.C., Thom, B., Brown, C., Edwards, E. and Mullan, M. (1990) Specialist versus general practitioner treatment of problem drinkers, *Lancet*, 336, 915–18.

Duffy, J. and Cohen, G. (1978) Total consumption and excessive drinking, *British Journal of Addiction*, 73, 259–64.

Duffy, J. and Pinot de Moira, A. (1996) Changes in licensing law in England and Wales and indicators of alcohol-related problems, *Addiction Research*, 4, 245–71.

Duffy, J. and Plant, M. (1986) Scotland's liquor licensing changes: an assessment, *British Medical Journal*, 292, 36–9.

Duffy, J.C. (ed.) (1992) *Alcohol and Illness* (Edinburgh, Edinburgh University Press).

Duffy, M. (1982) The effect of advertising on the total consumption of alcoholic drink in the United Kingdom: some econometric estimates, *Journal of Advertising*, 1, 105–17.

Duffy, M. (1983) The demand for alcoholic drink in the United Kingdom 1963–78, *Applied Economics*, 15, 125–40.

Duffy, M. (1987) Advertising and the inter-product distribution of demand: a Rotterdam model approach, *European Economic Review*, 31, 1051–70.

Duffy, M. (1989) Measuring the contribution of advertising to growth in demand: an econometric-accounting framework, *International Journal of Advertising*, 8, 95–110.

Duffy, M. (1991) Advertising and the consumption of tobacco and alcoholic drink: a system-wide analysis, *Scottish Journal of Political Economy*, 38, 369–85.

Duffy, M. (1995) Advertising in demand systems for alcoholic drinks and tobacco: a comparative study, *Journal of Policy Modelling*, 17, 557–77.

Duffy, S.W., and Sharples, L.D. (1992) Alcohol and cancer risk, in Duffy, J.C. (ed.) *Alcohol and Illness*, pp. 1–18 (Edinburgh, Edinburgh University Press).

Duncan, D. and Taylor, D. (1996) Chlormethiazole or chlordiazepoxide in alcohol detox-ification, *Psychiatric Bulletin*, 20, 599–601.

Dunn, C.W., Donovan, D.M. and Gentilello, L.M. (1997) Practical guidelines for performing alcohol interventions in trauma centers, *Journal of Trauma: Injury, Infection and Critical Care*, 42, 299–304.

Dunn, P.C., Glascoff, M.A. and Knight, S.M. (1993) Defining irresponsible drinking behaviours: an exploratory study using the diversity of five diverse groups, *Journal of Alcohol and Drug Education*, 38, 37–48.

Dunne, F. (1990) Alcohol abuse on skid row: in sight out of mind, *Alcohol and Alcoholism*, 25, 13–15.

Durant, R.H., Rome, E.S., Rich, M., Allred, E., Emans, S.J. and Woods, E.R. (1997) Tobacco and alcohol use behaviors portrayed in music videos: a content analysis, *American Journal of Public Health*, 87, 1131–5.

Eagles J. and Besson, J. (1985) Changes in the incidence of alcohol-related problems in North East Scotland 1974–82, *British Journal of Psychiatry*, 147, 39–43.

Eagles, J. and Besson, J. (1986) Scotland's licensing changes, *British Medical Journal*, 292, 486.

Edwards, G. (1995) Alcohol Policy and the Public Good (editorial), *Addiction*, 90, 173–80.

Edwards, G. (1998) If the drinks industry does not clean up its act, pariah status is inevitable, *British Medical Journal*, 317, 336.

Edwards, G., Anderson, A., Babor, T.F., Casswell, S., Ferrence, R., Giebrecht, N., Godfrey, C., Holder, H.D., Lemmens, P., Mäkelä, K., Midanik, L.T., Norström, T., Österberg, E., Romelsjö, A., Room, R., Simpura, J. and Skog, O. (1994) *Alcohol Policy and the Public Good* (Oxford, Oxford University Press).

Edwards, G. and Grant, M. (1980) *Alcoholism Treatment in Transition* (London, Croom Helm).

Edwards, G., Gross, M.M., Keller, M., Moser, J. and Room, R. (1987) *Alcohol-Related Disabilities*, WHO Offset Publication No. 32 (Geneva, WHO).

Edwards, G., Marshall, E.J. and Cook, C.C.H. (1997) The Treatment of Drinking Problems (3rd edition) (Cambridge, Cambridge University Press).

Edwards, G. and Unnithan, S. (1992) *Epidemiologically-based Needs Assessment: report No. 7, alcohol misuse* (London, National Health Service Management Executive).

Ellickson, P.L. and Bell, R.M. (1990) Drug prevention in junior high: a multi-site longitudinal test, *Science*, 247, 1299–305.

Ellickson, P.L., Bell, R.M., Thomas, M.A., Robyn, A.E. and Zellman, G.L. (1988) *Designing and Implementing Project ALERT: a smoking and drug prevention experiment* (Santa Monica, CA, RAND Corporation).

Ellickson, P.L. and Hays, R.D. (1991) Antecedents of drinking among young adolescents with different alcohol use histories, *Journal of Studies on Alcohol*, 52, 398–408.

Elliott, D.S., Huizinga, D. and Ageton, S.S. (1985) *Explaining Delinquency and Drugs Use* (London, Sage).

Elvy, G.A., Wells, J.E. and Baird, K.A. (1988) Counselling problem drinkers in medical wards: a controlled study, *British Journal of Addiction*, 83, 83–9.

Emrick, C.D. (1987) Alcoholics Anonymous: affiliation processes and effectiveness as treatment, *Alcoholism: Clinical and Experimental Research*, 11, 416–23.

English National Board (ENB) (1995) *Training Needs Analysis: project on 'meeting the education and training needs of nurses, midwives and health visitors in the field of substance misuse'* (London, ENB).

English National Board (1996a) *Creating Lifelong Learners: partnerships for care, curriculum guidelines for education programmes, substance misuse* (London, ENB).

English National Board (1996b) *Substance Use and Misuse: guidelines for good practice in education and training of nurses, midwives and health visitors* (London, ENB).

Enomoto, T., Takase, S., Yasuhara, M. and Takada, A. (1991) Acetaldehyde metabolism in different aldehyde dehydrogenase – 2 genotypes, *Alcoholism: Clinical and Experimental Research*, 15, 141–4.

Ensor, T. and Godfrey, C. (1993) Modelling the interactions between alcohol, crime and the criminal justice system, *Addiction*, 88, 477–87.

Ericksen, J.P. and Trocki, K.F. (1992) Behavioral risk factors for sexually transmitted diseases in American households, *Social Science Medicine*, 34, 843–53.

Eronen, M. (1995) Mental disorders and homicidal behavior in female subjects, *American Journal of Psychiatry*, 152, 1216–18.

Eronen, M., Tiihonen, J. and Hakola, P. (1996) Schizophrenia and homicidal behaviour, *Schizophrenia Bulletin*, 22, 83–9.

Etzioni, A. (1995) *The Spirit of Community* (London, Fontana).

Faculty of Public Health Medicine and Royal College of Physicians (1991) *Alcohol and the Public Health* (London, Macmillan).

Famularo, R., Stone, K., Barnum, R. and Wharton, R. (1986) Alcoholism and severe child maltreatment, *American Journal of Orthopsychiatry*, 56, 481–5.

Fanti, G. (1986) Study of field social workers' attitudes to problem drinkers: 1984 survey, *Social Services Research*, 2, 129–36.

Farrell, M.P. and David, A.S. (1988) Do psychiatric registrars take a proper drinking history? *British Medical Journal*, 296, 395–96.

Farrell, M.P. and Lewis, G. (1990) Discrimination on the grounds of diagnosis, *British Journal of Addiction*, 85, 883–90.

Fergusson, D.M., Lynskey, M.T. and Horwood, L.J. (1996) Alcohol misuse and juvenile offending in adolescence, *Addiction*, 91, 483–94.

Ferrence, R.G. (1995) Moderate drinking and public health, in Holder, H.D. and Edwards, G. (eds) Alcohol and Public Policy: evidence and issues, pp. 215–37 (Oxford, Oxford University Press).

Fillmore, K.M. (1988) *Alcohol Use Across the Life Course: review of seventy years of international longitudinal research* (Toronto, Addiction Research Foundation).

Fillmore, K.M., Golding, J.M., Graves, K.L., Kniep, S., Leino, E.V., Romelsjö, A., Shoemaker, C., Ager, C.R., Allebeck, P. and Ferrer, H.P. (1998a) Alcohol consumption and mortality, I: Characteristics of drinking groups, *Addiction*, 93, 183–203.

Fillmore, K.M., Golding, J.M., Graves, K.L., Kniep, S., Leino, E.V., Romelsjö, A., Showmaker, C., Ager, C.R., Allebeck, P. and Ferrer, H.P. (1998b) Alcohol consumption and mortality, III: Studies of female populations, *Addiction*, 93, 219–29.

Fillmore, K.M., Golding, J.M., Leino, E.V., Motoyoshi, M., Shoemaker, C., Terry, H., Ager, C.R. and Ferrer, H.O. (1997) Patterns and trends in women's and men's drinking, in Wilsnack, R.W. and Wilsnack, S.C. (eds) *Gender and Alcohol* (New Brunswick, NJ, Rutgers Center of Alcohol Studies).

Finney, J.W. and Monahan, S.C. (1996) The cost-effectiveness of treatment for alcoholism: a second approximation, *Journal of Studies on Alcohol*, 57, 229–43.

Finnigan, F. and Hammersley, R.H. (1992) Effects of alcohol on performance, in Jones, D.M. and Smith, A.P. (eds) *Handbook of Human Performance, Volume 2: health and performance*, pp. 73–126 (London, Academic Press).

Flay, B.R. (1986) Efficacy and effectiveness trials (and other phases of research) in the development of health promotion programs, *Preventive Medicine*, 15, 451–74.

Fleming, M.F., Barry, K.L., Manwell, L.B., Johnson, K. and London, R. (1997) Brief physician advice for problem alcohol drinkers: a randomized controlled trial in community-based primary care practices, *Journal of the American Medical Association*, 277, 1039–45.

Flett, R., Casswell, S., Brasch, P. and Silva, P.A. (1987) Alcohol knowledge and experience in children aged 9 and 11, *New Zealand Medical Journal*, 100, 747–9.

Fossey, E., Loretto, W. and Plant, M. (1996) Alcohol and youth, in Harrison, L. (ed.) *Alcohol Problems in the Community* (London, Routledge).

Foxcroft, D.R., Lister-Sharp, D.J. and Lowe, G. (1995) *Review of Effectiveness of Health Promotion Interventions: young people and alcohol misuse* (London, Alcohol Education and Research Council).

Foxcroft, D.R., Lister-Sharp, D. and Lowe, G. (1997) Alcohol misuse prevention for young people: a systematic review reveals methodological concerns and lack of reliable evidence of effectiveness, *Addiction*, 92, 531–7.

Franey, C. (1996) *Managing Patients with Dual Diagnosis in Ealing, Hammersmith and Hounslow* (London, Centre for Research on Drugs and Health Behaviour).

Franey, C. and Tober, G. (1999) Drug and alcohol education from a distance, *Drugs: Education, Prevention and Policy*, 6 (in press).

Franke, C. and Wilcox, C. (1987) Alcoholic beverages advertising and consumption in the United States, *Journal of Advertising*, 16, 22–30.

Fraser, R.C. (1992) Setting the scene, in Fraser, R.C. (ed.) *Clinical Method: a general practice approach* (2nd edition) (Oxford, Butterworth Heinemann).

Fremantle, N., Gill, P., Godfrey, C., Long, A., Richards, C., Sheldon, T., Song, F. and Webb, J. (1993) *Brief Interventions and Alcohol Use*, Effective Health Care Bulletin 7 (Leeds, Nuffield Institute for Health).

French, R.V. (1884) *Nineteen Centuries of Drink in England* (London, National Temperance Publication Depot).

Frezza, M., di Padova, C., Pozzato, G., Terpin, M., Baradna, E. and Lieber, C.S. (1990) High blood alcohol levels in women: the role of decreased gastric alcohol dehydrogenase activity and first-pass metabolism, *New England Journal of Medicine*, 322, 95–9.

Fuller, R.K. (1989) Antidipsotropic medications, in Hester, R.K. and Miller, W.R. (eds) *Handbook of Alcoholism Treatment Approaches: effective alternatives* (New York, Pergamon).

Galanter, M., Egelko, S., Edwards, H. and Vergaray, M. (1994) A treatment system for combined psychiatric and addictive illness, *Addiction*, 89, 1227–35.

Gelberg, L. and Leake, B. (1993) Substance abuse among impoverished medical patients: the effect of housing status and other factors, *Medical Care*, 31, 757–66.

Gentilello, L.M., Donovan, D.M., Dunn, C.W. and Rivara, F.R. (1995) Alcohol interventions in trauma centers: current practice and future directions, *Journal of the American Medical Association*, 274, 1043–8.

George, S.L., Shanks, N.J. and Westlake, L. (1991) Census of single homeless people in Sheffield, *British Medical Journal*, 302, 1387–9.

Gerstein, D.R. and Green, L.W. (eds) (1993) *Preventing Drug Abuse: what do we know?* (Washington, DC, National Academy Press).

Glass, I.B. (1989) Undergraduate training in substance abuse in the United Kingdom, *British Journal of Addiction*, 84, 197–202.

Glass, I.B. and Jackson, P. (1988) Maudsley Hospital survey prevalence of alcohol problems and other psychiatric disorders in a hospital population, *British Journal of Addiction*, 83, 1105–11.

Glatt, M.M. (1958) The English drink problem: its rise and decline through the ages, *British Journal of Addiction*, 55, 51–65.

Glatt, M.M. (1977) *Drug Dependence: current problems and issues* (Lancaster, Medical and Technical Publishing Co.).

Glatt, M.M. (1983) Conversation with Max Glatt (interview), *British Journal of Addiction*, 78, 231–43.

Glatt, M.M. (1997) Training general practitioners (Letter), *Alcohol and Alcoholism*, 32, 627–8.

Glen, D. and Carr-Hill, J. (1991) *Modelling the Demand for Alcoholic Drinks: a cointegration approach*, Working Papers in Economics 9 (London, Polytechnic of West London).

Godfrey, C. (1986) *Factors Influencing the Consumption of Alcohol and Tobacco*, Discussion Paper 17 (York, Centre for Health Economics, University of York).

Godfrey, C. (1988) Licensing and the demand for alcohol, *Applied Economics*, 20, 1541–58.

Godfrey, C. (1989) Factors influencing the consumption of alcohol and tobacco: the use and abuse of economic models, *British Journal of Addiction*, 84, 1123–38.

Godfrey, C. (1990) Modelling demand, in Maynard, A. and Tether, P. (eds) *Preventing Alcohol and Tobacco Problems, Volume 1: The Addiction Market: consumption, production and policy development* (Aldershot, Avebury).

Godfrey, C. (1994) Assessing the cost-effectiveness of alcohol services, *Journal of Mental Health*, 3, 3–21.

Godfrey, C. (1997) Lost productivity and costs to society, *Addiction*, 92, S49–54.

Godfrey, C. and Harrison, L. (1990) Preventive health objectives and tax policy, in Maynard, A. and Tether, P. (eds) *Preventing Alcohol and Tobacco Problems, Volume 1: The Addiction Market: consumption, production and policy development*, pp. 54–74 (Aldershot, Avebury).

Goel, R.K. and Morey, M.J. (1995) The interdependence of cigarette and liquor demand, *Southern Economic Journal*, 62, 451–9.

Gold, R.C. and Skinner, M.J. (1992) Situational factors and thought processes associated with unprotected intercourse in young gay men, *AIDS*, 6, 1021–30.

Golub, A. and Johnson, B.D. (1994) The shifting importance of alcohol and marijuana as gateway substances among serious drug-abusers, *Journal of Studies on Alcohol*, 55, 607–14.

Goodman, C. (1981) A Study of Social Workers' Knowledge and Attitudes to Alcohol-related Problems in Newcastle. Dissertation for Diploma in Alcohol and Drug Studies, Paisley College of Technology.

Gorman, D.M. (1993) A theory driven approach to the evaluation of professional training in alcohol abuse, *Addiction*, 88, 229–36.

Gormon, D.M. (1994) *Alcohol Education Programmes: a review of published evaluation studies (1983–1993)* (London, Alcohol Education and Research Council).

Green, M., Setchell, J., Hames, P., Stiff, G., Touquet, R. and Priest, R. (1993) Management of alcohol abusing patients in accident and emergency departments, *Journal of the Royal Society of Medicine*, 86, 393–5.

Greenaway, J.R. (1998) The 'improved' Public House, 1870–1950: the key to civilised drinking or the primrose path to drunkenness? *Addiction*, 93, 173–81.

Greenhalgh, N.M., Wylie, K., Rix, K.J.B. and Tamlyn, D. (1996) Pilot mental health assessment and diversion scheme for an English metropolitan petty sessional division, *Medicine, Science and the Law*, 36, 52–8.

Gronbaek, M., Deis, A., Sorensen, T.I.A., Becker, U., Schnohr, P. and Jesen, G. (1995) Mortality associated with moderate intakes of wine, beer and spirits, *British Medical Journal*, 310, 1165–9.

Grossman, M., Chaloupka, F., Saffer, H. and Laixuthai, A. (1993) *Effects of Alcohol Price Policy on Youth*, Working Paper 4385 (Cambridge, MA, National Bureau of Economic Research).

Grossman, M., Chaloupka, F. and Sirtalan, I. (1998) An empirical analysis of alcohol addiction: results from the Monitoring the Future Panels, *Economic Inquiry*, 36, 39–48.

Grossman, M., Coate, D. and Arluck, G. (1987) Price sensitivity of alcoholic beverages in the United States: youth alcohol consumption, in Holder, H. (ed.) *Advances in Substance Abuse, Behavioural and Biological Research: control issues in alcohol abuse prevention: strategies for states and communities*, pp. 169–98 (Greenwich, CT, JAI).

Grube, J.W. (1993) Alcohol portrayals and alcohol advertising on television: content and effects on children and adolescents, *Alcohol Health and Research World*, 17, 61–6.

Grube, J.W. (1997) Preventing sales of alcohol to minors: results from a community trial, *Addiction*, 92, S251–60.

Grube, J.W. and Wallack, L. (1994) Television beer advertising and drinking knowledge, beliefs, and intentions among schoolchildren, *American Journal of Public Health* 84, 254–9.

Gruenewald, P., Ponicki, W. and Holder, H. (1993) The relationship of outlet densities to alcohol consumption: a time series cross sectional analysis, *Alcoholism: Clinical and Experimental Research*, 17, 38–47.

Gruenewald, P., Treno, A., Nephew, T. and Ponicki, W. (1995) Routine activities and alcohol use: constraints on outlet utilisation, *Alcohol: Clinical and Experimental Research*, 19, 44–53.

Gustafson, R. (1993) What do experimental paradigms tell us about alcohol related aggressive responding? *Journal of Studies on Alcohol*, S11, 20–9.

Hagard, S., Chambers, J. and Killoran, A. (1991) Health education in England: a five-year strategy for the Health Education Authority, *Health Education Quarterly*, 18, 49–63.

Hammersley, R.H., Forsyth, A.J.M. and Levelle, T.L. (1990a) The criminality of new drug users in Glasgow, *British Journal of Addiction*, 85, pp. 1583–94.

Hammersley, R.H., Morrison, V.L., Davies, J.B. and Forsyth, A.J.M. (1990b) *Heroin Use and Crime: a comparison of heroin users and other substance users, in and out of prison* (Edinburgh, Scottish Office Central Research Unit).

Hammersley, R.H. and Pearl, S. (1997a) Temazepam misuse, violence and disorder, *Addiction Research*, 5, 213–22.

Hammersley, R. and Pearl, S. (1997b) Show me the way to go home: young homeless people and drugs, *Druglink*, 12 (1), 11–13.

Hannibal, J., van Inwaarden, M.J., Gefou-Madianou, D., Moskalaviez, J., Ritson, B. and Rud, M.G. (1995) *Alcohol and the Community* (Copenhagen, WHO Regional Office for Europe).

Hannum, H. (1998) Should industry sponsor research? Condemning the drinks industry rules out potentially useful research, *British Medical Journal*, 317, 335–6.

Hansen, A. (1985) Alcohol and drinking on television, in Institute of Alcohol Studies (ed.) *The Presentation of Alcohol in the Mass Media* (London, IAS).

Hansen, A. (1986) The portrayal of alcohol on television, *Health Education Journal*, 45, 249–79.

Hansen, A.C., Kristensen, I.B., Dragsholt, C. and Hansen, J.P.B (1996) Alcohol and drugs (medical and illicit) in fatal road accidents in a city of 300,000 inhabitants, *Forensic Science International*, 79, 49–52.

Hansen, W.B. (1992) School-based substance abuse prevention: a review of the state of the art in curriculum, 1980–1990, *Health Education Research: Theory and Practice*, 7, 403–30.

Hansen, W.B. (1993) School-based alcohol prevention programs, *Alcohol Health and Research World*, 17, 54–60.

Hansen, W.B. and Graham, J.W. (1991) Preventing alcohol, marijuana, and cigarette use among adolescents: peer pressure resistance training versus establishing conservative norms, *Preventive Medicine*, 20, 414–30.

Hansen, W.B., Johnson, C.A., Flay, B.R., Graham, J.W. and Sobel, J. (1988) Affective and social influences approaches to the prevention of multiple substance abuse among seventh grade students: results from project SMART, *Preventive Medicine*, 17, 135–54.

Harris, T.R., Wilsnack, R.W. and Klassen, A.D. (1994) Reliability of retrospective self-reports of alcohol consumption among women: data from a US national sample, *Journal of Studies on Alcohol*, 55, 309–14.

Harrison, B. (1971) *Drink and the Victorians* (London, Faber and Faber).

Harrison, L. (1989) The information component, in Robinson, D., Maynard, A. and Chester R. (eds) *Controlling Legal Addictions* (London, Macmillan).

Harrison, L. (ed.) (1992a) *Substance Misuse: guidance notes for the Diploma in Social Work*, Improving Social Work Education and Training 14 (London, CCETSW).

Harrison, L. (1992b) Substance misuse and social work qualifying training in the British Isles: a survey of CQSW courses, *British Journal of Addiction*, 87, 635–42.

Harrison, L. (ed.) (1993a) *Alcohol Problems: resource directory and bibliography* (London, CCETSW).

Harrison, L. (ed.) (1993b) *Substance Misuse: designing social work training* (London, CCETSW).

Harrison, L. (1995) *Health professionals and Substance Misuse Training in the United Kingdom* (Geneva, WHO).

Harrison, L. (1996) Introduction, in Harrison, L. (ed.) *Alcohol Problems in the Community* (London, Routledge).

Harrison, L. and Godfrey, C. (1989) Alcohol advertising controls in the 1990s, *International Journal of Advertising*, 8, 167–80.

Harrison, L., Harrison, M. and Adebowale, V. (1996) Drinking problems amongst black communities, in Harrison, L. (ed.) *Alcohol Problems in the Community* (London, Routledge).

Harrison, L. and Luck, H. (1996) Drinking and homelessness in the UK, in Harrison, L. (ed.) *Alcohol Problems in the Community* (London, Routledge).

Harrison, L., Manthorpe, J. and Carr-Hill, R. (1996) Alcohol and care of older people, in Harrison, L. (ed.) *Alcohol Problems in the Community* (London, Routledge).

Harrison, L., Sutton, M. and Gardiner, E. (1997) Ethnic differences in substance use and alcohol-related mortality among first generation migrants to England and Wales, *Substance Use and Misuse*, 32, 849–76.

Hartz, C. and Anderson, P. (1990) *Community Nurses and Alcohol* (Oxford, Alcohol Research Centre).

Havard, J. (1991) Off the rails, *British Medical Journal*, 303, 1006–7.

Hawker, A. (1978) *Adolescents and Alcohol* (London, Edsall).

Hayashida, M., Alterman, A.L., McLellan, A.T., O'Brien, C.P., Purtill, J.J., Volpicelli, J.R., Raphaelson, A.H. and Hall, C.P. (1989). Comparative effectiveness and costs of inpatient and outpatient detoxification of patients with mild-to-moderate alcohol withdrawal syndrome, *New England Journal of Medicine*, 320, 358–65.

Hays, R. and Ellickson, P. (1996) What is adolescent alcohol misuse in the United States according to the experts? *Alcohol and Alcoholism*, 31, 297–303.

Health Advisory Service (1996) *Children and Young People: substance misuse services: the substance of young needs* (London, HMSO).

Health Education Authority (HEA) (1992) *Today's Young Adults: 16–19 year olds look at alcohol, drugs exercise and smoking* (London, HEA).

Health Education Authority (1996) *Young People and Alcohol: a survey of attitudes and behaviour towards new types of alcoholic drinks in England* (London, HEA).

Health Education Authority (1997) *Health Update: alcohol* (2nd edition) (London, HEA).

Heath, D.B. (1962) Drinking Patterns of the Bolivian Camba, in Pittman, D.J. and Snyder C.R. (eds) *Society, Culture and Drinking Patterns* (New York, John Wiley and Sons).

Heath, D.B. (1995) Some generalizations about alcohol and culture, in Heath, D.B. (ed.) *International Handbook on Alcohol and Culture* (Westport, CT, Greenwood).

Heath, D.B. (1996) The war on drugs as a metaphor in American culture, in Bickel, W.K. and DeGrandpre, R.J. (eds) *Drugs Policy and Human Nature* (New York, Plenum).

Heath, D.B., Waddell, J.O. and Topper, M.D. (eds) (1981) *Cultural Factors in Alcohol Research and Treatment of Drinking Problems* (New Brunswick, NJ, Rutgers Center of Alcohol Studies).

Heather, N. (1982) Alcohol dependence and problem drinking in Scottish young offenders, *British Journal on Alcohol and Alcoholism*, 17, 145–54.

Heather, N. (1992) Economic evaluation of treatment for alcohol problems, in White, J., Ali, R., Christie, P., Cormack, S., Gaughwin, M. and Sweeney, R. (eds) *Drug Problems in Society: dimensions and perspectives* (Melbourne, Nepean Publishing).

Heather, N. (1995a) *Treatment Approaches to Alcohol Problems*. WHO Regional Publications, European Series 65 (Copenhagen, WHO Regional Office for Europe).

Heather, N. (1995b) Interpreting the evidence on brief interventions for excessive drinkers: the need for caution, *Alcohol and Alcoholism*, 30, 287–96.

Heather, N. (1996) The public health and brief interventions for excessive alcohol consumption: the British experience, *Addictive Behaviors*, 21, 857–68.

Heather, N. (1997) Where treatment and prevention merge: the need for a broader approach, *Addiction*, 92, S133–6.

Heather, N. (1998) Using brief opportunities for change, in Miller, W.R. and Heather, N. (eds) *Treating Addictive Behaviors* (2nd edition) (New York, Plenum).

Heather, N. and Robertson, I. (1997) *Problem Drinking* (3rd edition) (Oxford, Oxford University Press).

Heather, N., Robertson, I. and Davies, P. (1985) *The Misuse of Alcohol: crucial issues in dependence, treatment and prevention* (London, Croom Helm).

Heather, N., Rollnick, S., Bell, A. and Richmond, R. (1996) Effects of brief counselling among male heavy drinkers identified on general hospital wards, *Drug and Alcohol Review*, 15, 29–38.

Hegsted, D.M. and Ausman, L.M. (1988) Diet, alcohol and coronary heart disease in men, *Journal of Nutrition*, 118, 1184–9.

Herman, J. and Hirshman, L. (1981) Families at risk of father–daughter incest, *American Journal of Psychiatry*, 138, 967–70.

Hilton, M.E. (1991) The demographic distribution of drinking problems in 1984, in Clark, W.B. and Hilton, M.E. (eds) *Alcohol in America: drinking practices and problems*, pp. 87–101 (Albany, State University of New York Press).

Hingson, R., Heeren, T. and Winter, M. (1994) Lower legal blood alcohol limits for young drivers, *Public Health Reports*, 109, 738–44.

Hingson, R. and Howland, J. (1987) Alcohol as a risk factor for injury or death resulting from accidental falls: a review of the literature, *Journal of Studies on Alcohol*, 48, 212–19.

Hingson, R.W., Strunin, L., Berlin, B.M. and Heeren, T. (1990) Beliefs about AIDS, use of alcohol and drugs, and unprotected sex among Massachusetts adolescents, *American Journal of Public Health*, 80, 295–9.

Hodgins, D.C. and Lightfoot, L.O. (1988) Types of male alcohol- and drug-abusing incarcerated offenders, *British Journal of Addiction*, 83, 1201–13.

Hodgson, R. (1989) Low cost responses, in Robinson, D., Maynard, A. and Chester, R. (eds) *Controlling Legal Addictions* (London, Macmillan).

Holder, H.D. (1987) Alcoholism treatment and potential health care cost saving, *Medical Care*, 25, 52–71.

Holder, H.D. (1994) Mass communication as an essential aspect of community prevention to reduce alcohol-involved traffic crashes, *Alcohol, Drugs and Driving*, 3 (4), 295–307.

Holder, H.D. (1998) *Alcohol and the Community: a systems approach to prevention*, International Research Monographs in the Addictions (Cambridge, Cambridge University Press).

Holder, H.D. and Blose, J.O. (1986) Alcoholism treatment and total health care utilization and costs: a four-year longitudinal analysis of federal employees, *Journal of the American Medical Association*, 256, 1456–60.

Holder, H.D. and Blose, J.O. (1987) The impact of changes in distilled spirits availability on apparent consumption: a time series analysis of liquor by the drink, *British Journal of Addiction*, 82, 623–31.

Holder, H.D. and Blose, J.O. (1991) Typical patterns and costs of alcoholism treatment across a variety of populations and providers, *Alcoholism: Clinical and Experimental Research*, 15, 190–5.

Holder, H.D. and Blose, J.O. (1992) The reduction of health care costs associated with alcoholism treatment: a 14-year longitudinal study, *Journal of Studies on Alcohol*, 53, 293–302.

Holder, H.D. and Hallan, J.B. (1986) Impact of alcoholism treatment on total health care costs: a six-year study, *Advances in Alcohol and Substance Abuse*, 6, 1–15.

Holder, H., Janes, K., Mosher, J., Saltz, R., Spurr, S. and Wagenaar, A. (1993) Alcohol beverage server liability and the reduction of alcohol-involved problems, *Journal of Studies on Alcohol*, 54, 23–36.

Holder, H., Longabaugh, R., Miller, W.R. and Rubonis, A.V. (1991) The cost effectiveness of treatment for alcoholism: a first approximation, *Journal of Studies on Alcohol*, 52, 517–40.

Holder, H.D., Miller, W.R. and Carina, R.T. (1995) *Cost Savings of Substance Abuse Prevention in Managed Care* (Berkeley, CA, Center for Substance Abuse Prevention).

Holder, H.D. and Parker, R.N. (1992) Effect of alcoholism treatment on cirrhosis mortality: a 20-year multivariate time series analysis, *British Journal of Addiction*, 87, 1263–74.

Holder H.D., Saltz, R.F., Grube, J.W., Boas, R.B., Gruenewald, P.J. and Treno, A.J. (1997) A community prevention trial to reduce alcohol-involved accidental injury and death: overview, *Addiction*, 92, S155–71.

Holder, H.D. and Treno, A.J. (1997) Media advocacy in community prevention: news as a means to advance policy change, *Addiction*, 92, S189–99.

Holder, H. and Wagenaar, A. (1994) Mandated server training and the reduction of alcohol-involved traffic crashes: a time series analysis in the state of Oregon, *Accident Analysis and Prevention*, 26, 89–94.

Hollin, C.R. (1983) Young offenders and alcohol: a survey of the drinking behaviour of a Borstal population. *Journal of Adolescence*, 6, 161–74.

Holmila, M. (1997) *Community Prevention of Alcohol Problems* (London, Macmillan and WHO).

Holt, S., Stewart, I.C., Dixon, J.M.J., Elton, R.A., Taylor, T.V. and Little, K. (1980) Alcohol and the emergency service patient, *British Medical Journal*, 281, 638–40.

Holtermann, S. and Burchell, A. (1981) *Government Economic Service Working Party No. 37* (London, DHSS).

Home Office (1972) *Report of the Departmental Committee on Liquor Licensing* (the Erroll Report), Cmnd. 5154 (London, HMSO).

Home Office (1991) Mentally Disordered Prisoners (London, HMSO).

Home Office (1993) *Possible Reforms of the Liquor Licensing System in England and Wales: a consultation paper* (London, Home Office).

Home Office (1994) *Aspects of Crime: drunkenness 1993* (London, Home Office Research and Statistics Department).

Home Office (1996) *Liquor Licensing: children's certificates, England and Wales January 1995 to June 1996* (London, Home Office).

Home Office (1998) *Tackling Drugs to Build a Better Britain: the Government's 10-year strategy for tackling drug misuse* (London, The Stationery Office).

Homel, R., Tomsen, S. and Thommeny, J. (1992) Public drinking and violence: not just an alcohol problem, *Journal of Drug Issues*, 22, 679–97.

Homeless Network (1996) *Central London Street Monitor* (London, Homeless Network).

Honkanen, R. (1993) Alcohol in home and leisure injuries, *Addiction*, 88, 939–44.

Honkanen, R., Ertama, L., Kuosmanen, P., Linnoila, M., Alha, A. and Visuri, T. (1983) The role of alcohol in accidental falls, *Journal of Studies on Alcohol*, 44, 231–45.

Hope, T. (1986) Liquor licensing and crime prevention, *Home Office Research and Planning Unit Research Bulletin*, 20, 5–8.

Howland, J. and Hingson, R. (1987) Alcohol as a risk factor for injuries or death due to fires and burns: review of the literature, *Public Health Reports*, 102, 475–83.

Howland, J. and Hingson, R. (1988) Alcohol as a risk factor for drowning: review of the literature (1950–1985), *Accident Analysis and Prevention*, 20, 19–25.

Howland, J., Mangione, T., Hingson, R., Smith, G. and Bell, N. (1995) Alcohol as a risk factor for drowning and other aquatic injuries, in Watson, R.R. (ed.) *Alcohol, Cocaine and Accidents, Drug and Alcohol Abuse Reviews, Volume 7*, pp. 85–104 (Totowa, Humana Press).

Howse, K. and Ghodse, H. (1997) Hazardous drinking and its correlates among medical students, *Addiction Research*, 4, 355–66.

Hughes, J., Stewart, M. and Barraclough, B. (1985) Why teetotallers abstain, *British Journal of Psychiatry*, 146, 204–8.

Hughes, K., MacKintosh, A., Hastings, G., Wheeler, G., Watson, J. and Inglis, J. (1997) Young people, alcohol and designer drinks: quantitative and qualitative study, *British Medical Journal*, 314, 414–18.

Hutcheson, G., Henderson, M. and Davies, J. *(1995) Alcohol in the Workplace: costs and responses* (Glasgow, University of Strathclyde).

Institute of Medicine (1990) *Broadening the Base of Treatment for Alcohol Problems* (Washington, DC, National Academy Press).

International Agency for Research on Cancer (1988) *IARC Monograph on the Evaluation of Carcinogenic Risk to Humans: alcohol drinking* (Lyon, International Agency for Research on Cancer).

Irwin, S.T., Patterson, C.C. and Rutherford, W.H. (1983) Association between alcohol consumption and adult pedestrians who sustain injuries in road traffic accidents, *British Medical Journal*, 286, 522.

Isaacs, J. and Moon, G. (1985) *Alcohol Problems: the social work response* (Portsmouth, Social Services Research and Intelligence Unit).

Israel, Y., Hollander, O., Sanchez-Craig, M., Booker, S., Miller, V., Gingrich, R. and Rankin, J.G. (1996) Screening for problem drinking and counselling by the primary care physician–nurse team, *Alcoholism: Clinical and Experimental Research*, 20, 1443–50.

Jariwalla, A.G., Adama, P.H. and Hore, B.D. (1979) Alcohol and acute admissions to hospital, *Health Trends*, 11, 95–7.

Jarman, C.M.B. and Kellett, J.M. (1979) Alcoholism in the general hospital, *British Medical Journal*, II, 469–72.

Jeffs, B. and Saunders, W. (1983) Minimising alcohol-related offences by enforcement of the existing licensing legislation, *British Journal of Addiction*, 78, 67–77.

Jenkins, R., Bebbington, P., Brugha, T.S., Farrell, M., Lewis, G. and Meltzer, H. (1998) British psychiatric morbidity survey, *British Journal of Psychiatry*, 173, 4–7.

Jenson, J.M., Howard, M.O. and Yatte, J. (1995) Treatment of adolescent substance abusers: issues for practice and research, *Social Work in Health Care*, 21, 1–18.

Jessor, R. (1987) Problem-behaviour theory, psychosocial development and adolescent problem drinking, *British Journal of Addiction*, 82, 331–42.

Jessor, R. and Jessor, S.L. (1977) *Problem Behavior and Psychosocial Development: a longitudinal study* (New York, Academic Press).

Jewell, R.T. and Brown, R.W. (1995) Alcohol availability and alcohol-related motor vehicle accidents, *Applied Economics*, 27, 759–65.

John, H. (1992) *Facilitating the Prevention of Alcohol Misuse in General Practices* (Hillingdon, Hillingdon Family Health Service Authority).

Johnson, L.W. (1985) Alternative econometric estimates of the effect of advertising on the demand for alcoholic beverages in the United Kingdom, *International Journal of Advertising*, 4, 19–25.

Johnson, S. (1997) Dual diagnosis of severe mental illness: a case for specialist services? *British Journal of Psychiatry*, 171, 205–8.

Jones, A. (1989) A system approach to the demand for alcohol and tobacco, *Bulletin of Economic Research*, 41, 3307–78.

Jones, K.R. and Vischi, T.R. (1979) Impact of alcohol, drug abuse and mental health treatment on medical care utilization, *Medical Care*, 17, 1–82.

Julian, V. and Mohr, C. (1979) Father–daughter incest: profile of the offender, *Victimology*, 4, 348–60.

Justices' Clerks Society (1983) *Licensing Law in the Eighties* (Bristol, Justices' Clerks Society).

Kagle, J. (1987) Secondary prevention of substance abuse, *Social Work*, 32, 446–8.

Kaminer, Y. (1991) Adolescent substance abuse, in Frances, R.J. and Miller, R.I. (eds) *Clinical Textbook of Addictive Disorders*, pp. 320–46 (New York, Guilford Press).

Kaner, E., Haighton, C., Heather, N., McAvoy, B. and Gilvarry, E. (1998) *A Randomized Controlled Trial of Methods to Encourage Uptake and Utilization by General Practitioners of Brief Intervention Against Excessive Alcohol Consumption*, report to the Alcohol Education and Research Council (Newcastle upon Tyne, Department of Primary Health Care, University of Newcastle upon Tyne).

Kaner, E., McAvoy, B., Heather, N., Haighton, K. and Gilvarry, E. (1997) United Kingdom, in Saunders, J.B. and Wutzke, S. (eds) *WHO Collaborative Study on Implementing and Supporting Early Intervention in Primary Health Care, Report on Strand 1: the views and current practices of general practitioners regarding preventive medicine and early intervention for hazardous alcohol use* (Copenhagen, WHO Regional Office for Europe).

Kantor, G.K. and Strauss, M.A. (1987) The 'Drunken Bum' theory of wife beating, *Social Problems*, 34, 214–30.

Keene, J. (1997) Drug use among prisoners before, during and after custody, *Addiction Research*, 4, 343–53.

Kemm, J.R. and Rowe, C. (1992) Do people understand 'units of alcohol'? *Health Education Journal*, 51, 59–63.

Kendell, R.E., de Roumanie, M. and Ritson, E.B. (1983) Effect of economic changes on Scottish drinking habits 1978–82, *British Journal of Addiction*, 78, 365–79.

Kennedy, B.P., Isaac, N.E. and Graham, J.D. (1996) The role of heavy drinking in the risk of traffic accidents, *Society for Risk Analysis*, 565–69.

Kent, R. (1993) *Training for Alcohol Practitioners: a review and recommendations* (London, HEA).

Kerfoot, M. and Huxley, P. (1995) Suicide and deliberate self harm in young people, *Current Opinion in Psychiatry*, 8, 214–17.

Kerr, N. (1889) *Inebriety, its Etiology, Pathology, Treatment and Jurisprudence* (London, H.K. Lewis).

Kerr, W.C. (1997) The demand for alcohol by light, moderate, and heavy drinkers: estimates from the National Health Interview Survey. Paper presented at the Kettil Bruun Society Meeting, Iceland, 1997.

Kessel, N. (1961) Self-poisoning: part 1, *British Medical Journal*, II, 1265.

Kessell, N. and Walton, H. (1965) *Alcoholism* (Harmondsworth, Penguin).

Kessler, R.C., McGonagle, K.A., Zhao, S., Nelson, C.B., Hughes, M., Eshleman, S., Wittchen, H-U. and Kendler, K.S. (1994) Lifetime and 12-month prevalence of DSM-III-R psychiatric disorders in the United States, *Archives of General Psychiatry*, 51, 8–19.

Killen, J.D., Hayward, C., Wilson, D.M., Haydel, K.F., Robinson, T.N. and Taylor, C.B. (1996) Predicting onset of drinking in a community sample of adolescents: the role of expectancy and temperament, *Addictive Behaviors*, 21, 473–80.

Kirkpatrick, J. (1978) *Turnabout: new help for the woman alcoholic* (Garden City, NY, Doubleday).

Kishline, A. (1994) *Moderate Drinking: the new option for problem drinkers* (Tucson, AZ, Sharp Press).

Klatsky, A.L., Armstrong, M.A. and Friedman, G.D. (1990) Risk of cardiovascular mortality in alcohol drinkers, ex-drinkers and non-drinkers, *American Journal of Cardiology*, 66, 1237–42.

Klatsky, A., Armstrong, M. and Friedman, G. (1992) Alcohol and mortality, *Annals of Internal Medicine*, 117, 646–54.

Knibbe, R.A., Drop, M.J. and Muytjens, A. (1987) Correlates of stages in the progression from everyday drinking to problem drinking, *Social Science and Medicine*, 24, 463–73.

Knupfer, G. (1991) Abstaining for foetal health: the fiction that even light drinking is dangerous, *British Journal of Addiction*, 86, 1063–73.

Kohn, P.M. and Smart, R.G. (1987) Wine, women, suspiciousness and advertising, *Journal of Studies on Alcohol*, 48, 161–6.

Kohn, P.M., Smart, R.G. and Ogbourne, A.C. (1984) Effects of two kinds of alcohol advertising on subsequent consumption, *Journal of Alcohol and Drug Education*, 13, 34–40.

Kono, S., Ikeda, M., Tokudome, S., Nishizumi, M. and Karatsune, M. (1986) Alcohol and mortality: a cohort study of male Japanese physicians, *International Journal of Epidemiology*, 15, 527–31.

Kotch, J.B., Coulter, M.L. and Lipsitz, A. (1986) Does televised drinking influence children's attitudes toward alcohol? *Addictive Behaviours*, 11, 67–70.

Krausz, M. (1996) Old problems, new perspectives, *European Addiction Research*, 2, 1–2.

Kreitman, N. (1986) Alcohol consumption and the preventive paradox, *British Journal of Addiction*, 81, 353–63.

Kristenson, H., Ohlin, H., Hulten-Nosslin, M., Trell, E. and Hood, B. (1983) Identification and intervention of heavy drinking in middle-aged men: results and follow-up of 24:60 months of long-term study with randomized control, *Alcoholism: Clinical and Experimental Research*, 20, 203–9.

Lagerspetz, M. (ed.) (1994) *Social Problems in Newspapers* (Helsinki, Nordic Council for Alcohol and Drug Research).

Lamb, D. (1995) *Services for Street Drinkers: an initial overview* (London, National Street Drinking Network).

Lang, E., Stockwell, T., Rydon, P. and Lockwood, A. (1995) Drinking settings and problems of intoxication, *Addiction Research*, 3, 141–9.

Lattimore, P.K., Visher, C.A. and Linster, R.L. (1995) Predicting rearrest for violence among serious youthful offenders, *Journal of Research in Crime and Delinquency*, 32, 54–83.

Laugharne, R.A., Daniels, O.J. and Lutchman, R. (1997) The prevalence of alcohol problems amongst in-patients referred to the liaison psychiatrist, *Addiction Research*, 5, 379–82.

Lavik, N. and Onstad, S. (1986), Drug use and psychiatric symptoms in adolescence, *Acta Psychiatrica Scandinavica*, 73, 437–40.

Lawson, A. (1994) Identification of and responses to problem drinking amongst social services users, *British Journal of Social Work*, 24, 325–42.

Lazarus, N.B., Kaplan, G.A., Cohen, R.D. and Leu, D-J. (1991) Change in alcohol consumption and risk of death from all causes and ischaemic heart disease, *British Medical Journal*, 303, 553–6.

Leckie, T. (1990) Social work and alcohol, in Collins, S. (ed.) *Alcohol, Social Work and Helping* (London, Tavistock/Routledge).

Ledermann, S. (1956) *Alcool, Alcoolism, Alcoolisation, Vol. I* (Paris, Presses Universitaires de France).

Leedham, W. and Godfrey, C. (1990) Tax policy and budget decisions, in Maynard, A. and Tether, P. (eds) *Preventing Alcohol and Tobacco Problems, Volume 1: The Addiction Market: consumption, production and policy development*, pp. 96–116 (Aldershot, Avebury).

Leigh, B. (1990) The relationship of sex-related alcohol expectancies to alcohol consumption and sexual behaviour, *British Journal of Addiction*, 85, 919–28.

Leino, E.V., Romelsjö, A., Shoemaker, C., Ager, C.R., Allebeck, P., Ferrer, H.P., Fillmore, K.M., Golding, J.M., Graves, K.L. and Kniep, S. (1998) Alcohol consumption and mortality, II: Studies of male populations, *Addiction*, 93, 205–18.

Lemmens, P.H.H.M. (1995) Individual risk and population distribution of alcohol consumption, in Holder, H.D. and Edwards, G. (eds) *Alcohol and Public Policy* (Oxford, Oxford University Press).

Lemmens, P., Tan, E. and Knibbe, R. (1990) Comparing distributions of alcohol consumption: empirical probability plots, *British Journal of Addiction*, 85, 751–8.

Leonard, K.E. and Jacob, T. (1988) Alcohol, alcoholism and family violence, in Van Hasselt, V.B., Morrison, R.L., Bellack, A.S. and Hersen, M. (eds) *Handbook of Family Violence* (New York, Plenum).

Lessard, R.J., Harrison, P.A. and Hoffman, N.G. (1985) Costs and benefits of chemical dependency treatment, *Minnesota Medicine*, 68, 449–52.

Leung, S. and Phelps, E. (1993) My kingdom for a drink ... ? A review of estimates of the price sensitivity of demand for alcoholic beverages, in Hilton, M. and Bloss, M. (eds) *Economics and the Prevention of Alcohol-Related Problems*, Research Monograph No. 25, pp. 91–123 (Rockville, MD, US Department of Health and Human Services).

Lieber, C.S. (1982) Interaction of ethanol and drug metabolism, in *Medical Disorders of Alcoholism: pathogenesis and treatment* (Philadelphia, PA, W. B. Saunders Company).

Light, R. and O'Brien, J. (1995) *Fit and Proper Persons to Hold Justices' Licences* (Bristol, University of West of England).

Lightfoot, P.J.C. and Orford, J. (1986) Helping agents' attitudes towards alcohol related problems: situations vacant? A test and elaboration of a model, *British Journal of Addiction*, 81, 749–56.

Lindqvist, P. (1991) Homicides commited by abusers of alcohol and illicit drugs, *British Journal of Addiction*, 86, 321–6.

Lipsitz, A., Brake, G., Vincent, E.J. and Winters, M. (1993) Another round for the brewers: television ads and children's alcohol expectancies, *Journal of Applied Social Psychology*, 23 (6), 439–50.

Lister-Sharp, D. (1994) Underage drinking in the United Kingdom since 1970: public policy, the law, and adolescent drinking behaviour, *Alcohol and Alcoholism*, 29, 555–63.

Lloyd, G., Chick, J., Crombie, E. and Anderson, S. (1986) Problem drinkers in medical wards: consumption patterns and disabilities in newly identified male cases, *British Journal of Addiction*, 81, 789–95.

Lockhart, S.P., Carter, Y.H., Straffen, A.M., Pang, K.K., McLoughlin, J. and Baron, J.H. (1986) Detecting alcohol consumption as a cause of emergency general medical admissions, *Journal of the Royal Society of Medicine*, 79, 132–6.

London, J. (1903) *The People of the Abyss* London, Pluto Press (1998).

Lovatt, A. (1996) Soft City, Hard City?: The flexibility of permitted hours for UK cities. 24hour city conference, Leeds.

Luce, A., Heather, N. and McCarthy, S. (1998) *1996 Census of Alcohol Treatment Agencies in the UK*, report to the Society for the Study of Addiction (Newcastle upon Tyne, Centre for Alcohol and Drug Studies).

Luckey, J.W. (1987) Justifying alcohol treatment on the basis of cost savings: the 'offset' literature, *Alcohol Health and Research World*, 12, 8–15.

McAlister, A., Perry, C., Killen, J., Slinkard, L.A. and Maccoby, N. (1980) Pilot study of smoking, alcohol and drug abuse prevention, *American Journal of Public Health*, 70, 719–21.

McAllister, I. (1995) Public attitudes to the regulation of alcohol, *Drug and Alcohol Review*, 14, 179–86.

MacAndrew, C. and Edgerton, R.B. (1969) *Drunken Comportment: a social explanation* (Chicago, IL, Aldine).

McCarty, D. and Ewing, J.A. (1983) Alcohol consumption while viewing alcoholic beverage advertising, *International Journal of the Addictions*, 18, 1011–18.

McCrady, B.S. and Delaney, S.I. (1995) Self-help groups, in Hester, R.K. and Miller, W.R. (eds) *Handbook of Alcoholism Treatment Approaches: effective alternatives* (Needham Heights, MA, Allyn and Bacon).

McCusker, J., Westenhouse, J., Stoddard, A.M., Zapka, J.G., Zorn, M.W. and Mayer, K.H. (1990) Use of drugs and alcohol by homosexually active men in relation to sexual practices, *Journal of Acquired Immune Deficiency Syndrome*, 3, 729–36.

McEwan, R.T., McCallum, A., Bhopal, R.S. and Madhok, R. (1992) Sex and the risk of HIV infection: the role of alcohol, *British Journal of Addiction*, 87, 577–84.

McGarva, S. (1979) The Measurement of Alcohol Abuse in Social Workers' Caseloads. Dissertation for Diploma in Alcohol and Drug Studies, Paisley College of Technology.

McGowan, A. (1995) Developing a Community Health Promotion Initiative for Al Fresco Drinking. Master of Public Health thesis, University of Glasgow.

McGuinness, T. (1980) An econometric analysis of total demand for alcoholic beverages in the UK, 1956–1975, *The Journal of Industrial Economics*, 29, 85–109.

McGuinness, T. (1983) The demand for beer, spirits and wine in the UK, 1956–79, in Grant, M., Plant, M. and Williams, A. (eds) *Economics and Alcohol: consumption and controls*, pp. 128–39 (London, Croom Helm with Alcohol Education Centre).

McKeganey, N., Forsyth, A., Barnard, M., and Hay, G. (1996) Designer drinks and drunkenness among a sample of Scottish schoolchildren, *British Medical Journal*, 313, 401–2.

McKenna, M., Chick, J., Buxton, M., Howlett, H., Patience, D. and Ritson, B. (1996) The SECCAT Survey: I. the costs and consequences of alcoholism, *Alcohol and Alcoholism*, 31, 565–76.

McKeown, O., Forshaw, D., McGauley, G., Fitzpatrick, J. and Roscoe, J. (1996) Forensic addictive behaviours unit: a case study (part 1), *Journal of Substance Misuse*, 1, 27–31.

McLaughlin, P. (1988) *Managing Drunkenness in Scotland: criminal justice and social service responses to alcohol problems* (Edinburgh, Scottish Office Central Research Unit).

McLean, N.J. (1988) Early intervention in the general practice setting, *Australian Drug and Alcohol Review*, 7, 329–35.

McLellan, A.T., Luborsky, L., Woody, G.E., Druley, K.A. and O Brien, C.P. (1983) Predicting response to alcohol and drug abuse treatments: role of psychiatric severity, *Archives of General Psychiatry*, 40, 620–5.

McMurran, M. and Baldwin, S. (1989) Services for prisoners with alcohol-related problems: a survey of UK prisons, *British Journal of Addiction*, 84, 1053–8.

McMurran, M. and Hollin, C.R (1989) Drinking and delinquency: another look at young offenders and alcohol, *British Journal of Criminology*, 29, 386–94.

McMurran, M. and Hollin, C.R. (1993) *Young Offenders and Alcohol-related Crime* (Chichester, Wiley).

Madden, J.S. (1993) Alcohol and depression, *British Journal of Hospital Medicine*, 50, 261–4.

Magennis, P., Shepherd, J., Hutchison, I. and Brown, A. (1998) Trends in facial injury (editorial), *British Medical Journal*, 316, 325–6.

Maher, J. (1997) Exploring alcohol's effect on liver function, *Alcohol, Health and Research World*, 21, 5–12.

Mäkelä, K., Room, R., Single, E., Sulkunen, P. and Walsh, B. (1981) *Alcohol, Society and the State, Volume I* (Toronto, Addiction Research Foundation).

Makowsky, C.R. and Whitehead, P.C. (1991) Advertising and alcohol sales: a legal impact study, *Journal of Studies on Alcohol*, 52, 555–67.

Mann, R.E., Smart, R.G., Anglin, L. and Adlaf, E.M. (1991) Reductions in cirrhosis deaths in the United States: associations with per capita consumption and AA membership, *Journal of Studies on Alcohol*, 52, 361–5.

Mann, R.E., Smart, R.G., Anglin, L. and Rush, B.R. (1988) Are decreases in liver cirrhosis rates a result of increased treatment for alcoholism? *British Journal of Addiction*, 83, 683–8.

Manning, W., Blumberg, L. and Moulton, L. (1995) The demand for alcohol: the differential response to price, *Journal of Health Economics*, 14, 123–48.

Manthorpe, J. (1996) People with learning disabilities: alcohol and ordinary lives, in Harrison, L. (ed.) *Alcohol Problems in the Community* (London, Routledge).

Marmot, M. (1984) Alcohol and coronary heart disease, *International Journal of Epidemiology*, 13, 160–7.

Marmot, M. and Brunner, E. (1991) Alcohol and cardiovascular disease: the status of the U-shaped curve, *British Medical Journal*, 303, 565–8.

Marmot, M.G., Davey Smith, G., Stansfield, S., Patel, C., North, F., Head, J., White, I., Brunner, E. and Feeney, A. (1991) Health inequalities among British civil servants: the Whitehall II study, *Lancet*, 337, 1387–93.

Marmot, M.G., Elliott, P., Shipley, M.J., Dyer, A.R., Ueshima, H., Beevers, D.G., Stamler, R., Kesteloot, H., Rose, G. and Stamler, J. (1994) Alcohol and blood pressure: the INTERSALT study, *British Medical Journal*, 308, 1263–7.

Marmot, M.G., Rose, G., Shipley, M.J. and Thomas, B.S. (1981) Alcohol and mortality: a U-shaped curve, *Lancet*, I, 580–3.

Marttunen, M.J., Henriksson, M.M., Aro, H.M., Heikkinen, M.E., Isometsa, E.T. and Lonnqvist, J.K. (1995) Suicide among female adolescents: characteristics and comparison with males in the age group 13 to 22 years, *Journal of the American Academy of Child and Adolescent Psychiatry*, 34, 1297–307.

Mason, D., Birmingham, L. and Grubin, D. (1997) Substance use in remand prisoners: a consecutive case study, *British Medical Journal*, 315, 18–21.

Mason, P. (1997a) Alcohol counsellors in general practice, *Journal of Substance Misuse*, 2, 85–93.

Mason, P. (1997b) Alcohol counselling services in general practice (Part II): who uses them and how? *Journal of Substance Misuse*, 2, 210–16.

Mason, P. and Williams, K. (1990) *Evaluation of the Uptake, Acceptability and Effectiveness of the Cut Down on Drinking Pack in General Practices in Three Health Districts in the West Midlands*, Report to the Health Education Authority (Birmingham, Aquarius).

Mass Observation (1943) *The Pub and the People* (London, Victor Gollancz).

Mattick, R.P. and Jarvis, T. (eds) (1993) *An Outline for the Management of Alcohol Problems: quality assurance project*, National Drug Strategy Monograph Series No. 20 (Canberra, Australian Government Publishing Service).

Maynard, A. and Godfrey, C. (1994) Alcohol policy: evaluating the options, *British Medical Bulletin*, 50, 221–30.

Mayou, R. and Bryant, B. (1995) Alcohol and road traffic accidents, *Alcohol and Alcoholism*, 30, 709–11.

Measham, F. (1996) The 'big bang' approach to sessional drinking: changing patterns of alcohol consumption amongst young people in North West England, *Addiction Research*, 4, 283–99.

Mendenhall, C.L., Gartside, P.S., Roselle, G., Grossman, C.J., Weisner, R.E. and Chedid, A. (1989) Longevity among ethnic groups in alcoholic liver disease, *Alcohol and Alcoholism*, 24, 11–19.

Menezes, P.R., Johnson, S., Thornicroft, G., Marshall, J., Prosser, D., Bebbington, P. and Kuipers, E. (1996) Drug and alcohol problems among individuals with severe mental illnesses in South London, *British Journal of Psychiatry*, 168, 612–19.

Mental Health Foundation (1996) *Too Many for the Road: report of the Mental Health Foundation Expert Working Group on Persistent Street Drinkers* (London, Mental Health Foundation).

Meyer, R.E. (1996) The disease called addiction: emerging evidence in a 200-year debate, *Lancet*, 347, 162–6.

Midanik, L.T. (1995) Alcohol consumption and social consequences, dependence, and positive benefits in general population surveys, in Holder, H.D. and Edwards, G. (eds) *Alcohol and Public Policy: evidence and issues*, pp. 62–81 (Oxford, Oxford University Press).

Mill, J.S. (1859) *On Liberty* (London, Parker).

Miller, B.A., Downs, W.R. and Gondoli, D.M. (1989) Spousal violence among alcoholic women as compared to a random household sample of women, *Journal of Studies on Alcohol*, 50, 533–40.

Miller, G. and Agnew, N. (1974) The Ledermann model of alcohol consumption, *Quarterly Journal of Studies on Alcohol*, 39, 877–98.

Miller, P. and Plant, M. (1996) Drinking, smoking, and illicit drug use among 15 and 16 year olds in the United Kingdom, *British Medical Journal*, 313, 394–7.

Miller, P.M., Smith, G.T. and Goldman, M.S. (1990) Emergence of alcohol expectancies in childhood: a possible critical period, *Journal of Studies on Alcohol*, 51 (4), 343–9.

Miller, W. (1966) Violent crimes in city gangs, *Annals of American Academy of Political and Social Science*, 364, 97–112.

Miller, W.R., Andrews, N.R., Wilbourne, P. and Bennett, M.E. (1998) A wealth of alternatives: effective treatments for alcohol problems, in Miller. W.R. and Heather, N. (eds) *Treating Addictive Behaviors* (2nd edition) (New York, Plenum).

Miller, W.R. and Hester, R.K. (1986a) Inpatient alcoholism treatment: who benefits? *American Psychologist*, 41, 794–805.

Miller, W.R. and Hester, R.K. (1986b) The effectiveness of alcoholism treatment: what research reveals, in Miller, W.R. and Heather, N. (eds) *Treating Addictive Behaviors: processes of change* (New York, Plenum).

Ministerial Group on Alcohol Misuse (1989) *First Annual Report 1987–88* (London, MGAM).

Mintoff, K. and Drake, R.E. (eds) (1991) *Dual Diagnosis of Major Mental Illness and Substance Disorder* (San Francisco, Jossey Bass).

Moffitt, T.E., Newman, D.L. and Silva, P.A. (1996) Behavioral observations at age 3 years predict adult psychiatric disorders: longitudinal evidence from a birth cohort, *Archives of General Psychiatry*, 53,1033-9.

Moncrieff, J., Drummond, D.C., Candy, B., Checinski, K. and Farmer, R. (1996) Sexual abuse in people with alcohol problems: a study of the prevalence of sexual abuse and its relationship to drinking behaviour, *British Journal of Psychiatry*, 169, 355-60.

Moore, D. (1990) Drinking, the construction of ethnic identity and social process in a Western Australian youth subculture, *British Journal of Addiction*, 85, 1265-78.

Moore, D.T (1987) A class lesson in alcoholic malnutrition: the poor get sicker than the affluent, *Alcohol Health and Research World*, 11(4).

Moore, M. and Cook, P. (1995) *Habit and Heterogeneity in the Youthful Demand for Alcohol*. Working Paper 5152 (Cambridge, MA, National Bureau of Economic Research).

Moore, R.D., Bone, L.R., Geiler, G., Mamon, J.A., Stokes, E.J. and Levine, D.M. (1989) Prevalence, detection and treatment of alcoholism in hospitalized patients, *Journal of the American Medical Association*, 261, 403–7.

Morgan-Thomas, R., Plant, M.A., Plant, M.L and Sales, J. (1990) Risk of infection among clients of the sex industry in Scotland, *British Medical Journal*, 301, 525.

Moss, E.C. and Beresford-Davies, E. (1967) *A Survey of Alcoholism in an English County* (Cambridge, Geigy [UK] Ltd).

Mulford, H., Ledolter, J. and Fitzgerald, J. (1992) Alcohol availability and consumption: Iowa sales data revisited, *Journal of Studies on Alcohol*, 53, 487–94.

Murry, J.P., Stam, A. and Lastovicka, J.L. (1993) Evaluating an antidrinking and driving advertising campaign with a sample survey and time series intervention analysis, *Journal of the American Statistical Association*, 88, 50–6.

Myers, C. (1983) Alcohol and violence: self-reported alcohol consumption among violent and non-violent male prisoners, *British Journal of Addiction*, 77, 399–423.

National Association for the Care and Resettlement of Offenders (1992) *Mentally disturbed offenders*, NACRO Briefing, No. 74 (London, NACRO).

National Health Service Executive (1998) *Commissioning in the New NHS*. Health Service Circular 1998/198 (Wetherby, DoH).

Neff, J.A. and Husaini, B.A. (1982) Life events, drinking patterns and depressive symptomatology: the stress-buffering role of alcohol consumption, *Journal of Studies on Alcohol*, 43, 301–18.

Neuendorf, K.A. (1985) Alcohol advertising and media portrayals, *Journal of the Institute of Socioeconomic Studies*, 10, 67–78.

Newcombe, R., Measham, F. and Parker, H. (1995) A survey of drinking and deviant behaviour among 14–15-year-olds in north west England, *Addiction Research*, 2, 319–41.

Nordlund, S. (1985) Effects of Saturday closing of wine and spirits shops in Norway. Paper presented at the 31st International Institute on the Prevention and Treatment of Alcoholism, Rome, Italy.

Norris, N. (1984) *Integration of Special Hospital Patients into the Community* (Aldershot, Gower).

Norström, T. (1995) Alcohol and suicide: a comparative analysis of France and Sweden, *Addiction*, 90, 1463–9.

Northridge, D., McMurray, J. and Lawson, H. (1986) Association between liberalisation of Scotland's licensing laws and admissions for self-poisoning in West Fife, *British Medical Journal*, 293, 1466–8.

O'Brien, C.P. and McLellan, A.T. (1996) Myths about the treatment of addiction, *Lancet*, 347, 237–40.

Ockene, J.K. (1987) Physician-delivered interventions for smoking cessation: strategies for increasing effectiveness, *Preventive Medicine*, 16, 723–37

Office for National Statistics (ONS) (1996) *Health in England 1995: what people know, what people think, what people do: a survey of adults aged 16–74 in England carried out by Social Survey Division of ONS on behalf of the Health Education Authority* (London, The Stationery Office).

Office for National Statistics (1998a) *Living in Britain: results from the 1996 General Household Survey: a survey carried out by Social Survey Division* (London, The Stationery Office).

Office for National Statistics (1998b) *Regional Trends* 33 (London, The Stationery Office).

Office for National Statistics (1998c) *Mortality Statistics, Cause: England and Wales 1996* (London, The Stationery Office).

Office for National Statistics (various quarters and years) *Consumer Trends* (London, The Stationery Office).

Office of Population Censuses and Surveys (OPCS) (1986a) *Drinking and Attitudes to Licensing in Scotland* (London, HMSO).

Office of Population Censuses and Surveys (1986b) *Adolescent Drinking* (London, HMSO).

Office of Population Censuses and Surveys (1987) *Drinking in England and Wales in 1987* (London, HMSO).

Office of Population Censuses and Surveys (1991) *Drinking in England and Wales in the Late 1980s: an enquiry carried out by Social Survey Division of OPCS on behalf of the Department of Health in association with the Home Office* (London, HMSO).

Office of Population Censuses and Surveys (1994) *General Household Survey 1992: an interdepartmental survey carried out by OPCS between April 1992 and March 1993* (London, HMSO).

Office of Population Censuses and Surveys (1995a) *Health Survey for England 1993: a report carried out by the Social Survey Division of the OPCS on behalf of the Department of Health* (London, HMSO).

Office of Population Censuses and Surveys (1995b) *The Prevalence of Psychiatric Morbidity Among Adults Living in Private Households* (London, HMSO).

Office of Population Censuses and Surveys (1995c) *Occupational Health: Decennial Supplement: the Registrar General's decennial supplement for England and Wales* (London, HMSO).

Office of Population Censuses and Survey (1996a) *Living in Britain: results from the 1994 General Household Survey: an interdepartmental survey carried out by OPCS between April 1994 and March 1995* (London, HMSO).

Office of Population Censuses and Surveys (1996b) *Psychiatric Morbidity Among Homeless People* (London, HMSO).

Office of Population Censuses and Surveys (1996c) *Teenage Drinking in 1994* (London, HMSO).

Ogborne, A.C. and Smart, R.G. (1980) Will restrictions on alcohol advertising reduce alcohol consumption? *British Journal of Addiction*, 75, 293–6.

Oliver, J.E. (1985) Successive generations of child maltreatment: social and medical disorders in the parents, *British Journal of Psychiatry*, 147, 484–90.

Olsson, O. and Wikstrom, P. (1982) Effects of experimental Saturday closing of liquor retail stores in Sweden, *Contemporary Drug Problems*, 11, 325–53.

Orford, J. and Edwards, G. (1977) *Alcoholism: a comparison of treatment and advice with a study of the influence of marriage*, Maudsley Monographs No. 26 (Oxford, Oxford University Press).

Orford, J., Natera, G., Davies, J., Nava, A., Mora, J., Rigby, K., Bradbury, C., Bowie, N., Copello, A. and Velleman, R. (1998) Tolerate, engage or withdraw: a study of the structure of families coping with alcohol and drug problems in South West England and Mexico City, *Addiction*, 93, 1799–813.

Österberg, E. (1982) *Recorded consumption of alcohol in Finland 1950–75* (Helsinki, Social Research Institute of Alcohol Studies).

Österberg, E. (1994) Do alcohol prices affect consumption and related problems?, in Holder, H.D. and Edwards, G. (eds) *Alcohol and Public Policy: evidence and issues*, pp. 145–63 (Oxford, Oxford Medical Publications).

Parker, H. (1996) Young adult offenders, alcohol and criminological cul-de-sacs, *British Journal of Criminology*, 36, 282–98.

Parker, H., Aldridge, J. and Measham, F. (1998) *Illegal Leisure: the normalization of adolescent drug use* (London, Routledge).

Parr, D. (1957) Alcoholism in general practice, *British Journal of Addiction*, 54, 25–31.

Patience, D., Buxton, M., Chick, J., Howlett, H., McKenna, M. and Ritson, B. (1997) The SECCAT Survey: II. the Alcohol-related Problems Questionnaire as a proxy for resource costs and quality of life in alcoholism treatment, *Alcohol and Alcoholism*, 32, 79–84.

Pendleton, L.L., Smith, C. and Roberts, J.L. (1990) Public opinion on alcohol policies, *British Journal of Addiction*, 85, 125–30.

Pendleton, L.L., Smith, C. and Roberts, J.L. (1991) Drinking on television: a content analysis of recent alcohol portrayal, *British Journal of Addiction*, 86, 769–74.

Perry, C.L., Grant, M., Ernberg, G., Florenzano, R.U., Langdon, M.C., Myeni, A.D., Waahlberg, R., Berg. S., Andersson, K., Fisher, K.J., Blaze-Temple, D., Cross, D., Saunders, B., Jackobs, D.R. and Schmid, T. *et al.* (1989) WHO collaborative study on alcohol education and young people: outcomes of a four country pilot study, *International Journal of the Addictions*, 24, 1145–71.

Phillips, J. (1995) *Licensing Law Guide* (London, Butterworths).

Pierce, J.P., Choi, W.S., Gilpin, E.A., Farkas, A.J. and Berry, C.C. (1998) Tobacco industry promotion of cigarettes and adolescent smoking, *Journal of the American Medical Association*, 279, 511–15.

Pihl, R.O. and Peterson, J. (1995) Drugs and aggression: correlations, crime and human manipulative studies and some proposed mechanisms, *Journal of Psychiatry and Neuroscience*, 20, 141–9.

Pinot de Moira, A. and Duffy, J. (1995) Changes in licensing law in England and Wales and alcohol-related mortality, *Addiction Research*, 3, 151–64.

Pittman, D.J. and Snyder, C.R. (1962a) Drinking in anthropological perspective: introductory note, in *Society, Culture and Drinking Patterns* (New York, John Wiley and Sons).

Pittman, D.J. and Snyder, C.R. (eds) (1962b) *Society, Culture and Drinking Patterns* (New York, John Wiley and Sons).

Plant, M., Bagnall, G., and Foster, J. (1990) Teenage heavy drinkers: alcohol-related knowledge, beliefs, experiences, motivation and the social context of drinking, *Alcohol and Alcoholism*, 25, 691–8.

Plant, M.A. and Foster, J. (1991) Teenagers and alcohol: results of a Scottish national survey, *Drug and Alcohol Dependence*, 28, 203–10.

Plant, M.L., Plant, M.A. and Morgan-Thomas, R. (1990) Alcohol, AIDS risks and commercial sex: some preliminary results from a Scottish study, *Drug and Alcohol Dependence*, 25, 51–5.

Platt, S. (1987) Association between liberalisation of Scotland's licensing laws and admissions for self poisoning, *British Medical Journal*, 294, 116–17.

Platt, S. and Robinson, A. (1991) Parasuicide and alcohol: a 20 year study of admissions to a regional poisoning treatment centre, *International Journal of Social Psychiatry*, 37, 159–72.

Poikolainen, K. (1995) Alcohol and mortality: a review, *Journal of Clinical Epidemiology*, 48, 455–65.

Pollack, B. (1989) Primary health care and the addictions: where to start and where to go, *British Journal of Addiction*, 84, 1425–32.

Ponicki, W. (1990) *The Price and Income Elasticities of the Demand for Alcohol: a review of the literature*, Working Paper, WP801 (Berkeley, CA, Prevention Research Center).

Porter, R. (1985) The drinking man's disease: the pre-history of alcoholism, *British Journal of Addiction*, 80, 385–96.

Portman Group (1993) *Keeping the Peace: a guide to the prevention of alcohol-related disorder* (London, Portman Group).

Portman Group (1995) Legal entrapment, *Solutions, the Portman Group Newsletter*, 2.

Potamianos, G., North, W.R., Meade, T.W., Townsend, J. and Peters, T.J. (1986) Randomised trial of community based centres versus conventional hospital management in the treatment of alcoholism, *Lancet*, II, 797–9.

Pratt, O. (1981) Alcohol and the woman of childbearing age: a public health problem, *British Journal of Addiction*, 76, 383–90.

Prest, A.R. (1949) Some experiments in demand analysis, *Review of Economics and Statistics*, 21, 33–49.

Prochaska, J.O. and DiClemente, C.C. (1986) Toward a comprehensive model of change, in Miller, W.R. and Heather, N. (eds) *Treating Addictive Behaviors: processes of change* (New York, Plenum).

Prochaska, J.O. and DiClemente, C.C. (1992) Stages of change in the modification of problem behaviors, in Hersen, M., Eisler, R.M. and Miller, P.M. (eds) *Progress in Behavior Modification* (Newbury Park, CA, Sage).

Project MATCH Research Group (1997) Matching alcoholism treatments to client heterogeneity: Project MATCH post-treatment drinking outcomes, *Journal of Studies on Alcohol*, 58, 7–29.

Quayle, M. and Clarke, F. (1992) The role of alcohol in the offences of special hospital patients. Internal Report, Broadmoor Hospital.

Quinn, M.A. and Johnston, R.V. (1976) Alcohol problems in acute male medical admissions, *Health Bulletin*, 34, 253–6.

Raistrick D.S. (1988) The 'combined approach': still an important debate, *British Journal of Addiction*, 83, 349–50.

Raistrick, D. and Heather, N. (forthcoming) *Review of Effectiveness of Treatment for Alcohol Problems* (London, DoH).

Ramayya, A. and Jauhar, P. (1997) Increasing incidence of Korsakoff's psychosis in the East End of Glasgow, *Alcohol and Alcoholism*, 32, 281–5.

Ramsay, M. (1989) *Downtown Drinkers: the perceptions and fears of the public in a city centre*, Home Office Crime Prevention Unit Paper 19 (London, Home Office).

Rao, R. and Miller, P. (1975) Advertising/sales response functions, *Journal of Advertising Research*, 15, 7–15.

Rasanen, P., Hakko, H. and Vaisanen, E. (1995) The mental state of arsonists as determined by forensic psychiatric examinations, *Bulletin of the American Academy of Psychiatry and the Law*, 23, 547–53.

Rasmussen, K. and Levander, S. (1996) Crime and violence among psychiatric patients in a maximum security psychiatric hospital, *Criminal Justice and Behavior*, 23, 455–71.

Reed, A., Ramsden, S., Marshall, J., Ball, J., O Brien, J., Flynn, A., Elton, N., El-Kabir, D. and Joseph, P. (1992) Psychiatric morbidity and substance abuse among residents of a cold weather shelter, *British Medical Journal*, 304, 1028–9.

Reid, A.L.A., Webb, G.R., Hendrikus, D., Fahey, P.P. and Sanson-Fisher, R.W. (1986) Detection of patients with high alcohol intake by general practitioners, *British Medical Journal*, 293, 735–7.

Reid, D. (1996) Tobacco control: overview, *British Medical Bulletin*, 52, 108–20.

Regier, D.A., Farmer, M.E., Rae, D.S., Locke, B.Z., Keith, S.J., Judd, L.L. and Goodwin, F.K. (1990) Comorbidity of mental disorders with alcohol and other drug abuse: results from the Epidemiologic Catchment Area (ECA) study, *Journal of the American Medical Association*, 264, 2511–18.

Renaud, S. and de Lorgeril, M. (1992) Wine, alcohol, platelets and the French paradox for coronary heart disease, *Lancet*, 339, 1523–6.

Reutzel, T.J., Becker, F.W. and Sanders, B.K. (1987) Expenditure effects of changes in Medicaid benefit coverage: an alcohol and substance abuse example, *American Journal of Public Health*, 77, 503–4.

Richmond, R. and Anderson, P. (1994) Research in general practice for smokers and excessive drinkers in Australia and the UK. III Dissemination of interventions, *Addiction*, 89, 49–62.

Richmond, R. and Heather, N. (1990) General practitioner interventions for smoking cessation: past results and future prospects, *Behaviour Change*, 7, 110–19.

Richmond, R., Heather, N., Wodak, A., Kehoe, L. and Webster, I. (1995) Controlled evaluation of a general practice-based brief intervention for excessive drinking, *Addiction*, 90, 119–32.

Rimm, E.B., Klatsky, A., Grobbee, D. and Stampfer, M.J. (1996) Review of moderate alcohol consumption and reduced risk of coronary heart disease: is the effect due to beer, wine or spirits? *British Medical Journal*, 312, 731–6.

Ritson, B. (1996) *Community and Municipal Action on Alcohol* (Copenhagen, WHO Regional Office for Europe).

Robertson, G., Gibb, R. and Pearson, R. (1995) Drunkenness among police detainees, *Addiction*, 90, 793–803.

Robins, L.N. and McEvoy, L. (1991) Conduct problems as predictors of substance abuse, in Rutter, M. and Robins, L.N. (eds) *Straight and Devious Pathways from Childhood to Adulthood* (Cambridge, Cambridge University Press).

Robinson, D. (1979) *Talking Out of Alcoholism: the self-help process of Alcoholics Anonymous* (London, Croom Helm).

Rohde, P., Lewinsohn, P. and Seeley J. (1996) Psychiatric comorbidity with problematic alcohol use in high school students, *Journal of the American Academy of Child and Adolescent Psychiatry*, 35, 101–9.

Rohrbach, L.A., Graham, J.W. and Hansen, W.B. (1997) A controlled trial of educational strategies to teach medical students brief intervention skills for alcohol problems, *Preventive Medicine*, 26, 78–85.

Roizen, J. (1989) Alcohol and trauma, in Giesbrecht, N., Gonzalez, R., Grant, M., Österberg, E., Room, R., Rootman, I. and Towle, L. (eds) *Drinking and Casualties: accidents, poisonings and violence in an international perspective* (London, Routledge).

Romelsjö, A. (1995) Alcohol consumption and unintentional injury, suicide, violence, work performance, and inter-generational effects, in Holder, H.D. and Edwards, G. (eds) *Alcohol and Public Policy: evidence and issues* (Oxford, Oxford University Press).

Room, R. (1984) Alcohol and ethnography: a case of problem deflation? *Current Anthropology*, 25, 169–91.

Room, R. (1989) Alcoholism and Alcoholics Anonymous in US films, 1945–1962: the party ends for the 'wet generations', *Journal of Studies on Alcohol*, 50, 368–83.

Room, R. (1991) Cultural changes in drinking and trends in alcohol problems indicators: recent US experience, in Clark, W.G. and Hilton, M.E. (eds) *Alcohol in America*, pp. 149–63 (Albany, State University of New York).

Room, R. (1998) Thirsting for attention, *Addiction*, 93, 797–8.

Rorstad, P. and Checinski, K. (1996) *Dual Diagnosis: facing the challenge* (Kenley, Wynne Howard Publishing).

Rose, G. (1985) Sick individuals and sick populations, *International Journal of Epidemiology*, 14, 32–8.

Rose, G. (1992) *The Strategy of Preventive Medicine* (Oxford, Oxford University Press).

Rose, G. and Day, S. (1990) The population mean predicts the number of deviant individuals, *British Medical Journal*, 301, 1031–4.

Rosenbaum, D.P., Flewelling, R., Bailey, S., Ringwalt, C. and Wilkinson, D. (1994) Cops in the classroom: a longitudinal evaluation of drug abuse resistance education, *Journal of Research in Crime and Delinquency*, 31, 3–31.

Rosenheim, Lord (1970) Foreword, in Glatt, M., *The Alcoholic and the Help he Needs*, pp. v–vii (Royston, Priory Press).

Rossow, I. (1996) Alcohol-related violence: the impact of drinking pattern and drinking context, *Addiction*, 91, 1651–61.

Rowland, N., Maynard, A., Kennedy, P., Stone, W. and Wintersgill, W. (1988) Doctors and alcohol screening: the gap between attitudes and action, *Health Education Journal*, 47, 133–6.

Rowntree, J. and Sherwell, A. (1903) *Public Control of the Liquor Traffic* (London, Grant Richards).

Royal College of General Practitioners (1986) *Alcohol: a balanced view* (London, Royal College of General Practitioners).

Royal College of General Practitioners (1996) *Information Sheet No. 3: general practitioner workload* (London, Royal College of General Practitioners).

Royal College of Physicians (1987) *A Great and Growing Evil: the medical consequences of alcohol abuse* (London, Tavistock).

Royal College of Physicians (1994) *Alcohol and Ill-health* (London, Royal College of Physicians).

Royal Colleges of Physicians, Psychiatrists and General Practitioners (1995) *Alcohol and the Heart in Perspective: sensible limits re-affirmed* (London, Royal Colleges).

Royal College of Psychiatrists (1979) *Alcohol and Alcoholism* (London, Tavistock).

Royal College of Psychiatrists (1986) *Alcohol: our favourite drug* (London, Tavistock).

Royal College of Psychiatrists (1997) *Educational Policy*, Occasional Paper OP36 (London, Royal College of Psychiatrists).

Rundell, O.H., Jones, M.S. and Gregory, D. (1981) Practical benefit cost analysis for alcoholism programs, *Alcoholism: Clinical and Experimental Research*, 5, 497–508.

Rutherford, D. (1991) The drinks cabinet: UK alcohol policy, *Contemporary Record*, 5, 450–67.

Rychtarik, R. G. (1990) Alcohol training in south-east England: a survey and evaluation, *Alcohol and Alcoholism*, 25, 699–709.

Rychtarik, R.G., Fairbank, J.A., Allen, C.M. and Foy, D.W. (1983) Alcohol use in television programming: effects on children's behavior, *Addictive Behaviors*, 8, 19–22.

Saffer, H. (1991) Alcohol advertising bans and alcohol abuse: an international perspective, *Journal of Health Economics*, 10, 65–79.

Saffer, H. (1996) Studying the effects of alcohol advertising on consumption, *Alcohol Health and Research World*, 20, 266–72.

Saffer, H. (1997) Alcohol advertising and motor vehicle fatalities, *Review of Economics and Statistics*, 79, 431–42.

Saffer, H. and Grossman, M. (1987) Beer taxes, the legal drinking age, and young motor vehicle fatalities, *Journal of Legal Studies*, 16, 351–74.

St Leger, A.S., Cochrane, A.L. and Moore, F. (1979) Factors associated with cardiac mortality in developed countries with particular reference to the consumption of wine, *Lancet*, I, 1017–20.

Salisu, M. and Balasubramanyam, V. (1997) Income and price elasticities of demand for alcoholic drinks, *Applied Economics Letters*, 4, 247–51.

Saunders, J.B., Haines, A., Portmann, B., Wodak, A.D., Powell-Jackson, P.R. and Williams, R. (1982) Accelerated development of alcoholic cirrhosis in patients with HLA B8, *Lancet*, I, 1381–4.

Saunders, J.B., Wodak, A.D. and Williams, R. (1985) Past experience of advice and treatment for drinking problems of patients with alcohol liver disease, *British Journal of Addiction*, 80, 51–6.

Saunders, W. (1985) Licensing law, the Scottish experiment: a reply to Clayson, *Triple A Review*, July–August.

Saxe, L., Dougherty, D., Esty, K. and Fine, M. (1983) *The Effectiveness and Costs of Alcoholism Treatment*. Health Technology Case Study 22, Congress of the United States Office of Technology Assessment (Washington, DC, US Government Printing Office).

Scally, G. and Donaldson, L.J. (1998) Clinical governance and the drive for quality improvement in the new NHS in England, *British Medical Journal*, 317, 61–5.

Scammon, D.L., Mayer, R.N. and Smith, K.R. (1991) Alcohol warnings: how do you know when you have had one too many? *Journal of Public Policy and Marketing*, 10, 214–28.

Scheffler, A., Fawcett, A., Pushkin, J., Zahir, K. and Morgan, M.Y. (1987) Alcohol-related problems amongst selected hospital patients and the cost incurred in their care, *British Journal of Addiction*, 82, 275–83.

Schooler, C., Basil, M.D. and Altman, D.G. (1996) Alcohol and cigarette advertising on billboards: targeting with social cues, *Health Communication*, 82, 109–29.

Schuckit, M.A. and Monteiro, M.A. (1988) Alcoholism, anxiety and depression, *British Journal of Addiction*, 83, 1373–80.

Scott, E. and Anderson, P. (1991) Randomized controlled trial of general practitioner intervention in women with excessive alcohol consumption, *Drug and Alcohol Review*, 10, 313–21.

Scottish Council on Alcohol (1994) *United Kingdom Alcohol Statistics: 1994* (Glasgow, SCA).

Scottish Home and Health Department (1973) *Report of the Departmental Committee on Scottish Licensing Laws* (The Clayson Report), Cm. 5354 (Edinburgh, HMSO).

Scottish Office (1993) *Towards a National Strategy for Substance Misuse* (Edinburgh, HMSO).

Scottish Office and Department of Health (1997) *Designed to Care: renewing the National Health Service in Scotland*, Cm. 3811 (Edinburgh, The Stationery Office.)

Scottish Office and Department of Health (1998) *Working Together for a Healthier Scotland: a consultation document*, Cm. 3584 (London, The Stationery Office).

Scribner, R., MacKinnon, D. and Dwyer, J. (1994) Alcohol outlet density and motor vehicle accidents in Los Angeles county cities, *Journal of Studies on Alcohol*, 55, 447–53.

Scribner, R., MacKinnon, D. and Dwyer, J. (1995) The risk of assaultative violence and alcohol availability in Los Angeles County, *American Journal of Public Health*, 85, 335–40.

Seale, J.P., Amodei, N., Bedolla, M., Ortiz, E., Lane, P. and Gaspard, J. (1995) Evaluation of addiction training for psychiatric residents, *Substance Abuse*, 16, 1–8.

Select Committee (1834) *Select Committee on the Prevailing Vice of Drunkenness* (London, House of Commons).

Selvanathan, E. (1988) Alcohol consumption in the UK, 1955–85: a system-wide analysis, *Applied Economics*, 20, 1071–86.

Selvanathan, E. (1989) Advertising and alcohol demand in the UK: further results, *International Journal of Advertising*, 8, 181–8.

Selvanathan, E. (1991) Cross-country consumption comparison: an application of the Rotterdam demand system, *Applied Economics*, 23, 1613–22.

Shadwell, A. (1902) *Drink, Temperance and Legislation* (London, Longmans, Green).

Shaffer, D., Gould, M., Fisher, P., Trautman, P., Moreau, D., Kleinman, M. and Flory, M. (1996) Psychiatric diagnosis in child and adolescent suicide, *Archives of General Psychiatry*, 53, 339–48.

Shanks, N.J., George, S.L., Westlake, L. and Al-Kalai, D. (1994) Who are the homeless? *Public Health*, 108, 11–19.

Shaper, A.G. (1990) Alcohol and mortality: a review of prospective studies, *British Journal of Addiction*, 85, 837–47.

Shaper, A.G., Walker, M. and Wannamethee, G. (1988) Alcohol and mortality in British men: explaining the U-shaped curve, *Lancet*, II, 1267–73.

Shaper, A.G., Wannamethee, G. and Walker, M. (1994) Alcohol and coronary heart disease: a perspective from the British Regional Heart Study, *International Journal of Epidemiology*, 23, 482–94.

Sharkey, J., Brennan, D. and Curran, P. (1996) The pattern of alcohol consumption of a general hospital population in North Belfast, *Alcohol and Alcoholism*, 31, 279–85.

Shaw, S., Cartwright, A., Spratley, T. and Harwin, J. (1978) *Responding to Drinking Problems* (London, Croom Helm).

Shawcross, M., Robertson, S., Jones, A., McIver, J. and de Souza, R. (1996) *Family and Alcohol Project: report on a pilot project* (Edinburgh, Lothian Regional Council Social Work Department).

Shepherd, J. (1994a) Violent crime: the role of alcohol and new approaches to the prevention of injury, *Alcohol and Alcoholism*, 29, 5–10.

Shepherd, J. (1994b) Preventing injuries from bar glasses: temper the nonik, *British Medical Journal*, 308, 933.

Sherman, D.I.N. and Williams, R. (1994) Liver damage: mechanisms and management, in Edwards, G. and Peters T.J. (eds) *Alcohol and Alcohol Problems*, British Medical Bulletin 50, pp. 124–38 (London, Churchill Livingstone).

Shibuya, A. and Yoshida, A. (1988) Genotypes of alcohol metabolising enzymes in Japanese with alcoholic liver disease: a strong association with the usual caucasian-type aldehyde dehydrogenase gene (ALDH21) with the disease, *American Journal of Human Genetics*, 43, 744–8.

Shope, J.T., Dielman, T.E., Butchart, A.T., Campanelli, P.C. and Kloska, D.D. (1992) An elementary school-based alcohol misuse prevention program: a follow-up evaluation, *Journal of Studies on Alcohol*, 53, 106–21.

Siegel, K., Mesagno, F.P., Chen, J.Y. and Christ, G. (1989) Factors distinguishing homosexual males practising risky and safer sex, *Social Science Medicine*, 28, 561–9.

Signorielli, N. (1987) Drinking, sex, and violence on television: the cultural indicators perspective, *Journal of Drug Education*, 17, 245–60.

Simes, R.J. (1986) Publication bias: the case for an international registry of clinical trials, *Journal of Clinical Oncology*, 4, 1529–41.

Simpson, M., Williams, B. and Kendrick, A. (1994) Alcohol and the elderly: an overview of the literature for social work, *Ageing and Society*, 14, 575–87.

Simpura, J. (1995) Trends in alcohol consumption and drinking patterns: lessons from world-wide development, in Holder, H.D. and Edwards, G. (eds) *Alcohol and Public Policy*, pp. 9–37 (Oxford, Oxford University Press).

Simpura, J. (1996) Trends in alcohol consumption in the EU countries, in Peters, T.J. (ed.) *Alcohol Misuse: a European perspective* (Amsterdam, Harwood).

Simpura, J. (1997) Alcohol and European transformation, *Addiction*, 92, S33–41.

Skog, O.J. (1971) *Alkoholkonsumets Fordeling I Befolkninger* (Oslo, National Institute for Alcohol Research).

Skog, O.J. (1980) Is alcohol consumption lognormally distributed? *British Journal of Addiction*, 75, 169–73.

Skog, O.J. (1985) The collectivity of drinking cultures: a theory of the distribution of alcohol consumption, *British Journal of Addiction*, 80, 83–99.

Skog, O.J. (1991) Epidemiological and biostatistical aspects of alcohol use, alcoholism, and their complications, in Erickson, P.C. and Kalant, H. (eds) *Windows on Science 40* (Toronto, ARF).

Slater, M.D., Rouner, D., Murphy, K., Beauvais, F. and Van Leuven, J. (1996) Adolescent counterarguing of TV beer advertisements: evidence for effectiveness of alcohol education and critical viewing discussions, *Journal of Drug Education*, 26, 143–58.

Smart, R.G. (1988) Does alcohol advertising affect overall consumption? A review of empirical studies, *Journal of Studies on Alcohol*, 49, 314–23.

Smart, R.G. (1989) Is the postwar drinking binge ending? Cross national trends in per capita alcohol consumption, *British Journal of Addiction*, 84, 743–8.

Smart, R.G. and Cutler, R.E. (1976) The alcohol advertising ban in British Columbia: problems and effects on beverage consumption, *British Journal of Addiction*, 71, 31–21.

Smart, R.G., Mann, R.E. and Anglin, L. (1989) Decreases in alcohol problems and increased Alcoholics Anonymous membership, *British Journal of Addiction*, 84, 507–13.

Smart, S. (1974) The effect of licensing restrictions during 1914–1918 on drunkenness and liver cirrhosis deaths in Britain, *British Journal of Addiction*, 69, 109–21.

Smith, C., Roberts, J.L. and Pendleton, L.L. (1988) Booze on the box. The portrayal of alcohol on British television: a content analysis, *Health Education, Research, Theory and Practice*, 3, 267–73.

Smith, D. (1989) Social work with problem drinkers, *Practice*, 2, 301–10.

Smith, D. and Burvill, P. (1987) Effect on juvenile crime of lowering the drinking age in three Australian states, *British Journal of Addiction*, 82, 181–8.

Smith, J. and Hucker, S. (1993) Dual diagnosis patients substance abuse by the severely mentally ill, *British Journal of Hospital Medicine*, 50, 650–4.

Smith, S.G.T., Touquet, R., Wright, S. and Das Gupta, N. (1996) Detection of alcohol misusing patients in accident and emergency departments: the Paddington alcohol test (PAT), *Journal of Accident and Emergency Medicine*, 13, 308–12.

Smith, S.J. (1990) The impact of product usage warnings in alcoholic beverage advertising, *Journal of Public Policy and Marketing*, 9, 16–29.

Snyder, C.R. (1978) *Alcohol and the Jews* (Carbondale, Southern Illinois University Press).

Sobell, L.C., Sobell, M.B., Toneatto, T., Leo, G.I., Pavan, D. and Cancilla, A. (1986) Effect of television programming and advertising on alcohol consumption in normal drinkers, *Journal of Studies on Alcohol*, 47, 333–40.

Sobell, L.C., Sobell, M.B., Toneatto, T. and Leo, G.I. (1993) Severely dependent alcohol abusers may be vulnerable to alcohol cues in television programs, *Journal of Studies on Alcohol*, 54, 85–91.

Sobell, M.B. and Sobell, L.C. (1999) Stepped care for alcohol problems: an efficient method for planning and delivering clinical services, in Tucker, J.A., Donovan, D.A. and Marlatt, G.A. (eds) *Changing Addictive Behavior* (New York, Guilford Press.)

Social Services Inspectorate of the Department of Health (1997) *Inspection of Social Services for People Who Misuse Alcohol and Drugs: standards and criteria* (London, DoH).

Stall, R., McKuisick, L., Wiley, J., Coates, T.J. and Ostrow, D.G. (1986) Alcohol and drug use during sexual activity and compliance with safe sex guidelines for AIDS: the AIDS Behavioral Research Project, *Health Education Quarterly*, 13, 359–71.

Stampfer, M.J., Colditz, G.A., Willett, W.C., Speizer, F.E. and Hennekens, C.H. (1988) A prospective study of moderate alcohol consumption and the risk of coronary disease and stroke in women, *New England Journal of Medicine*, 319, 267–73.

Standing Conference on Crime Prevention (1987) *Report of the Working Group on Young People and Alcohol* (London, Home Office).

Steele, B.F. and Pollock, C.P. (1974) A psychiatric study of parents who abuse infants and small children, in Helfer, R.E. and Kempe, C.H. (eds) *The Battered Child* (2nd edition) (Chicago, IL, University of Chicago Press).

Steele, C.M. and Josephs, R.A. (1990) Alcohol myopia: its prized and dangerous effects, *American Psychologist*, 45, 87–91.

Stockwell, T. (1987) The Exeter Home Detoxification Project, in Stockwell, T. and Clement, S. (eds) *Helping the Problem Drinker: new initiatives in community care* (London, Croom Helm).

Stockwell, T. (1993) Influencing the labelling of alcoholic beverage containers: informing the public, *Addiction*, 88, S53–60.

Stockwell, T. (1997) Liquor outlets and prevention policy: the need for light in dark corners, *Addiction Research*, 92, 925–30.

Stockwell, T. and Bolderstone, H. (1987) Alcohol and phobias, *British Journal of Addiction*, 82, 971–9.

Stockwell, T., Bolt, L., Milner, I., Pugh, P. and Young, I. (1990) Home detoxification for problem drinkers: acceptability to clients, relatives, general practitioners and outcome after 60 days, *British Journal of Addiction*, 85, 61–70.

Stockwell, T., Lang, E. and Rydon, P. (1993) High risk drinking settings: the association of serving and promotional practices with harmful drinking, *Addiction*, 88, 1519–26.

Stockwell, T., Somerford, P. and Lang, E. (1992) The relationship between licence type and alcohol-related problems attributed to licensed premises in Perth, Western Australia, *Journal of Studies on Alcohol*, 53, 495–8.

Stone, R. (1945) The analysis of market demand, *Journal of the Royal Statistical Society*, 108, 286–382.

Stone, R. (1951) *The Role of Measurement in Economics* (Cambridge, Cambridge University Press).

Stonham, Rt. Hon. Lord (1969) Introductory address, in Cook, T., Gath, D. and Hensman, C. (eds) *The Drunkenness Offence*, pp. 1–5 (Oxford, Pergamon).

Strachan, V.P.N. (various months and years) *HM Customs and Excise annual report* (London, The Stationery Office).

Strang, J., Clee, W.B., Gruer, W. and Raistrick, D. (1997) Why Britain's drug czar mustn't wage war on drugs: aim for pragmatism, not dogma (editorial), *British Medical Journal*, 315, 325.

Strang, J. and Sheridan, J. (1998) Effect of government recommendations on methadone prescribing in south east England: comparison of 1995 and 1997 surveys, *British Medical Journal*, 7171, 1489–90.

Strickland, D.E. (1983) Alcohol exposure, alcohol advertising and the misuse of alcohol, in Grant, M., Plant, M. and Williams, A. (eds) *Economics and Alcohol: consumption and controls* (London, Croom Helm).

Strickland, D.E. (1984) Content and effects of alcohol advertising: comment on NTIS pub. no. PB82-123142, *Journal of Alcohol Studies*, 45, 87–93.

Sutherland, I. and Willner, P. (1998) Patterns of alcohol, cigarette and illicit drug use in English adolescents, *Addiction*, 93, 1199–208.

Sutton, S. (1992) Shock tactics and the myth of the inverted U, *British Journal of Addiction*, 87, 517–19.

Sutton, M. and Godfrey, C. (1995) A grouped data regression approach to estimating economic and social influences on individual behaviour, *Health Economics*, 4, 237–47.

Suzuki, K., Takeda, A. and Matsusshita S. (1995) Coprevalence of bulimia with alcohol abuse and smoking among Japanese male and female high school students, *Addiction*, 90, 971–5.

Teplin, L.A., Abram, K.M. and McClelland, G.M. (1994) Does psychiatric disorder predict violent crime among released jail detainees?: a 6-year longitudinal study, *American Psychologist*, 49, 335–42.

Tether, P. and Godfrey, C. (1990) Liquor licensing, in Godfrey, C. and Robinson D. (eds) *Preventing Alcohol and Tobacco Problems, Volume 2: Manipulating Consumption: information, law and voluntary controls*, pp. 116–38 (Aldershot, Avebury).

Tether, P. and Robinson, D. (1986) *Preventing Alcohol Problems: a guide to local action* (London, Tavistock).

Thom, B., Brown, C., Drummond, D.C., Edwards, G. and Mullan, M. (1992) The use of services for alcohol problems: general practitioner and specialist alcohol clinics, *British Journal of Addiction*, 87, 613–24.

Thom, B. and Green, A. (1996) Services for women: the way forward, in Harrison, L. (ed.) *Alcohol Problems in the Community* (London, Routledge).

Thom, B. and Tellez, C. (1986) A difficult business: detecting and managing alcohol problems in general practice, *British Journal of Addiction*, 81, 405–18.

Thomas, G. and MacMillan, M. (1993) Alcohol related offending in male special hospital patients, *Medicine, Science and the Law*, 33, 29–32.

Thornton, L. and Holding, A. (1990) *Alcohol Misuse: a study of social work practice* (London, Social Services Inspectorate, DoH).

Tober, G. and Raistrick, D. (1990) Development of a district training strategy, *British Journal of Addiction*, 85, 1563–70.

Tolley, K. and Rowland, N. (1991) Identification of alcohol-related problems in a general hospital setting: a cost-effectiveness evaluation, *British Journal of Addiction*, 86, 429–38.

Torres, M.I., Mattick, R.P., Chen, R. and Baillie, A. (1995) *Clients of Treatment Service Agencies: March 1995 census findings* (Canberra, Australian Government Publishing Service).

Treno, A., Parker, R. and Holder, H. (1993) Understanding US alcohol consumption with social and economic factors: a multivariate time series analysis, 1950–1986, *Journal of Studies on Alcohol*, 54, 146–56.

Trice, H. and Beyer, J. (1984) Work-related outcomes of constructive confrontation strategies in a job based alcoholism program, *Journal of Studies on Alcohol*, 45, 393–404.

Trimpey, J. (1991) *Rational Recovery from Alcoholism: the small book* (3rd edition) (California, Lotus Press).

Trotter, T. (1804) *An Essay, Medical, Philosophical and Chemical, on Drunkenness and its Effects on the Human Body* (London, Longman, Hurst, Rees and Orme).

Tuck, M. (1989) *Drinking and Disorder: a study of non-metropolitan violence*, Home Office Research Study 108 (London, HMSO).

Tucker, L.A. (1985) Television's role regarding alcohol use among teenagers, *Adolescence*, 20, 593–98.

Turner, J. (1980) State purchase of the liquor trade in the First World War, *Historical Journal*, 23, 589–615.

Tyler, A. (1986) *Street Drugs* (London, New English Library).

Tylor, E.B. (1873) *Primitive Culture: researches into the development of mythology, philosophy, religion, language, art and custom, Volume 1* (2nd edition) (London, John Murray).

UK Alcohol Forum (1997) *Guidelines for the Management of Alcohol Problems in Primary Care and General Psychiatry* (London, Tangent Medical Education).

Unger, J.B., Johnson, C.A. and Rohrbach, L.A. (1995) Recognition and liking of tobacco and alcohol advertisements among adolescents: relationships with susceptibility to substance use, *Preventive Medicine*, 24, 461–6.

US General Accounting Office (1987) *Drinking Age Laws: an evaluation synthesis of their impact on highway safety* (Washington, DC, US Superintendent of Documents).

Vaillant, G.E. (1995) *The Natural History of Alcoholism Revisited* (Cambridge, MA, Harvard University Press).

Valdez, A., Kaplan, C.D., Cuyrtis, R.L. and Yin, Z. (1995) Illegal drug use, alcohol and aggressive crime among Mexican-American and white male arrestees in San Antonio, *Journal of Psychoactive Drugs*, 27, 135–43.

Valdiserri, R.O., Lyter, D., Leviton, L.C., Callahan, C.M., Kingsley, L.A. and Rinaldo, C.R. (1988) Variables influencing condom use in a cohort of gay and bisexual men, *American Journal of Public Health*, 78, 801–5.

Vasse, R.M., Nijhuis, F.J.N. and Kok, G. (1998) Associations between work stress, alcohol consumption and sickness absence, *Addiction*, 93, 231–41.

Wagenaar, A. (1993) Research affects public policy: the case of the legal drinking age in the United States, *Addiction*, 88, S75–81.

Wagenaar, A. and Holder, H. (1991) A change from public to private sale of wine: results from natural experiments in Iowa and West Virginia, *Journal of Studies on Alcohol*, 52, 162–73.

Wagenaar, A. and Holder, H. (1993) A response to Mulford, Ledolter and Fitzgerald, *Journal of Studies on Alcohol*, 54, 251–2.

Wagenaar, A. and Langley, J.D. (1995) Alcohol licensing system changes and alcohol consumption: introduction of wine into New Zealand grocery stores, *Addiction*, 90, 773–83.

Wagenaar, A., Toomey, T., Murray, D., Short, B., Wolfson, M. and Jones-Webb, R. (1996) Sources of alcohol for underage drinkers, *Journal of Studies on Alcohol*, 57, 325–33.

Wake, M. (ed.) (1992) *Homelessness and Street Drinking* (London, Arlington Housing Association).

Wallace, P., Cutler, S. and Haines, A. (1988) Randomized controlled trial of general practitioner intervention in patients with excessive alcohol consumption, *British Medical Journal*, 297, 663–8.

Wallace, P.G. and Haines, A.P. (1984) General practitioners and health promotion: what patients think, *British Medical Journal*, 289, 534–6.

Wallack, L. (1994) Media advocacy: a strategy for empowering people and communities, *Journal of Public Health Policy*, 15, 420–36.

Walsh, B. (1982) The demand for alcohol in the UK: a comment, *Journal of Industrial Economics*, 30, 439–46.

Walsh, M.E. and Macleod, D.A.D. (1983) Breath alcohol analysis in the accident and emergency department, *Injury: the British Journal of Accident Surgery*, 15, 62–6.

Wannamethee, G. and Shaper, A.G. (1988) Men who do not drink: a report from the British Regional Heart Study, *International Journal of Epidemiology*, 17, 307–16.

Ward, M. and Applin, C. (1998) *The Unlearned Lesson* (London, Wynne Howard Books).

Warner, J. (1995) Good help is hard to find: a few comments about alcohol and work in pre-industrial England, *Addiction Research*, 2, 259–69.

Waterson, J. (1996) Gender divisions and drinking problems, in Harrison, L. (ed.) *Alcohol Problems in the Community* (London, Routledge).

Watson, J.P. (1969) Alcohol and the accident department, *British Journal of Addiction*, 64, 223–30.

Wattis, J. (1983) Alcohol and old people, *British Journal of Psychiatry*, 143, 306–7.

Watts, R. and Rabow, J. (1983) Alcohol availability and alcohol problems in 213 California cities, *Alcoholism: Clinical and Experimental Research*, 7, 47–58.

Waxer, P.H. (1992) Alcohol consumption in television programming in three English-speaking cultures, *Alcohol and Alcoholism*, 27, 195–200.

Weatherburn, P., Davies, P.M., Hickson, F.C.I., Hunt, A.J., McManus, T.J. and Coxon, A.P.M. (1993) No connection between alcohol use and unsafe sex among gay and bisexual men, *AIDS*, 7, 115–19.

Weaver, K. (1997) Homelessness is habit forming, *Inside Housing*, February, 14–15.

Webb, E., Ashton, C.H., Kelley, P. and Kamali, F. (1996) Alcohol and drug use in UK university students, *Lancet*, 348, 922–5.

Webster, P., Mattick, R.P. and Baillie, A.J. (1992) Characteristics of clients receiving treatment in Australian drug and alcohol agencies: a national census, *Drug and Alcohol Review*, 11, 111–19.

Webster, R. and Chappell, I. (1995) *Breaking into the System: a guide for alcohol services on partnership with the police, probation and prison services* (London, Alcohol Concern).

Wechsler, H., Kasey, E.H., Thum, D. and Demone, H.W. (1969) Alcohol level and home accidents, *Public Health Reports*, 84, 1043–50.

Welsh Office and Department of Health (1998) *Putting Patients First: the future of the NHS in Wales*, Cm. 3841 (London, The Stationery Office).

Welte, J.W. and Abel, E.L. (1989) Homicide: drinking by the victim, *Journal of Studies on Alcohol*, 50, 197–201.

Wight, D. (1993) *Workers Not Wasters* (Edinburgh, Edinburgh University Press).

Wiley, J.A. and Weisner, C. (1995) Drinking in violent and nonviolent events leading to arrest: evidence from a survey of arrestees, *Journal of Criminal Justice*, 23, 461–76.

Wilkins, R.H. (1974) *The Hidden Alcoholic in General Practice* (London, Elek Science).

Wilkinson, J. (1987) Reducing drunken driving, *Southern Economic Journal*, 54, 322–34.

Williams, C.L., Toomey, T.L., McGovern, P., Wagenaar, A.C. and Perry, C.L. (1995) Development, reliability, and validity of self-report alcohol-use measures with young adolescents, *Journal of Child and Adolescent Substance Abuse*, 4, 17–40.

Williams, G.P. (1975) Off-licences in supermarkets open a new door for many, *Journal of Alcoholism*, 10, 122–31.

Williams, G.P. and Brake, G.T. (1980) *Drink in Great Britain 1900–1979* (London, Edsall).

Williams, L. (1960) *Tomorrow Will Be Sober* (London, Casswell).

Williams, R. (1976) *Keywords: a vocabulary of culture and society* (London, Fontana).

Williams, R. and Morgan, H. (1994) *Suicide Prevention: the challenge confronted*, NHS Health Advisory Service (London, HMSO).

Wilson, G.B. (1940) *Alcohol and the Nation* (London, Nicholson and Watson).

Wilson, P. (1980) *Drinking in England and Wales* (London, HMSO).

Windle, R.C. and Windle, M. (1995) Longitudinal patterns of physical aggression: associations with adult social, psychiatric, and personality functioning and testosterone levels, *Development and Psychopathology*, 7, 563–85.

Wittchen, H-U., Perkonigg, A. and Reed, V. (1996) Comorbidity of mental disorders and substance use disorders, *European Addiction Research*, 2, 36–47.

Wober, J.M. (1986) *Alcohol on Television and in Viewers' Experience: a study of links between attitudes and behaviour* (London, Research Department, Independent Broadcasting Authority).

Wolfson, M., Toomey, T., Murray, D., Forster, J., Short, B. and Wagenaar, A. (1996) Alcohol outlet policies and practices concerning sales to underage people, *Addiction*, 91, 589–602.

Wong, A. (1988) *The Demand for Alcohol in the UK 1920–1938: an econometric study*, Discussion Paper No. 88.13 (Perth, University of Western Australia).

World Health Organization (1993) *European Alcohol Action Plan* (Copenhagen, WHO Regional Office for Europe).

World Health Organization (WHO) (1995) *European Charter on Alcohol*, adopted at the European Conference on Health, Society and Alcohol, Paris, France.

Wright, S.J. (1985) SOS: alcohol, drugs and boating, *Alcohol Health and Research World*, 9, 28–33.

Yamada, T., Kendix, M. and Yamada, T. (1993) *The Impact of Alcohol Consumption and Marijuana Use on High School Graduation*, Working Paper No. 4497 (Cambridge, MA, National Bureau of Economic Research).

Yancey, G.B. and Kelly, L. (1990) The inappropriateness of using participants' reactions to evaluate effectiveness of training, *Psychological Reports*, 66, 937–8.

Yano, K., Rhoads, G.G. and Kagan, A. (1977) Coffee, alcohol and risk of coronary heart disease among Japanese men living in Hawaii, *New England Journal of Medicine*, 297, 405–9.

Yates, D.W., Hadfield, J.M. and Peters, K. (1987) The detection of problem drinkers in the accident and emergency department, *British Journal of Addiction*, 82, 163–7.

Yu, J. and Williford, W.R. (1994) Alcohol, other drugs and criminality: a structural analysis, *American Journal of Drug and Alcohol Abuse*, 20, 373–93.

Yuan, J-M., Ross, R.K., Gao, Y-T., Henderson, B.E. and Yu, M.C. (1997) Follow-up study of moderate alcohol intake and mortality among middle-aged men in Shanghai, China, *British Medical Journal*, 314, 18–23.

Zador, P.L. (1991) Alcohol-related risk of fatal driver injuries in relation to driver age and sex, *Journal of Studies on Alcohol*, 52, 302–10.

Index

Compiled by Sue Carlton